Accounting

Made Simple

The Made Simple series
has been created
primarily for self-education
but can equally well
be used as
an aid to group study.
However complex the subject,
the reader is taken
step by step,
clearly and methodically
through the course. Each volume
has been prepared by experts,
taking account of
modern educational requirements,
to ensure the most
effective way of
acquiring knowledge.

In the same series

Accounting
Acting and Stagecraft
Additional Mathematics
Administration in Business
Advertising
Anthropology
Applied Economics
Applied Mathematics
Applied Mechanics
Art Appreciation
Art of Speaking
Art of Writing
Biology
Book-keeping
Britain and the European Community
British Constitution
Business and Administrative Organisation
Business Calculations
Business Economics
Business Law
Business Statistics and Accounting
Calculus
Chemistry
Childcare
Commerce
Company Law
Company Practice
Computer Programming
Computers and Microprocessors
Cookery
Cost and Management Accounting
Data Processing
Economic History
Economic and Social Geography
Economics
Effective Communication
Electricity
Electronic Computers
Electronics
English
English Literature
Financial Management
French
Geology
German
Housing, Tenancy and Planning Law
Human Anatomy
Human Biology
Italian
Journalism
Latin
Law
Management
Marketing
Mathematics
Metalwork
Modern Biology
Modern Electronics
Modern European History
Modern Mathematics
Modern World Affairs
Money and Banking
Music
New Mathematics
Office Administration
Office Practice
Organic Chemistry
Personnel Management
Philosophy
Photography
Physical Geography
Physics
Practical Typewriting
Psychiatry
Psychology
Public Relations
Public Sector Economics
Rapid Reading
Russian
Salesmanship
Secretarial Practice
Social Services
Sociology
Spanish
Statistics
Teeline Shorthand
Twentieth-Century British History
Typing
Woodwork

Accounting

Made Simple

Joseph P. Simini
Wilfred Hingley, BSc(Econ), FCMA

Made Simple Books
HEINEMANN : London

Made and printed in Great Britain
by Richard Clay (The Chaucer Press), Ltd, Bungay, Suffolk
for the publishers William Heinemann Ltd
10 Upper Grosvenor Street, London, W1X 9PA

First Edition, October 1969
Reprinted, December 1972
Reprinted, January 1974
Reprinted, February 1975
Reprinted, April 1977
Reprinted, August 1978
Reprinted, March 1980
Reprinted, April 1981
Reprinted, April 1982
Second Edition, May 1984

British Library Cataloguing in Publication Data

Simini, J. P.
Accounting made simple.—2nd ed.—
(Made simple books, ISSN 0265–0541)
1. Accounting
I. Title II. Hingley, Wilfred
657 HF5635

ISBN 0–434–98469–8

Foreword to Second Edition

As stated in the first edition, edited by A. J. Grant, *Accounting Made Simple* was prepared primarily for two kinds of students: those having some knowledge of book-keeping or elementary accounting and those having no knowledge at all, but needing accounting as part of a business or professional course. As the book has been reprinted eight times since the First Edition it seems reasonable to assume that those for whom it was written, and others such as the more general reader who wishes to become familiar with the basic principles and techniques of accounting, have found the style and content appropriate. The emphasis throughout is on accounting procedures, also on the significance of accounting statements, their uses and their interpretation.

Chapters 1–10 are devoted primarily to financial accounts and culminate in Chapter 14 with a copy of the published accounts annotated with page references to the text where a particular item is discussed. This provides an index for readers primarily interested in the interpretation of accounts. It is suggested that these chapters are first read through as a whole, and then re-worked in consecutive order—possibly before attempting the exercises. The reason for this approach is that a large number of the principal items and terminology introduced in the first three chapters are developed in detail in the subsequent chapters. The remaining Chapters 11–13 form an introduction to cost and management accounting and are concerned with records and procedures for control and decision-making purposes.

The exercises are given in two series. In the first the questions are, in general, short and straightforward, designed to test the reader's understanding of the subject matter. Worked solutions are provided for these. The questions in the second series are wider in scope and include examples from the examinations of professional bodies and other organisations. They have been chosen to develop the reader's understanding of the topics discussed, and also to provide teachers with appropriate material for class use.

The references to law and practice, except where otherwise specified, are to English law and practice. There is continuous and expanding updating of company legislation and recommended practice such as that contained in the Standards referred to in the text. Emphasis is therefore placed upon how and why accounts are prepared rather than treatment in detail of the precise legal requirements at a particular time and place.

Accounting Made Simple is suggested as appropriate reading for students working on such courses as:

BTEC Diploma and Certificate courses
Foundation and Intermediate stages of:
- Professional accounting bodies
- Banking and insurance
- London Chamber of Commerce
- Business studies and accounting degrees
- Diploma in Management Studies
- Institute of Commercial Management
- Institute of Management Services
- Chartered Institute of Transport
- Institute of Industrial Management

It is also suitable for the non-specialist or general reader requiring an appreciation of the accounting function.

WILFRED HINGLEY

Acknowledgements

Thanks for their generosity and assistance are recorded as follows:

To the Senate of the University of London, London Chamber of Commerce and Society of Company and Commercial Accountants for permission to reproduce past examination questions.

To the Transport Development Group PLC for permission to reproduce substantial parts of their published Report and Accounts.

To *Investors Chronicle* and *Financial World* for permission to reproduce examples of business ratios.

To Mrs P. Higgins for efficiently transcribing the amendments to manuscript and tabulations.

The following books in the Made Simple series may be found useful for further reading, and development of the main divisions and levels of the subject covered in this book.

Book-keeping or *Business Statistics and Accounting*
for more intensive study of recording processes

Cost and Management Accounting
for development of areas mentioned in Chapters 11–13

Financial Management
for advanced treatment of company financial control and decision-making

W.H.

Contents

1
Financial Statements

Owners, managers, suppliers, granters of credit and others interested in a business enterprise are generally confronted with financial statements prepared by accountants. These include the **Balance Sheet**, showing the firm's condition on the last day of the accounting period, a **Profit and Loss Account**, which may include an **Appropriation Section** showing how the profit (if any) has been utilised. The Profit and Loss Account is sometimes referred to as the **Operations Statement** which may be accompanied by a statement telling of changes in the equity of the owner or owners. In this chapter each of these financial statements will be discussed.

Balance Sheet

A Balance Sheet always shows the business as being in a condition of equality: what it owns equals what it owes to either its creditors or its owners. This can be expressed in the form of an equation:

Assets = Liabilities + Owners' Equity

This relationship does not of itself imply that the business is in a satisfactory financial condition. The equality may have been preserved by treating a loss as a fictitious asset or deducting it from the owners' equity. It may also be preserved by leaving assets at values which are no longer realistic, or by ignoring liabilities. **Assets** are those resources that the business owns. **Liabilities** are obligations owed by the business to persons (or businesses) other than its owners. **Owners' Equity**, shown as **Capital and Reserves**, is what the business owes to the owners. The Balance Sheet shows all of these elements at the last day of an accounting period.

If the Balance Sheet were to contain only one total each for assets, liabilities, and owners' equity, it would be completely uninformative. If assets of a different nature were included in one total—such as land and buildings, and patents—this would be of little use. The land and buildings could be expected to have a fair market value if the business were to close down. The patents might well be valueless in those circumstances. The Balance Sheet would give no indication as to the proportion of the total represented by land and buildings and the proportion represented by patents. Deliberately misleading Balance Sheets have sometimes been prepared in this way when assets or liabilities of completely different kinds have been combined.

Balance Sheets now normally show assets and liabilities classified so that they give adequate information to those who use them. With Limited Companies in the United Kingdom, this has been largely brought about by the various Companies Acts of 1948, 1967, 1976, 1980 and 1981—subsequently referred to as Companies Acts 1948–81—which lay down how assets and liabilities shall be valued and classified in a Company's Balance Sheet. (Readers in the UK should refer to Schedules 1–4 of the Companies Act, 1981 for fuller details.) The London Stock Exchange exercised further control by making certain additional requirements of a company seeking a Stock Exchange quotation for its shares. In the United States legislation is less influential than the Stock Exchanges, and preparing a Balance Sheet for the Securities and Exchange Commission is practically reduced to filling in the appropriate detailed forms.

The amount of detail contained in the Balance Sheets of other businesses is influenced by the need to present them to the taxation authorities to confirm the owners' income, and to bankers and other lending institutions when the owner wants to borrow money.

The items on a Balance Sheet are consequently classified into groups. The reader should first study the classification referring to the simple Balance Sheet on page 5, and then repeat the process referring to the more realistic example provided by the accounts of the Transport Development Group PLC on page 182.

Current Assets

Some assets are of greater immediate utility than others because they can be converted into cash or other kinds of asset comparatively quickly. These are called 'current assets', and include cash and the kind of asset that can be turned into cash, or be sold or consumed reasonably soon. **Cash** includes currency, bank balances and money equivalents (cheques, money orders, etc.). Other assets that can reasonably be expected to be converted to cash in the current financial period are **debtors** (sometimes referred to as *accounts receivable*).

Debtors are sometimes separated into **trade debtors** (representing amounts due from customers for purchases of goods or services in the ordinary course of business) and **other debtors** (representing amounts due from transactions of any other types).

Also included in this group of assets are **bills receivable**, which are amounts due from customers for which Bills of Exchange are held.

Assets which can reasonably be expected to be sold in the following financial period in a trading business come under the heading of **stocks** (or **merchandise inventory**). Work-in-progress (partly processed goods) is sometimes shown as a separate item. Other assets which can reasonably be expected to be used in the following period are **sundry stores**, such as stationery, and **prepaid expenses**. Examples of prepaid expenses are insurance premiums and rentals paid during the current period although the benefit, or service required, extends into the following accounting period.

Current assets, therefore, are assets which may be expected to be used within one year of the date of the Balance Sheet.

Fixed Assets

Tangible assets which have a relatively long life (more than one year), are relatively fixed (in size, shape, or form), are permanent in nature and used by the business in its operation, are called 'fixed assets'. Examples are **freehold land and buildings, leasehold land and buildings, plant and machinery**, and **motor vehicles**. These assets are generally relatively expensive and will be used over long periods of time. The fact that the life of these assets extends over many accounting periods makes it necessary for the accountant to **allocate** the cost of the asset to current and future operations on some rational basis. This allocation is called **depreciation accounting** and will be discussed in Chapter 8. Fixed assets will initially appear on the Balance Sheet at their cost price. In a period of rising prices it is legitimate, and may be deemed expedient, to revalue these assets on the basis of current prices.

If the business has borrowed on the security of a particular asset or group of assets, the amount so borrowed is sometimes deducted from the value of the asset on the Balance Sheet.

Other Assets

This category includes all assets that cannot be classified as 'current' or 'fixed'. It includes investments in other corporate bodies and may be divided into **quoted investments, unquoted investments**, and shares in and amounts owing from **subsidiary companies**. Quoted investments are investments which are quoted on a recognised stock exchange. Unquoted investments are those which are not so quoted and are therefore more difficult to value. Subsidiary companies are those in which the company concerned has a controlling interest, as defined in the Companies Acts, 1948–81. In the United Kingdom a company with one or more subsidiaries is normally required to prepare also a **Consolidated Balance Sheet** (discussed in Chapter 3, page 34).

Current Liabilities

Those liabilities owing to creditors that must be paid within the following accounting period (the same period as for current assets) are called 'current liabilities'. Current liabilities evidenced by a formal document are called **bills payable**. When a business knows that it owes money to someone other than the owners but has received no account, such amounts are called **accrued liabilities**. Included under this description are **salaries and wages** earned by employees but not yet paid, **interest due** on obligations of the business, **taxes**, and **proposed dividends**.

Long-term Liabilities

All liabilities that are not due to be paid in the following accounting period are called 'long-term liabilities'. Businesses are sometimes partly financed by this use of long-term credit obtained from sources other than the proprietors. These may be in the form of a **loan** from an individual or financial institution, or in the form of an issue of **debentures**. The rate of interest payable and the first and last dates of repayment will be shown on the Balance Sheet. Each item or issue of debentures will be shown separately.

The Owners' Equity

The third section of the Balance Sheet tells what the business owes to its owners. There are three main basic types of business:

(*a*) *The Sole Trader*, an unincorporated business owned by one person.

(*b*) *The Partnership*, an unincorporated business owned by two or more persons.

(*c*) *The Limited Company*, a business which is a separate legal entity from its owners, whose rights and obligations are determined by the shares they hold. They comprise two categories:

(i) the public limited company indicated by the abbreviation PLC or plc immediately after the name of the company and (ii) the private limited company indicated by the abbreviation Ltd indicating limited liability. Essentially the plc are large companies with shares quoted on the stock exchange whilst the private limited companies tend to be smaller, are unquoted and have certain restrictions imposed upon them in return for the privilege of limited liability (see page 37).

On the Balance Sheet, this section shows how much the business owes its owners on the balance date. The equity is shown in different ways, depending on the type of ownership, and is discussed in Chapter 2, page 19. In the event of the business being liquidated, the owners will receive the amount of the equity shown on the Balance Sheet only if the assets are sold for their exact book-value; they will receive less if the assets happen to have been overvalued, and more if they have been undervalued.

The Balance Sheet of a Sole Trader is shown in Fig. 1(a).

The layout in Fig. 1(a) is one of many. In it the total liabilities are shown beneath the total assets. They could have been, and frequently are, shown side by side as on page 25. The order of the items may also be varied. In Fig. 1(a) the assets are listed beginning with the most liquid first, i.e. those in cash or quickly convertible into cash. It was traditional to extract Balance Sheets side by side since as the name implies they are primarily a list of balances from the ledgers. In some countries assets are shown on the right-hand side and liabilities on the left, whilst in others the reverse is the case. In respect of published accounts—those of companies listed on a Stock Exchange—preference has arisen over the last few years for a vertical format.

It is claimed that accounts in this form are more intelligible to the non-specialist. Additionally there has been a tendency to subtract Current liabilities from Current assets and show a net working capital balance to indicate immediately the short-term liquid position. With the introduction of the Companies Act, 1981 this form of layout has become mandatory for public limited companies. A revised version of the Balance Sheet from Fig.

CENTRAL PROVISION STORE
BALANCE SHEET
(as at December 31st, 19..)

ASSETS

	£	£	£
CURRENT ASSETS			
Cash		1,000	
Debtors		3,000	
Bills Receivable		1,500	
Stocks		40,000	
Office Supplies		200	
Store Supplies		300	
Prepaid Insurance		500	
Total Current Assets			46,500
Investments		50,000	
Patents		10,000	
Goodwill		5,000	65,000
FIXED ASSETS			
Store Equipment	20,000		
Less Accumulated Depreciation	6,000		
		14,000	
Buildings	76,000		
Less Accumulated Depreciation	3,000		
		73,000	
Land		5,000	
Total Fixed Assets			92,000
TOTAL ASSETS			£203,500

LIABILITIES

	£	£	£
CURRENT LIABILITIES			
Accrued Salaries		1,000	
Creditors		15,000	
Bills Payable		5,000	
Accrued Taxes		2,000	
Total Current Liabilities			23,000
LONG-TERM LIABILITIES			
Loan		20,000	
Mortgages		50,000	
Total Long-term Liabilities			70,000
TOTAL LIABILITIES			93,000

OWNERS' EQUITY

William Jones, Capital			110,500
TOTAL LIABILITIES AND CAPITAL			£203,500

Fig. 1(a). Balance Sheet of a sole trader

1(a) in the required format is shown in Fig. 1(b). This represents exactly the same financial position as before in spite of the totals being considerably lower. The reader should trace the comparable position of each item and this layout should specifically be used for all references to published accounts. Where double-sided Balance Sheets are used in the following pages they are either to emphasise the source of the figures or are in respect of non-quoted companies.

Balance-Sheet Analysis

It is often useful to compare the financial position of a business at two different dates, or to compare the position of one business with that of another. This is facilitated by the use of ratios. The most widely used are outlined below.

Current Ratio

The formula

$$\textit{Current Ratio} = \frac{\textit{Current Assets}}{\textit{Current Liabilities}}$$

tells us how many times the current liabilities could be paid out of the current assets. It is a measure of the risk that a business may not be able to meet its liabilities promptly in the near future.

The current ratio of the Central Provision Store (see Fig. 1(a)) is:

$$\frac{\textit{Current Assets}}{\textit{Current Liabilities}} = \frac{46{,}500}{23{,}000} = 2.0$$

This is sometimes (confusingly) referred to as the Working Capital Ratio but the term Working Capital should preferably be restricted to the *difference* between Current Assets and Current Liabilities as defined below.

Working Capital

The formula

$$\textit{Working Capital} = \textit{Current Assets} - \textit{Current Liabilities}$$

tells us how much of the current assets would be left over if all current liabilities were paid out of them. This relationship is a guide to the capital requirements of a business. Creating additional long-term liabilities and employing the funds in current assets will increase the working capital, whereas creating additional short-term liabilities and using the funds for the acquisition of fixed assets will reduce it. The greater the working capital, the more stable will be the business. We must, however, consider the possibility of the business requiring additional fixed assets when assessing the adequacy of the working capital.

CENTRAL PROVISION STORE BALANCE SHEET
(as at December 31st, 19..)

	£	£	£
FIXED ASSETS			
Intangible Assets			
Goodwill		5,000	
Patents		10,000	
		——	15,000
TANGIBLE ASSETS			
Land		5,000	
Buildings	76,000		
Less Accumulated Depreciation	3,000		
	——	73,000	
Store Equipment	20,000		
Less Accumulated Depreciation	6,000		
	——	14,000	
		——	92,000
LONG-TERM INVESTMENTS			50,000
Current Assets			
Stocks			
Consumables for Office and Stores	500		
Finished Goods	40,000		
	——	40,500	
DEBTORS			
Trade	3,000		
Bills Receivable	1,500		
	——	4,500	
INVESTMENTS			
Short-Term			
Cash at bank and in hand		1,000	
PREPAYMENTS AND ACCRUED INCOME			
Prepayments			
Insurance prepaid		500	
		46,500	
CREDITORS: AMOUNTS FALLING DUE WITHIN ONE YEAR			
Trade Creditors	15,000		
Bills Payable	5,000		
Taxation	2,000		
Salaries Accrued	1,000		
	——	23,000	
		——	23,500
TOTAL ASSETS LESS CURRENT LIABILITIES			£180,500
REPRESENTED BY:			
CREDITORS: AMOUNTS FALLING DUE AFTER MORE THAN ONE YEAR			
Loan		20,000	
Mortgages		50,000	
		——	70,000
CAPITAL AND RESERVES			
Capital			110,500
			£180,500

Fig. 1(b). Balance Sheet of a sole trader

The working capital of the Central Provision Store (see Fig. 1(a)) is:

£46,500 − £23,000 = £23,500

Acid-test Ratio

The formula

$$\textit{Acid-test Ratio} = \frac{\textit{Cash + Debtors + Readily Marketable Securities}}{\textit{Current Liabilities}}$$

tells how many times the current liabilities can be paid with the so-called 'liquid' current assets. Some current assets—such as stocks and, in the case of a manufacturing business, raw materials and work-in-progress—may take longer to turn into cash than the period within which the current liabilities must be met. This may be an important consideration during a period of economic restriction. The acid-test ratio gives the ratio between the amount of cash that can be realised in a hurry and the current liabilities.

The acid-test ratio of the Central Provision Store (Fig. 1(a)) is:

$$\frac{1{,}000 + 3{,}000 + 1{,}500}{23{,}000} = \frac{5{,}500}{23{,}000} = 0.2$$

If the level of business fell severely, Central Provision Store would have difficulty in meeting its obligations. The current assets omitted from this calculation, stocks, will only be turned into cash as trading takes place. If trade falls off, stocks will be converted into cash more slowly.

All of these relationships are measures of the financial strength of a business and are used by owners, managers, lenders, and others in evaluating the firm's ability to meet its obligations. The ratios that might be indications of healthy financial strength vary from one type of business to another. The working capital of a business will depend on the type of business and its size. Fig. 3, extracted from the *Investors Chronicle* dated June 17th, 1983, gives an indication of the ratios which are calculated and published.

Revenue Accounts

The owners and other interested parties will want to know how much profit (or loss) was generated by the manufacturing or trading operations of their business. In other words, did the running of a provision store this year prove profitable or not? What were the sales and expenses? The Profit and Loss Account for the period answers these questions.

Income and Expenditure

The net increase in assets due to operations (sales of goods or services) is called **net income** or **net revenue**. Because a business has sold goods or rendered a service, assets in the form of cash, debtors or bills receivable are increased. If the business is earning a profit, this increase is greater than the reduction in assets involved in producing or buying the goods or rendering the service. The reduction in assets is reflected in the costs which expire while the income is being earned. Costs which do not expire during the earning period, e.g. goods not yet sold and insurance cover not yet used up, are treated as assets and appear as such on the Balance Sheet.

It should be borne in mind that Revenue Accounts are prepared to show the results of operations over a period of time, and not at one moment of time (like the Balance Sheet). This fact is reflected in the heading: 'Revenue Account for the period ended December 31st, 19..'.

There are two bases on which income can be measured:

(*a*) *The accrual basis*. If income and expenditure are measured when the transactions occur, regardless of the physical flow of cash, the business is said to be *operating on an accrual basis*. This basis is almost invariably used by manufacturing and trading businesses.

(*b*) *The cash basis*. If income is measured when cash is received and expenses are measured when cash is spent, the business is said to be *operating on a cash basis*. This basis is sometimes used in a service business, such as a professional practice.

Types of Business

The three basic types of business are classified according to the nature of their operations.

(*a*) The *Service Business* which gives advice or services exclusively and in which there is no transfer of title to goods.

(*b*) The *Trading Business* which acquires goods for sale to its customers, e.g. a departmental store or a wholesaler.

(*c*) The *Manufacturing Business* which changes the form of goods by analysis or which assembles goods, e.g. a refinery (analysis), steel mill (synthesis), or car-assembly plant.

There is a section of the Revenue Account for each of these types of activity, namely:

(*a*) the Manufacturing Account
(*b*) the Trading Account
(*c*) the Profit and Loss Account.

These accounts are usually prepared separately in the financial books of the business, but are often combined (in the so-called **narrative** form of account) when printed and published.

The Manufacturing Account

In a manufacturing business all three sections of the Revenue Account are required. The section exclusive to the manufacturing business is the Manufacturing Account, two types of which are given on page 12.

Fig. 2. Companies/Analysis

Company	*Performance*					*Financial Status*					
	Year end	*Return on assets %*	*Profit margin %*	*Stock turnover*	*Debtor turnover*	*Cash flow £000*	*Gross debt/ shareholders funds %*	*Net debt/ shareholders funds %*	*Interest cover*	*Current ratio*	*Acid test*
Allied Plant	12–82	Nil	Nil (5.0)	10.9	4.2	27	278.7	221.1	0.2	1.0	0.8
Associated British Foods	3–83	19.0	5.1 (5.1)	10.5	12.8	130,684	30.7	25.6	6.2	1.2	0.6
British Home Stores	3–83	23.4	9.4 (9.3)	8.5	—	28,179	15.8	Nil	18.0	1.7	0.8
A. Caird	1–83	Nil	Nil (Nil)	3.9	13.8	*−161*	Nil	Nil	Nil	6.2	3.7
Costain	12–82	15.1	5.9 (7.7)	10.4	8.3	30,187	42.6	Nil	3.3	1.3	1.0
De Vere Hotels and Restaurants	12–82	2.7	3.6 (2.4)	17.4	7.8	507	Nil	Nil	13.6	1.5	1.3
Duport	1–83	Nil	Nil (2.3)	9.9	5.6	*−772*	26.9	20.7	Nil	1.7	1.1
Eucalyptus Pulp Mills	12–82	2.3	6.0 (21.8)	3.9	4.4	475	71.6	68.1	1.0	1.3	0.7
Fidelity Radio	3–83	1.1	2.2 (1.1)	6.7	6.8	530	43.5	43.2	1.1	1.1	0.5
Flight Refuelling	12–82	19.1	12.3 (13.8)	3.4	5.1	3,365	0.6	Nil	76.0	2.6	1.4
Foseco Minsep	12–82	10.6	4.8 (7.6)	5.2	4.2	9,293	41.2	29.1	2.4	1.6	0.95
Grampian Television	2–83	11.2	8.3† (8.5†)	20.8	6.8	1,042	25.5	25.4	17.7†	0.6	0.5
Matthew Hall	12–82	26.7	1.7 (1.8)	7.6	20.1	8,813	16.0	Nil	16.3	1.3	0.7
P. C. Henderson	2–83	22.6	8.6 (8.1)	5.7	4.6	2,616	31.8	15.2	9.3	1.4	0.9
House of Fraser	1–83	7.0	4.9 (4.5)	6.8	4.4	22,139	18.2	14.6	4.1	2.0	1.3
Hunting Gibson	12–82	23.0	0.6 (8.7)	3.3	4.0	970	157.9‡	101.2‡	1.0	0.9‡	0.6‡
John Laing	12–82	22.1	1.9 (1.2)	6.6	11.2	16,098	42.1	Nil	4.3	1.1	0.6
Lee Cooper	12–82	34.7	12.1 (13.4)	4.9	4.8	5,457	53.0	25.1	10.7	1.8	1.0
London and Liverpool Trust	3–83	62.5	25.8 (10.4)	6.2	3.9	4,736	46.2	37.0	11.7	1.1	0.7
Midland Industries	12–82	5.8	6.6 (7.6)	6.3	4.0	1,239	69.8	64.6	1.3	0.9	0.6
Modern Engineers of Bristol	12–82	Nil	Nil (Nil)	2.8	5.9	*−266*	211.1	210.0	Nil	1.1	0.3
Neil & Spencer	11–82	Nil	0.5 (Nil)	3.9	4.2	*−445*	125.6	121.7	0.2	1.2	0.6
Prince of Wales Hotels	12–82	8.5	9.4 (10.8)	27.1	14.2	602	67.3	67.1	2.2	0.4	0.3
Ropner	12–82§	15.7‖	18.0 (17.7)	5.1‖	6.4‖	4,076	106.4	61.7	4.2	1.7	1.3
Walter Runciman	12–82	6.2	5.2 (7.4)	7.8	4.8	2,711	149.4	104.1	7.4	1.1	0.8
Sears	1–83	14.3	7.0 (6.8)	6.8	14.7	66,067	16.7	Nil	9.0	1.8	0.9
Silentnight	1–83	22.5	7.0 (6.7)	10.3	5.8	5,576	13.9	10.2	28.3	1.2	0.8

Stylo	1–83	5.5	4.3 (4.8)	4.1	20.0	1,163	31.9	31.4	1.7	1.1	0.2
Tilbury	12–82	15.4	5.5 (3.7)	5.9	10.9	2,660	1.2	Nil	161.4	1.3	0.6
Tootal	1–83	11.1	5.8 (5.3)	3.7	6.3	11,691	51.1	45.9	2.1	1.7	0.7
Turriff Corporation	12–82	24.1	2.1 (2.0)	7.4	13.5	1,653	2.5	Nil	42.5	1.5	0.9
Wettern Brothers	12–82	9.9	1.6 (Nil)	30.3	6.4	263	25.9	15.7	3.2	0.9	0.8
George Wimpey	12–82	9.5	3.5 (3.8)	3.3	6.7	75,400	23.7	16.2	3.0	1.9	0.7

Notes: * Previous year in brackets. † Before charging exchequer levy and channel 4 subscription. ‡ Excluding net assets in interest in property development partnership. § 9 Months. || Annualised.

Statistical Definitions

[T] indicates trustee status under the Trustee Investments Act, 1961.

Investment

Nil price/earnings (PE) ratio: The number of years' purchase of latest nil earnings per share represented by the current share price.

Nil earnings: Net profits per share after tax and minorities and preference dividends, ignoring advance corporation tax on equity dividends. Where allowances reduce corporation tax, a notional full tax charge is assumed.

Cash earnings: Profits attributable to the ordinary shareholders plus depreciation.

Net assets per share: Book value of assets (after deducting intangibles such as goodwill) attributable to the ordinary capital, divided by the number of ordinary shares in issue.

Dividend cover: The net earnings shown by the company (amended only for prior year's tax adjustments) divided by the net cost of the dividend (ignoring any waivers).

Pre-tax profit: Total profits adjusted to allow for all items exceptional to normal trading (including above-the-line redundancy payments) and subject only to the tax charge shown in the accounts.

Dividend per share: Gross dividend (i.e. the net payment plus tax credit).

Performance

Return on assets: Pre-tax profits plus loan stock interest expressed as a percentage of the issued capital, reserves, loan capital, deferred tax and minorities less intangibles.

Profit margin: Profits before interest and tax as a percentage of turnover.

Stock turnover: The number of times the balance sheet figure for stocks can be divided into the turnover.

Debtor turnover: The number of times the balance sheet figure for debtors can be divided into the turnover. Where firms sell both for cash and for credit, only credit sales are used for this ratio.

Financial Status

Cash flow: Retained profits plus depreciation (excluding exceptional and extraordinary items).

Gross debt/shareholders' funds: Borrowings, including all debentures and loans plus bank overdrafts, as a percentage of shareholders' funds less intangibles.

Net debt/shareholders' funds: Borrowings, including all debentures and loans plus bank overdrafts less liquid assets, as a percentage of shareholders' funds less intangibles.

Interest cover: Loan interest divided into earnings before interest and tax.

Working capital: Gross—the same as current assets; **Net**—Current assets less current liabilities.

Current ratio: Current liabilities divided into current assets.

Acid test: Current liabilities divided into current assets less stock.

Source: Investors Chronicle dated June 17th, 1983.

Type 1

MANUFACTURING ACCOUNT
(for the year ended December 31st, 19. .)

	£		£
Work-in-Progress at Beginning of Year	40,000	Cost of Goods Manufactured (transferred to Trading Account)	420,000
Plus Direct Labour used During Year	180,000		
Plus Direct Materials used During Year	115,000		
Plus Overheads for Year	130,000		
	465,000		
Less Work-in-Progress at End of Year	45,000		
	£420,000		£420,000

This type of Manufacturing Account arrives at the *cost* of goods manufactured in exactly the same way that the *cost* of goods sold is arrived at in a trading business. It can then be included in the Trading Account (see page 13).

In Type 2 (see below), the *value* of the goods manufactured is introduced and the difference between the cost and the value of goods manufactured is shown as the **manufacturing profit**. This type of account can be used only when there is some basis available for valuing the goods manufactured, for example, where there is a market for the goods or the opportunity of buying manufactured goods from competitors. The account can then be used for assessing whether it is more profitable to manufacture or to buy in manufactured goods and concentrate on trading. Very great care is necessary in allocating costs as between items in the Manufacturing Account and the other sections of the Revenue Account if it is to be used for this purpose.

Type 2

MANUFACTURING ACCOUNT
(for the year ended December 31st, 19. .)

	£		£
Work-in-Progress at Beginning of Year	40,000	Value of Goods Manufactured	465,000
Plus Direct Labour used During Year	180,000		
Plus Direct Materials used During Year	115,000		
Plus Overheads for Year	130,000		
	465,000		
Less Work-in-Progress at End of Year	45,000		
	420,000		
Manufacturing Profit	45,000		
	£465,000		£465,000

The Trading Account

Both a manufacturing and a trading business will require a Trading Account. It is drawn up as follows:

TRADING ACCOUNT
(for the year ended December 31st, 19..)

	£		£
Opening Stock of Finished Goods	25,000	Sales	665,000
Cost of Goods Manufactured	420,000		
Cost of Goods Purchased	175,000		
	620,000		
Less Closing Stock of Finished Goods	30,000		
Cost of Goods Sold	590,000		
Gross Profit	75,000		
	£665,000		£665,000

The above account includes both the goods manufactured by the business (as indicated in the previous Manufacturing Account) and manufactured goods bought from outside suppliers. The item 'Cost of Goods Purchased, £175,000' includes all the costs directly involved in preparing the goods for sale, but not the cost of selling them. Thus the delivery charges on goods purchased, the costs of breaking bulk and of packing will be included, but any selling expenses are left out.

The Trading Account above follows the type-1 Manufacturing Account. If it were to follow the type-2 Manufacturing Account, the item 'Cost of Goods Manufactured, £420,000' would be replaced by the item 'Value of Goods Manufactured, £465,000.' The 'Gross Profit, £75,000' would become 'Trading Profit, £30,000', and the Manufacturing Profit (£45,000) would be credited directly to the Profit and Loss Account. The total profit transferred to the Profit and Loss Account would be the same in both cases.

The Profit and Loss Account

A Profit and Loss Account is required for all types of business. The Profit and Loss Account following the above Trading Account might be as follows:

PROFIT AND LOSS ACCOUNT
(for the year ended December 31st, 19..)

	£		£
Administrative Expenses	15,000	Gross Profit	75,000
Selling Expenses	20,000		
Financial Expenses	5,000		
Net Profit	35,000		
	£75,000		£75,000

The 'Administrative Expenses' and 'Selling Expenses' each represent the total of a considerable number of items, and at an earlier stage a Profit and Loss Account would have been prepared incorporating a greater amount of detail.

These sections of the Revenue Account can be built up into a unified narrative account, as shown below. In the form already illustrated, most of the items are placed on the same side as they appear in the double-entry accounting records of the business (see page 20). In the form shown below, the items are arranged solely with a view to ease of understanding.

PROFIT AND LOSS ACCOUNT
(for the year ended December 31st, 19..)

	£	£	£
Sales			665,000
Opening Stock of Finished Goods		25,000	
Work-in-Progress at Beginning of Year	40,000		
Direct Labour used During Year	180,000		
Direct Materials used During Year	115,000		
Overheads for Year	130,000		
	465,000		
Less Work-in-Progress at End of Year	45,000		
Cost of Goods Manufactured		420,000	
Cost of Goods Purchased		175,000	
		620,000	
Less Closing Stock of Finished Goods		30,000	
Cost of Goods Sold			590,000
Gross Profit			75,000
Administrative Expenses		15,000	
Selling Expenses		20,000	
Financial Expenses		5,000	
			40,000
Net Profit			£35,000

The Profit and Loss Account of a professional business may be prepared either on a cash or an accrual basis. Whichever basis is used, it might well appear as follows:

PROFIT AND LOSS ACCOUNT
(for the year ended December 31st, 19..)

EXPENSES	£		£
Salaries	6,000	Fee Income	60,000
Rent	4,000		
Telephone	600		
Supplies	2,000		
Car Rental	2,400		
Net Profit	45,000		
	£60,000		£60,000

The examples given are simple ones. In most businesses a fuller classification of expenses will be necessary, and with more complicated businesses, supporting schedules can be used to make the statement easier to grasp. The Companies Acts, 1948–81, lay down the minimum amount of detail to be included in published Revenue Accounts of Limited Companies, but a company will invariably prepare more detailed Final Accounts for internal consideration. The Profit and Loss Account of the Transport Development Group (shown on page 195) illustrates how details may be incorporated in notes rather than in the Account itself.

Revenue Account Analysis

A great deal can be learnt from a Revenue Account by comparing one item with another in the form of a ratio. Seven of the most commonly used ratios are given below.

(*a*) **Cost of Goods to Sales.** The formula is

$$\frac{\textit{Cost of Goods Sold}}{\textit{Sales}} \times 100\%$$

In the accounts which we have already discussed, the cost of goods sold is £590,000 and the figure for sales is £665,000. Hence the cost of goods to sales in this example is

$$\frac{590{,}000}{665{,}000} \times 100 = 88.7\%$$

(*b*) **Gross Profit to Sales.** The formula is

$$\frac{\textit{Gross Profit}}{\textit{Sales}} \times 100\%$$

In the accounts illustrated, the gross profit to sales is

$$\frac{75{,}000}{665{,}000} \times 100 = 11.3\%$$

Ratios *a* and *b* are alternatives, since the 'Cost of Goods to Sales' is the complement of the 'Gross Profit to Sales'.

(*c*) **Selling Expenses to Sales.** The formula is

$$\frac{\textit{Selling Expenses}}{\textit{Sales}} \times 100\%$$

From the accounts illustrated, $\frac{20{,}000}{665{,}000} \times 100 = 3.0\%$

(*d*) **Administrative Expenses to Sales.** The formula is

$$\frac{\textit{Administrative Expenses}}{\textit{Sales}} \times 100\%$$

From the accounts illustrated, $\frac{15{,}000}{665{,}000} \times 100 = 2.3\%$

(*e*) **Net Profit to Sales.** The formula is

$$\frac{\textit{Net Profit}}{\textit{Sales}} \times 100\%$$

From the accounts illustrated, $\frac{35{,}000}{665{,}000} \times 100 = 5.3\%$

These ratios have been developed by trade associations, banks, accountants, managers and other organisations to help the businessman determine whether his business is more efficient, or less, than others in the same trade. They also serve to compare the efficiency of one year's operations with those of another.

The business man will seek to keep ratios *a*, *c*, and *d* as low as possible, and ratios *b* and *e* as high as possible, subject to the following considerations.

The aggregate net profit (which is what really matters) is determined partly by the ratios described and partly by the volume of sales. In some cases it may be desirable to accept a low ratio of profit to sales if thereby a more than proportionate increase in sales is possible. Also the expense ratios can be kept to a minimum by a careful control of expenditure, but a more worthwhile approach may be to seek an increase in the volume of business without incurring a proportionate increase in expenses. Similarly it may be possible to reduce the cost of goods sold by increasing the volume of business alone, thus enabling the business to buy in larger quantities, or on more attractive terms.

(*f*) **Sales to Stock** (sometimes called the Rate of Stock Turnover). The formula is

$$\frac{\textit{Sales}}{\frac{1}{2}\,(\textit{Opening Stock} + \textit{Closing Stock})}$$

Stock should preferably be valued at selling price, but the cost of market price is sometimes the only value available. This is adequate if it is used consistently. Alternatively both sales and stock should be expressed at cost in which case the rate of stock turnover would be

$$\frac{\textit{Cost of Sales}}{\frac{1}{2}\,(\textit{Opening Stock} + \textit{Closing Stock})}$$

Note that either method assumes that there is an opening stock. In the first period of operating the initial purchases may be high and it is therefore preferable to ascertain the average over the whole period or use the closing stock figure as a base for the divisor. Greater accuracy can be obtained by taking the average of the quarterly or monthly stock levels, but often only the details of the stock at the beginning and end of the year are available. From the accounts illustrated, the ratio for finished goods is

$$\frac{665{,}000}{\frac{1}{2}\,(25{,}000 + 30{,}000)} = 24.2$$

A similar ratio could be calculated for the cost of raw material used, to the stock of raw material.

A low ratio may indicate that the company is in general holding a higher level of stocks than is necessary, or it may be that there is a proportion of dead stock which is no longer selling. This will only become manifest by further analysis of the stock position. The remedy is of course to dispose of such stock for what it will fetch, thereby releasing working capital and storage space.

(*g*) **Sales to Trade Debtors.** The formula which reveals how many times a year their debts are paid up by our debtors is

$$\frac{\textit{Sales}}{\frac{1}{2}\,(\textit{Trade debtors and bills receivable at beginning of year} + \textit{Trade debtors and bills receivable at end of year})}$$

In our example trade debtors and bills receivable at the end of the year only are available, so the nearest approximation is

$$\frac{\textit{Sales}}{\textit{Trade debtors and bills receivable at end of year}}$$

From the accounts illustrated, the ratio is

$$\frac{665{,}000}{3{,}000 + 1{,}500} = 148 \text{ times a year}$$

The formula can be inverted and multiplied by 12, 52, or 365 go give the *average collection period* in months, weeks, or days, respectively. From the accounts illustrated, the average collection period is

$$\frac{4{,}500}{665{,}000} \times 365 = 2.5 \text{ days}$$

Sales to trade debtors should be kept as high as possible (or the average collection period as short as possible) both to conserve working capital and to minimise bad debts.

A similar ratio can be calculated for creditors.

In using these percentages and ratios it is important to compare similar businesses (not, say, a grocer with a furniture dealer) and to compare businesses in the same type of locality (not a high-street supermarket with a remote village store). Information is collected on a considerable scale for the calculation of these ratios, and the results are published in tabular form as shown in Fig. 2, which is reproduced by courtesy of *Investors Chronicle* dated June 17th, 1983. Other specialist agencies such as Dun and Bradstreet can supply information on individual firms and summaries are published in newspapers and journals such as the *Financial Times* and by organisations such as the Centre for Inter Firm Comparison.

2
The Owners' Equity

In the example of the Balance Sheet of Central Provision Store in the previous chapter (see page 5), the *equity* or interest of the proprietor in the business was shown as:

'William Jones, Capital . . . £110,500'

Normally it is useful to have more detail of the equity on the Balance Sheet; indeed, for partnerships and limited companies it is essential. We shall therefore consider the equity of each type of business separately.

The Sole Trader

It is usual to include on the Balance Sheet of a sole trader a summary of the dealings between the *owner* and the *business* during the past accounting period. This will include details of any capital put into the business during the period and the drawing of any amounts either surplus to the requirements of the business or in anticipation of profits.

It would appear in this form:

CAPITAL, WILLIAM JONES		£
Capital at Beginning of Year		90,100
Plus Capital Introduced During Year		10,000
		100,100
Plus Profit for the Year	13,400	
Less Drawings	3,000	
		10,400
Capital at End of Year		£110,500

It will be noticed that the capital as shown on the previous Balance Sheet as well as the capital as shown on the latest balance are included in this statement.

A Balance Sheet may be prepared by taking the values of all the assets and **external** liabilities of a business on a particular date and entering the equity as a balancing item in the equation

Assets = External Liabilities + Owner's Equity

If two such Balance Sheets are available, and details of the proprietor's drawings and any introduction or withdrawal of capital are available for the intervening period, it is possible to calculate the profit for the period even if no complete details of transactions have been recorded. The statement can be prepared now as a **Statement of Profit** as follows:

STATEMENT OF PROFIT, WILLIAM JONES
(for the year ended December 31st, 19..)

	£	£
Capital at End of Year		110,500
Plus Drawings		3,000
		113,500
Less Capital at Beginning of Year	90,100	
Capital Introduced During Year	10,000	
		100,100
Profit for the Year		£13,400

This is not a very satisfactory way of assessing the profit as there is no check upon its accuracy. Nor does this statement give any indication whatsoever of the efficiency or otherwise of the business.

Double-entry Book-keeping

To overcome the shortcomings of a Profit Statement calculated in the way just described, the double-entry system of book-keeping has come into almost universal use. It involves a dual classification of all business transactions, organised so that for each transaction a debit entry is recorded on the left and a credit entry on the right in a set of two-sided accounts.

In this way a partial check of the arithmetical accuracy of the records is provided by extracting a **Trial Balance** which lists and totals all the debit and credit balances. A specimen of such a Trial Balance is incorporated in Exercise 2 on page 223. If the totals of the debits and credits are not equal, there must be at least one error either in balancing the accounts or in the original entries; the agreement of the totals of the Trial Balance does not, however, preclude compensating errors, omission of transactions, and the posting of items to wrong accounts.

The procedure is based on the fact that all business dealings fit into one of a limited number of types of transaction, one part of which is represented by a **debit entry** (left-hand) and the other by a **credit entry** (right-hand).

DEBIT	CREDIT
1. Receipt or recognition of an asset 2. Recording an expense or a loss 3. Extinguishing a liability 4. Withdrawal of capital or profits by owners	5. Disposal of an asset 6. Reduction in value of an asset 7. Incurring or recognition of a liability 8. Receipt of revenue 9. Introduction of capital by owners 10. Reducing an expense

In the affairs of a business any change listed as a debit must also be associated with one of the changes listed as a credit. Thus if a business parts with cash (credit entry 5), it will either receive an asset in exchange (debit entry 1), or it will have an expense to record (debit entry 2), or it will have extinguished a liability (debit entry 3). On the other hand, if a business receives cash (debit entry 1), it may have borrowed (credit entry 7), or it may have received income (credit entry 8), or it may have disposed of an asset (credit entry 5). In most cases both the Revenue Account and the Balance Sheet will be affected by each transaction.

The categories in the preceding Table are subdivided by the opening of as many separate accounts as required for transactions of different types. Thus for the receipt or recognition of an asset (debit entry 1), separate accounts will be opened for (*a*) Freehold Land and Buildings, (*b*) Leasehold Land and Buildings, (*c*) Plant and Machinery, (*d*) Motor Vehicles, (*e*) Stocks, (*f*) Cash, as well as for any other items which need to be entered separately in the Balance Sheet or on a note appended to it.

In preparing a Revenue Account the balances of all accounts representing income are set against the balances of all accounts representing expenses; this shows the balance as a profit or loss, whichever it may be. The form in which these items are set out has already been shown in Chapter 1 (page 14).

In preparing the Revenue Accounts the following additional debit-and-credit entries may be necessary:

(*a*) Assets will deteriorate (depreciate) with use and the passage of time. This will not automatically be reflected in the accounting records, and a credit entry (6) with a debit entry (2) will be required to convert the reduction in the value of an asset to an expense. This is dealt with more fully in Chapter 8 (page 95).

(*b*) Not all the benefits from some expenditure may have been received during the period. An annual insurance premium may have been paid halfway through the year. Since half the benefit has not yet been received, half the premium should be an expense and the other half an asset (prepaid expense). Consequently, a credit entry (10) with a debit entry (1) will be required.

(*c*) The accounting records may show that goods to the value of £200,000 have been purchased and goods to the value of £250,000 have been sold; but this gives no indication of what proportion of the goods purchased have been sold, since they are valued on different bases. We transfer the purchases to the Revenue Account as an expense, and the sales as income, so it is necessary to make some record of the value of goods not yet sold (the stock or inventory). The value must be calculated by a physical stock-taking then incorporated by a debit entry (1) and a credit entry (10).

(*d*) A debit-and-credit entry may be used merely to transfer an amount from one account to another without any transaction taking place at all. This will happen, for instance, when the balances of various expense accounts are transferred to the Profit and Loss Account at the end of the accounting period.

All the remaining balances represent liabilities or assets and will, with the balance of the Revenue Account (either profit or loss), still preserve the equality of debits and credits. From these the Balance Sheet is prepared by grouping the assets, liabilities, and equity into the appropriate classes. With large businesses it is usually more convenient to limit detail in the Balance Sheet itself but include it where appropriate in supporting schedules, as illustrated on page 203 and described in Chapter 8, page 95.

The debit-and-credit form of account is maintained for the Revenue Accounts, and the balances are transferred from the appropriate accounts to the same side of the Revenue Accounts by appropriate debit-and-credit entries. In the Balance Sheet, however, these terms disappear, and in the United Kingdom the side on which the items appear is opposite to that on which they appear in the Ledger Accounts. Many countries do, however, record the item on the same side as in the ledger—opposite to the way in which it would be recorded in the United Kingdom. This distinction is becoming less significant with today's growing practice of presenting a Balance Sheet in the form of a report with the liabilities and capital shown below the assets, as in the accounts of Transport Development Group PLC, given on page 196 and, indeed, is required in the UK by the 1981 legislation for public limited companies.

The Partnership

The business partnership is complicated by the fact that capital has been provided by more than one person and the profits have to be shared. It is left to the partners, on the formation of their partnership, to determine the basis upon which capital and profits are to be shared. There are, however, provisions in the Partnership Act, 1890, for dealing with the sharing of capital and profits where a partnership agreement has not been drawn up.

The sharing of profits is influenced by the fact that the partners may vary in the experience or goodwill they bring with them, and in the amount of time they devote to the partnership. Any desired result can be achieved by modifying the following variables:

(*a*) the proportion and amount of capital the partners are deemed to have provided;
(*b*) the rate of interest (if any) allowed on their capital;
(*c*) the salary to be paid to each partner;
(*d*) the proportion in which they share the residual profits.

Since the business may be detrimentally affected if a partner withdraws excessive amounts of capital, each partner's capital is often divided into two parts. These are recorded in two accounts in his name:

(i) **The Capital Account.** This is the amount of capital which he has agreed to keep in the business.

(ii) **The Current Account.** This shows the balance over and above the amount in the Capital Account. The partner's interest, salary, and share of the profits are credited to this account and his drawings are debited.

Sometimes a third account, a **Drawings Account**, is opened for each partner. This is done where profits are credited to the partners at the end of the year, and any drawings made before then are subject to interest charge. The total interest charge from all partners is added to the firm's profit and subsequently divided between them in the ratio in which they share profits.

To facilitate the sharing of the profit, the Revenue Account is supplemented by a **Profit and Loss Appropriation Account**. Let us now assume that the Central Provision Store is in the form of a partnership. The Profit and Loss Appropriation Account and the proprietors' accounts might be as shown below.

It should be noted that if losses are sustained, these are shared in the same way as profits. There is no limit to the extent to which a partner may be liable for such losses except in the case of a limited partnerhsip, and even in this case only the limited partner has the privilege of limited liability. There are always one or more partners who are responsible without limit for the losses of the firm.

PROFIT AND LOSS APPROPRIATION ACCOUNT
(for the year ended December 31st, 19..)

	£	£		£
Salaries				
Brown	1,250		Trading Profit for the Year	13,400
Black	1,500			
Green	2,000			
		4,750		
Interest on capital (at 5%)				
Brown	1,250			
Black	1,250			
Green	3,000			
		5,500		
Share of profits				
Brown ($\frac{2}{10}$)	630			
Black ($\frac{3}{10}$)	945			
Green ($\frac{1}{2}$)	1,575			
		3,150		
		£13,400		£13,400

CAPITAL ACCOUNT—BROWN

		£
	Balance	22,500
	Cash—Additional Capital	2,500
		£25,000

CAPITAL ACCOUNT—BLACK

			£
		Balance	22,500
		Cash—Additional Capital	2,500
			£25,000

CAPITAL ACCOUNT—GREEN

			£
		Balance	45,000
		Cash—Additional Capital	5,000
			£50,000

CURRENT ACCOUNT—BROWN

	£		£
Cash—Drawings	1,000	Salary	1,250
Balance c/f	2,130	Interest	1,250
		Profits	630
	£3,130		£3,130

CURRENT ACCOUNT—BLACK

	£		£
Cash—Drawings	1,000	Balance b/f	100
Balance c/f	2,795	Salary	1,500
		Interest	1,250
		Profits	945
	£3,795		£3,795

CURRENT ACCOUNT—GREEN

	£		£
Cash—Drawings	1,000	Salary	2,000
Balance c/f	5,575	Interest	3,000
		Profits	1,575
	£6,575		£6,575

It will be seen that each partner receives a salary and interest on his capital and then a predetermined share of the residual profits. During the year each partner has put in some additional capital, but each has drawn £1,000 in cash in anticipation of salary, interest, and profits. The total amounts are the same as when we considered William Jones as sole proprietor on page 19.

The equity section of the Balance Sheet will in this case appear either as:

BALANCE SHEET

CAPITAL				
	Current A/c	Capital A/c		
	£	£		£
Brown	2,130	25,000	Total Assets	203,500
Black	2,795	50,000		
Green	5,575	50,000		
	10,500	100,000		
		10,500		
		110,500		
Total External Liabilities		93,000		
		£203,500		£203,500

or as:

BALANCE SHEET

CAPITAL					
		£	£		£
Brown:	Capital A/c	25,000		Total Assets	203,500
	Current A/c	2,130			
			27,130		
Black:	Capital A/c	25,000			
	Current A/c	2,795			
			27,795		
Green:	Capital A/c	50,000			
	Current A/c	5,575			
			55,575		
			110,500		
Total External Liabilities			93,000		
			£203,500		£203,500

The Limited Company

There are different requirements under the 1981 Companies Acts depending upon whether the company is private or public, i.e. shares quoted on a stock exchange. Anyone can purchase shares in a public company but the opportunity of share sale and transfer in a private limited company is restricted. The public limited company (PLC) is used in most instances throughout the book as it is the form of company to whose final accounts most people would have access.

Rules on the form and content of annual accounts for companies are set out in the first schedule of the 1981 Act. This replaces Schedule 8 of the 1948 Act as subsequently amended. There are exceptions in the case of size and certain types of business have special requirements notably banks, insurance companies and building societies.

Dealing with the equity of a limited-liability company presents problems different from those of a sole trader or a partnership since

(*a*) there may be a very large number of shareholders;
(*b*) there may be more than one class of shares;
(*c*) the rights and obligations of shareholders are closely defined by law;
(*d*) share capital can be repaid to shareholders only in exceptional circumstances and, even then, is subject to the conditions laid down by law.

This situation is met by opening only one Capital Account for each class of shareholder. The details of individual shareholdings are contained in a separate register of members and not in the books of account which form part of the double-entry system. Once the shares have been fully paid up, the balance of the capital would not vary, so nothing would be gained by bringing into the double-entry system an account for each customer. Thus, while there may be frequent entries in the Register of Members as shares are bought and sold, there will be entries in the Share Capital Account only when amounts are due to be paid up on existing shares, or when more shares of the same class are issued.

If we assume that the Central Provision Store was organised as a limited-liability company, Central Provision Store PLC., and that 90,200 shares of £1.00 each had been issued and called up by the beginning of 19*x*8, the Share Capital Account would appear as

ORDINARY SHARE CAPITAL ACCOUNT

		Balance	£90,200

Issuing of Shares

When an amount becomes due on shares, either when first issued or by way of an instalment or call, the total amount is entered in a temporary account (really a Sundry Shareholders' Account) which is known as an Application and Allotment Account, a Call Account, or an Instalment Account. Thus, if Central Provision Stores PLC had issued 90,200 shares of £1.00 each in 19*x*7, payable £0.5 on allotment, the entries would have been:

ORDINARY SHARE CAPITAL ACCOUNT

		Application and Allotment A/c	£45,100

APPLICATION AND ALLOTMENT ACCOUNT

Ordinary Share Capital A/c	£45,100	By Cash—Application and Allotment moneys	£45,100

Since making an issue of shares, or a call on shares issued, means receiving money from a large number of shareholders, a company will normally make arrangements for these amounts to be paid directly to its bankers. The amounts are paid into a separate account and, after an appropriate interval, are transferred to the company's ordinary Bank Account. In this way the company avoids having to deal with a large number of remittances over a short period, and the difficulties such extra work might cause. When this is done the entries would be as follows for a call of £0.5 per share:

ORDINARY SHARE CAPITAL CALL ACCOUNT

	£		£
Ordinary Share Capital A/c	45,100	Cash	45,000
		Calls in arrear	100
	£45,100		£45,100

CALLS IN ARREAR ACCOUNT

Share Capital Call A/c	£100		

In this case the holder of 200 shares had failed to pay the Call of £0.5 per share and thus owes the company £100. This first shows up on the Call Account, but is later transferred to the Calls in Arrear Account, opened specifically for the purpose.

In practice journal entries would be required before making any entries in the Ledger Accounts.

The Balance Sheet of Central Provision Store PLC would include the following items:

	£
Capital and Reserves	
Called up Share Capital	
90,200 shares of £1 each fully called	90,200
Current Assets (would include)	
Debtors	
Called up Share Capital not paid	100
The authorised share capital	
125,000 Ordinary shares of £1.00 each	£125,000

The paid up capital is therefore £90,100, i.e. called up share capital (£90,200) less in assets (£100).

Alternatively the Share Capital called up but unpaid can be shown as a separate *asset* immediately preceding the Fixed Assets.

It will be noticed that in addition to details of the shares actually issued there are shown the details of the shares which the company is authorised by its Memorandum of Association to issue. This is required under the Companies Acts.

Often it is found desirable to remove a considerable amount of detail from the Balance Sheet itself and to append this in notes. The Transport Development Group Balance Sheet on page 196 represents a considerable amount of detail shown in notes which appear after it. There is also certain financial information which does not appear on the Balance Sheet but which must be disclosed in order to give a correct view of the company's affairs. This is mainly concerned with contingent liabilities such as commitments for capital expenditure and under leases. The Companies Acts require certain specific items of this nature to be stated. This is illustrated in the note on page 209.

Appropriation of Profits

As in the case of a partnership, an account (sometimes regarded as part of the Profit and Loss Account) is opened to show the appropriation of profit. This is called the **Profit and Loss Appropriation Account**. With a limited company not all the profit for the year is necessarily appropriated, and any balance is carried forward from the Appropriation Account of one year to that of the next year. Any such balance will be shown on the Balance Sheet as part of the equity in the form of a **Revenue Reserve**.

The procedure for the payment of dividends is similar to the procedure for receiving payments from the shareholders on their shares. A special Dividend Account is opened by crediting a Dividend Payable Account and debiting the Profit and Loss Appropriation Account with the total amount. On the payment day the Cash Book is credited with the total amount of the dividend, and the Dividend Account is debited. At the same time the amount involved is transferred to a special account at the bank and the dividend warrants are paid by the bank from this account.

An interim dividend may be paid during the course of the year when the directors are satisfied that there is sufficient accumulated profit to meet it. In this case the Profit and Loss Appropriation Account will be debited with the amount before the profit for the year has been credited to it. The Interim Dividend Account will be balanced by the payment before the end of the year. The only record of such a dividend in the Final Accounts will be a debit entry in the Profit and Loss Appropriation Account.

A final dividend will not be payable until after the end of the company's financial year, when the profit (or loss) for the year has been ascertained. In preparing the Final Accounts a **Proposed Final Dividend Account** will be credited with the amount which the directors propose to pay, but it will not be closed by the recording of the payment as this has not yet taken place. Hence the proposed final dividend will appear in the Final Account as a debit entry in the Profit and Loss Appropriation Account and also on the Balance Sheet as a 'Current Liability'.

After an appropriate period, any balance on the bank account opened for the payment of dividends will represent unclaimed dividends. The amount will be credited to an 'Unclaimed Dividend Account'.

Just as separate Capital Accounts are opened for each class of share, so separate Dividend Accounts are opened for each dividend on each class of share.

Looking again at Central Provision Store PLC, and assuming that an interim dividend of $3\frac{1}{3}$ per cent was paid during the year and that the directors propose paying a final dividend of $6\frac{2}{3}$ per cent for the year on fully paid shares (90,000 shares), the accounts would appear as follows:

INTERIM DIVIDEND ACCOUNT

Cash	£3,000	Profit and Loss Appropriation A/c	£3,000

PROPOSED FINAL DIVIDEND ACCOUNT

		Profit and Loss Appropriation A/c	£6,000

PROFIT AND LOSS APPROPRIATION ACCOUNT
(for the year ended December 31st, 19..)

	£		£
Interim Dividend	3,000	Balance b/f	—
Proposed Final Dividend	6,000	Profit for the Year	13,400
Balance c/f	4,400		
	£13,400		£13,400

Assuming that prior to the end of the year a further 10,000 shares at £1 each had been issued the summarised balance sheet would appear as follows:

CENTRAL PROVISION STORE PLC

BALANCE SHEET
(as at December 31st, 19..)

	£
Total Assets (including £100 Called up Share Capital not paid)	£203,600
Creditors: Accounts falling due within one year	29,000
Creditors: Amounts falling due after one year	70,000
Capital	
Called up Share Capital	
100,200 Shares of £1 each	100,200
Revenue Reserves	4,400
	£203,600

or in full as follows:

CENTRAL PROVISION STORE PLC

BALANCE SHEET
(as at December 31st, 19..)

	£	£	£
FIXED ASSETS			
Intangible Assets			
Goodwill		5,000	
Patents		10,000	
			15,000

Continued over.

	£	£	£
b/f			15,000
Tangible Assets			
Land		5,000	
Buildings	76,000		
less Accumulated Depreciation	3,000		
		73,000	
Store Equipment	20,000		
less Accumulated Depreciation	6,000		
		14,000	
			92,000
Long Term Investment			50,000
CURRENT ASSETS			
Stocks			
Consumables for Office and Stores	500		
Finished goods	40,000		
		40,500	
Debtors			
Trade	3,000		
Bills Receivable	1,500		
		4,500	
Investments			
Short Term			
Cash at Bank and in hand		1,000	
Called up share capital not paid		100	
Prepayments and Accrued Income			
Prepayments			
Insurance prepaid		500	
		46,600	
CREDITORS: AMOUNTS FALLING DUE WITHIN ONE YEAR			
Trade Creditors	15,000		
Bills Payable	5,000		
Taxation	2,000		
Salaries Accrued	1,000		
Dividend Proposed (Final)	6,000		
		29,000	
Net Current Assets			17,600
TOTAL ASSETS LESS CURRENT LIABILITIES			£174,600
(including proposed final dividend of £6,000)			
CREDITORS: AMOUNTS FALLING DUE AFTER MORE THAN ONE YEAR			
Loan		20,000	
Mortgage		50,000	
			70,000
			£104,600
Capital and Reserves			
Issued Share Capital			
100,200 Ordinary Shares of £1.00 each	100,200		
Share Premium account		—	
Revaluation Reserve		—	
Other Reserves		—	
Profit and Loss account		4,400	£104,600

Note:
Authorised Capital
125,000 Ordinary Shares of £1. £125,000

Classes of Shares

A company may issue shares of different types. With the exception of Redeemable Preference Shares, the company may not normally repay capital to the shareholders unless it is liquidated, and then only in accordance with the provisions of the Companies Acts. The main differences relate to:

(*a*) The priority in the return of capital to the shareholders if the company is liquidated.
(*b*) The priority in the receipt of dividends and limitations on the maximum rate for preference shares.
(*c*) Whether, if the company pays dividends on preference shares below the maximum permitted rate, such deficiencies are cumulative or non-cumulative.
(*d*) Whether the shares have a par value. Companies in Great Britain are not permitted to issue shares of no par value.

Capital Gearing

The return on capital used in the business may depend entirely on the profits available, as with ordinary shares, or the return on it may be purely contractual, as with debentures where interest is payable whether or not the company makes profits. In some instances, e.g. preference shares, it represents a compromise. The relationship between capital raised by way of ordinary shares and that on which there is a prior charge for interest or dividends is known as the 'capital gearing' of the company. It is said to be low when a large proportion of the capital is in the form of ordinary shares, and high when a large proportion is in the form of preference shares and debentures.

The capital gearing has a marked effect on the performance of the ordinary shares. The higher the capital gearing, the greater will be the variation between good years and bad in the return on the ordinary shares. Again, if the capital gearing is high, the ordinary shareholders will benefit more from inflation and suffer more as a result of falling prices. This follows from the fact that the return on prior capital is fixed in money terms, and not on the level of profits which will tend to reflect changes in the price level.

The capital gearing of Central Provision Store PLC at December 31st, 19. . is fairly low, being approximately £100,000 of Ordinary Share Capital to £70,000 of Long-term Liabilities. If it had been £50,000 of Ordinary Share Capital to £120,000 of Long-term Liabilities, it would have been high. Any increase in profits over the present level would be divisible over 50,000 shares instead of 100,000 shares, and the increase in dividend could have been double that in the former case. On the other hand, if profits declined the sum available for distribution as dividends to ordinary shareholders would fall by twice as much as with the existing capital structure.

3
Changes in the Owners' Equity

The Sole Trader

No difficulties arise over equity changes with the sole trader, as he may introduce or withdraw capital from the business at will. This is not of direct concern to creditors or others since the proprietor remains liable for the debts of the business to the full extent of his possessions, whether earmarked by him for the use of the business or not.

The Partnership

Although partners are personally liable for the debts of the partnership, and creditors are not directly concerned, any changes in the ownership of the business will affect a partner's individual share. The most usual changes will be the introduction of a new partner or the retirement of an existing one.

Goodwill

Since most of the assets of the business are included on the basis of their cost less depreciation written off, and some on the basis of a valuation at a particular date, it would be a coincidence if the current value of the assets all corresponded with their book-values. Moreover, a business will often be worth more as a going concern than as a group of unrelated assets.

When a partner retires he is entitled to the appropriate share of the value of the business. This is achieved by valuing the business as a **going concern** and introducing into the Balance Sheet an intangible asset called 'Goodwill'.

Let us go back and reconsider the Central Provision Store as a partnership, the Balance Sheet being shown on page 25. It is proposed to introduce a new partner, Amber, who will provide capital in the form of £35,000 cash, and to revise the profit-sharing ratio so that it will become: Brown 2/10, Black 3/10, Green 3/10, Amber 2/10.

The business is first valued as a **going concern**. The net worth of the business on the basis of the Balance Sheet is:

Total Assets – Total Liabilities
£203,500 – £93,000 = £110,500

By definition this is equal to the owners' equity. If the current value of the business is £130,200, the Goodwill is £130,200 – £110,500 = £19,700.

The Balance Sheet and accounts are first adjusted to include the Goodwill, which is divided between the existing partners in their profit-sharing ratio. (This is how the Goodwill would have been divided between them if the business had been sold as a going concern.) The accounts involved are

GOODWILL ACCOUNT

Sundries	£19,700		

CAPITAL ACCOUNT—BROWN

			£
		Balance	25,000
		Goodwill ($\frac{2}{10}$ of £19,700)	3,940
			£28,940

CAPITAL ACCOUNT—BLACK

			£
		Balance	25,000
		Goodwill ($\frac{3}{10}$ of £19,700)	5,910
			£30,910

CAPITAL ACCOUNT—GREEN

			£
		Balance	50,000
		Goodwill ($\frac{5}{10}$ of £19,700)	9,850
			£59,850

Having recorded the current position, the new partner, Amber, can now be introduced as follows:

CAPITAL ACCOUNT—AMBER

		Cash	£35,000

CASH ACCOUNT

Amber	£35,000		

The Balance Sheet will now appear like this:

BALANCE SHEET
(as at January 1st, 19..)

	Current A/c	Capital A/c		
	£	£	Total Assets (including £35,000 additional cash)	238,500
Brown	2,130	28,940	Goodwill	19,700
Black	2,795	30,910		
Green	5,575	59,850		
Amber	—	35,000		
	10,500	154,700		
		10,500		
		165,200		
Total Liabilities		93,000		
		£258,200		£258,200

It is always possible to check whether the appropriate entries have been made by considering what would happen if the partnership were dissolved immediately after the admission of the new partner, the business being sold for the amount estimated. The new partner should receive back exactly the amount which he introduced into the business. The current value of the business, £130,200, plus the additional cash, £35,000, gives a total of £165,200, which is the exact amount required to repay old and new partners their capital as shown on the Balance Sheet.

Sometimes partners choose to delete the Goodwill after the change in the equity. This is done by dividing the Goodwill in the new profit-sharing ratio, taking it out of the Balance Sheet, and reducing each of the partner's Capital Accounts by their share. It would mean the following adjustments to the Capital Accounts:

	Capital	Goodwill	Reduced Capital
	£	£	£
Brown	28,940	3,940	25,000
Black	30,910	5,910	25,000
Green	59,850	5.910	53,940
Amber	35,000	3,940	31,060
	£154,700	£19,700	£135,000

An alternative method is to calculate the value of the Goodwill but not to introduce it into the Partnership Accounts of the Balance Sheet. Instead, the new partner uses part of the cash he has available to pay the existing partners for the share of the Goodwill which will become his on the basis of the share of profits that he is due to receive. The calculation would be:

	£
Goodwill	19,700
Amber's Share ($\frac{2}{10}$)	3,940
(to be paid to existing partners in their old profit-sharing ratio)	
Brown ($\frac{2}{10}$)	788
Black ($\frac{3}{10}$)	1,182
Green($\frac{5}{10}$)	1,970
	£3,940
Cash Provided by Amber	35,000
Less Paid to Existing Partners	3,940
Cash Remaining, Introduced as Capital	£31,060

The existing partners may either retain the amount they receive for Goodwill or pay it into the partnership. If they retain it, the Balance Sheet will appear as:

BALANCE SHEET
(as at January 1st, 19..)

	Current A/c	Capital A/c	Total Assets (including	£
	£	£	£31,060 additional cash)	234,560
Brown	2,130	25,000		
Black	2,795	25,000		
Green	5,575	50,000		
Amber	—	31,060		
	10,500	131,060		
		10,500		
		141,560		
Total Liabilities		93,000		
		£234,560		£234,560

The accuracy of this can be checked by assuming that the business was sold for £130,200, plus the amount of additional cash introduced, and then calculating the sum that would be due to the new partner Amber. It would amount to:

	£
Capital	31,060
$\frac{2}{10}$th of Goodwill (excess of current value of business over book value)	
$\frac{2}{10}$th of £19,700	3,940
Total	£35,000

resulting in Amber receiving exactly the amount he had paid for the privilege of joining the business and sharing the Goodwill.

Dissolution

At the dissolution of a partnership the assets are all transferred to a **Realisation Account**. Whether they are disposed of either separately or as a going concern, the proceeds are credited to this account. The expenses of disposing of the assets are debited and any profit or loss on realisation is divided between the partners in their profit-sharing ratios. Special rules apply when the partners are not able to make the contribution necessary to meet the obligations of the partnership.

If we assume that instead of introducing a new partner, the business was sold on December 31st for £131,000, and the expenses incurred in selling the business were £800, the entries would be as follows (with Brown's Capital Account as example):

CAPITAL ACCOUNT—BROWN

	£		£
Cash	31,070	Balance	25,000
		Balance of Current Account Transferred	2,130
		Profit on Realisation	3,940
	£31,070		£31,070

REALISATION ACCOUNT

		£		£
Total Assets		203,500	Total Liabilities	93,000
Cash—Realisation Expenses		800	Cash—Sale of Business	131,000
Profit on Realisation				
Brown ($\frac{2}{10}$)	3,940			
Black ($\frac{3}{10}$)	5,910			
Green ($\frac{5}{10}$)	9,850			
		19,700		
		£224,000		£224,000

CASH ACCOUNT

	£		£
Sale of Business	131,000	Realisation Expenses	800
		Brown	31,070
		Black	33,705
		Green	65,425
	£131,000		£131,000

The balance of the partners' Current Accounts are transferred to their Capital Accounts. The profit or loss on realisation, divided in the profit-sharing ratio, is also transferred to the Capital Accounts.

If the payment for the business has been in cash, the balance of the Cash Account will be just sufficient to permit payment to the partners of the balance of their Capital Accounts. If, on the other hand, the business has been sold partly or entirely for the shares of a company, an account (Shares in X Co. Ltd) will be debited with the value of the shares when the business is sold. This account will be closed by credit entries when the shares are transferred to the partners, and the partners' Capital Accounts will be debited with the value of the shares which have been transferred to them in payment or part payment for the business. (This value will not necessarily be the same as the nominal value of the shares.) The final settlement of the Capital Accounts will still be made by a cash payment.

The Limited Company

Any change in the equity of a company will normally result in the issue of additional shares. Shares of a class different from those already on the market may be issued in the normal way provided that the rights attaching to the new issue do not conflict with those of existing shares. If further shares of a class already issued are created, they will normally be at a premium (i.e. the market value will be above the paid-up value). If it were not so, they would not be taken up and issuing at a discount is not permitted.

It would obviously be a better proposition for a prospective shareholder to buy existing shares on the Stock Exchange at a price below the paid-up value than to subscribe for new shares which cannot be issued below the par value. If a company's £1.00 shares stood at £0.75 on the Stock Exchange, no buyer would contemplate subscribing for new shares which could not be issued below £1.00.

Share Premiums

Where shares stand above the paid-up value, it would be unfair to the existing shareholders to issue further shares of the same class at the par value. The new shares would carry the same rights as the existing shares, and the new shareholders would receive in effect a bonus equal to the difference between the market price and the par value.

When, for example, a company's £1.00 shares stand at £1.50 there are apparently investors willing to pay £1.50 for these shares and the company could therefore issue more shares of the same class at a price a little below £1.50, say £1.40. If £1.00 shares were issued at £1.40, £0.40 of the price would represent a **share premium**.

From time to time the company may make a **rights issue**. This means that the shares are issued at a price considerably below the market price, but existing shareholders are given the right to subscribe for them in proportion to the number of shares held and to be issued. Thus if 500,000 shares had already been issued and a further 100,000 were to be issued, shareholders would be given the right to subscribe for one share for every five already held.

In this case the shares would still be issued at a premium, but not such a large one as in the former case. The existing shareholders would, however, benefit either from obtaining shares at a price below the market price or from selling the rights for the difference between the issue price and the market price.

In the United Kingdom the Companies Acts do not permit a company to distribute share premium by way of dividend to the shareholders. It may only be used for certain clearly defined purposes. Hence the amount so received is always credited to a Share Premium Account and this item is included in the Balance Sheet as a Capital Reserve (a reserve not available for distribution to shareholders by way of dividend).

By way of example let us assume our Central Provision Store PLC, whose Balance Sheet appears on pages 29 and 30, is thinking of acquiring an interest in another business and to raise a further £50,000. For various reasons the shares are standing at £1.30, so it is decided to issue 40,000 shares at £1.25 to raise the amount required. The issue of the shares would involve the same procedures as with the original issue except that the first £0.25 per share would be credited to the Share Premium Account and the remaining £1.00 to the Ordinary-Share Capital Account. The result would be:

ORDINARY SHARE CAPITAL ACCOUNT

	Balance	£100,200
	Cash	£40,000

SHARE PREMIUM ACCOUNT

	Cash	£10,000

CENTRAL PROVISION STORE PLC

BALANCE SHEET

(as at January 1st, 19..)

	£	£
Total Assets (including £50,000 additional cash and £100 calls in arrear)		253,600
Total Creditors		99,000
		£154,600
Capital and Reserves		
Called up Share Capital		
140,200 Shares of £1 each	140,200	
Share Premium	10,000	
Balance of Profit and Loss	4,400	
		£154,600

Note:
Authorised Share capital
200,000 Ordinary Shares of £1 each £200,000

'No-Par-Value' Shares

Although it is illegal in the United Kingdom, some countries permit the issue of shares of no par value. In the first instance such shares are issued at a price determined by the company and the proceeds are credited to a 'No-Par-Value Share Capital Account'. If further no-par-value shares are issued at a later date, they are issued at a price as close to the market price as possible and the proceeds are credited to the No-Par-Value Share Capital Account. Consequently, the total amount received from the issue of shares accumulates in this account, and there is no question of any share premium arising. The use of no-par-value shares is advocated on the grounds that after a company has been successful for a considerable period and has ploughed back profits, the par value of the shares gives no guide to the value of the assets representing the shareholder's interest in the company.

No complications arise since each no-par-value share is entitled to the same voting rights and the same amount of dividend at each distribution of profit. There is no par value to mislead anyone trying to work out the asset value of the shares.

Redemption or Purchase of Shares

A major change introduced by the Companies Act, 1981 was the granting of permission for a company to purchase its own shares—a practice which had been legal for some time in many EEC countries and the USA. There are limitations—primarily that some of the remaining shares *must* be irredeemable, the dealing must be permitted by the articles of association, shareholders' approval must be obtained and disclosure of the dealings must be made. Prior to this the only shares which could be redeemed were Preference Shares specifically indicated to be redeemable at the time of the original issue. So that the position of creditors shall not be unfavourably affected by the redemption, the funds required for the purpose may only come out of profits which would be available for distribution or out of the proceeds of a further issue of shares or share premium.

When such shares are redeemed out of profits it is necessary to open a Capital Redemption Reserve, crediting this account with the amount paid in redemption of the shares and debiting the account or accounts where the undistributed profits are recorded (usually the Revenue Reserve Account or the Profit and Loss Appropriation Account). For example, had the only entries been in the Cash Account and the Redeemable Preference Share Capital Account, the revenue reserves would remain on the Balance Sheet and there would be nothing to prevent the company distributing them later by way of dividend. If this were done, the cash for the repayment of the shares would have come from other resources of the company, thus reducing the amount which creditors could expect to be available to meet the company's debts.

If we assume that Central Provision Store PLC had raised the additional capital by an issue of 50,000 6 per cent Redeemable Preference Shares repayable ten years later, the Balance Sheet would have appeared as:

CENTRAL PROVISION STORE PLC

BALANCE SHEET
(as at January 1st, 19..)

	£	£
Total Assets		£253,600
Total External Liabilities		99,000
Capital and Reserves		
Called up Share Capital		
100,200 Ordinary Shares of £1.00 each	100,200	
50,000 6% Redeemable Preference Shares of £1 each	50,000	
		150,200
Revenue Reserves		
Balance of Profit and Loss Account		4,400
		£253,600

Let us now look into the future and assume that in ten years £60,000 profits have been ploughed back into the company and that by a happy coincidence these profits are reflected by an increase in cash of £60,000 while all other items have remained unchanged. The company is going to repay the Redeemable Preference Shares in cash on January 1st, 1989.

The Balance Sheet at December 31st, 1988 will differ from the one at January 1st, 1979, only in the following respects:

	1979 £	1988 £
Total Assets	253,500	313,500
General Reserve and Balance of Profit and Loss A/c	4,400	64,600

The entries on redeeming the shares would be

6% REDEEMABLE PREFERENCE SHARE CAPITAL ACCOUNT

Cash	£50,000	Balance b/f	£50,000

CASH ACCOUNT

Balance	?	Redeemable Preference Share Capital	£50,000

GENERAL RESERVE

	£		£
Redeemable Preference Share Capital Reserve	50,000	Balance b/f	60,000
Balance c/f	10,000		
	£60,000		£60,000
		Balance b/f	£10,000

CAPITAL REDEMPTION RESERVE ACCOUNT

	General Reserve	£50,000

On January 1st, 1989, after the shares have been redeemed, the Balance Sheet would appear as:

CENTRAL PROVISION STORE PLC
BALANCE SHEET
(as at January 1st, 1989)

	£	£
Total Assets		
(£313,600 less £50,000)		£263,600
Total External Liabilities		99,000
Capital and Reserves		
Called up Share Capital		
100,200 Ordinary Shares of £1	100,200	
Reserves		
Capital Redemption Reserve	50,000	
General Reserve	10,000	
Balance of Profit and Loss Account	4,400	
		164,600
		£263,600

The Capital Redemption Reserve may be used for the issue of **Bonus Shares.**

Bonus Shares

Over a number of years a company may plough back part of its profits, or after a number of years of rising prices a company may revalue its assets. The result will be an increase in reserves and will normally cause a rise in the market price of the company's shares. Companies may not like the market price of their shares to be much above the par value. They are not in a position to distribute their reserves by way of dividend because the resources involved are invested in the business; the cash is not available. The alternative is the issue of 'bonus shares' to the existing shareholders, the company paying for them in full out of the reserves. Thus, a company whose capital is £100,000 and which has £50,000 in the form of reserves (Share Premium, Capital Redemption Reserve and/or balance of the Profit and Loss Account), may issue 50,000 Bonus Shares of £1.00 each. This will raise the issued capital to £150,000 and reduce the reserves by £50,000. Such an action is usually contemplated when the company is in a position to continue paying the same rate of dividend on the enlarged capital. In the example given, it would mean increasing the amount of profits distributed by 50 per cent.

Holding and Subsidiary Companies

The equity of the company may be affected when its shares are acquired by another company. Where a substantial proportion of such shares are acquired, the interests of the remaining shareholders (the *minority interest*) may be affected. In the United Kingdom the Companies Acts provide certain safeguards and require that the company acquiring such shares (known as the **holding company**) should prepare and circulate a consolidated Balance Sheet and Profit and Loss Account. The company whose shares are thus acquired is known as a **subsidiary company**. The Companies Acts define the circumstances in which this relationship is deemed to exist. A holding company may have more than one subsidiary company, and in such cases the subsidiary companies are required to indicate on the Balance Sheets any amounts owing to or from fellow subsidiaries as well as to or from the holding company.

Basically the **consolidated Balance Sheet** of the group differs from the Balance Sheet of the holding (or parent) company in that the 'Assets and liabilities of the subsidiary company' replaces that part of the asset group 'Investments' which represents 'Shares in Subsidiary Companies at cost'. It is unlikely that the holding company will have paid an amount for the shares corresponding exactly to the equity (capital and reserves) of the subsidiary company. Merely replacing the item 'Shares in subsidiary companies' by the 'Assets and liabilities' from the subsidiary company's Balance Sheet would leave the consolidated Balance Sheet unbalanced. An additional item is therefore inserted, being the difference between the holding company's share of the equity of the subsidiary company and the amount paid by the holding company. This is described as **Cost of Control** (sometimes **Goodwill on Consolidation**) if there is a deficiency on the asset side, or **Reserve on Consolidation** if there is a deficiency on the liability and equity side. The simplest case is where the holding company acquires all the shares of the subsidiary company.

By way of illustration let us assume that Central Provision Store PLC, after raising the additional capital, acquired all the shares in Northern Provision Store Ltd, on January 1st, 19.9.

The Balance Sheet of Northern Provision Store Ltd at the end of 19.8, showing only sufficient detail to illustrate the process of consolidation, was

NORTHERN PROVISION STORE LTD

BALANCE SHEET

(as at December 31st, 19..)

	£	£
Fixed Assets		18,000
Current Assets		
Stock	4,500	
Debtors	4,800	
Cash	700	
	10,000	
Creditors		
Trade Creditors	5,000	
Net Current Assets		5,000
		£23,000
Capital and Reserves		
Called Up Share Capital		20,000
Reserves		3,000
Note:		
Authorised Capital		£25,000

The Balance Sheet of Central Provision Store PLC after raising additional capital is shown on page 38 and in full on page 44.

CENTRAL PROVISION STORE PLC

BALANCE SHEET

(as at December 31st, 19. .)

	£	£	£	£
Fixed Assets				
Intangible Assets				
Goodwill		5,000		
Patents		10,000		
			15,000	
Tangible Assets				
Land		5,000		
Buildings	76,000			
less Accumulated depreciation	3,000			
		73,000		
Stores Equipment	20,000			
less Accumulated depreciation	6,000			
		14,000		
			92,000	
Investments			50,000	
				157,000
Current Assets				
Stocks			40,500	
Debtors and Bills Receivable		4,500		
Called up Share capital not paid		100		
Prepayments		500		
			5,100	
Cash			51,000	
			96,600	
Creditors: amounts falling due within one year				
Trade Creditors, etc.			29,000	
Net Current Assets				67,600
Total Assets *less* current liabilities				£224,600
Creditors: amounts falling due after one year				
Loan			20,000	
Mortgages			50,000	
				70,000
				£154,600
Capital and Reserves				
Called up Share Capital				140,200
Share Premium				10,000
Balance of Profit and Loss				4,400
				£154,600

Assuming that Central Provision Store PLC acquired all the shares of Northern Provision Store Ltd (20,000 £1.00 shares) for £25,000, the Balance Sheet of the Central Provision Store PLC, now becomes:

CENTRAL PROVISION STORE PLC

BALANCE SHEET

(as at January 1st, 19.9)

	£	£	£	£
Fixed Assets				
Intangible Assets				
Goodwill		5,000		
Patents		10,000		
			15,000	
Tangible Assets				
Land		5,000		
Buildings	76,000			
less Accumulated depreciation	3,000			
		73,000		
Stores Equipment	20,000			
less Accumulated depreciation	6,000			
		14,000		
			92,000	
Investments				
Shares in Group Companies (*Northern Provision Store at cost*)		25,000		
Quoted Investments		50,000		
			75,000	
				182,000
Current Assets				
Stocks			40,500	
Debtors and Bills Receivable		4,500		
Called up share capital not paid		100		
Prepayments		500		
			5,100	
Cash			26,000	
			71,600	
Creditors: amounts falling due within one year				
Trade Creditors			29,000	
Net Current Assets				42,600
Total Assets *less* Current Liabilities				224,600
Creditors: falling due after more than one year				
Loan			20,000	
Mortgages			50,000	
				70,000
				154,600
Capital and Reserves				
Called up Share Capital				140,200
Share Premium				10,000
Balance of Profit and Loss				4,400
				£154,600

It is important to realise that this is the Balance Sheet of the parent (or holding) company only. The only change from the previous balance sheet is the substitution of the investment in Northern Provision Ltd (at cost), for the £25,000 cash paid for the shares, i.e. we have changed one form of asset for another. If we were to substitute the assets and liabilities of Northern Provision Store Ltd (£28,000 – £5,000 = £23,000) which incidentally is equal by definition to the Owners Equity (Capital and Reserve) there would be a deficiency of £2,000 in the assets. This will be represented by the Cost of Control, £2,000, but such adjustment will only by shown on the *Consolidated* Balance Sheet. In a Consolidated Balance Sheet the individual assets and liabilities of the companies concerned are *added together* hence the necessity for any difference between the price paid and the value of the company acquired to be shown as an asset (Cost of Control) or if the price paid is less than the value of assets acquired as a liability (Capital Reserve).

The Consolidated Balance Sheet will appear as follows on page 47.

Additional information may well indicate that further adjustments are necessary to produce a satisfactory Consolidated Balance Sheet.

(*a*) We may find that Central Provision Store PLC has sold goods to Northern Provision Store Ltd for £1,500 which cost £1,200, and half of these goods have not yet been sold.

If we consider the group as a whole, goods costing Central Provision Store PLC £600 (½ of £1,200) are still unsold by the group but appear in the assets of Northern Provision Store Ltd at £750 (½ of £1,500). This contravenes the convention of valuing stock at cost or net realisable value, whichever is the lower, and consequently the profit of the group must be reduced by £150. The value of the stocks on the Consolidated Balance Sheet must be reduced by this amount. Normally the profits of the group will be reduced accordingly, but in this case as the shares have only just been acquired, the Cost of Control must be increased by £150. Once the Cost of Control or the reserve arising on consolidation has been correctly established the only circumstances in which it is altered are:

(i) If it is decided to write down the value of any of the assets of the subsidiary company when consolidating its accounts with those of the holding company. The reserve arising on consolidation will be reduced by the total amount written off the subsidiary company's assets. (This will not affect the Balance Sheet of the subsidiary company itself.)

(ii) If the company distributes by way of dividend any reserves which had already been accumulated by the date on which the holding company acquired its shares. These are not earnings on the holding company's investment, they represent assets which the subsidiary company had already acquired. They must therefore be treated as a repayment of part of the price paid for the investment, and any such dividends received must be used to reduce the Cost of Control or increase the reserve arising on consolidation. Such amounts are known as **pre-acquisition profits**.

(*b*) We may find that Northern Provision Store Ltd owes Central Provision Store Ltd £800. This amount is included in the creditors of the Northern Provision Store Ltd PLC and the debtors of the Central Provision

CENTRAL PROVISION STORE PLC

CONSOLIDATED BALANCE SHEET

(as at January 1st, 19.9)

		£	£	£
Fixed Assets				
Intangible Assets				
Goodwill	CPS	5,000		
Cost of Control		2,000		
		7,000		
Patents		10,000		
			17,000	
Tangible Assets				
Land, Buildings, Plant etc.,	CPS	92,000		
	NPS	18,000		
			110,000	
Investments				
Quoted Investments			50,000	
				177,000
Current Assets				
Stocks	CPS	40,500		
	NPS	4,500		
			45,000	
Debtors and Bills Receivable	CPS	4,500		
	NPS	4,800		
		9,300		
Called up share capital not paid	CPS	100		
Prepayments		500		
			9,900	
Cash	CPS	26,000		
	NPS	700		
			26,700	
			81,600	
Creditors: amounts falling due within one year				
Trade Creditors	CPS	29,000		
	NPS	5,000		
			34,000	
Net Current Assets				47,600
Total Assets *less* Current Liabilities				224,600
Creditors: amounts falling due after more than one year				
Loan			20,000	
Mortgages			50,000	
				70,000
				154,600
Capital and Reserves				
Called up Share Capital				140,200
Share Premium				10,000
Balance of Profit and Loss				4,400
				£154,600

Note: The separate values of each type of asset belonging to CPS (Central Provision Store) and NPS (Northern Provision Store) have been included to make clearer the sources of the consolidated figure. In practice this would not be shown.

Store PLC. As the Consolidated Balance Sheet stands, the group is shown as owing itself £800 and this amount must be deducted from debtors and creditors. It may happen on occasion that one of the companies has surplus funds which it lends to another. Any such loan must be treated in the same way as the debt arising from trading between the companies already mentioned.

The Consolidated Balance Sheet with these two adjustments is shown on page 49:

The Minority Interest

It is quite common for the holding company to acquire only a part of the share capital of the subsidiary company: the holding company will then have only a part interest in the assets and liabilities of the subsidiary. Rather than include only a part of the assets and liabilities of the subsidiary company on the Consolidated Balance Sheet, it is usual to include the full amount and to show the interest of the other shareholders as a liability. This may be described as the *Minority Interest* or the *Outside Shareholders Interest*.

Let us assume that Central Provision Store PLC now acquires an interest in Suburban Provision Store Ltd, whose skeleton Balance Sheet is as follows:

SUBURBAN PROVISION STORE LTD

BALANCE SHEET
(as at December 31st, 19.8)

	£	£
Fixed Assets		
Current Assets		15,000
Stock	8,000	
Debtors	5,500	
Prepaid Expenses	300	
Cash	200	
	14,000	
Creditors: amounts falling due within one year		
Creditors	4,000	
		10,000
Total Assets *less* Current Liabilities		£25,000
Capital and Reserves		
Called up Share Capital (£1 shares)		20,000
Reserves		5,000
		£25,000

CENTRAL PROVISION STORE PLC AND SUBSIDIARY

CONSOLIDATED BALANCE SHEET

(as at January 1st, 19.9)

		£	£	£
Fixed Assets				
Intangible Assets				
Goodwill	CPS	5,000		
Cost of Control		2,150		
		7,150		
Patents		10,000		
			17,150	
Tangible Assets				
Land and Buildings Plant, etc.	CPS	92,000		
	NPS	18,000		
			110,000	
Investments				
Quoted Investments			50,000	
				177,150
Current Assets				
Stock		45,000		
less Adjustment (a)		150		
			44,850	
Debtors and Bills Receivable		9,300		
Less Adjustment (b)		800		
		8,500		
Called up share capital not paid		100		
Prepayments		500		
			9,100	
Cash			26,700	
			88,650	
Creditors: amounts falling due within one year				
Creditors		34,000		
less Adjustment (b)		800		
			33,200	
Net Current Assets				47,450
Total Assets *less* Current Liabilities				224,600
Creditors: falling due after one year				
Loans			20,000	
Mortgages			50,000	
				70,000
				154,600
Capital and Reserves				
Called up Share Capital				140,200
Share Premium				10,000
Balance of Profit and Loss				4,400
				£154,600

Central Provision Store PLC acquired 12,000 shares for £14,000 and immediately lent to Suburban Provision Store Ltd £5,000 as the company was short of funds. The interest acquired by Central Provision Store PLC can be calculated as follows:

Total number of shares = 20,000
Acquired by Central Provisions Store PLC = 12,000

$\therefore$ proportion of holding $= \frac{12,000}{20,000} = \frac{6}{10}$

	Central Provision Store PLC	Minority	Total
	£	£	£
Proportionate Interest in SPS	$\frac{6}{10}$	$\frac{4}{10}$	$\frac{10}{10}$
Share Capital and Reserve of SPS	15,000	10,000	25,000
Cost of Shares in SPS	14,000		
Reserve Arising on Consolidation	£1,000		
Minority Interest		£10,000	

The Consolidated Balance Sheet including both Northern Provision Store Ltd and Suburban Provision Store Ltd is given below. (We start from the Consolidated Balance Sheet shown on page 49.) As there is already an item 'Cost of Control, £2,150', the reserve on consolidation would be deducted from this item rather than shown separately. This can be calculated as follows:

We have acquired 12,000 shares which is 12,000 ÷ 20,000 or 60 per cent. Since this is the proportion of the equity or ownership interest we shall simultaneously acquire the same proportion of the reserves, i.e. 60 per cent of the *Net Worth* will belong to CPS. Note that the authorised capital of SPS is not relevant. In other words we made a gain on acquiring SPS because we acquired shares with a value of £15,000 for £14,000 and the £1,000 can be used to reduce the cost of control of acquiring the first subsidiary thus:

Original cost of control on acquiring NPS Ltd (pages 46–7)

	£	£
Total Assets	28,000	
less liabilities	5,000	
	23,000	
Amount paid	25,000	
Cost of Control of NPS		2,000
Add unrealised Profit in stock		150
		2,150
less Reserve on consolidation (SPS)		1,000
Net Cost of Control		1,150

CENTRAL PROVISION STORE PLC AND SUBSIDIARY

CONSOLIDATED BALANCE SHEET
(as at January 1st, 19.9)

		£	£	£
Fixed Assets				
Intangible Assets				
Goodwill		5,000		
Goodwill Cost of Control		1,150		
		6,150		
Patents		10,000		
			16,150	
Tangible Assets				
Land and Buildings, Plant, etc.		110,000		
	SPS	15,000		
			125,000	
Investments				
Quoted Investments			50,000	
				191,150
Current Assets				
Stocks		44,850		
	SPS	8,000		
			52,850	
Debtors and Bills Receivable		8,500		
	SPS	5,500		
		14,000		
Called up Share Capital not paid		100		
Prepayments		500		
Prepayments	SPS	300	14,900	
Cash		12,700		
	SPS	200		
			12,900	
			80,650	
Creditors amounts falling due within one year				
Creditors		33,200		
	SPS	4,000		
			37,200	
				43,450
				234,600
Creditors amounts falling due after one year				
Loans		20,000		
Mortgages		50,000		
				70,000
				£164,600
Capital and Reserves				
Called up Share Capital				140,200
Share Premium				10,000
Balance of Profit and Loss				4,400
				154,600
Minority Interest				10,000
				£164,600

The loan made by Central Provision Store PLC to Suburban Provision Store Ltd would mean changes in the individual Balance Sheet of each company, but would not have any effect on the Consolidated Balance Sheet: it is a transaction within the group.

Consolidated Profit and Loss Account

Just as all the assets and liabilities of a subsidiary are included in the Consolidated Balance Sheet, so all the profit (or loss) of the subsidiary company is included in the Consolidated Profit and Loss Account. If the subsidiary company is only partly owned, that part of the profits due to the minority shareholders must be segregated. Of the remaining profit, part will normally be distributed by way of dividend and will have been (or will shortly be) paid over to the holding company; the rest will be retained by the subsidiary company.

It is necessary to consider whether any of the dividend received by the holding company represents the distribution of profits earned before the holding company acquired the shares. The method of treatment was explained on page 46. Where goods sold by one company to another are in stock at the end of the year, the proportion of such goods reflecting the group interest must be reduced in value to the *cost* of the goods to the supplying company, and the profit of the group reduced accordingly.

It is also necessary to make adjustments where dividends paid or about to be paid by the subsidiary company to the holding company are provided for in the accounts of the holding company. Such amounts must not be included in the holding company's profit when consolidating the profit figures or there will be double counting. The undistributed profits proportionate to the Minority Interest must be deducted from the amounts added to the group's reserves and shown as an increase in the Minority Interest.

Consolidated accounts can be extremely complicated in practice: the subsidiary company may have acquired shares in the holding company before it became a subsidiary company; the holding company may have acquired shares in the subsidiary company at various dates at various prices; the subsidiary company may itself have subsidiary companies, and there may be other cross-shareholdings.

Overseas Subsidiaries

The accounts of subsidiary companies formed overseas will be kept in a different currency. If the currency is fully convertible, the Balance Sheet and Profit and Loss Accounts will be converted to sterling using defined policies and rules. Recommendations as to acceptable bases are given in the Statement of Standard Accounting Practice No. 20 (SSAP 20) first published in April 1983. The most common basis of conversion is the closing rate/net investment method. Under this method:

(*a*) Balance sheet items are translated into sterling using the rate of exchange ruling at the balance sheet date.

(*b*) Amounts in the profit and loss account are translated at the closing rate or at an average rate for the accounting period. The use of either method is permitted provided that the one selected is applied consistently from one period to another.

(*c*) Exchange differences arise if the rate used in (*a*) differs from that ruling at the previous balance sheet date. These are normally treated as a movement in reserves. The treatment used is disclosed in the *accounting policies*. See the note on basis of consolidation in the specimen accounts on page 209. Similarly if an average rate has been used and this differs from the closing rate a difference will arise which should be dealt with through reserves.

The Source and Application of Funds Statement

This is a statement which shows the source of funds flowing into a business, the way in which they have been utilised and the net deficiency or surplus arising in the accounting period to which it relates. It supplements the other main statements—the Balance Sheet and Profit and Loss Account—and provides an essential link between them. In the UK it forms part of the audited accounts of a company and is the subject of Statement of Standard Accounting Practice (SSAP) No. 10. This has a suggested format to which most companies adhere in respect of published accounts. An example is given for a single company to illustrate the derivation and format.

X LTD

PROFIT AND LOSS ACCOUNT
(for year ended December, 31st 19.7)

	£000	*£000*
Sales		900
Depreciation	100	
Loss on sale of fixed assets	50	
Sundry expenses	600	
		750
Net profit		150
Taxation	40	
Proposed dividends	50	
		90
Retained Profit		60
Balance brought forward		35
Balance carried forward		95

X LTD

BALANCE SHEETS

(at year end)

	31st December, 19.6	31st December, 19.7
	£000	£000
Fixed Assets		
Cost	500	400
Depreciation	200	280
	300	120
Current Assets		
Stocks	400	700
Debtors	140	250
Cash	20	135
	860	1,205
Share Capital	600	800
Profit and Loss Account	35	95
	635	895
Long Term loan	100	150
Taxation	30	40
Creditors	60	70
Proposed dividend	35	50
	860	1,205

Notes:

1. No fixed assets were purchased during the year.
2. Fixed assets sold originally cost £100,000 and had a written down value of £80,000.

X LTD

SOURCE AND APPLICATION OF FUNDS STATEMENT

(for year ended December 31st, 19.7)

	£000	£000
Source of funds:		
Adjusted Net profit (see below)	300	
Issue of shares	200	
Increase in loan	50	
Increase in creditors	10	
Sale of fixed assets	30	
Total source of funds	590	
Application of funds:		
Payment of taxation	30	
Payment of dividend	35	
Increase in stocks	300	
Increase in debtors	110	
Increase in cash	115	
Total application of funds	£590	

Workings

(1) Calculation of net profit for source and application of funds statement:

	£000	
Net Profit and Loss Account	150	before provision for tax and dividend
Add : Depreciation	100	
Loss on sale of fixed assets	50*	derived from (2) below
	300	

(2) Changes in fixed assets:

	£000 Cost	£000 Dep.	£000 NBV
Balance December 31st, 19.6	500	200	300
Less Disposal of assets	100	20* (bal. fig.)	80
Position after disposal	400	180	220
Depreciation for year		100	
	400	280	120

Calculation of loss on disposal	£000
NBV of asset sold	80
Loss on sale	50
∴ sales value	30*

(3) Other items:

	19.6 £000	19.7 £000	S & A Statement £000
Fixed Assets	300	120	See 2 above
Current Assets			
Stocks	400	700	−300
Debtors	140	250	−110
Cash	20	135	−115
Share Capital	600	800	+200
Profit and Loss Account	35	95	See 1 above
Long-term loan	100	150	+50
Taxation	30	40	−30 (a)
Creditors	60	70	10
Proposed dividend	35	50	−35 (a)

Notes:

(a) The previous year taxation and proposed dividends are applications of funds this year.

(b) + = source of funds.
− = application of funds.

Presentation of source and application of funds statements

SSAP 10 does not make any special form of presentation obligatory. However, it does suggest that a distinction be drawn when presenting the statement between:

(1) Funds generated from operations.
(2) Funds obtained from other sources.
(3) Funds absorbed/released by changes in working capital.
(4) Funds applied in areas other than working capital.
(5) Funds absorbed/released by changes in liquid funds. Consequently, the answer above could be redrafted as follows:

X LTD

SOURCES AND APPLICATION OF FUNDS STATEMENT

	£000	*£000*	
Net Profit	150		
Plus/minus items not involving movement in funds:			
Depreciation	100		
Loss on sale of Fixed Assets	50		
Total generated from operations		300	
Funds from other sources:			
Issue of shares for cash	200		
Increase in loan	50		
Sale of fixed assets	30	280	
Total funds generated			580
Application of funds:			
Payment of taxation	30		
Payment of dividends	35		
		65	
Movement in working capital			
Increase in stocks	300		
Increase in debtors	110		
Increase in creditors	(10)		
		400	
			465
			115
Changes in liquid funds			
Opening cash		20	
Closing cash		135	115

The Funds Statement has been a topic of much discussion in recent accounting literature. When prepared, it gives the reader information about the business that a traditional set of comparative statements (such as those shown in Chapter 1) cannot supply. The Funds Statement can be prepared from the traditional set of statements if there is sufficient detail.

The example below is a form of Funds Statement which might be used where a group of companies, whose liquid funds have been increased by the acquisition of an additional subsidiary, is dependent for working capital on bank advances.

SOURCES AND USE OF FUNDS

	£000	£000	£000
Net Overdrawn Position at January 1st, 19.8			2,647
Source of Funds:			
Net Cash Assets Arising on Acquisition of Smalltown Co. Ltd	520		
Sale of Part of Investment in a Subsidiary	615		
Cash Flow (Retained Profits, Depreciation, etc.)	4,983		
		6,118	
Use of Funds:			
Capital Expenditure (net)	2,743		
Net Increase in Working Capital (other than cash)	1,830		
		4,573	1,545
Net Overdrawn Position at December 31st, 19.8			£1,102

Another possible form in which the statement might be prepared is as follows:

GROUP CASH GENERATION AND DISPOSITION OF FUNDS

	£000
Cash Generation:	
Retained Earnings	429
Depreciation	511
Sale of Assets	243
	£1,183
Disposition of Funds:	
Cost of Acquiring New Interests	462
Other Expenditure by Group Companies on Fixed Assets	897
Additional Working Capital	220
	£1,579

The difference was financed by:

Debenture Proceeds, *Less* Short-term Investments	234
Increased Borrowings	162
	£396

In this case also the form of statement is appropriate for a group of companies. The method of preparation is the same as for an individual company, except that the Consolidated Balance Sheets are used and any changes resulting from the acquisition or disposal of interests in subsidiary or associated companies are segregated and shown as a separate item as, for instance, *Sale of part of investment in a subsidiary* in the first example and *Cost of acquiring new interests* in the second example.

Uses of sources and application of funds statements

(*a*) *External use.* As stated earlier SSAP 10 requires that a source and application of funds statement be included in a company's annual report and accounts. This enables users of company accounts; shareholders, prospective investors, creditors, trade unions, etc., to identify clearly the sources from which a company has generated funds during the year, and the ways in which the funds have been applied.

Much of the information shown in the funds flow statement could be obtained from the Profit and Loss Account, Balance Sheet and relevant notes to the accounts. But this would be a tedious task and extremely difficult for users with little accounting knowledge. Consequently, the sources and applications of funds statement is included to show clearly and concisely the inflows and outflows of funds during an accounting period.

(*b*) *Internal use.* Source and application statements are frequently used by company management as part of the company's budgeting and planning system. Forecast statements are prepared, on a monthly, quarterly or annual basis, and statements showing actual results are later prepared thereby allowing the extraction of variances between actual or budget. Appropriate action is then taken by management to deal with the variances that have arisen.

Value Added Statements

It is becoming increasingly common to include a value added statement in corporate reports as an addition to the final accounts and funds flow. Value added is defined as 'the increase in realisable value resulting from an alteration in form, location or availability of a product or service, excluding the cost of purchased materials or services; unlike conversion cost value added includes profit' (ICMA). It is a result of the shift of emphasis of corporate reporting away from reporting shareholders' profits to accounting for performance of all contributors to the organisation—workers and investors. An example of a value added statement is given in the reproduced accounts of the Transport Development Group on page 214. The analysis expressed in percentage terms is of particular interest as the relative contribution of each of the groups can be compared between various companies and industries.

4

Branch Accounts

When a business operates from more than one location certain complications arise both as regards keeping appropriate records and exercising adequate control. Let us look at the problems of Central Provision Store PLC when it contemplates opening a number of branches.

Branch Books Kept at Head Office

The first plan is to open branches in town. These are to be organised as simply as possible. All payments including wages will be paid by headquarters and all the merchandise will be provided by the central warehouse. In this case all the accounting records can be kept at the head office, and the only financial records which must be kept at the branch are of cash takings and the value of the stock. Since the selling price of all items is predetermined, the stock will be charged to the branch at the selling price. (This would not be possible for a butcher, a greengrocer or someone in a similar business.)

Initially the branch will be provided with a cash float so that it can give change to customers. All cash takings will be paid into the bank daily, leaving the cash float intact. The branch manager will have to account for the value of the goods sent to his branch for sale in terms of cash takings and/or stock-on-hand (at selling price). Thus if a branch were provided with a float of £25 and goods (at selling price) £3,500 and the cash takings were £2,975, the branch manager would be expected to have a stock valued at £3,500 − £2,975 = £525 in addition to his cash float. Any deficiency would be the result of deterioration of stock, wastage, pilfering, or mistakes.

Let us assume our company has opened its first branch in Lime Street, and the results of the first month's operations were as follows:

		£
Cash Float Provided, January 1st, 19. .		25
Goods Sent to Branch during January (at Selling Price)		3,500
Cost of Goods Sent to Branch During January		2,800
Cash Takings During the Month Paid into Bank		2,975
Goods Returned by Branch:		
	Cost Price	50
	Selling Price	70
Stock-on-Hand at the End of the Month:		
	Selling Price	440
	Cost	400

It will be obvious that the records of goods sent to the branch must contain two sets of values: cost price and selling price.

First, there must be an account to record goods sent to the branch or branches at cost price, so as to be able to deduct such amounts from the cost of goods sold at the main shop. This will be as follows:

GOODS-TO-BRANCHES ACCOUNT

Lime Street Branch (returns)	£50	Lime Street Branch	£2,800

At the end of the year the balance of this account will be credited to the Purchase Account, Trading Account or Stock Account.

The double entries will be completed by entries in the Branch Account. As these entries are at cost price, additional columns will be provided in the Branch Account to record the corresponding selling prices. These are not part of the double entry but are provided for control purposes; the balance will represent the shortage (if any) of goods or cash. In practice there will always be some deficiency of this nature and the aim of the branch manager must be to keep it as small as possible.

The account will appear as follows:

LIME STREET BRANCH ACCOUNT

	Invoice Price £	£		Invoice Price £	£
Goods to Branches	3,500	2,800	Cash Paid into Bank	2,975	2,975
Gross Profit for Month		625	Returns from Branches	70	50
			Stock c/d	440	400
			Shortage	15	
	£3,500	£3,425		£3,500	£3,425
Stock brought down	£440	£400			

All the expenses of the branch are paid by the head office and they will be debited as they arise to the Branch Expenses Account in such detail as deemed appropriate. It will then be possible to prepare a Branch Profit and Loss Account. If this were done at the end of the month it might appear as follows:

PROFIT AND LOSS ACCOUNT FOR LIME STREET BRANCH
(for month of January, 19..)

	£		£
Rent	150	Gross Profit for Month	625
Wages	180		
Sundry Expenses	170		
Net Profit for Month	125		
	£625		£625

The gross profit has been transferred from the Lime Street Branch Account and the expenses from the Lime Street Branch Expenses Account. The net profit for the branch is transferred to the Profit and Loss Account of the company with the net profit from any other branches. Although an interim Profit and Loss Account may be prepared at more frequent intervals the final accounts with the appropriate ledger entries will normally be made only once a year.

Sometimes it is decided to charge goods to the branches at cost plus some loading to cover the general expenses of the company, including the costs of administering the branches. Where the goods are charged to the branches on this basis it is necessary to make an adjustment for the closing stock, as the Branch Account will then show a balance which represents the value of the stock including the loading mentioned above. This is provided for by opening a Branch Adjustment Account.

If the price at which the goods sent to the Lime Street Branch had included a loading of £36 towards such expenses it would mean that the balance of stock, £400, included this loading. It would be necessary to make the following entry:

LIME STREET BRANCH ADJUSTMENT ACCOUNT

		Stock Reserve	£36

The debit entry would be in the Lime Street Branch Account, reducing the gross profit for the month from £625 to £589. (If this were not done, the loading on goods not yet sold would be treated as profit.)

Consignment Accounts

An opportunity arises for Central Provision Store PLC to send a consignment of kitchen gadgets to France, where they are to be sold by an agent. The financial records required for this type of transaction are similar in many ways to the records required for the Lime Street Branch. The main difference lies in that this is an isolated transaction rather than a continuing one, and that many expenses will of necessity have to be paid by the foreign agent.

The details of the consignment are as follows:

	£
1,000 CENPRO kitchen gadgets @ £1.25 each	1,250 (at cost)
Expenses paid by Central Provision Store Ltd:	
Insurance	40
Freight	110
Expenses paid by Paris Importeurs:	
Duty	280
Freight	65

Paris Importeurs are to receive a commission of 15 per cent on sale, and 800 gadgets had been sold by the end of the year for £2,000.

First, a 'Goods on Consignment Outwards Account' is required to perform a similar function to a 'Goods Sent to Branches Account'.

GOODS ON CONSIGNMENT OUTWARDS ACCOUNT

		Goods to Paris Importeurs	£1,250

The dispatch of all consignments to this and other consignees will be recorded in this account.

Secondly, a 'Consignment to Paris Importeurs Account' is required, in which are recorded all the expenses and revenue arising out of this consignment, whether paid by the consignor, Central Provision Store PLC, or by the consignee, Paris Importeurs. This will form the Trading Account for the consignment, and the balance will provide the Gross Profit for transfer to the Profit and Loss Account. If the goods are not all sold by the end of the financial year, the balance will, however, be part profit and part the value of the goods not yet sold. This (including an appropriate proportion of the expenses incurred on the *whole* consignment) will be segregated and carried down on the Consignment Account, and the amount will be included on the Balance Sheet as an asset (Stock—Goods on Consignment).

CONSIGNMENT TO PARIS IMPORTEURS ACCOUNT

	£		£
Goods on Consignment	1,250	Paris Importeurs	2,000
Cash:		Value of Goods Unsold, c/d	349
Insurance	40		
Freight	110		
Paris Importeurs:			
Duty	280		
Freight	65		
Commission (15% of £2,000)	300		
Profit on Sales (to P & L A/c)	304		
	£2,349		£2,349
Value of Goods Unsold, b/d	349		

The balance brought down represents one-fifth of the cost of the goods and expenses paid on the consignment as follows:

	Total	Per gadget
	£	£
Goods	1,250	1.25
Expenses	495	0.49
	£1,745	£1.74

$\frac{1}{5}$ of £1,745 = £349.

The profit of £304 represents the profit on the gadgets already sold.

If we found that the remaining 200 gadgets could only be sold at a price less than £1.74 plus the 15 per cent commission to the consignee, it would be necessary to reduce the value of the goods unsold so that this loss would be anticipated.

Thirdly, it is necessary to open an account for the consignee to record the expenses he has incurred on the consignment, the revenue he has received and his commission. This information will have to be provided by the consignee. It would appear as:

PARIS IMPORTEURS

	£		£
Sales Revenue	2,000	Duty on Consignment	280
		Freight on Consignment	65
		Commission on Consignment	300
		Cash, Payment on Account	1,200
		Balance c/d	155
	£2,000		£2,000
Balance, b/d	£155		

In this case Paris Importeurs made a payment on account at the end of the year of £1,200 leaving a balance outstanding of £155. The account would be settled later when the remaining gadgets were sold.

There occurs an opportunity later for a reciprocal arrangement, and Paris Importeurs sends a consignment of French kitchen gadgets to Central Provision Store PLC for them to dispose of.

The details so far as they concern the Central Provision Store PLC are: 1,000 'CONTINENTAL' kitchen gadgets to be sold at £2.75 each, Central Provision Store PLC to receive 15 per cent commission and to charge all expenses on the consignment to Paris Importeurs.

The financial records of Central Provision Store PLC are simple in this case. The goods are not theirs and are not included in their stocks. Their obligation is to account to Paris Importeurs for the cash received for the goods consigned to them less their expenses and commission. Thus if 500 gadgets are sold at £2.75 each and Central Provision Store PLC pays £750 custom duty and £60 freight, the only additional account necessary is a personal account in the name of Paris Importeurs as follows:

PARIS IMPORTEURS

	£		£
Cash: Customs Duty	750.00	Cash: Sale of Gadgets	1,375.00
Freight	60.00		
Commission Receivable	206.25		
Balance c/d	358.75		
	£1,375.00		£1,375.00
		Balance b/d	£358.75

There is an amount of £358.75 due to Paris Importeurs; this will increase as further gadgets are sold. It would have been agreed when the consignment was arranged as to how and when the amounts due should be remitted.

Branches Keeping Their Own Records

Meanwhile Central Provision Store PLC has been contemplating opening more branches, but as the branches are to be some distance away, a different form of organisation is necessary. The branch manager will have to be responsible for the financial records of the branch and for paying expenses. He will also have discretion to buy merchandise from outside suppliers direct. Capital expenditure will, however, be controlled by headquarters.

It will be necessary for each branch to open accounts to be kept on the double-entry system. But instead of capital being supplied directly by the proprietor, fixed assets, supplies of merchandise and funds will be provided from within the organisation. Instead of opening a Capital Account the branch will open a 'Head Office Current Account' to record all dealings between the branch and the head office. Apart from this, the records will be kept in the same way as they would be by an independent business.

As the head office will be supplying the branch with funds and goods, it is necessary to provide an account in the head office books to record such transactions. This is the 'Branch Current Account'.

The following is a summary of the transactions between the head office and Othertown Branch up to the end of June 19. .

	£	£
Cash Remitted by Head Office to Branch		5,000
Goods sent by Head Office to Branch:		
Received by June 30th	6,200	
Not Received by June 30th	600	
		6,800
Cash Remitted Back by Branch to Head Office:		
Received by June 30th	4,100	
Not Received by June 30th	400	
		4,500
Goods returned by Branch to Head Office		200

The account in the **branch** books will appear

HEAD OFFICE CURRENT ACCOUNT

	£		£
Returns	200	Cash	5,000
Cash	4,500	Goods	6,200
Balance c/d	6,500		
	£11,200		£11,200
		Balance b/d	£6,500

The account in the **head office** books will appear

OTHERTOWN BRANCH CURRENT ACCOUNT

	£		£
Cash	5,000	Returns	200
Goods	6,800	Cash	4,100
		Balance c/d	7,500
	£11,800		£11,800
Balance b/d	£7,500		

The final accounts for the business as a whole can be prepared by combining the trial balances of the head office and the branch, but this can only be done if the balances of the Head Office Current Account and the Branch Current Account are equal and opposite so that they can be cancelled out. In the above accounts the balances differ by £1,000 because goods to the value of £600 had been dispatched by head office but had not been received by the end of June, and a cash remittance of £400 had been dispatched by the branch but had not been received by the head office by the end of June.

The first step is to bring about an equality in the balance of the two accounts. This is achieved by opening two temporary accounts in the head office books as follows:

GOODS-IN-TRANSIT ACCOUNT

Othertown Branch Current Account	£600		

CASH-IN-TRANSIT ACCOUNT

Othertown Branch Current Account	£400		

Continuing the entries in the Branch Current Account we have

OTHERTOWN BRANCH CURRENT ACCOUNT

	£		£
Balance b/d	7,500	Goods in Transit	600
		Cash in Transit	400
		Balance c/d	6,500
	£7,500		£7,500
Balance b/d	6,500		

The two current accounts now offset each other and the final accounts can be prepared. Afterwards the Cash-in-Transit Account and the Goods-in-Transit Account are closed by making reverse entries; in due course the goods and cash will arrive at the branch and head office respectively.

It is quite straightforward to prepare a Trading and Profit and Loss Account for the business as a whole and also a Balance Sheet. If it is desired to prepare accounts showing the position of the branch or branches separately, additional work is involved. Some expenses incurred at head office will be for the benefit of the branch. Since fixed assets are all recorded in the books of the head office, depreciation will be written off in the head office books also. This will have to be allocated between the head office and branches.

Foreign Branches

Although it would not be a feasible procedure for a business such as Central Provision Store PLC, there are occasions when a business might choose to open a branch or branches abroad. We shall therefore briefly review the issues.

The main complication arises because the financial records of the branch will be kept in a different currency from that of the head office. No difficulties would arise if all the items on the branch trial balance could be converted to the currency of the head office at the same rate. In most cases, and certainly when there has been a marked alteration in the rate of exchange, this would not give the correct results. Moreover, remittances between the branch and head office will have to be converted at the rate actually ruling when the transfer took place, or else the Branch Current Account and Head Office Current Account cannot be made to agree. Since fixed assets have to be shown on the Balance Sheet at cost, these must be converted to the home currency at the rate ruling when the assets were purchased. Revenue and expenditure items may be deemed to have taken place evenly through the year and the rate of exchange used for converting these will consequently be the average rate ruling through the year.

Having converted all the items on the branch trial balance at these varying rates it would be a coincidence if the totals of the trial balance still agreed. An item has therefore to be inserted in the trial balance in respect of the difference. This difference will be treated on a conservative basis. If it is a debit balance it will be treated as an expense in the Profit and Loss Account, but if it is a credit balance it will be included in the Balance Sheet as a reserve.

5
Departmental Accounting

In a company that handles different lines of merchandise, the management will want to know about sales and expenses of each line in order to analyse better the results of business operations. The Revenue Account of Central Provision Store PLC for the current year can be presented as follows:

TRADING AND PROFIT AND LOSS ACCOUNT
(for the year ended December 31st, 19..)

	£	£	
Sales		200,000	100%
Opening Stock	30,000		
Purchases	121,000		
	151,000		
Closing Stock	40,000		
Cost of Goods Sold		111,000	55%
Gross Profit on Sales		89,000	45%
Operating Expenses:			
Selling Expenses	50,000		
Administrative Expenses	25,600	75,600	38%
Net Profit		£13,400	7%

If there is a variation in percentages of profit and the cost of sales in each line of goods, the Revenue Account as presented above may be practically useless to management as a control tool. Where there are two departments, the sales and cost of sales can be analysed more usefully to give a statement as on page 68.

From this type of analysis we can readily see that each £1.00 increase in sales in the household-goods department makes a greater **contribution** to net profit than each £1.00 increase in sales in the tools department. Contribution is the amount available for fixed expenses and profit. If the figures for the gross profit in each line were available for the industry as a whole, it might be possible to see which line is better or worse than the national average. If we had details for the industry or for associated companies we could analyse the selling expenses by department and make comparisons.

TRADING AND PROFIT AND LOSS ACCOUNT
(for the year ended December 31st, 19..)

	Groceries		Hardware		Total	
	£		£		£	
Gross Sales	120,000	100%	80,000	100%	200,000	100%
Opening Stock	20,000		10,000		30,000	
Purchases	66,000		55,000		121,000	
	86,000		65,000		151,000	
Closing Stock	25,000		15,000		40,000	
Cost of Goods Sold	61,000	51%	50,000	62%	111,000	55%
Gross Profit on Sales	59,000	49%	30,000	38%	89,000	45%
Selling Expenses	32,000	27%	18,000	23%	50,000	25%
Departmental Income	27,000	22%	12,000	15%	39,000	20%
Administrative Expenses					25,600	13%
Net Profit					£13,400	7%

Sales Analysis

For retail trading businesses there are two main ways by which departmental analyses may be made. In the departmental store, the physical space is divided into separate areas, each having its own cash register (or bill books), so that figures can easily be accumulated for the various departments. In the supermarket, however, there is no such physical division of space. The goods are collected by the shopper, and the analysis must take place at the check-out points where the cash registers are designed to accumulate sub-totals for different classes of goods. The accuracy of the analysis will of course depend upon the care taken by the cashiers to depress the key representing the correct category of goods for each item. In modern computerised systems this analysis can be prepared automatically by use of scanning apparatus which reads coded details from the package and feeds the data into the computerised files. This type of analysis permits a day-to-day comparison of the sales of each category of goods, thus whatever action is considered appropriate, e.g. rearrangement of the display of goods or adjustment of stock levels, it can be done quickly.

In businesses where sales are normally on credit, the analysis may be obtained by an examination of the items on sales invoices. Where records are kept manually, analysis columns for each department will be kept in the Sales Day Book. Accounting machines used for the Sales Ledger must have sufficient adding registers to be able to accumulate the total sales for each department as well as the overall total sales. Sometimes a more elaborate analysis of sales, say by areas or salesmen, is undertaken as a separate operation. Most data processing systems have programs which can produce easily and quickly such analyses without the tedium associated with other forms of recording.

Expenditure Analysis

It is necessary to study the components of expenditure and to classify them properly in just the same way as with sales analysis. Here, however, the problem is a bit more complex. In a supermarket, the effort of the workers is spread over all lines, and the lines are intermixed on the display floor. It would be hard to assign the wages of the cashier to 'groceries', 'meats', etc., because she probably handles all items in the supermarket on the one register. The same can be said of the shelf filler. However, in a departmental store, wages can be classified because a sales person is assigned to a specific department.

Expenses other than wages can also be classified by department. Equipment can be classified by location, and other items can follow departmental classification, such as bags, string, tape, etc., charged to a department according to storeroom requisition. **Where possible, expenses should always be charged to a department directly, so that a more accurate distribution of costs can be obtained.**

There are some selling expenses that are more difficult to assign to individual departments because all departments use the facility and only a single price is paid for the total facility. An example would be rent (or rates) for a seven-storey department store. All floors have the same area but some floors are more desirable. Should all floors be allocated the same rent factor per square foot or should it vary from floor to floor? If the rent factor varies from floor to floor, should it depend upon location on the floor? What about heat for the building? How do we allocate lift and escalator depreciation and maintenance? We might begin by saying that no allocation system will please everyone in the company. If a department is charged £500 per month rent, the department manager will think the rent charge is too high while other department managers will think it is too low.

Top management must realise that in these situations there are two kinds of departmental expenses:

(*a*) Direct—those that can be controlled by the departmental manager.
(*b*) Allocated—those that cannot be controlled by the departmental manager.

Where the difference is realised, the operating statement can be changed to show the controllable apart from the non-controllable. In this way responsibility can be assigned to the department manager for those expenses over which he can exercise control, and management must assume responsibility for those over which only they can exercise control.

With a supermarket, where the use of selling space is flexible, it is common to measure the profit of each section in relation to the floor space occupied.

Departmental Profit or Loss

When the Income Statement is presented in departmental form, copies of the departmental results can be sent to the manager with comparisons: this year with last year same period; total to date with last year same period; actual performances with budgeted performances, etc. Each manager can see the results of his department's performance and can initiate actions that will increase his department's contribution to the total company profit. With the statement, the management may send an evaluation of the departmental results with commendations for good performance (rarely done—but so essential to good employee morale) and recommendations for improving performance.

In some businesses there may be departments that operate at a loss. The management should know what the loss for the department is and review the advisability of maintaining the operation of that department. One such department may be a restaurant that serves both customers and employees. What might the total profit be if the restaurant were discontinued? Would the employees take more time for lunch and tea breaks? Where would a shopper meet her friend if a meeting place is not provided? The management has to answer these questions, but it might not even be aware of a problem if departmental statements are not prepared.

Special Statements for Decision-making Purposes

If fundamental changes are being contemplated, the departmental Trading and Profit and Loss Account shown on page 68 may not be adequate. If, for instance, the question of whether to close the hardware department and expand the groceries department were being considered, it would be necessary to prepare a special statement before an enlightened decision could be made. The following are some of the points which would have to be considered:

(*a*) Would the administrative expenses remain the same if there were only one department?

(*b*) Would there be sufficient sales area to replace £80,000 sales of hardware by £80,000 sales of groceries?

(*c*) Would it be necessary to increase the scale of selling expenses to achieve such an increase in sales of groceries?

(*d*) Would the company lose groceries customers because they had to go elsewhere to buy their hardware?

The projected Profit and Loss Account for the following year, assuming the tools department were closed down, might be that shown opposite. It can be seen that:

(*a*) the sales of hardware (£80,000) are expected to be only partly replaced by sales of groceries (+ £60,000);

(*b*) selling expenses of groceries would increase more than proportionately (+ £2,000); and

(*c*) administrative expenses would fall (– £2,600).

	£	£
Gross Sales		180,000
Opening Stock	25,000	
Purchases	106,500	
	131,500	
Closing Stock	40,000	
Cost of Goods Sold		91,500
Gross Profit on Sales		88,500
Selling Expenses	50,000	
Administrative Expenses	23,000	73,000
Net Profit on Groceries		15,500
Costs of Closing the Hardware Dept. and Liquidation of Stocks		3,500
		£12,000

The overall result would be an increase in profit of £2,100 in a normal year, but against this must be set the costs of closing the hardware department (£3,500) which would result in a fall in profit for the year in which the change took place. A special statement would have to be prepared when considering each suggested fundamental change in the administration of the business.

6
Credit Sales

Increasing Sales

Every business strives to increase sales. With increased sales there is generally an increase in the amount of gross profit but a smaller increase in expenses, resulting in a larger net profit.

Operating expenses generally rise so little because they include rent, rates on property, depreciation on equipment, and other items that do not change in amount as sales vary. These are the **fixed charges**. Also included in operating expenses may be salesmen's salaries, heat and light, store supplies, and other items that do vary as sales vary.

As long as a business can increase its sales at a greater rate than it increases its operating expenses, it tries to do so because the net profit will be increasing at an even greater rate than sales income.

One of the easiest ways to increase sales is by extending **credit** to the customer. This extension of credit, however, has some drawbacks. One is a delay between the time of sale and the time of collection. The Table below shows the difference between a sale for cash and a sale for credit with a subsequent payment.

After the customer pays, the account balances are the same; but in the time that has elapsed between the sale and the receipt of the payment, the business has had no use of the cash resulting from the sale. This lack of cash may have a decided effect on the success of the business.

	Cash Sale			*Credit Sale*		
Date of Sale	Cash Sales	£500	 £500	Trade Debtors Sales	£500	 £500
				(passage of some time period)		
Date of Collection				Cash Trade Debtors	£500	 £500

Credit Risks

Another disadvantage of credit sales is that the customer may never pay the amount that is owed. In other words, the business has extended credit to the wrong customer. The business must decide to whom it will extend credit. The extension of credit to most business customers is largely granted on the basis of ratings compiled by such credit-reference organisations as Dun & Bradstreet Ltd. The Dun & Bradstreet rating is related to the size of the company in terms of tangible net worth and a composite credit appraisal.

The extension of credit to small businesses and to individuals may be on the basis of a report from a credit-rating bureau or on the basis of such factors as the potential customer's earnings, past credit record, marital status, ownership of a home or car, or character references. When these factors are studied, each customer is rated as to his 'creditability', an estimate of the assurance that a customer granted credit will pay the amount he owes. The lower 'creditability' a business is willing to accept, the more customers it may have, but the greater the possible loss from non-collection of accounts receivable. So the business must draw the line at some point. No matter where the line is drawn, there will be some persons included in the acceptable 'creditability' group who will not pay if they become customers. There will also be some persons not included in the acceptable 'creditability' group who would pay if they had been permitted to become customers.

There are two pressures on the credit manager or other person who determines to whom credit will be extended and to whom it will be denied. One is the sales manager, who wants an ever-expanding source of potential customers. The other is the accountant who wants to collect for every sale made. The successful sales manager must expand the group of potential customers without unduly increasing losses due to bad debts.

Credit Control

In any company selling on credit, some effort should be made to establish a system for the collection of accounts receivable. The collection effort should start with a clearly defined policy that is explained to the customer when credit is granted. The customer is reminded of the policy at the time of sale by the printing of its major features on the sales invoice, or by a complete explanation of the credit policy on the credit-card or monthly statement.

There are numerous variations of credit terms. 'Net 30 days' means that the amount due is payable in full 30 days after the invoice date. The terms might well be 2½ per cent discount if paid before the 15th of the month, otherwise terms strictly net.

When the customer fails to send in a payment on the due date, some form of reminder should be sent to him. The reminders should be made often and they should be more forceful as time goes by.

An understandable credit policy, firmly administered, is a valuable resource to a business. It helps in reducing losses from bad debts, in creating goodwill, and in keeping the business financially healthy.

Cash Discount

When a credit sale is made, it is obviously not known whether the customer will pay within the period entitling him to deduct the permitted cash discount. The entry recording the discount allowed (if any) must therefore be made at the time when the customer settles the account.

It is usual to provide an additional column in the cash book to record the amount of discount that is allowed. The sum of the cash received and discount allowed is posted to the customer's account. The discount is accumulated in the cash book, and when the cash book is balanced the total of the discount column is transferred to the debit side of the Discount Allowed Account. Thus the double entry consists of the individual entries in the customer's accounts (credit) or Sales Ledger Control Account and the total entry in the Discount Allowed Account (debit).

Example. Smith has bought goods to the value of £500, the terms being 2 per cent discount for settlement within 30 days. Payment is made within this period. The total receipts from customers during the month were £4,700 and the total discount allowed £65.

SALES LEDGER CONTROL ACCOUNT

Balance		Cash (including Smith's £490)	£4,700
		Discount allowed (including Smith's £10)	£65

SMITH

Goods	£500	Cash and Discount	£500

CASH BOOK

	Discount	Cash	
Smith	£10	£490	
	£65	£4,700	

DISCOUNT ALLOWED ACCOUNT

Cash Book	£65		

When preparing the Final Accounts it is necessary to recognise that some of the customers with outstanding accounts at the end of the year will be entitled to deduct cash discount. So as not to overstate assets, provision must be made for this and the total of the debtors reduced on the Balance Sheet. The amount of the provision so made will be debited to the Profit and Loss Account as an expense. The amount of the provision necessary can be assessed from the debtors outstanding at the end of the year, and from the terms of payment established by the business. (Obviously any debts which have run beyond the period allowed for cash discount would be ignored for this purpose.)

When payments are received from customers it would be a waste of time to separate payments and discount on the previous year's sales and to debit the Provision for Cash Discount Allowed and to post discounts arising from the current year's sales to the Discount Allowed Account. So the amount required as a Provision for Cash Discount Allowed is calculated at the end of the year, and no further entries are made in the account until the end of the following year when the balance of the Provision Account is increased or reduced to the amount appropriate for the debtors at the end of that year.

Example. The Provision for Cash Discount Allowed at the end of 19.7 was £145. At tne end of 19.8 the debtors totalled £7,500, of which £6,750 could be subject to 2 per cent cash discount. During the year cash discount of £420 had been allowed. The entries in the Provision for Cash Discount and the charge to the Profit and Loss Account will be:

PROVISION FOR CASH DISCOUNT ALLOWED

	£		£
19.8 Profit and Loss A/c	10	19.7 Balance	145
Balance c/d (2% of £6,750)	135		
	£145		£145
		19.8 Balance b/d	£135

PROFIT AND LOSS ACCOUNT

Cash Discount	£420		
Less Adjustment to Provision	£10		
		£410	

Bad Debts

When a customer fails to pay what he owes, and all collection efforts have been made, it is advisable to remove the account from the General Ledger and the Subsidiary Ledger. One method of removing the account is called the **direct write-off**. In this method, an account called Bad Debts Account is debited and the Sales Ledger Control Account is credited. The loss in asset value is taken at the time it is determined that the debt is valueless.

Example. During 19.8 Jones buys £500 worth of goods from a firm whose total sales on account totalled £100,000 for that year. The General Ledger Accounts are prepared as follows:

SALES LEDGER CONTROL ACCOUNT

19.8	£100,000 (including Jones's £500)	

SALES

Closed-to-Trading A/c	19.8	£100,000 (including Jones's £500)

and the following entry is made in the Sales Ledger Account:

JONES

19.8 £500	

In 19.9 it is determined that Jones will not pay, and it is necessary to enter the bad debt of £500 in the General Ledger Account as follows:

SALES LEDGER CONTROL ACCOUNT

Balance (including Jones's £500)	19.9 Bad Debts £500

BAD DEBT EXPENSE ACCOUNT

19.9 £500	Closed-to-Trading A/c

while the following entry is made to close the Sales Ledger Account:

JONES

Balance (£500)	19.9 Bad Debts £500

This method is the simplest for recording losses on trade debtors. It has, however, the disadvantage of not measuring income and its related expense in the same year.

Provision for Bad Debts

As we saw in the above example, the sale was made in 19.8 but the expense related to the sale was recognized in 19.9. The direct write-off overstates 19.8 net income and understates 19.9 net income. A method that is used to estimate losses from bad debts in the year of sale is called the **provision and write-off** method.

In this method an estimate is made of those accounts that will not be paid, and this amount is charged to the Bad Debt Expense Account and is credited to the Provision for Bad Debts Account. This latter is an asset-valuation account, appears in the asset section of the Balance Sheet, and normally has a credit balance. (It is sometimes called a Contra-asset Account.) The estimated amount may be determined:

(*a*) As a percentage of the year's credit sales.

(*b*) As a percentage of the year's total sales (where there is a fairly constant relationship between cash and credit sales from year to year).

(*c*) As a percentage of the year-end trade debtors.

(*d*) By an analysis of the year-end trade debtors.

When the debt is determined later to be 'uncollectable', the account is written off against the allowance previously established.

Example. During 19.8 Jones buys £500 worth of goods from a firm whose sales on account totalled £100,000 for that year. The General Ledger Accounts are prepared as follows:

SALES LEDGER CONTROL ACCOUNT

19.8	£100,000 (including Jones's £500)		

SALES

Closed-to-Trading A/c		19.8	£100,000 (including Jones's £500)

and the following entry is made in the Sales Ledger:

JONES

19.8	£500		

It is estimated on some basis that £4,000 of the 19.8 sales will not be collected, and an adjusting entry is made in the General Ledger Accounts:

PROVISION FOR BAD DEBTS ACCOUNT

		19.8	£4,000

BAD DEBT EXPENSE

1968	£4,000		

Thus in 19.8 there is recorded £100,000 of sales and a concurrent expense of £4,000 due to the expected loss from bad debts. In 19.9, after it has been determined that Jones will not pay, the General Ledger Accounts are prepared as follows:

SALES LEDGER CONTROL ACCOUNT

Balance (including Jones's £500)		19.9	£500

PROVISION FOR BAD DEBTS

19.9	£500	Balance (which might include some of the 19.8 allowance)	

while the following entry is made to close the Sales Ledger Account:

JONES

Balance	(£500)	19.9	£500

Recovery of Bad Debts

Occasionally a debt that has been written off will be paid by the customer. When this happens the original entry writing off the debt is reversed and the regular entry for the receipt of cash from trade debtors is then made. If the debt was written off originally by the 'direct write-off' method, the reversing entry will be as follows:

Jones	£500	
Bad Debt Expense		£500

This, in effect, represents a reduction in the current year's expenses or, if there is no other bad-debt expense, an extraordinary income.

If the debt was written off originally by the 'provision and write-off' method, the reversing entry will be as follows:

Jones	£500	
Provision for Bad Debts		£500

Since this is an *intra Balance-Sheet entry*, i.e. an entry within the Balance Sheet, it does not affect the income statement.

Whichever method of write-off was used, the entry to record the receipt of cash is:

Cash	£500	
Jones		£500

Using Trade Debtors as a Source of Cash

A business having trade debts that will fall due at some future time can often arrange with a financial institution to use these debts as a source of cash. This may be done in one of three ways:

(*a*) *Pledging* the debts. Under this arrangement, the financial institution selects certain debts as a pledge against a loan of money to the business. Usually, the business collects the accounts and applies the money collected against the loan balance.

(*b*) *Assigning* the debts. Under this arrangement, the financial institution selects the debts to be used as security for the loan of money to the business. The business may continue to collect the debts and apply the money received against the loan balance, or the lending institution may do the collecting. When the financial institution collects the debts, the method is called **factoring**, and the financial institution is called a **factor**. The factor usually accepts the debts **with recourse**; that is, if the debt is considered bad the business will allow the factor to return the debt and select another in its place. After the loan is paid off, all unpaid debts are returned to the business.

(*c*) *Selling* the debts. Under this arrangement, the financial institution selects debts and pays the business for those selected. The financial institution charges a fee for this service.

Credit Cards

Some financial institutions and banks have established a credit-card system. The credit application is made to the institution that approves the credit and issues the credit card. The business pays a fee to become part of the system. When the sale is made, a credit-sales slip is prepared and the business turns this slip over to the institution for cash, receiving the amount of the sale less a predetermined charge. Familiar examples of this system are Access, American Express, and Barclaycard.

All these methods cost money to the business, but the increased sales, less service charges and loan interest, may be such that a substantial increase in net profit can result.

Extended Credit and Hire-purchase

The sales of durable more-expensive household goods are likely to be restricted unless our company can offer its customers extended terms of some kind. There are a number of possibilities such as hire-purchase contracts or instalment sales. The legal implications must in each case be considered, as must the current Government regulations regarding the amount of the initial deposit and the period over which the instalments may be spread. We are, however, concerned with the accounting implications.

Normally the total price paid by the customer is greater when payments are spread over a period than when one immediate cash payment is made. The period over which the payments become due often extends beyond the current financial year, and the financial year in which the profit is deemed to have been earned must be decided upon. There are two basic methods: profits are recognised at the time of sale or they are recognised over the life of the contract.

Recognition of Profit

(*a*) *In Period of Sale*. The department store sells on short-term credit and recognizes the profit at the time of sale. This procedure is followed because the payment period is short-term—one, two, or three months. The sale is recorded as follows:

Trade Debtors	£100	
Sales		£100

and in the same period the cost of sales is deducted to determine the gross profit.

It is easy to extend this concept to instalment sales, but there is one difference—the time period for payment is longer, and the fact that a buyer might not pay will not be known at the time of sale or even during the financial year in which the sale is made. But one method of accounting for instalment sales ignores the objections that arise because of the protracted payment schedule and records the sale and the profit in the year of sale. The entry in this case is:

Instalment Contracts Receivable	£100	
Sales		£100

In the same period the cost of sales is deducted to determine the gross profit.

(*b*) *During Contract Term*. Some time ago accountants recognised that in the event of losses on instalment contracts in future years there would be a lack of matching of revenue and expenditure and the financial situation would be distorted. The following methods were therefore devised to recognise the profit during the contract term.

(i) The payments at the beginning of the contract term are considered to be recoveries of the cost price. After the cost price is recovered, the balance of the payments is profit. This is a conservative treatment and has the effect of putting all the profit at the end of the contract term.

(ii) The payments at the beginning of the contract term are considered to be profit. After the profit is recovered, the balance of the payments are considered to be recoveries of cost. This treatment is less conservative than accountants may like and has the effect of putting all the profit at the beginning of the contract term, even before the cost is recovered.

(iii) All payments to the seller are considered to be recovery of cost and profit in the same proportion that cost and profit are to the total sale price. This method is called the **instalment method** and is explained in detail below.

Instalment Method

In the instalment method of accounting for sales made in one period with collections made in the current and subsequent periods, it is necessary to record instalment sales separately from regular sales and to record cost of instalment sales separately from cost of regular sales. This is done by introducing three new accounts: Instalment Contracts Receivable—(Year); Instalment Sales—(Year); and Cost of Instalment Sales—(Year).

Assume the seller has an article that cost him £175 which carries a price of £200. A customer wants to buy the article, agreeing to pay £45 down and the balance in 12 monthly instalments of £15 each (total amount of sale is £225). The sales entry is recorded as follows:

Cash	£45	
Instalment Contracts Receivable—19.8	£180	
Instalment Sales—19.8		£225

The cost-of-sales entry (using the perpetual inventory method) is recorded as follows:

Cost of Instalment Sales—19.8	£175	
Merchandise Inventory or stock		£175

The entry to close the operating account is:

Instalment Sales—19.8	£225	
Cost of Instalment Sales—19.8		£175
Gross Profit on Instalment Sales—19.8		£45

The total gross profit to be realised in the current and future periods is £45 or 20 per cent of the total sales price. Therefore, 20 per cent of all the collections on this contract is profit in the period in which the collection is made.

Assume that in the year the contract was made the following payments were received:

Down payment	£45	
Five instalments of £15 each	75	£120

We have seen above how the down payment was recorded at the time of the sale. Let us now examine the recording of the subsequent payments.

Cash	£15	
Instalment Contracts Receivable—19.8		£15
(for each payment received)		

At the end of the year the Instalment Contracts Receivable—19.8 account would appear as follows:

INSTALMENT CONTRACTS RECEIVABLE—19.8

	£		£
Sale Balance	180	Payment	15
		,,	15
		,,	15
		,,	15
		,,	15
		Balance c/d	105
	£180		£180
Balance b/d	105		

Of the total contract (£225), the company has collected £120. The amount of profit is 20 per cent of the year's collections or £24. The entry to record the profit earned this year is:

Gross Profit on Instalment Sales—19.8	£24	
Instalment Sales Gross Profits Realised		£24

The Gross Profit on Instalment Sales—19.8 would appear as follows:

GROSS PROFIT ON INSTALMENT SALES—19.8

	£		£
Realised	24	Total	45
Balance c/d	21		
	£45		£45
		Balance b/d	21

The balance is correct because it is 20 per cent of £105, the remaining balance in the Instalment Contracts Receivable—19.8 account.

On the Balance Sheet are found the accounts Instalment Contracts

Receivable—(Year) and Gross Profit on Instalment Sales—(Year). The receivable account is shown by year and in total as follows:

	£	£	£
Cash			10,000
Trade Debtors		£150,000	
Instalment Contracts Receivable			
19.6	20,000		
19.7	80,000		
19.8	160,000	260,000	410,000
	etc.		

or the yearly details may be shown as a separate exhibit.

The unearned gross profit may be shown in one of three ways:

(*a*) As a current liability, like any other unearned income.

(*b*) As a part of the equity accounts, on the proposition that only collection is needed to realise profit to the owners.

(*c*) As a contra-asset or valuation account to be subtracted from the receivable account, on the proposition that there may be some accounts which will not be collected.

In the Trading Account the total sales may be shown or the regular sales may be shown, and the amount of profit earned on instalment sales may be shown. If all sales are shown, the Trading Account appears as follows:

	Sales		
	Regular	*Extended Credit*	*Total*
	£	£	£
Sales	£200,000	£300,000	£500,000
Cost of Sales (detailed)	140,000	180,000	320,000
Gross Profit	60,000	120,000	180,000
Less Unrealised Gross Profit on 19.8 Sales		64,000	64,000
	£60,000	£56,000	£116,000
Profit Realised on Previous Instalment Sales (detailed), etc.			66,600 etc.

If only the regular sales are shown, the income statement appears as follows:

	£	£
Regular Sales		200,000
Cost of Regular Sales		140,000
Gross Profit on Regular Sales		60,000
Profit Realised on Instalment Sales (detailed), etc.		122,600
		182,600 etc.

The details would show:

19.6 Instalment Sales Income (collections of £90,000 × 34%)		£30,600
19.7 Instalment Sales Income (collections of £100,000 × 36%)		36,000
		£66,600
19.8 Instalment Sales	£300,000	
Less Cost of Sales	180,000	
Gross Profit (40% of Sales)	£120,000	
(Collection of £140,000 × 40%)		56,000
		£122,600

Part Exchange

Because instalment sales are used for relatively high-priced items, it is not unusual to find the seller accepting a used piece of merchandise as a trade-in down payment. The amount given as a 'trade-in' allowance may vary from customer to customer for an almost identical piece of used merchandise. How a particular part-exchange value is arrived at for a particular prospect for a particular piece of used merchandise is unimportant to this discussion. What is important is the implication of the part-exchange value. The part-exchange may be priced so that it can be resold (after reconditioning) at a fair profit. Or it may be priced at a figure higher than one that would bring a fair profit on resale.

Let us assume that a used piece of equipment is to be traded in as a down payment on a new piece of equipment. The used equipment could be sold for £1,000 (assuming a 25 per cent mark-up on cost). It should then be carried on the books at £800 when reconditioned. The estimated cost of reconditioning should be subtracted from £800 to obtain the part-exchange value. So long as the amount allowed is less than the figure thus obtained, the part-exchange is properly priced. The trade-in and cash receivable from the customer are debited and Instalment Sales is credited.

Example. A customer wants to purchase a new machine and offers a used machine in trade. The dealer shows a new machine priced at £10,000 to the customer and offers a trade-in value of £1,000 for the used machine with £9,000 cash. The normal mark-up is 25 per cent on the selling price. It will take £400 to repair and recondition the used machine, which can then be sold for £2,000.

The following schedule may be used to determine whether the part-exchange value is correct:

	£
Sale Price of Used Equipment	2,000
Less Profit on Sale (25%)	500
	1,500
Less Reconditioning Cost	400
Part-exchange Value	£1,100

The part-exchange allowance is less than £1,100; therefore, the £1,000 is used as the value of the trade-in. The entry is:

Used Machinery Inventory	£1,000	
Cash	9,000	
Instalment Sales		£10,000

Let us now assume that the piece of used equipment is given a part-exchange value higher than the sale price of the reconditioned equipment, less mark-up, less reconditioning costs. In this case the part-exchange value is to be written down and the instalment sale is to be reduced by a like amount.

Example. A customer wants to purchase a new machine and offers a used one in exchange. The dealer shows a new machine priced at £20,000 to the customer and offers a trade-in value of £2,500 for the used machine, with £17,500 in cash. The normal mark-up on used equipment is 20 per cent on the selling price. It will take £1,000 to repair and recondition the used machine, which can then be sold for £4,000.

The following schedule may be used to determine whether the part-exchange value is correct:

	£
Sale Price of Used Equipment	4,000
Less Profit on Sale (20%)	800
	3,200
Less Reconditioning Cost	1,000
Part-exchange Value	£2,200

The part-exchange value allowed is greater than the £2,200 calculated above; therefore, the £2,500 is not recorded as the value of the trade-in. The entry is:

Used Machinery Inventory	£2,200	
Cash	17,500	
Instalment Sales		£19,700

Defaults and Repossessions

When the buyer of merchandise on an instalment contract stops payment before the contract is completely paid off, it is said to be in **default** and the seller may be able to repossess the merchandise subject to any legal restrictions. When the goods are repossessed, the seller sets them up on the books at the sales price less mark-up and reconditioning costs. The remainder of the entry is the write-off of the debt and the unrealised portion of income and the recognition of loss due to repossession.

Example. A customer owes £500 on an instalment contract. The gross profit ratio is 20 per cent of the selling price. The contract is in default due to cessation of payments by the buyer and the goods are repossessed by the seller. When reconditioned at a cost of £100, the goods can be sold for £550. The gross profit ratio for used equipment is 10 per cent of the selling price.

The amount of unrealised income on the original sale is £100 (£500 × 20%). The value of the repossessed goods is:

	£
Selling Price	550
Gross Profit (10%)	55
	495
Reconditioning Cost	100
Value of the Repossessed Item	£395

The entry to record the repossession is:

Repossessed Goods Inventory	£395	
Gross Profit on Instalment Sales	100	
Loss on Repossessions	5	
Instalment Contracts Receivable		£500

Interest on Instalment Sales

The seller recognises in making instalment sales that the buyer has use of the goods before full payment is made. The seller generally charges the buyer for extended credit terms, so that the total amount paid by the buyer will exceed the price if it had been paid in cash at the time of purchase. The difference is the **interest** or **carrying charge**. This additional amount may be added in various ways; two of the most popular are:

(*a*) Equal payments for a specified number of terms covering both interest and principal.

(*b*) Equal payments on the principal each term plus interest on the principal since the last payment.

The first is the type of loan one might secure from a bank by way of a personal loan, a finance company, or a retailer. Suppose the purchaser buys a piece of equipment priced at £2,600 and pays £1,100 down in cash. The balance is £1,500 to be paid £70 per month for 24 months. This means there is £180 of interest and service charges. Each month part of the £180 is earned. The entry to record the sale would be:

Cash	£1,100	
Instalment Contracts Receivable	1,680	
Instalment Sales		£2,600
Deferred Interest Income		180

When a payment is made the entry to record the receipt of cash is:

Cash	£70	
Instalment Contracts Receivable		£70

An adjusting entry might be made now (or prepared at the end of the period for all payments) as follows:

Deferred Interest Income	£XX	
Interest on Instalment Sales		£XX

The amount would probably be determined by a schedule from which the instalment contract was prepared. The account 'Interest on Instalment Sales' may be titled differently to reflect properly the composition of the additional charge.

The second method is the type of financing one might secure from a bank by way of overdraft. Suppose a purchaser buys furniture priced at £2,600, paying £1,100 down in cash. The balance is to be paid at £70 per month and the seller will charge 1 per cent on the unpaid balance per month. The entry to record the sale is:

Cash	£1,100	
Instalment Contracts Receivable	1,500	
Instalment Sales		£2,600

The payment of £70 is made by the purchaser and is recorded as follows:

Cash	£70	
Instalment Contracts Receivable		£70

An entry is made to record the interest earned as follows:

Instalment Contracts Receivable	£15	
Interest Income (1% × £1,500)		£15

In the following month the interest is £14.45 (1% × £1,445). The amount of interest is computed each month and reduces by 1 per cent of the amount applied on the principal.

The type of financing used for instalment sales varies with the nature of the seller, the type of merchandise being sold, credit practices in the industry, and so on.

7
Stock or Inventory Valuation

In a trading business, one of the larger current assets is **merchandise** or **stocks**. These are the goods owned by the company that are for sale to customers. They may include clothing, furniture, motor-cars, food and drink, kitchenware, garden supplies, and many more items. They may include items for sale in a shop or by mail order. They may include general merchandise (such as a department store would carry) or they may be limited to only one item, such as dresses. They may include goods from all over the world or they may be specialised (Italian imports).

Physical Stock-taking Methods

Periodic Inventory Method

In the days when most owners ran their own businesses and the size of their stocks was small, there was little need for establishing elaborate control systems for stocks because the owners 'knew' their stock. Once a year (or some other time period), the stock was counted and priced out. Each owner (or his accountant) determined the cost of goods sold by the formula:

	£
Opening Stock (same as last year's Closing Stock)	5,962
+ Purchases During the Year	37,622
= Goods Available for Sale	43,584
– Closing Stock (will be next year's Opening Stock)	7,264
= Cost of Goods Sold	£36,320

If the Cost of Goods Sold had the proper percentage relationship to Sales, an owner assumed his stock was all right.

This type of system requires that the store be closed for stock-taking (although it might be taken at night or over the weekend) and affords little accounting control because the ratio of Cost of Goods Sold to Sales is not known until the end of the period, after the stock-taking. The reliance for control is on individual alertness on the part of the owner or manager with respect to size and movement of stock.

Perpetual Inventory Method

When business has a more extensive stock than the owner or management can 'know' intimately, a more positive control, the **perpetual inventory system,** is used. Here, a card or other form of record such as a computer file for each type of item is used. (There may or may not be prices on these records.)

As items are received, the number of units is placed in the 'receipts' column, and the balance is accordingly increased. As items are sold, the number of units is placed in the 'sold' column, and the balance is reduced. In this way the owner or manager can tell how much of any item is on hand simply by checking the inventory card.

This system requires an investment in cards and card files and the services of someone to keep the card file up to date. It requires the processing of data when goods are received and when they are sold. But it enables the management to control the relationship between Sales and Cost of Goods Sold on a current basis. It also permits a closer control of stocks through the accounting records. It permits the use of cyclic rather than year-end stock-taking.

Transaction	*Periodic Method*			*Perpetual Method*		
		£	£		£	£
Purchase of goods	Purchases Cash (or Creditors)	1,000	 1,000	Inventory Cash (or Creditors) (An entry is made on the item card)	1,000	 1,000
Sales	Cash (or Debtors) Sales	2,000	 2,000	Cash (or Debtors) Sales	2,000	 2,000
Cost of Goods Sold	No entry of sale at this time. The Cost of Goods Sold is determined at year end by use of the Cost of Goods Sold formula			Cost of Goods Sold Inventory (An entry is made on the item card)	1,500	 1,500
Deficiency of inventory item	Not determinable during year except by chance			Inventory Over and Short A/c Inventory	150	 150
Surplus of inventory item	Not determinable during year except by chance			Inventory Over and Short A/c	200	 200

If all sales tickets are priced out with the Cost of Goods Sold when the entry for removal of the goods is made, the current relationship between Sales and Cost of Sales can be established. Any error in sales price can be determined immediately, and corrective action can be taken.

When accounting control is kept over stocks by use of this system, pilferage is less likely to occur, because employees do not know when a count of the item they are taking will be made and the shortage discovered. This is in contrast to the periodic system, in which the counting time is definitely established in the future, permitting pilfering in the interim with comparative safety from detection.

When inventory is controlled under the perpetual inventory system, a count of stock at any time can be compared with the balance shown on the card (plus adjustments on the card balance for recent receipts and sales not recorded). In this system, the inventory is 'cycled' for physical counting, or a count can be made when purchase requisitions are prepared. In any event, all goods should be counted at least once a year.

When a discrepancy is noted between the physical count and the adjusted card balance, the situation should be analysed and the reasons for the discrepancy established. Corrective action should be taken to remedy the situation, and an adjustment made on the card to reconcile it with the reality of the physical count. The difference in meaning of the terms should be noted since they are often confused. Perpetual Inventory is a system of recording stock receipts and issues and computing the balance after each transaction—manually or otherwise. Cyclic or Continuous Stocktaking is a system for physically checking the stock levels and is usually, but not necessarily, complementary to the perpetual inventory recording system.

Price-level Changes and Pricing Methods

Before the Second World War, when the price-level rise was relatively small, prices were thought to follow the flow of goods. The oldest goods were sold first and the newest goods were kept in stock. The oldest prices, therefore, were applied to Cost of Goods Sold, and the newest prices applied to stock. This system was a natural extension of the physical movement phenomenon and became known as the FIFO Inventory Method, although the more proper name would be the FIFO Cost of Goods Sold Pricing Method. The term 'FIFO' comes from the initial letters of 'First In First Out'.

A closer analysis of price movements shows that prices do not remain steady or move upward or downward at a fixed rate. Rather, they move around a trend line. During periods of small fluctuations if may be better to determine the **average** price of a type of item on hand and use this average for pricing Cost of Goods Sold and the closing stock. The average price is changed as new stock is purchased.

In periods of stable prices, or in periods of relatively small upward or downward trends in prices, the 'FIFO' and 'average' methods yield fairly realistic Cost of Goods Sold and Closing-Stock values. In the changed economic conditions brought about by the Second World War, prices began to rise steeply and this trend has continued ever since. The use of

	Purchases			*Sales*		
			£			£
19.8	Jan. 2	100 @ £0.10	10.00	Jan. 15	50 @ £0.20	10.00
	Feb. 10	50 @ £0.11	5.50	April 20	70 @ £0.20	14.00
	May 19	150 @ £0.12	18.00	Oct. 12	80 @ £0.21	16.80
		300	£33.50		200	£40.80
19.9	April 9	75 @ £0.12	9.00	May 12	100 @ £0.22	22.00
	June 10	75 @ £0.11	8.25	July 15	150 @ £0.21	31.50
		150	£17.25		250	£53.50

	FIFO		*Average*		*LIFO*	
19.8		£		£		£
	Sales (200)	40.80	Sales (200)	40.80	Sales (200)	40.80
	Cost of Sales:		Cost of Sales:		Cost of Sales:	
	100 @ £0.10	10.00	$\frac{£33.50}{300}$ = £0.11$\frac{1}{6}$ each		150 @ £0.12	18.00
	50 @ £0.11	5.50			50 @ £0.11	5.50
	50 @ £0.12	6.00	200 @ £0.11$\frac{1}{6}$	22.33	200	23.50
	200	21.50				
	GROSS PROFIT	£19.30	GROSS PROFIT	£18.47	GROSS PROFIT	£17.30
	December 31 Stock		December 31 Stock		December 31 Stock	
	100 @ £0.12	£12.00	100 @ £0.11$\frac{1}{6}$	£11.17	100 @ £0.10	£10.00
19.9	Sales (250)	53.50	Sales (250)	53.50	Sales (250)	53.50
	Cost of Sales:		Cost of Sales:		Cost of Sales:	
	100 @ £0.12	12.00	100 £11.17		75 @ £0.11	8.25
	75 @ £0.12	9.00	150 17.25		75 @ £0.12	9.00
	75 @ £0.11	8.25	250	28.42	100 @ £0.10	10.00
	250	29.25			250	27.25
	GROSS PROFIT	£24.25	GROSS PROFIT	£25.08	GROSS PROFIT	£26.25
	Gross Profit for both years	£43.55	Gross Profit for both years	£43.55	Gross Profit for both years	£43.55

the FIFO and average methods did not yield realistic Cost of Goods Sold and income-expense matching. So a method of pricing was devised that would more closely match current income and expense in an inflationary period. This method uses more recent prices for Cost of Goods Sold and leaves older prices in the inventory and is called LIFO, from 'Last In First Out'.

Comparison of FIFO, Average and LIFO

Let us assume a company has no inventory of item X at January 1st, 19.8, purchases 300 units in 19.8, sells 200 units in 19.8, purchases 150 units in 19.9, and sells 250 units in 19.9, leaving no inventory at December 31st, 19.9. This information can be presented in tabular form, as illustrated on page 90, so that the detailed time sequence can be more clearly shown.

It can be seen that in a period of inflation (19.8 in the illustration), FIFO yields higher profits than LIFO. In a period of deflation (19.9 in the illustration), LIFO yields higher profits than FIFO. (Note that we are discussing pure price movement and cost pricing with no modification.) Profits using average price will generally fall between the FIFO and the LIFO profits.

Note that the profit over the extended period of time (two years) is the same for all methods because, in the illustration, all sales are the same (therefore total sales are the same), and all purchases are the same (therefore total purchases are the same), and there is no opening and no closing stock. The effect of using the various pricing systems is to match income and expense more closely, or for ease in the accounting process. The effect on the records in the short run is to shift income between years; in the long run, there is no effect on income.

Cost or Net Realisable Value (NRV), whichever is the Lower

After the inventory or stock cost is determined, using FIFO, average, or LIFO, the stock value is compared to the net realisable value. The original basis of stock valuation for historic profit determination was cost or market value, whichever was lower. In introducing the Statement of Standard Accounting Practice No. 9 (SSAP 9) the term net realisable value was preferred. Net realisable value is defined as the price at which goods in stock could be currently sold, less any further costs which would be incurred to complete the sale. This elimination of excess prices gives the most conservative stock value and reduces the profit of the current period by the amount the stock is written down. This can be done in three ways.

(*a*) *Item by Item.* By comparing the book cost of each item to the net realisable value, taking the lower of the two costs, and multiplying that cost by the number of units on hand.

(*b*) *Group by Group.* Multiplying the number of units on hand in an inventory group by the book cost and getting a total; then multiplying the same number of units on hand by the net realisable value and getting a total, and taking the smaller total, for each inventory group.

(c) *Total Stocks.* Multiplying each item on hand in the inventory by its book cost and adding these, getting a total; then multiplying the same units on hand by the net realisable value and adding these and getting a total; and taking the smaller total.

Examples. Assume three classes of inventory (Groups A, B, and C). Assume two items in each group and prices as shown:

A1 100 units—cost £10—NRV £11
A2 200 units—cost 55—NRV 50

B1 200 units—cost 14—NRV 12
B2 300 units—cost 15—NRV 17

C1 150 units—cost 22—NRV 21
C2 200 units—cost 21—NRV 22

The inventory value using the Item by Item method:

		£
A1	100 × £10	1,000
A2	200 × 50	10,000
B1	200 × 12	2,400
B2	300 × 15	4,500
C1	150 × 21	3,150
C2	200 × 21	4,200
		£25,250

The stock value using the Group by Group method:

		£		£	£
A1	100 × £10	1,000	× £11	1,100	
A2	200 × 55	11,000	× 50	10,000	
		£12,000		£11,100	11,100
B1	200 × 14	2,800	× 12	2,400	
B2	300 × 15	4,500	× 17	5,100	
		£7,300		£7,500	7,300
C1	150 × 22	3,300	× 21	3,150	
C2	200 × 21	4,200	× 22	4,400	
		£7,500		£7,550	7,500
					£25,900

The stock value using the Total Stocks method:

		£		£
A1	100 × £10	1,000	× £11	1,100
A2	200 × 55	11,000	× 50	10,000
B1	200 × 14	2,800	× 12	2,400
B2	300 × 15	4,500	× 17	5,100
C1	150 × 22	3,300	× 21	3,150
C2	200 × 21	4,200	× 22	4,400
		£26,800		£26,150

In comparing the stock values determined by these three methods we have:

Item by Item	£25,250
Group by Group	25,900
Total Stocks	26,150

The spread between the lowest (Item by Item) and highest (Total Stocks) value is less than 4 per cent. The Item by Item method is often used because the lower cost is selected first and only one multiplication step is performed; whereas in the other two methods the multiplication is performed for both the book cost and the NRV and then the comparison is made.

The adjusting entry to reduce inventory cost from book cost to cost or NRV, whichever is lower, is:

Loss Due to Decline in NRV	XXX	
Stocks		XXX

Other Pricing Methods

There are two additional methods that use other than invoice price to determine closing stock value.

Retail Method

This method requires that a detailed record be kept of the difference between cost (invoice) price and the retail price. When an item is purchased, the retailer changes the price to a higher one for use in sales to his customers. This increase in price is called **mark-up** or **mark-on**. The retail price can be increased further or it can be decreased, even below cost, if the situation suggests such action (competition, popularity of product, etc.). A pair of columns are used on a worksheet to summarise opening stock, purchases, and goods available for sale at both cost and retail. When the ratio of cost to retail price of goods available for sale is known, the closing stock is determined by multiplying the retail price of the stock by that ratio. To determine Cost of Goods Sold, the formula Opening Stock + Purchases − Closing Stock is used.

Gross Profit Method

Another method for determining stock value without using invoice prices is the gross profit method, which is based on the assumption that if the percentage of Gross Profit to Sales is known the Cost of Goods Sold can be determined from Sales, and the Closing Stock can be found by using the Cost of Goods Sold formula. This method should be avoided unless the stock value is determined in some other manner for purposes of comparison. The lack of control and the possibility of overlooking stock shortages when this method is used can make the apparent savings in accounting costs very expensive indeed.

Presentation of Stock on the Balance Sheet

The stock-in-trade is a current asset and is usually shown before the Accounts and Notes Receivable in the following manner:

Stocks are stated at the lower of cost and net realisable value £XXX.

8
Assets Used in Operations Over Long Periods

Some businesses need equipment and other assets that will be used over long periods of time. An example of this might be a delivery van. The entry to record the purchase of such a vehicle for £500 cash would be:

Motor Vehicles	£500	
Cash		£500

Note that the debit was not made to an expenditure account. Although the asset will be used up by the business in its operation, the debit to expense comes at a later time with another entry.

Another example might be the purchase of ten vans costing £500 each under an agreement to pay £1,500 in cash and £3,500 in three months. The entry would be:

Motor Vehicles	£5,000	
Cash		£1,500
Creditors		3,500

Again, note that the debit was not made to an expense account.

In assets of this type, the problem of accounting is twofold: to determine the cost of the asset (not difficult in the examples above) and to allocate, on some mathematical basis, the cost of the asset to the financial periods of its expected economic life.

This type of asset might be defined as a tangible asset of a relatively fixed or permanent nature used in the operation of the business, or as an intangible asset used by the business in its operation.

Types of Asset

Basically, there are five types of these assets:

(*a*) **Land.** In this sense land is considered as industrial or commercial property: a building site, a site for a car park. It does not include farmland, which is treated differently and is outside the scope of this volume.

(*b*) **Buildings.** Buildings are shelters for housing operations or protecting assets: office buildings, factories, garages, hotels, storage warehouses.

(*c*) **Man-made Assets.** These include all tangible assets other than buildings: office equipment, factory equipment, sales furniture and fixtures, delivery van, cars.

(*d*) **Natural Assets.** All assets produced by nature which man converts to his own use. There are two sub-types:

(i) *Extractive resources:* gold, oil, coal, etc.
(ii) *Regenerative resources:* trees, cattle, crops.

(*e*) **Intangible Assets.** These are non-physical assets created by legal contract, statutory operation, or other such means. There are two sub-types:

(i) *Limited life:* patents, copyrights.
(ii) *Unlimited life:* goodwill, trademarks.

These assets have certain distinguishing characteristics. Buildings have a relatively longer life as compared to other man-made assets. Equipment assets are of varying types, are used for different purposes, and have very different lives. In general, such equipment asset lives will be shorter than building lives, and equipment assets may have a scrap value that is a larger percentage of cost than would be the resale value of a building.

Those businesses that extract natural assets must build physical facilities so that operations can begin or continue. The cost of the physical facilities and the cost of the natural assets must be allocated to the years of expected economic extraction, although the physical facilities may last much longer. In the regenerative natural assets, there are rules for plant assets approximating to those in use with office and factory assets.

Intangible assets are written off over their contractual term, or over a shorter period if the economic life of the intangible asset is shorter than the stated term. Those intangible assets having no term can be kept at their original cost until the economic value has shrunk, but are often written off over several years.

Property

Land and buildings can be acquired on either a leasehold or freehold basis. Where a business acquires leasehold property it will have to be handed back in the same condition at the end of the lease. The value of this property must therefore be written off or depreciated over the period of the lease in the same way as other fixed assets.

Land acquired on a freehold basis will not be depreciated unless it has been acquired for mining, or extracting its natural resources in other ways, when its value must be written down as the ores are extracted. Freehold buildings may be written down, but in periods of inflation—such as the past few decades—any fall in value is usually offset by increasing property values in general. Each case must be decided on its merits.

Freehold and leasehold property are normally shown separately on a Balance Sheet: in fact, this is legally required of limited-liability companies.

Completion Statements

When industrial or commercial premises change hands there are usually a number of adjustments to be made. It would be unlikely that the vendor would have paid rates (payable in advance) up to the date on which the transfer takes place. It would be unlikely that a sitting tenant in part of the property would have paid rent up to the date of the transfer. It may even happen that the purchaser takes possession of the premises either before or after the date of the legal transfer. Adjustments will accordingly be required in some or all of these matters, and these adjustments will be incorporated in a Completion Statement, an example of which is given below.

COMPLETION STATEMENT OF PROGRESS WAREHOUSE
(May 31st, 19..)

	£	£
Purchase Price as Agreed		18,000.00
Less Deposit Paid January 1st, 19..		1,800.00
		16,200.00
Add Proportion of Water Rate Paid for Period Jan. 1st to Dec. 31st, 19..		
$\frac{7}{12}$th of £54.00	31.50	
Proportion of General Rates Paid for Half Year to Sept. 30th, 19..		
$\frac{4}{6}$th of £150.00	100.00	
Proportion of Fire Insurance Paid for Year Ending June 30th, 19..		
$\frac{1}{12}$th of £30.00	2.50	134.00
		16,334.00
Less Proportion of Rent Paid for Part Occupation of Premises for Quarter Ending June 30th		
$\frac{1}{3}$rd of £120.00		40.00
		£16,294.00

Of the total of £18,094 paid to the vendor, only £18,000 represents the cost of the property. The sum of £134 added represents expenses which would have fallen on the purchaser if they had not already been paid by the vendor, and consequently must be debited to the appropriate expense accounts. The sum of £40 deducted represents rent paid to the vendor of the property, two months previously, to cover the quarter to the end of June. If it had not been paid in advance it would be paid to the purchaser and would be a source of income associated with the property. It must therefore be credited to the appropriate income account.

The accounts of the purchase would appear as follows:

VENDOR'S ACCOUNT

	£		£
Cash	1,800.00	Water Rate	31.50
Rent Receivable	40.00	General Rates	100.00
Cash	16,294.00	Insurance	2.50
		Freehold Warehouse	18,000.00
	£18,134.00		£18,134.00

FREEHOLD WAREHOUSE

Vendor	£18,000.00		

WATER RATES

Vendor	£31.50		

GENERAL RATES

Vendor	£100.00		

INSURANCE

Vendor	£2.50		

RENT RECEIVABLE

		Vendor	£40.00

If a piece of property is purchased with a building on it for £10,759, but the building is torn down because only the land is wanted, the total purchase price of the land is the cost of the parcel plus the cost of demolishing the building and preparing the land for use. If, in the example above, land was purchased on which there was a building that was demolished at a cost of £7,500, the entry for removal would be:

Land	£7,500	
Cash or Debtors		£7,500

The cost of the property would be £18,259.

Sometimes a piece of property is purchased with a building that is to be removed, but a demolition company will pay to remove it. If, in the original example above, the building is to be demolished and the demolition company pays £6,000 to salvage the building, the entry would be:

Cash	£6,000	
Land		£6,000

The cost of the property would be £4,759.

Cost of a New Building

When a building is put up on bare land, the cost of the building includes soil tests, architect's fees, excavation costs, cost of in-progress alterations, interest on the money borrowed for the building during construction, and the attributed portion of the rates to the time of completion. When the contractor completes the job and the owner accepts it as completed, the construction is at an end. All amounts paid and liabilities assumed up to that time are costs of construction.

Cost of a Remodelled Building

When a building is purchased with the intention of converting or remodelling it before use, all the costs of design, conversion or remodelling, painting, decoration, repairs to roofs and windows, etc., up to the time the building is ready for occupation in its refurbished condition, are part of the cost.

Capital Expenditures vs *Revenue Expenditures*

After the initial cost has been determined for fixed assets, expenditures will be made in connection with these fixed assets. Expenditures made to repair the asset for the purpose of maintaining its utility are **revenue** expenditures chargeable to income for that period. Expenditures made to change the utility character of the asset are **capital** expenditures and are added to fixed-asset cost.

Other Fixed Assets

Purchases of tangible assets other than land and building include:

Office Equipment: typewriters, desks, chairs, filing cabinets, adding machines, calculators, etc., used in general offices. (Some larger companies might classify further into Accounting Office Equipment, Factory Office Equipment, Sales Office Equipment, etc.)

Store (*or Sales*) *Equipment:* sales counters, display counters, sales-floor shelving, cash registers, display racks or fixtures, used in displaying and selling goods and in storing the merchandise for sale. (For purposes of control, this group of equipment assets could be further classified into Dept. 1 Sales Equipment, Dept. 2, etc.)

Factory Equipment: lathes, drills, presses, looms, pickling tanks, conveyor belts, fork-lift trucks, used to produce finished goods or used in the movement of goods round the factory. (This might be further classified into Production Equipment, Factory Transport Equipment, Factory Storeroom Equipment, etc.)

Delivery Equipment: vans and other vehicular equipment used to deliver the produce in external transport. The term usually refers to delivery from the store to the customer. When the equipment is used to deliver materials from a supplier to the factory, a separate category called Factory Transport Equipment is sometimes set up.

Jigs and Fixtures: tools, fixtures, jigs, gauges, and other specially-designed and accurately-made devices that are used in production.

Small Tools: an inventory of stock tools that the company has on hand for use by the employees in furthering productive effort. Since this class includes hammers, wrenches, pliers, etc., that are subject to pilferage, special controls must be established to prevent loss.

The cost of these assets includes all costs necessary to get the asset in the place wanted in the condition wanted. Therefore, if a business buys a machine FOB New York for £10,000 but must spend £200 for freight and insurance during transit and £500 for installation and testing, the cost of this machine is not £10,000 but £10,700. If a van costs £600 but the business orders a special colour and lettering at £20 extra, the asset cost is £620.

Depreciation

Although the purchase of an asset occurs at one time, the use of the asset goes on into future periods. Therefore, the asset's cost must be allocated to the periods that receive benefit from the expenditure so that the net income, in the year of purchase, is not distorted, as it would be if the total cost was charged to expense in that one period. The distribution should be equitable so that each period bears its fair share during the lifetime of the asset. The allocation should be based on some rational mathematical system which is determined at the beginning of use so that varying personal judgements over the years of the asset's life will not affect the charging procedure.

Factors Involved in Depreciation

To determine what use might be had from an asset, we must examine those factors that would make the asset less useful. These factors fall into two classes, physical and functional. Physical factors include:

(*a*) *Wear and tear:* the lessening in utility that comes from normal use of the asset.
(*b*) *Decay:* the lessening in utility by the effect of nature.
(*c*) *Destruction:* the lessening of utility due to the asset's physical destruction.

Functional factors include:

(*a*) *Obsolescence:* the reduction of utility that results from the development of a better machine or process.
(*b*) *Inadequacy:* the reduction in utility that comes about because more production is needed than this asset or combination of assets can give. (Such a situation may force an earlier retirement of this asset or combination of assets than was originally contemplated.)

When we determine the economic utility of a fixed asset so that the concepts of depreciation accounting can be applied, all of the factors listed above should be taken into consideration. They are generally reduced to a statement expressing utility for a definite number of years or for the production of a definite number of units.

Depreciation Formulas

After the utility statement is expressed, the question of how much to charge the present period, and each succeeding period, has to be resolved. The amount to be charged is the cost less the estimated scrap value that the asset will bring after its utility has been dissipated. Various mathematical methods have been devised for the allocation; the ones currently in use are discussed below.

(*a*) *Straight-line.* This method is based on the proposition that each time period should be charged the same amount as any other similar time period. It is the easiest method to use from a record-keeping and computational standpoint. The formula used is:

$$\frac{\textit{Cost less estimated scrap value}}{\textit{Expected number of terms of utility}} = \textit{Depreciation charge per term}$$

'Terms of utility' can be expressed as months or years, depending upon the nature of the asset.

(*b*) *Hourly*. This method is based on the same proposition as the straight-line method—that is, each time period should have an equal charge. But the time period is an hour, rather than years or months as in the straight-line method. This requires that a record be kept of the number of hours of use of the asset in each financial period. When the rate per hour is multiplied by the number of hours of use in a financial period, the resultant figure is the depreciation charge for that particular financial period. The formulas used are:

$$\frac{\textit{Cost less estimated scrap value}}{\textit{Estimated number of hours of utility}} = \textit{Depreciation charge per hour}$$

and

$$\begin{matrix}\textit{Depreciation charge} \\ \textit{per hour}\end{matrix} \times \begin{matrix}\textit{Actual hours of use in} \\ \textit{the financial period}\end{matrix} = \begin{matrix}\textit{Depreciation charge for} \\ \textit{the financial period}\end{matrix}$$

In this method, the depreciation charge for the financial period varies as the usage of the fixed asset varies.

(*c*) *Output*. This method is based on the proposition that each unit of output should bear an equal share of the allocated cost. It requires that a record be kept of the output in the financial period. When the rate per unit of output is multiplied by the number of units produced, the resultant figure is the depreciation charge for the financial period. The formulas used are:

$$\frac{\textit{Cost less estimated scrap value}}{\textit{Estimated number of units of output}} = \textit{Depreciation charge per unit of output}$$

and

$$\begin{matrix}\textit{Depreciation charge} \\ \textit{per unit of output}\end{matrix} \times \begin{matrix}\textit{Actual units produced in} \\ \textit{the financial period}\end{matrix} = \begin{matrix}\textit{Depreciation charge for} \\ \textit{the financial period}\end{matrix}$$

In this method, the depreciation charge for the financial period varies as production from the usage of the fixed asset varies.

At this point it might be well to show the accounting entries used to record the depreciation charge, to show the related accounts involved, and to discuss a few other concepts before returning to depreciation formulas.

The Accounting Entry

The depreciation expense is recorded in the books by means of a journal entry at the end of each financial period. The entry is:

Depreciation—Asset	£XXX	
Accumulated Depreciation—Asset		£XXX

(Where the word 'Asset' appears above, the account title will be Office Equipment, Store Equipment, Delivery Equipment, etc., as appropriate.)

When a fixed asset is acquired during the year or disposed of during the year, the depreciation charge should be calculated *pro rata* when the straight-line method and the methods discussed below are used. (This calculation is not needed for the hourly or output methods.) The calculation can be modified so that anything purchased in a financial period will (or will not) be depreciated for the entire financial period, which might be a month, a quarter, or a year. A similar statement would be established for its disposal. The rule is a matter of company policy, not accounting principle.

The General Ledger Accounts

The cost is recorded as shown previously and is posted to the General Ledger Account:

OFFICE EQUIPMENT (OR STORE EQUIPMENT, ETC.)

Date of purchase	Cost	
Date of Improvement	Cost	

The account remains at original cost until a capital expenditure is made, at which time the amount of this expenditure is added to cost. No other entry is made to this account in relation to a specific asset until that asset is disposed of in some fashion. The two accounts affected by the depreciation charge entry are Accumulated Depreciation—Asset (Office Equipment, Store Equipment, etc., as appropriate) and Depreciation—Asset:

ACCUMULATED DEPRECIATION—ASSET

	Year 1	Depreciation	£XXX
	Year 2	Depreciation	£XXX etc.

As the entry is made each year, the credit is posted to the Accumulated Depreciation Account which is a contra-asset or asset valuation account. The balance keeps getting larger, ultimately equalling cost less estimated scrap value (except when an asset is disposed of before the end of its full expected life). This account balance tells how much of the cost of particular assets has been charged to operations.

DEPRECIATION—ASSET

Year 1	£XXX	Closed to Revenue A/c	£XXX
Year 2	£XXX	Closed to Revenue A/c	£XXX

Note that this account operates in the same manner as any other expense account. It is closed and transferred to the Manufacturing, Trading, or Profit and Loss Account, as appropriate, so that no balance is carried over from one year to the next.

Another account that can be used in connection with fixed assets is Repairs and Maintenance. When revenue expenditure is incurred for fixed assets the entry is:

Repairs and Maintenance Expense	£XXX	
Cash or Creditors		£XXX

The posting is made to the Repairs and Maintenance Expense Account as follows:

REPAIRS AND MAINTENANCE EXPENSE

19.8 charges		Closed to Revenue A/c	
19.9 charges		Closed to Revenue A/c	

Note that this account also operates in the same manner as any other expense account. It is closed and transferred to the Manufacturing, Trading, or Profit and Loss Account, as appropriate, so that no balance is carried over from one year to the next.

Book Value

On the Balance Sheet, assets are shown at cost less accumulated depreciation. One method used to show this is:

	£	£
Fixed Assets:		
Land		50,000
Building	100,000	
Less Accumulated Depreciation	20,000	80,000
Office Equipment	25,000	
Less Accumulation Depreciation	6,000	19,000
TOTAL FIXED ASSETS		£149,000

Another method is:

	Cost	Accumulated Depreciation	Book-Value
	£	£	£
Fixed Assets:			
Land	50,000	—	50,000
Building	100,000	20,000	80,000
Office Equipment	25,000	6,000	19,000
	£175,000	£26,000	£149,000

Note that land has no accumulated depreciation because it is not subject to depreciation accounting, as we saw earlier.

Book-value is a term that is used to indicate how much of the cost of fixed assets has not yet been depreciated. The question of book-value of fixed assets has been the subject of much discussion in professional accounting circles in the past few years. The normal accounting procedure is to report fixed assets at cost less accumulated depreciation, the latter determined by some rational mathematical system. However, since fixed assets are relatively long-lived, changes in price level generally affect the market value of the asset. Under the principle of conservatism, accountants will reduce the value of the asset from book-value to current market value in periods of declining prices. This reduction in value is taken as an extraordinary loss in the period in which it occurs.

In periods of rising prices, however, conservative practice leaves the fixed-asset book-value at cost less accumulated depreciation. But this might not reflect current market value and, in fact, may be lower by thousands of pounds. At present, accountants are aware of the fact that this practice distorts the financial statements, but they have reached no generally accepted method of showing this on the financial statements. The reader of financial statements, therefore, should be aware that discrepancies between the present realistic values of fixed assets and those recorded on the books do sometimes exist, and that they tend to show fixed-asset values at a price lower than the realistic price. This is part of the wider problem of accounting under consistent inflationary conditions, which is still the subject of debate and experiment.

More Depreciation Formulas

(*d*) *Declining Balance*. In using this method, a constant factor is applied to the reducing book-value of the asset (the declining balance). A formula which may be used in obtaining the ratio is:

$$\frac{100\%}{\textit{Expected number of periods of use}} \times 2 = \textit{Rate to be applied to the declining balance (book-value)}$$

Assume that an asset costing £20,000 has an expected economic life of five years; the rate to be applied would be: $\frac{100}{5}\% \times 2 = 40\%$. This factor is then applied to the reducing book-value, giving a successively smaller depreciation charge each year.

Applying the 40 per cent factor to the figures given above, we have:

	Depreciation Expense for the Year	Cost	Accumulated Depreciation	Book-Value
	£	£	£	£
Purchase		20,000		20,000
1st Year's Depreciation (40% × 20,000)	8,000		8,000	12,000
2nd Year's Depreciation (40% × 12,000)	4,800		12,800	7,200
3rd Year's Depreciation (40% × 7,200)	2,880		15,680	4,320
4th Year's Depreciation (40% × 4,320)	1,728		17,408	2,592
5th Year's Depreciation (40% × 2,592)	1,037		18,445	1,555
	£18,445			

The above method is an approximate one. The correct variables can be deduced from the following formula:

Let C = Cost of the asset
R = Residual value
n = Life of asset in periods
P = Proportion of cost of asset to be written off per period

then $P = 1 - \sqrt[n]{\frac{R}{C}}$

Note that if the residual value is nil then a nominal figure of, say, £1 must be attributed to R otherwise the whole equation would be zero. Either variable can be determined by transposing the formula.

(*e*) *Sum-of-the-Years-Digits*. This method applies a reducing fraction to the original cost minus salvage value. The formula for finding the fraction is: Let n be the number of periods of expected economic life. The denominator of the fraction is the sum of $n + (n - 1) + (n - 2) + \ldots + 1$. The numerator for the first year is n; the second year, $n - 1$; . . .; the last year, 1. Therefore, each year the fraction becomes smaller but the total of all the fractions equals 1.

Assume that an asset costing £20,000 has an expected economic life of five years and a scrap value of £2,000:

Denominator = 5 + 4 + 3 + 2 + 1 = 15.
Fractions are $\frac{5}{15}$, $\frac{4}{15}$, $\frac{3}{15}$, $\frac{2}{15}$ and $\frac{1}{15}$.
Cost minus salvage value £20,000 − £2,000 = £18,000

1st Year's Depreciation:	18,000 × $\frac{5}{15}$ =	6,000
2nd Year's Depreciation:	18,000 × $\frac{4}{15}$ =	4,800
3rd Year's Depreciation:	18,000 × $\frac{3}{15}$ =	3,600
4th Year's Depreciation:	18,000 × $\frac{2}{15}$ =	2,400
5th Year's Depreciation:	18,000 × $\frac{1}{15}$ =	1,200
		£18,000

The illustrations of these last two methods show that they have the effect of bringing into the earlier years of the useful life of an asset a greater proportional amount of depreciation expense than would be the case under the straight-line method.

(*f*) *Annuity Method.* None of the methods hitherto mentioned have considered the interest charges on the funds needed to acquire the asset or the interest that might be earned on the funds if they were otherwise employed. Consider a transport-modernisation programme costing £10 million, which it is decided should be written off over 40 years. If this were done using the straight-line method, the depreciation charge would be £250,000 per annum.

Let us assume that the money for the programme has to be borrowed at 6 per cent per annum, and that it is necessary to borrow the full £10 million for 40 years. If £10 million were borrowed initially and £250,000 (the amount of the annual depreciation charge) were repaid annually, the interest charge would be far higher in the first year than in the 40th year. It would be misleading to regard the annual cost of the programme as being

Interest @ 6% on £10M	600,000
Annual Depreciation	250,000
Total	£850,000

since this would gradually reduce with the annual repayments until in the 40th year the annual cost would be

Interest @ 6% on £250,000	15,000
Annual Depreciation	250,000
Total	£265,000

This is illustrated in Fig. 3.

The annuity method is based on the reasoning that both depreciation and interest charges should be considered together and that they should form a combined charge which remains constant over the life of the assets involved. If this is to be achieved, the depreciation charge must begin at a low figure and increase year by year by the amount of the annual reduction in interest charges.

The appropriate figure can be obtained by the use of the 'annuity factor' (see page 177) from compound-interest tables calculated on the rate of interest payable (or able to be earned) on the funds. The appropriate symbol is $a\frac{6\%}{\overline{40|}}$ where 40 is the term and 6 per cent is the rate of interest. The tables give the present value of one unit per term for *n* terms assuming that interest at the given rate is earned on the amount not yet paid out. From this we can calculate the 40 annual payments that can be made out of £10M assuming interest is earned at 6 per cent as follows:

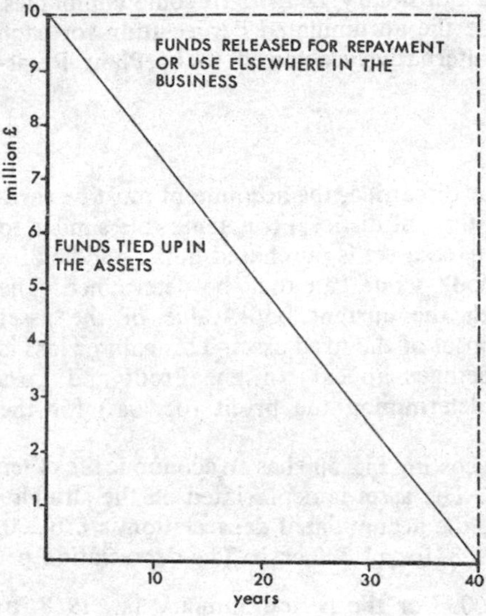

Fig. 3.

$$\begin{aligned}&\pounds 10{,}000{,}000 \div a_{\overline{40}|}\\ &= 10{,}000{,}000 \div 15.04629687\\ &= \pounds 664{,}615\end{aligned}$$

This figure will cover both the interest on the funds tied up and also the depreciation charge. They can be separated like this:

	Annuity	Interest on Balance, at Beginning of Year	Balance, being Depreciation
Year 1	£664,615	£600,000	£64,615
Year 40	664,615	15,000	649,615

Thus, whether the funds released are repaid or are used elsewhere in the business, the depreciation charge can be so allocated over the life of the assets as to reflect the release of these resources and the saving of interest charges or earning power of the funds released. The mathematics involved in this method of calculation is beyond the scope of this book, but is discussed in the companion book *Financial Management Made Simple*.

Asset Registers and Subsidiary Ledgers

For purposes of control, to help prevent theft, to aid in the location of assets, and for purposes of insurance claims processing, among other reasons, many companies keep a detailed card file or a detailed listing (sometimes called a register) of all assets in a group. If this card file or register is totalled to equal the Control Account in the General Ledger, the detailed records can constitute a Subsidiary Ledger. In some companies, the data are expanded to include the accumulated depreciation for each asset item. These records are alternatively referred to as Plant Registers.

Selling and Discarding Assets

When fixed-asset items are sold or discarded, the accountant must be careful to depreciate the asset to the time of disposal (on some rule similar to the one discussed earlier when a fixed asset is purchased in the middle of a financial period). The current book value can then be determined. The amount received compared with the current book-value of the asset measures the gain or loss on disposal of the fixed asset. This gain or loss is an extraordinary item and sometimes appears on the Profit and Loss Account as a deduction after determining the profit (or loss) for the year.

Assume that a factory machine costing £12,500 has an economic life of ten years and a scrap value of £500. The asset is depreciated on the straight-line basis. On January 1st, 19.8, the accumulated depreciation is £10,200. The asset is sold on April 1st, 19.8, for £1,300 cash. The depreciation per year is $\frac{£12{,}500 - £500}{10}$ or £1,200. For the period January 1st, 19.8, to April 1st, 19.8 (three months), the depreciation is £300. The entry to record this is:

Depreciation Expense— Factory Equipment	£300	
Accumulated Depreciation— Factory Equipment		£300

The allowance for depreciation is now £10,500 and the book-value is £2,000. The loss from disposal is £700. The entry to record this is:

Accumulated Depreciation— Factory Equipment	£10,500	
Cash	1,300	
Loss on Disposal of Fixed Assets	700	
Factory Equipment		£12,500

The depreciation expense entry is prepared first; then the entry is prepared debiting the assets received (in this case cash), debiting the corrected accumulated depreciation, debiting the loss on disposal, if any, crediting the asset at cost, and crediting the gain on disposal, if any.

If the asset is discarded and there is no asset received in return, the loss on disposal is the current book-value of the asset.

Assets Fully Depreciated Still Used in Production

When fixed assets are fully depreciated down to scrap value and are still used by the business in its operation, the current period has income but no matching depreciation expense, thereby increasing net income. Some accountants suggest that fixed assets fully depreciated still used in production be so noted on the balance sheet. It should be pointed out to the statement reader that the income was produced with fully depreciated assets if their amount is significant.

Part Exchange of Assets

In many cases in which assets are traded for newer assets, the dealer offers a trade-in or part-exchange allowance for the old piece of equipment. Trade-in is a sales device and should not be recognised in the books of the company trading the old asset. Rather, the accounting records should reflect the true cost of the new asset acquired which is the current book-value of the old asset plus the cash or assets paid and the liabilities assumed.

Assume that a van costing £780 has an estimated scrap value of £60 and an economic life of six years (straight-line basis is used). The balance in the Accumulated Depreciation—Van Account on January 1st, 19.8, is £520. On June 1st, 19.8, the van is traded in for a new one with a list price of £800. A trade-in allowance of £250 is given by the dealer; the remainder is paid in cash.

To bring the allowance up to date:

$$\frac{£780 - £60}{6 \times 12} = £10 \text{ depreciation per month.}$$

January 1st to June 1st = 5 months or £50 depreciation.

Depreciation Expense—Van	£50	
Accumulated Depreciation—Van		£50

(Balance in the Accumulated Depreciation account is now £570.) To record the purchase of the new vehicle:

Van (new)	£760	
Accumulated Depreciation—Van	£570	
Van (old)		£780
Cash (£800 – £250)		£550

The value determined for the new van (£760) is the amount needed to establish debit–credit equality in the purchase entry. This is called the 'adjusted basis' and is the cost that will be depreciated over the economic life of the new asset after subtracting scrap value.

Obsolescence and Inadequacy

When a fixed asset loses its economic value before it is depreciated down to scrap value, because of obsolescence or inadequacy, there is a **write-down** of the asset to scrap in the financial period in which this change in asset utility occurs. **Obsolescence** is the condition of having the utility of an asset lost as a result of the discovery or development of a better asset that has made the present one less useful. An example would be a propeller aeroplane being replaced by a jet plane for long-distance flights. When the jet plane was developed for commercial use, the economic life of the propeller aircraft was shortened. The airlines had to purchase jet aircraft prior to the time the propeller planes would be depreciated to scrap value in order to compete with airlines equipped with jets. The depreciation schedules had to be revised to reflect this fact.

Inadequacy is the condition of possessing an asset that cannot adequately handle anticipated production, with the result that a new asset must be acquired to meet production needs. An example would be a situation in which a company has a machine that was purchased to produce 100,000 units per year in normal operation. With overtime, production can be increased to 125,000 units. But the level of sales is such that future production requirements are 200,000 units per year. The old facility is inadequate and must be replaced if the company wants to take advantage of the market potential.

Management must always be aware of the state of development in facilities in its industry and must be aware of changing market potentials. This requires that owners and managers have a communication system efficient enough to enable them to recognise these factors. Sales literature and representatives from manufacturers, trade periodicals, business magazines and newspapers, trade conventions, courses established by manufacturers, business groups, or schools of business administration all are sources of information which management must consider. Sales analyses, modern projection techniques, budgeting and forecasting, salesmen's reports, and other market information must be continually used to assess market potential. The results of this information-gathering and -evaluation system must be communicated internally to the policy-makers if the company is to improve its position in the future.

Natural Assets and Depletion

Natural assets are those assets produced by nature which man converts to his own use. There are two sub-types: extractive resources and regenerative resources.

The extractive industries (oil, coal, gold, etc.) must locate the natural deposits, determine the value of the deposit, and determine the cost of building and operating physical facilities. The total cost to be expended must be less than the sale value of the resource extracted if the company is to make a profit. Once all the resource is extracted, the physical facility built to extract it becomes useless (except for items that can be moved or sold for scrap value). The rules of fixed-asset cost allocation discussed above are modified so that the allocation is made during the time of extraction.

The whole question of the extractive industries is a specialised field of accounting and is mentioned only because large capital investments are made in physical facilities, and many of its rules of accounting are analogous to those of depreciation accounting. These principles form what is known as **depletion accounting.**

The industries that deal in regenerative natural assets include crop farming, forestry, fishing, poultry farming and the like. In these industries, physical facilities are treated as they are in industrial situations. The problem of land preparation arises for crop farming, but again this is a specialised field of accounting and is mentioned here only because many rules of accounting in these industries parallel rules of depreciation accounting in concept.

Intangible Assets and Amortisation

Intangible assets are non-physical assets that are created by legal contract, statutory operation, or other such concepts. These intangible assets are valuable rights for the business and are enforceable in law (except perhaps for goodwill, which is a special intangible asset). Included in intangible assets are two sub-types: limited-life (patents and copyrights), and unlimited life (trademarks and goodwill).

The limited-life intangibles may be purchases (such as a patent) or may be developed (a patent or copyright). Where they are purchased, usually one charge is made to the intangible account. Thus, if a company pays £10,000 for a franchise to run a pier for ten years in a seaside town, the entry is:

	Dr	Cr
Franchise	£10,000	
Cash		£10,000

Each year, franchise amortisation expense is charged, and the Franchise Account is credited with a portion of the cost:

$$\frac{£10{,}000}{10 \text{ yrs}} = £1{,}000/\text{yr}$$

	Dr	Cr
Franchise Amortisation Expense	£1,000	
Franchise		£1,000

When the intangible is developed, there may be a series of charges that will eventually result in the accumulation of the cost of the intangible in an appropriate account. If a patent is secured, the cost is allocated over the term of the patent or its economic life, whichever is shorter. The entries are the same as those shown above except that 'patent' would be used rather than 'franchise'.

Where the intangible is for an unlimited life the asset is charged with the cost, but there is no charge to operations on a regular basis. Sometimes, in the interest of accounting conservatism, the asset is written down to a nominal value of £1.00.

Valuations

One of the major problems in accounting today is determining how to change accounting principles so that assets purchased in years gone by, which have been recorded at cost and have been depreciated under the concepts described in this chapter, can be shown at nearer their present value rather than at book-value. There is no current requirement, in generally accepted accounting principles, that the present value must be shown. However, when cost less accumulated depreciation only is shown, there can be a great disparity between the book-value and the present value. In the UK the accountancy profession has produced recommendations for a formal system of updating published accounts called Current Cost Accounting and described in SSAP 16. This is, however, not universally accepted and is subject to ongoing debate.

Let us assume that 25 years ago a company purchased a building (exclusive of land) for £200,000, paying £50,000 down and taking out a mortgage for £150,000 (now paid off). The building has been depreciated on a straight-line basis to £20,000 book-value; the recording has all been done on a cost basis. If the company decides to remortgage the building (for whatever reason), it would want to show more than £20,000, especially if the building is now worth £300,000. So on the financial statement the book-value is shown as £20,000, but the company would want the bank to know that the building is actually worth £300,000 today.

There are ways of telling what present values are. One is just knowing that the property is worth so much today—really a hunch or an unscientific sampling of local information. Another is getting a valuation from an estate agent or a professional valuer. The latter is perhaps the most accurate because the valuer's fee is based upon the time spent on the assignment and he is usually more objective. Those who are interested parties, such as estate agents, quite often bring into the valuation situation their personal biases of property values.

Once some realistic value is decided upon, the unrecorded excess of valuation over book-value can be recorded in the following manner:

Sole Trader:		
Excess of Present Value over Book-Value	£280,000	
Jones, Capital		£280,000
Partnership:		
Excess of Present Value over Book-Value	£280,000	
Brown, Capital		£140,000
Smith, Capital		140,000
Limited Company:		
Excess of Present Value over Book-Value	£280,000	
Capital Reserve (Surplus on revaluation)		£280,000

In this manner the statements more nearly reflect the facts of present value, yet the statement reader is put on notice that there are some values that have not been arrived at in the generally accepted method of sale or value transfer.

Statement Presentation

BALANCE SHEET

	£	£	£
FIXED ASSETS:			
Land		50,000	
Buildings	200,000		
Less Accumulated Depreciation	75,000	125,000	
Factory Machinery	500,000		
Less Accumulated Depreciation	200,000	300,000	
Small Tools		55,000	
Store Equipment	100,000		
Less Accumulated Depreciation	60,000	40,000	
Office Equipment	75,000		
Less Accumulated Depreciation	15,000	60,000	
TOTAL FIXED ASSETS			630,000
NATURAL ASSETS:			
Wasting Asset (Mineral Deposit)		100,000	
Less Accumulated Depletion		25,000	75,000
INTANGIBLE ASSETS:			
Franchise		20,000	
Patent		15,000	
			35,000

Another method for showing the fixed assets might be:

FIXED ASSETS

	Cost £	Accumulated Depreciation £	Book Value £	£
Land	50,000	—	50,000	
Buildings	200,000	75,000	125,000	
Factory Machinery	500,000	200,000	300,000	
Small Tools	55,000	—	55,000	
Store Equipment	100,000	60,000	40,000	
Office Equipment	75,000	15,000	60,000	
	£980,000	£350,000		£630,000

PROFIT AND LOSS STATEMENT

	£	
Factory Machinery Depreciation Expense	35,000	
Patent Amortisation Expense	7,000	
Franchise Amortisation Expense	3,000	
Small Tools Expense	12,000	
Sales Equipment Depreciation Expense	5,000	
Office Equipment Depreciation Expense	2,000	
Loss From Disposal of Depreciable Assets	15,000	
Gain From Disposal of Depreciable Assets		5,000
Loss From Natural Calamity (Fire, etc.)	12,000	
Gain From Natural Calamity (Fire, etc.)		6,000

Leasing and Hiring

To avoid tying up capital in fixed assets, a company may enter into an arrangement whereby a financial institution buys the asset, perhaps a computer, which is then leased to the company on an annual basis over its useful life. Where this is done the total commitments of the company are not substantially different from those incurred if the asset were bought outright, but the effect on the company's Balance Sheet is marked.

The Balance Sheet of our company before acquiring an asset (as given on page 38) can be summarised as follows:

CENTRAL PROVISION STORE PLC

BALANCE SHEET
(as at January 1st, 19..)

	£		£
Capital and Reserves	154,500	Fixed Assets, etc.	157,000
Liabilities	99,000	Current Assets	96,500
	£253,500		£253,500

If now the company purchases for £50,000 an item of equipment with a life of five years, the Balance Sheet would appear:

CENTRAL PROVISION STORE PLC

BALANCE SHEET
(as at January 1st, 19..)

	£		£
Capital and Reserves	154,500	Fixed Assets, etc.	207,000
Liabilities	99,000	Current Assets	46,500
	£253,500		£253,500

If, on the other hand, it were arranged for a financial institution to purchase the item of equipment for £50,000 and lease it to Central Provision Store PLC for five years at an annual charge of £15,000 payable at the beginning of each year, the Balance Sheet would appear as follows:

CENTRAL PROVISION STORE PLC

	£		£
Capital and Reserves	154,500	Fixed Assets, etc.	157,000
Liabilities	99,000	Current Assets	96,500
	£253,500		£253,500

The only change would be in the current assets, where cash would be reduced by £15,000 (the first payment to the financial institution) and an increase of £15,000 in prepaid expenses (as this payment is to cover the use of the asset for the year just beginning).

On comparing these two Balance Sheets, the second appears to show a more favourable situation than the former, since the total of liquid assets is £50,000 greater and the cash balance is £35,000 greater. The second would certainly seem to be better able to weather adverse circumstances or to increase its investment in fixed assets, and the rate of return on the fixed assets shown on the Balance Sheet would also be considerably greater.

Taken by themselves, one or other of the Balance Sheets must therefore be misleading, and it is quite obviously the second. We should have been informed of the continuing commitment to lease the asset concerned for the annual sum of £15,000 over the next four years.

Similar consideration arises when a company has entered into a contract involving capital expenditure. The company may have signed a contract for the building of a new factory, but at the date of the Balance Sheet no payment or only a small payment has been made and no asset has yet been acquired. Apart from any deposit the Balance Sheet will not be affected in any way, but a company with such a commitment is most certainly in a different position from one which has no such commitment. If trade increases the first company will be better placed; if a prolonged recession occurs the second will be better able to withstand it. The Companies Act now requires a note to be attached to the Balance Sheet giving details of both these types of commitment.

Investments

Investments are assets of a rather special nature in that they consist of legal claims of various descriptions rather than physical assets. We have already considered investments in subsidiary companies in Chapter 3. These have to be shown as a separate item on the Balance Sheet, along with any intercompany indebtedness. This will normally arise when one company within the group has surplus cash resources while another is short of funds: indeed, an interest may be acquired in a company to obtain use of its surplus funds.

Other investments have to be separated into Quoted Investments and Unquoted Investments. Quoted Investments are those which are quoted on a recognised stock exchange. Although one total is shown for each type on the Balance Sheet, a separate Ledger Account will be opened for each item in the Ledger. Since the income from quoted and unquoted investments has to be shown separately in the Profit and Loss Account, two income accounts will normally be opened: Quoted Investment Income Account and Unquoted Investment Income Account.

With a company which acquires and disposes of investments frequently, a special form of account is often used. This is because in such circumstances it is necessary to be able to separate the income on the investment from the capital cost. When, for instance, debentures are acquired after the due date for the payment of interest, part of the price paid will represent accrued interest; the reverse applies when they are sold. The calculations are facilitated by having three columns on each side of the account for Nominal Value, Income and Capital, respectively.

Thus if a company acquires £4,000 nominal of 5 per cent Stock for

£3,500 on January 1st, the interest being payable on April 1st and October 1st, after deduction of income tax at 0.40 in the £1.00 the Investment Account would appear as

INVESTMENT 5% STOCK

	Nominal £	Income £	Capital £		Nominal £	Income £	Capital £
Jan. 1st. Cash	4,000	50	3,450	Apr. 1st Cash		60	
				Oct. 1st Cash		60	
Dec. 31st Quoted-investment income		200		Dec. 31st Income Tax A/c		80	
				Dec. 31st Bal. c/d	4,000	50	3,450
	£4,000	£250	£3,450		£4,000	£250	£3,450
Jan. 1st Balance b/d	£4,000	£50	£3,450				

9
Liabilities

Most businesses use credit to purchase stocks, supplies, goods and services, and fixed assets. The business or persons to whom moneys are owed are called **creditors** and the amounts owed are called **liabilities**. The creditors are not owners of the business and do not share in its profits; they expect to get paid only for the goods and services rendered.

There are two types of liabilities:

(*a*) *Current liabilities:* Those liabilities that, by their credit terms, are due to be paid during the next financial period (usually defined as one year from the balance-sheet date).

(*b*) *Long-term liabilities:* Those liabilities that, by their credit terms, are not due to be paid until after the end of the next financial period.

It is not when the business *plans* to pay a liability that determines its classification as current or long-term; the governing factor is the **due date**.

In this chapter various types of current and long-term liabilities will be discussed.

Current Liabilities

Creditors or Accounts Payable

When a business wants to purchase on open credit, it makes arrangements with a supplier who extends the credit after ensuring, to the best of his knowledge, that the business asking for credit is a good risk. After the credit relationship is established, the business asks the supplier to furnish goods or services with payment to be made at some future date according to the credit terms. The supplier may require that the buyer sign some form of receipt, and the supplier will later send an invoice to the purchaser. But the arrangement of credit is such that the purchaser is to pay for all purchases in any amount, not just one particular invoice.

When open credit is used to purchase goods or services, the entry is:

Assets Stocks Expenses Other appropriate account	} £XXX	
Creditors, or Accounts Payable		£XXX

Internal Control of Accounts-Payable Transactions

To ensure that the company will only order goods and services needed, and that the amounts owing will be paid only once, two internal control mechanisms are used. The first is **a purchasing procedure**, which can be described as follows:

(*a*) The person needing goods or services prepares a **purchase requisition** which is given to the Purchasing Agent or Department after proper approval. This requisition should state clearly what is requested—it should include type of material, drawings, delivery schedules, quantity schedules, and any other data that will assist the Purchasing Agent in locating vendors who can supply the material.

(*b*) The Purchasing Agent or Department combs the market for a vendor (in some cases he may invite tenders for the items required) and, after selecting one who can deliver the goods as stated, issues a **purchase order** to the vendor. Copies of the purchase order can be made for distribution as follows:

Receiving Department: to give the receiving clerk an idea of what is coming in and when the goods are to arrive, and so that sufficient space is available to take delivery from the carrier. The quantities of the materials ordered can be masked out; this requires the receiving clerk actually to count the material and not simply assume that what has been ordered matches what is received.

Inspection Department: to enable the department to schedule testing of materials received, if required.

Accounting Department: to ensure that the cash required for payment of the invoice is available by the date of projected payment.

The Purchasing Department keeps a copy of the purchase order for purposes of follow-up if materials are not delivered on time.

(*c*) As the goods flow from the vendor to the purchaser, they are accompanied by a packing slip or similar document. The goods are received, counted, examined, and forwarded to the inspection department or storage areas for ultimate use or sale.

The receiving clerk prepares a receiving report that is sent to the Purchasing Department for the purpose of comparing the actual shipment received with the original purchase order. If the goods go to the inspection department, they are examined for quality and an inspection report is completed and forwarded to the Purchasing Department, and then the goods go to the storage areas.

(*d*) After receiving each document from the vendor, the receiving department, and the inspection department (if appropriate), the Purchasing Department checks them against the original purchase order to see if all conditions as stated in the purchase order have been complied with by the vendor, and that the goods were received as called for in the purchase order.

(*e*) The Purchasing Department notifies the accounting department that the vendor's invoice (which he has received directly from the vendor or indirectly through the accounting department) is a proper liability for the company.

The second internal control mechanism is the **voucher system procedure**, which can be described as follows:

(*a*) When an invoice is approved by proper authority as a company liability, the accounting department prepares a voucher. This is a standardised company form on which is transcribed all pertinent data from the approved invoices. The voucher clerk is generally familiar with the location of the necessary information on the different invoices that come into the business, and he places the information on the voucher form so that a specific item found on an invoice, such as price, will always be found in the same place on the voucher. The voucher clerk also shows the accounts to be debited, and the total amount of the invoice is credited to the supplier. This distribution is generally approved by the voucher clerk's supervisor, who also approves the voucher for correctness.

(*b*) After the approval, the voucher is entered into the Voucher Register (a form of Purchase Journal) which shows credits to the supplier and the appropriate debits. At the end of the month the register is cast and cross-cast, and the entry shown on page 117 is made. (Sometimes the General Ledger is posted directly from the register.)

(*c*) When time for payment arrives, the voucher is approved for payment and is given to the cashier's office where a cheque is prepared. The voucher and the cheque are presented to the cashier for review of the correctness of the charge and for signature on the cheque. The voucher and the invoice are then marked 'Paid'. There are two possible entries:

(i) Invoice paid net (no discount):

Supplier	£5,000	
Cash		£5,000

(ii) Invoice paid net of discount (e.g. 2%):

Supplier	£5,000	
Cash		£4,900
Purchase Discount		100

Sometimes the invoices rendered by the suppliers are used instead of a voucher prepared within the firm.

Controlling Cash Discount on Purchases

When an invoice is rendered with discount terms (2 per cent discount for cash within 30 days or net within 60 days or similar terms), it is important that discounts should not be missed. After voucher or invoice is entered, a note is made (perhaps on a calendar) of the day on which the invoice must be paid. Alternatively, the vouchers are filed in the order of payment due. On that day the invoice is located and paid, taking the discount allowed. The entries using this procedure are the ones shown above. The Purchase Discount Account might be shown in the Revenue Accounts as a reduction of purchases or as Other Income in the Profit and Loss Account.

This practice is common in many firms but has the disadvantage of not showing when a discount has been missed. Another system, employing the **exception principle**, records invoices net of discount on the assumption that all discounts will be taken. If a discount is missed, then the total invoice must be paid, and the discount not taken will show in an account called

Discounts Lost. If the company made a purchase of merchandise of £4,000 on credit with terms 2 per cent discount for cash within 30 days or net within 60 days, the entry for the purchase would be:

Purchase (£4,000 − £80)	£3,920	
Creditors		£3,920

When the invoice is paid within the discount period, the entry is:

Creditors	£3,920	
Cash		£3,920

If, however, the payment was made after the discount period and the cash discount savings were lost, the entry would be:

Creditors	£3,920	
Discount Lost	80	
Cash		£4,000

Management could analyse the Discounts Lost Account to ascertain why the discount was not taken and could then take corrective action to ensure that discounts were not missed in the future.

The Discounts Lost item is shown on the Trading Account as an addition to purchases or as Other Expense in the Profit and Loss Account.

Bills of Exchange

When goods are sold on credit, particularly to a foreign customer, it is a common practice to make use of a Bill of Exchange. A Bill of Exchange is a legal document drawn up and signed by the seller requiring the customer to pay a definite sum on a predetermined future date, often three or six months from the date of the bill. Although it is not essential bills are usually accepted by the customer by signing his name on the face of it. Sometimes a bank is authorised to act on behalf of a customer for this purpose. The seller is then able to sue the acceptor of the Bill of Exchange without reference to the transaction out of which it arose.

If the seller of the goods holds the bill until it is due for payment, no problems arise. The procedure is to debit the customer in the usual way for the goods sold and, when the bill is accepted, to credit the customer's account and debit the Bills Receivable Account. If goods to the value of £1,200 were sold to B. Brown who then accepted a three-month bill, the entries would be as follows:

B. BROWN

Goods	£1,200	Bills Receivable	£1,200

BILLS RECEIVABLE ACCOUNT

B. Brown	£1,200		

If the company's financial year ended before the end of the three months, the balance of the Bills Receivable Account would appear on the Balance Sheet among the Current Assets following the Trade Debtors. When in due course the bill was met, the Bills Receivable Account would be credited, thus offsetting the previous entry.

If, however, our company is short of funds it may be decided to discount the bill. This is done by transferring the bill to a bank, which would immediately pay an amount less than the face value of the bill to our company. The bank would collect payment of the bill in due course and the difference between the face value and the amount paid to the company would be discount. The discount is the interest charge which is made by the bank for advancing the money. It should be noted that discount is calculated on the face value of the bill and not on the amount of money advanced. A given rate of discount is therefore equivalent to a slightly higher rate of interest.

If the bill previously mentioned had immediately been discounted for three months at 8 per cent per annum, the company would have received £1,176, the discount being £24. (In practice it is calculated with precision on a daily basis.) The entries would be:

BILLS RECEIVABLE ACCOUNT

	£		£
B. Brown	1,200	Cash (from Bank)	1,176
		Discount Payable	24
	£1,200		£1,200

DISCOUNT PAYABLE ACCOUNT

Bills Receivable	£24		

In this case there would be no balance on the Bills Receivable Account nor would such an item appear on the Balance Sheet. This would not give the full picture since, if B. Brown failed to meet the bill on its due date, the bank would be entitled to recover the value of the bill (£1,200) from our company. Since no indication of this appears on the Balance Sheet, one would be justified in assuming the cash had been received direct from the customer . The transaction has given rise to a **contingent liability**, a liability that may arise in certain circumstances. A company is required to append to the Balance Sheet a note of any contingent liabilities. An alternative procedure adopted by financial institutions where contingent liabilities often arise, is to include the amounts involved on both sides of the Balance Sheet: with the current liabilities and with the current assets, respectively.

Accrued Liabilities

At the end of the financial period there are often liabilities that have not been entered on the books because the time for computation of the liability has not arrived (payroll) or the supplier has not yet invoiced for the goods or services delivered (credit purchases of petrol or long-distance telephone charges).

Accrued Payroll

If the payroll is computed on a weekly basis on Friday and the financial period ends on a Wednesday, the company must accrue the amount earned by the employees for work done on Monday, Tuesday, and Wednesday. An analysis of the time charges for the three days may be made (or an estimate based on the full week's payroll is made, if this is more practicable), and an adjusting entry is made as follows:

Sales Salaries	£1,000	
Office Salaries	800	
Factory Salaries	7,100	
(or other appropriate salary accounts)		
Accrued Salaries or Accrued Salaries Payable or Salaries Payable		£8,900

and the entry is reversed in the following period.

When the next payroll is prepared, the total distribution will be made to the proper accounts as debits, the reversing entry will have credited the accounts, and the balance in the account will be the salary expense for the new period only.

Accrued Liabilities for Goods

If goods are invoiced on a monthly basis (as in credit-card purchases) and the monthly statement received in December was dated December 15th, then all credit-card purchases not appearing on the statement should be accrued as of December 31st with an adjusting entry as follows:

Car (or Van) Expense	£50	
(or other appropriate expense)		
Accrued Liabilities		£50

This entry is reversed in the following period.

If goods are received prior to the end of the financial period but no invoice has been received, the amount owed must be accrued. If a £500 consignment of goods is received on December 29th but the invoice is received on January 5th of the following year, an adjusting entry is made as follows:

Stock Account	£500	
(or other appropriate account)		
Accrued Liabilities		£500

If a £300 consignment of goods is received on January 6th but the invoice was received on December 28th and recorded on that date, an adjusting entry must be made to remove the liability in the year the invoice was received. The entry is as follows:

Creditors	£300	
Stock Account (or Purchases Account) (or other appropriate account)		£300

and in the following year, an entry is made as follows:

Stock Account (or Purchases Account) (or other appropriate account)	£300	
Creditors		£300

Provisions or Estimated Liabilities

Some companies may have an obligation to customers under a guarantee or under an agreement to redeem coupons. The liability is certain, but the amount is not. An estimate must be made of the amount and the proper liability balance must be established. After reviewing all the facts, the business will prepare an entry as follows:

Guarantee Expense	£3,000	
Provision for Estimated Guarantee Liability		£3,000

or

Coupon Redemption Expense	£5,000	
Provision for Estimated Coupon Redemption Liability		£5,000

When, in later periods, the liability is paid by rendering service (for a guarantee), the entry is:

Provision for Estimated Guarantee Liability	£100	
Wages Account, Materials Account (or other appropriate account)		£100

When, in later periods, the liability is paid by rendering cash (for a guarantee or coupon redemption), the entry is:

Provision for Estimated Guarantee Liability Provision for Estimated Coupon Liability }	£300	
Cash		£300

Note that the expense is recorded when the liability is established, even though the amount of liability is estimated. At each year end, the Estimated Liability Account is reviewed and adjusted upward (if there are new guarantees or coupons issued) or downward (for those guarantees or coupons that have expired).

Unearned Income

In some businesses, customers may pay for goods or services before their receipt. Examples of this type of transaction include magazine subscriptions and prepaid travel vouchers.

When a magazine subscription is received, an entry is made as follows:

Cash (or Subscriptions Receivable)	£15	
Prepaid Subscriptions		£15

This recording is made for all subscriptions which, let us assume, total £5,000 for the year. Upon analysis of the Prepaid Subscription account at the year end, it is determined that £2,200 of the subscription contracts have been earned. The entry to record the conversion of liability to income is:

Prepaid Subscriptions	£2,200	
Subscriptions Income		£2,200

When a book of travel vouchers is sold, the entry is:

Cash	£10	
Prepaid Travel Vouchers		£10

This recording is made for all vouchers sold; let us say £3,000 for the year. Here, however, the earning of the income is not a function of time, as it is in the case of the magazines. Fare income arises when the passenger uses vouchers in payment of a fare. The entry to record the receipt of vouchers in payment of the fare is:

Prepaid-voucher Liability	£1	
Fare Income		£1

(Such an entry would not be made for each voucher received but would be summarised for a month or similar period.)

Because vouchers may be lost by the purchaser and never used in the payment of fares, an adjustment can be made in the Prepaid-voucher Liability Account to reduce the voucher liability to the amount expected to be used in payment of fares. This adjustment will require the analysis of sales and redemption of vouchers on a detailed basis.

These are only two examples of the type of transaction in which payment is made before goods or services are received. There are others, and it might be a good idea for management to review the operations of any business to see if perhaps some such system of prepayment by the customer might not be used to good advantage.

Contingent Liabilities

In some businesses, situations arise in which there is the possibility that a liability will come about because of some circumstance that has not been provided for by insurance. One example might be the loss of a lawsuit. When the action is brought against the business, there is the possibility that the business may not be able to defend itself successfully—the liability is possible but not certain. From a review by the business' lawyers there can be some basis for assessing chances of success in the case and the amount of the award to the plaintiff.

Preparing an entry before the decision is rendered is premature because the decision might be in favour of the business. But to ignore the possibility of loss may mislead the reader of the financial statements. Therefore, two solutions to this problem are possible:

(*a*) A footnote can be added to the equity section stating the circumstances and what would happen in the event of loss.
(*b*) For a company only, an entry such as the following can be prepared:

Revenue Reserve	£XXX	
Reserve for Contingencies		£XXX

Long-term Liabilities

We have already defined long-term liabilities as those liabilities that do not become due in the next financial year. This definition does not mean that we cannot pay long-term liabilities in the next financial year: it means that we are not *required* to pay them in the next financial year. Long-term liabilities may be of the type that require periodic reduction of the amount due by some form of instalment payments, or they may be of the type that require one payment at a fixed future time to liquidate the amount owed.

These loans to the company must be separated on the Balance Sheet into

(*a*) those not repayable by instalments, but repayable after five years from date of the Balance Sheet;
(*b*) those repayable by instalments, any of which fall due for payment after five years from the date of the Balance Sheet.

A company may find that it needs large sums of money for the purchase of fixed assets, or to increase its working capital, or for the purchase of shares in other companies. Borrowings for any of these purposes may be made on the general credit of the company. In such cases the amount involved will appear on the Balance Sheet in the group of items headed Long-term Liabilities. Borrowing for the acquisition of fixed assets, and sometimes for the increase of working capital, is made on the security of particular assets. In this case it is usual to deduct the amount borrowed from the value of the asset on the Balance Sheet. It might appear as follows:

	£	£
Freehold Land and Buildings		
Cost	246,785	
Less Depreciation	51,264	
	195,521	
Less 7% Mortgage Repayable by Instalments Expiring in 1978	102,136	
		93,385

Debentures

Debentures are similar to shares in that a large number of persons may lend to a company amounts on similar terms. There will be only one entry in the financial records for the total amount borrowed, and the records of the amount of debentures held by individuals will be recorded in a separate register of debenture holders.

Debentures are different from shares in this way: while shareholders are members of the company entitled to vote at shareholders' meetings (unless the shares are not voting shares) and to receive such dividends as the directors may recommend only out of profits, the debenture holders are creditors and are entitled to receive interest on their debentures whether or not the company has accumulated any profits. In the last resort, debenture holders can petition for the winding up of the company if the interest is not paid or the capital is not repaid at the due date. The debentures may be

(*a*) Unsecured, when they are normal debts of the company.

(*b*) Secured by a floating charge, when they are normal debts of the company until such time as interest or capital repayments are overdue, when the debenture holders may claim control over all the company's assets at the particular date.

(*c*) Secured by a charge on particular asset or assets; the company cannot dispose of such assets without the permission of the debenture holders.

Types (*a*) and (*b*) will appear as long-term liabilities on the Balance Sheet. Type (*c*) may be deducted from the value of the asset or assets on which the debentures are secured.

Debentures Issued at a Discount

Frequently debentures are issued at a discount, thus enabling the rate of interest to be fixed at a round figure and permitting the precise terms of issue to be determined at the last moment by adjusting the amount of the discount.

Thus if the market rate of interest for a company such as Central Provision Store PLC were about 5 per cent on January 1st, 1979, the company might well issue £40,000 of 7 per cent debentures at £98. In other words, a debenture holder paying £98 would be treated as if he had paid £100: the interest would be calculated on £100, and £100 would be repaid in 1989. £800 would be debited to the debenture discount A/c and credited to the 7 per cent debenture A/c. (The debentures are assumed to be for 10 years.)

The discount on the issue of debentures must be written off by the time that the debentures are repaid. Normally it is written off over a much shorter period. If in this case it were written off over four years, the entries would be:

DEBENTURE DISCOUNT ACCOUNT

	£		£
1979 7% Debentures	800	1979 Profit and Loss Appropriation A/c	200
		Balance c/d	600
	£800		£800
1980 Balance b/d	600	1980 Profit and Loss Appropriation A/c	200
		Balance c/d	400
	£600		£600

and similarly for the remaining two years.

Until such time as the discount has been written off, the item must appear on the Balance Sheet. It is grouped with 'Preliminary Expenses' (the expenses incurred in bringing a company into existence) and the expenses arising out of the issue of shares or debentures, which are written off in a similar way.

These assets used to be grouped together as 'Fictitious Assets'—a rather unsatisfactory term. Today they are normally shown as a group following the company's assets. Although they are not assets in the normal sense of the word, this is the appropriate place for them since the assets side of the Balance Sheet shows how the funds available to the company have been utilised. From another point of view, one can regard such items as expenses which do not relate particularly to the year in which they are incurred, and provide deferred benefits to the company. The company would in fact never have come into existence without incurring preliminary expenses.

Redemption of Debentures

A company with an issue of debentures, all of which are repayable at the same date, may wish to repay some of them from time to time as funds become available. In the case of a large debenture issue, which is dealt in on the Stock Exchange, this becomes possible by buying debentures on the open market.

The amount to be repaid when the debentures fall due for payment is fixed when the issue is made. However, when debentures are purchased on the open market the price paid is determined by the state of the market. If the market value of interest has risen since the issue of the debentures the price of the debentures will have fallen, and vice versa. It would therefore be an unlikely coincidence that the debentures were purchased at their face value, and normally there will be a difference to be taken into account. If the debentures were purchased at a discount, the amount of the discount would be transferred to a Reserve Account. If they were purchased at a premium, this would be set against the reserve finally credited when purchasing debentures at a discount. If there were not such a reserve, it would be permissible to set the premium against a Share Premium Reserve. Otherwise the premium would be charged as an expense in the Profit and Loss Account.

10
Taxation

Hitherto we have ignored taxation, apart from its appearance in the examples of published accounts to which we have referred. Taxation of profits is, however, a fact of life and it is necessary for us to consider how it affects a firm's accounts. The two taxes which we shall be concerned with are:

(*a*) *Income Tax*, which is a tax on personal incomes,

(*b*) *Corporation Tax*, which is a tax levied on the profits of companies in addition to the tax credit available to shareholders on the dividends which they may receive. We shall consider these taxes in relation to the three types of business organisation.

The Sole Trader

The total income of the sole trader, including his business profits, is assessed as a whole, taking into account any personal allowances to which he is entitled. The profits on his business which are included in his income for tax purposes will not necessarily be calculated on the same basis as in his accounts.

The assessment year for **income tax** purposes runs from April 6th to the following April 5th. This is the year of assessment and all income under the various schedules, e.g. Schedule A for rents and Schedule D Case 1/11 for profits, would be summed to provide the total income upon which the tax demand would be based.

The Partnership

The profits of the partners form part of their individual total incomes, each of which is assessed as a whole, taking into account any personal allowances to which they are entitled. To make the necessary calculations it is necessary to have details both of the profits of the partnership and of the individual circumstances and other sources of income of each of the partners. The amount due from each partner will be debited to his Drawings Account and credited to a Taxation Account. When the amount involved is paid over to the Inland Revenue the Taxation Account will be closed. The applicable dates and schedules would be as described for the sole trader.

Aspects of Company Taxation

Introduction

Companies pay **Corporation Tax** on their assessable profits. At the outset it is important to understand that assessable profit and net profit have different definitions. To arrive at assessable profit the net profit earned by a company is adjusted for certain items, e.g. depreciation charged against net profits is added back and substituted by capital allowances. It is not proposed to deal with the detailed rules relating to the calculation of assessable profits as this is a specialised topic best covered in a book dealing specifically with taxation. In this book we are more concerned with those aspects of company taxation which affect the **presentation** of companies' annual accounts.

The rate of corporation tax is fixed by the Chancellor of the Exchequer, usually in his annual budget. The tax year for companies runs from April 1st to the following March 31st. The rate fixed in the budget (usually in March or April) is applied to the assessable profits earned by companies during the twelve months previous to the 31st March.

Example. In the budget announced in April 19.4 the corporation tax rate was fixed at 50 per cent. Therefore assessable profits earned by companies from April 1st, 19.3 to March 31st, 19.4 (i.e. the Government's fiscal year) would be subject to a corporation tax rate of 50 per cent. Consequently, where a company's financial year spans two fiscal years then two rates of corporation tax may apply.

Rate of corporation tax for the fiscal year ended March 31st, 19.6 50%
Rate of corporation tax for the fiscal year ended March 31st, 19.7 40%

Company A Ltd: assessable profits for the financial year ended December 31st, 19.6 £48,000.

Rate of tax applicable:

January 1st, 19.6 to March 31st, 19.6: $50\% \times \left(£48{,}000 \times \frac{3}{12}\right) =$ £6,000

April 1st, 19.6 to December 31st, 19.6: $40\% \times \left(£48{,}000 \times \frac{9}{12}\right) =$ £14,400

£20,400

Payment of Corporation Tax

The dates on which a company pays corporation tax to the Inland Revenue depend on whether the payment relates to Advance Corporation Tax or Mainstream Corporation Tax.

Advance Corporation Tax (ACT)

When a company pays a dividend to its shareholders, a sum equal to a fraction of the dividend must be paid to the Inland Revenue within 14 days of the end of the quarter in which the dividend is paid. The fraction applied to the dividend payment depends on the standard rate of income tax applicable at the time, and is calculated as follows:

$$\frac{\text{standard rate of income tax}}{100 - \text{standard rate}}$$

Thus, if the standard rate is 30 per cent the ACT fraction applied to dividends will be:

$$\frac{30}{100 - 30} = \frac{3}{7}$$

Consequently, if a company pays a dividend of £21,000, and the standard rate of income tax is 30 per cent, the ACT payable within three months is 3 ÷ 7 × £21,000 = £9,000. It must be emphasised that the ACT is *not* deducted from the dividend paid to the shareholders, they will receive a total of £21,000 from the company. (All dividends are declared and paid net.)

The ACT paid is later deducted from the total corporation tax due on the assessable profits of the company's financial year from which the dividend was paid—up to an arithmetical maximum and any excess is available for carry forward or carry back.

Example. For the year ended March 31st, 19.6 A Ltd had assessable profits of £200,000. During the year A Ltd paid a dividend of £42,000. The corporation tax rate is 50 per cent and the standard rate of income tax is 30 per cent.

Advance corporation tax payable = £42,000 × 3 ÷ 7 = £18,000

Total corporation tax liability for the year £200,000 × 50% =	£100,000
Less ACT already paid	18,000
Leaving mainstream corporation tax to pay of:	£82,000

Mainstream Corporation Tax (MCT)

As shown in the examples above MCT is the amount of corporation tax owing to the Inland Revenue after deducting the ACT paid from the total tax liability. The date of payment of MCT depends on whether or not the company in question was trading before April 1st, 19.5.

For companies in existence before April 1st, 19.5 the date of payment of MCT is the January 1st following the end of the fiscal year in which the company's financial period ended. Thus if the financial year of A Ltd ended on December 31st, 19.5, then the end of the relevant fiscal year would be April 5th, 19.6. Thus the MCT is due for payment on January 1st, 19.7.

For companies who began trading after April 1st, 19.5 the mainstream corporation tax is due for payment nine months after the company's financial year end.

Income Tax

As stated above, companies pay corporation tax on their assessable profits. In addition they may also make payments of income tax to the Inland Revenue. However, the income tax payments do not relate to the company's profits, instead they represent income tax deduction on certain payments made by the company. If, for example, a company pays debenture interest, income tax at the standard rate is deducted from the amount paid to the debenture holder and the tax so deducted is paid over directly to the revenue. This system simplifies the collection of taxes, although adjustments will have to be made directly between the revenue and the individual taxpayer if the standard rate of tax is not applicable to a particular taxpayer. Where a company receives income from which income tax has been deducted at source, the tax so deducted may be offset against the tax deducted and collected by the company itself, thereby leaving the balance only to be paid over to the Inland Revenue.

The Imputation System

As explained in the earlier section on MCT when a company pays a dividend no tax is deducted from the amount paid to shareholders, although advance corporation tax is paid to the Inland Revenue by the company. The ACT so paid is regarded as a tax credit from the shareholders' viewpoint so that no additional tax liability will fall on the shareholder if the standard rate of income tax is applicable to his circumstances.

Example. A Ltd pays a dividend of £28,000; standard rate of income tax is 30 per cent.

The ACT fraction in this case is $\frac{30}{100 - 30} = \frac{3}{7}$

Therefore the ACT paid to the inland revenue by the company is $3 \div 7 \times$ £28,000 = £12,000.

Thus if an individual shareholder receives a dividend of £70 he will disclose on his tax return an income of £70 plus £30 ($3 \div 7 \times$ £70) tax credit. At a basic rate of income tax of 30 per cent the tax due on £100 is £30, but the shareholder is allowed to offset the tax credit against the tax charge. Clearly if the standard rate of tax is not applicable to the shareholder a tax repayment or additional charge will be made.

Where a UK resident company receives a dividend from another UK resident company, the dividend received plus the tax credit is called **Franked Investment Income**. Similarly the amount of dividend paid plus the tax credit is termed a **Franked Payment**. During an accounting period a company receiving Franked Investment Income can offset the tax credit against the advance corporation tax due on dividends paid, the balance only being paid over to the Inland Revenue. Where the franked investment income exceeds the franked payment the excess tax credit so arising can be set off against the advance corporation tax payable in the next accounting period.

PAYE

In addition to deducting income tax from payments made in respect of dividends, interest on debentures and similar terms, a company (or any employer) is required to deduct income tax on payments of wages or salaries. But while the deduction of tax from dividends and interest is always made at the standard rate, the deduction from salaries and wages is related to the personal circumstances and total income of the employee.

This is achieved through the PAYE (Pay As You Earn) system. The Inland Revenue undertakes the work of assessing the tax-free allowances to which a person is entitled and the extent to which tax on income from other sources covers the tax liability of that person. This is estimated in advance for the fiscal year ending on April 5th. The results of these calculations are expressed in the form of a code number which is notified to the employer. Knowing the code number, the employer can, with the aid of tax tables supplied by the Inland Revenue, determine the tax-free pay to which the employee is entitled for that proportion of the fiscal year which has passed. Since certain amounts of income may be taxable at less than the standard rate, further tables are provided to indicate how much tax is due after making allowances for the reduced rate payable on part of the taxable pay.

This involves keeping certain information on a cumulative basis. The items are as follows:

(*a*) Gross pay for the week or month.
(*b*) Total gross pay since the beginning of the tax year.
(*c*) Tax-free pay to date (from the tax tables).
(*d*) Taxable pay to date.
(*e*) Total tax due (from the tax tables).
(*f*) Total tax paid since the beginning of the tax year.
(*g*) Tax due or repayable for the week or month.

These items will be incorporated in the Wages Book and on each employee's tax record. So far as the accounts are concerned, the significant item is the tax due or overpaid at the end of the week or month, which is deducted or added when paying wages and salaries. The total amount involved is credited to a PAYE Account, and the monthly remittance to the Inland Revenue is debited to this account. The entries for the last month of the company's financial year might well be:

PAYE ACCOUNT

	£		£
December 31st Balance c/d	837.30	December 7th Weekly Wages	128.25
		14th „ „	132.50
		21st „ „	130.40
		21st Monthly Salaries	314.40
		28th Weekly Wages	131.75
	£837.30		£837.30
January 15th Cash—Inland Revenue	£837.30	January 1st Balance b/d	£837.30

When the Balance Sheet is prepared at December 31st the amount of £837.30 deducted from the December wages and salaries will not as yet have been paid over to the Inland Revenue. It will consequently appear on the balance sheet as a Current Liability.

Value Added Tax (VAT)

VAT is a tax on goods and services introduced in 1973. Firms are required to add tax at the rate enacted to their sales when invoicing their customers. When remitting the tax to the Customs and Excise they are permitted to deduct the tax they have paid on their purchases of goods and services. It is necessary to accumulate the tax collected and paid either in analysis columns or in separate accounts and to transfer the totals to a VAT Account in preparation for the payment of the tax each quarter. The VAT Account might appear as follows:

VAT ACCOUNT

	£		£
Input Tax		Output Tax (tax charged on sales)	10,000
Imported goods	800		
Purchase of UK goods	4,500		
Plant and Equipment	600		
Telephone Service	100		
Balance c/d	4,000		
	£10,000		£10,000
		Balance being net amount payable to Customs and Excise	£4,000

Certain businesses are zero rated which means that they are not required to add tax to their sales, but are entitled to reclaim tax paid on their 'inputs'. If this applied in the above case, no tax would be charged and there would be no credit entry. The business is able to collect £6,000 from the Customs and Excise. Other businesses are exempt. As with zero rated businesses, these do not add tax to their sales, but are not able to collect tax paid on inputs from the Customs and Excise. If a business only makes exempt transactions it will not require to open a VAT Account; the amounts involved will be treated as expenses.

Foreign Taxation

When a company receives income from abroad, the foreign country will normally have subjected the income to some form of taxation. There are double-taxation agreements with some countries whereby a company is permitted to set the payment of overseas taxation off in part against the corporation tax levied at home. There will in any event remain some foreign taxation which has to be borne by the company. This item is required to be shown separately in the Profit and Loss Appropriation Account or in the notes attached to it. The subject of double-taxation is a complex one and a matter for specialists.

11
Management Accounting: Budgeting and Financial Planning

The accounting system provides information for both internal and external use. That part of the system which deals with the relationship of the business to outsiders and owners is normally termed financial accounting and has been emphasised in previous chapters. Management accounting is concerned with providing information for planning, controlling and decision-making. Cost accounting is that part of management accounting which deals primarily with recording and analysis and is described in Chapter 12. The term costing is used also to describe this part of an accounting system but is more generally understood to refer to the processes of cost ascertainment described in Chapter 13.

Planning is a simple concept—so simple that only very few persons are unaware of it, at least in its rudimentary form and use. But when the word 'plan' is changed to 'budget' and the word 'financial' is placed before it, panic ensues.

Let us look, then, at a budget and see what it is. A budget is a plan of future action measured in terms of quantifiable units—pounds, work-hours, tons, years, days, etc. Financial planning is nothing more than planning the financial facet of the business—sources of future income, future expenditures, future obligations, etc.

Budget Preparation

The preparation of the budget is the first step in preparing a plan of control. The budget may be prepared at the level of the chief executive, or it may be prepared at the level of the operating departments. When it is prepared at the level of the operating departments, it must be reviewed at the top and co-ordinated with the budgets of other departments. The sales budget, as prepared by the sales department, is based on past performance and a consideration of expected future conditions. But the sales department may tend to underestimate sales so that the actual performance exceeds the budget, thereby making the department 'look good'. The production budget, on the other hand, also based on past performance and a consideration of expected future conditions may tend to overestimate production costs so that the actual performance is less than the budget, thereby making the production department 'look good'. The reviewing group (budget committee or similar group) has the task of making the budget as realistic as possible in the light of expected future conditions.

The sales budget may start with last year's sales in units, adjusted for style and model changes and priced at expected sales prices. The production budget may start with the adjusted unit-sales budget and from it may be prepared a materials budget, showing quantity of materials, price, and, perhaps, delivery dates; a labour budget, showing the types of skills needed, with wage rates; a factory-overhead budget, showing all costs in the factory other than direct labour and direct material; and a capital budget, showing what must be spent for factory rearrangement of new equipment. From this it can be seen that various departments within the company are involved in budgeting—sales, production, production engineering, purchasing, personnel, and others. It is these various budgets that are then reviewed and co-ordinated by the budget committee. When a company-wide budget is established, the accounts office may prepare a cash budget showing expected income by source, expected expenditure by object, and loan requirements, if any.

Example. It is decided to prepare a budget for the following year based on past experience. Last year the figures developed from accounting and collateral records were as follows:

	Item A	Item B	Item C	Total
Sales:				
Units	100,000	200,000	150,000	
Income	£300,000	£200,000	£300,000	£800,000
Cost of Sales (£):				
Direct Labour	£125,000	£100,000	£160,000	£385,000
Direct Material	75,000	45,000	60,000	180,000
Production Overhead	50,000	30,000	40,000	120,000
	£250,000	£175,000	£260,000	£685,000
Gross Profit on Sales (£)	£50,000	£25,000	£40,000	£115,000
Gross Profit (per cent)	16.7%	12.5%	13.3%	
Selling Expenses				£20,000
Administrative Expenses				25,000
				£45,000
Net Operating Profit				£70,000

It is estimated that unit sales of items A, B and C will increase by 15 per cent, 20 per cent and 10 per cent respectively, while prices per unit advance 5 per cent. The labour force in the factory will receive pay increases of 5 per cent; direct materials will advance 3 per cent in price; Production overheads will increase 4 per cent. Selling expenses will advance 3 per cent while administrative costs will rise 2 per cent.

Item A

Sales: 100,000 × 1.15	115,000 units
Income: £300,000 × 1.15 × 1.05	£362,250.00
Direct Labour: £125,000 × 1.15 × 1.05	150,937.50
Direct Materials: £75,000 × 1.15 × 1.03	88,837.50
Production Overhead: £50,000 × 1.15 × 1.04	59,800.00
	£299,575.00
Gross Profit on Sales	£62,675.00

Item B

Sales: 200,000 × 1.20	240,000 units
Income: £200,000 × 1.20 × 1.05	£252,000.00
Direct Labour: £100,000 × 1.20 × 1.05	126,000.00
Direct Materials: £45,000 × 1.20 × 1.03	55,620.00
Production Overhead: £30,000 × 1.20 × 1.04	37,440.00
	£219,060.00
Gross Profit on Sales	£32,940.00

Item C

Sales: 150,000 × 1.10	165,000 units
Income: £300,000 × 1.10 × 1.05	£346,500.00
Direct Labour: £160,000 × 1.10 × 1.05	184,800.00
Direct Materials: £60,000 × 1.10 × 1.03	67,980.00
Production Overhead: £40,000 × 1.10 × 1.04	45,760.00
	£298,540.00
Gross Profit on Sales	£47,960.00

Putting this data into statement form:

	Item A	Item B	Item C	Total
Sales:				
Units	115,000	240,000	165,000	
Income (£)	£362,250.00	£252,000.00	£346,500.00	£960,750.00
Cost of Sales (£):				
Direct Labour	£150,937.50	£126,000.00	£184,800.00	£461,737.50
Direct Materials	88,837.50	55,620.00	67,980.00	212,437.50
Production Overhead	59,800.00	37,440.00	45,760.00	143,000.00
	£299,575.00	£219,060.00	£298,540.00	£817,175.00
Gross Profits on Sales	£62,675.00	£32,940.00	£47,960.00	£143,575.00
Gross Profit per cent	17.3%	13.1%	13.8%	
Selling Expenses	(£20,000 × 1.03)			£20,600.00
Administrative Expenses	(£25,000 × 1.02)			25,500.00
				£46,100.00
Net Operating Income				£97,475.00

A detailed analysis of all costs may give more accurate estimates, but it is more expensive. As in every control situation, the additional profit benefits must be measured against added costs to ascertain if an increase in net profit results. An advantage of detailed analysis that is often overlooked is the discovery of situations in which improvements in methods may result in savings.

Collecting Performance Data

In planning the budget, it is important that performance information be collected so that it can be compared with the budget figures. This specific collection may mean that there should be changes in the methods of collecting accounting data to fit the budget plan. The definitions used for budget purposes should be the same as those used for the collection of accounting data. If they are not, comparisons between budget and performance cannot be readily made, or if made without correction, may even be misleading.

The redesigning of account classifications to match the budget classifications may require some thought as well as the redesign of forms, but in the long run it should give better control. Where in the past sales were collected in total pounds, the use of a budget may require an analysis by units and pounds for each product sold as well as total pounds. The classification of expense accounts may be divided into controllable and non-controllable expenses for purposes of corrective action.

The use of specific definitions for budgeting is not incompatible with good accounting technique; rather it is a logical extension of the accounting system. Records must be kept for historical purposes; if they can be used for control purposes as well, the additional cost of record-keeping should be more than compensated for by additional profits that result from increased knowledge of the business and its operation.

Comparisons and Corrective Action

After the budget is prepared and the accounting collection system is made compatible with it, the actual performance of the company should be compared with the estimated performance and the differences noted and analysed. A budget by itself will not solve many problems, although additional knowledge of the operation is always useful. But the analysis and study of differences can awake an awareness in management of the need for efforts to increase efficiency, reduce costs, and increase income. The problem areas of a business are more clearly shown and can be studied.

After the study has been made, it is management's responsibility to initiate corrective action. Without this action the company loses most of the value of the budgetary effort. Why are sales lower than expected? What can we do to increase them? Why are sales higher than expected? What can we do to sustain this additional volume? Can techniques for selling one product be extended to other product lines? Why are costs higher than expected? How can we decrease them? Why are costs lower than expected? What can we do to continue these lower costs? Can cost reductions in one area be applied to other areas? The answers to these and similar questions should bring forth corrective action that will benefit the company. The company moves from a relatively unplanned organisation to one that has some form of guide to future action as related to present performance. The company has added a powerful tool of control to its inventory of management techniques. It is almost sure to improve because of the depth of analysis that has been made in the initial preparation of the budget and because of the analytic study of the differences between budgeted and actual performance.

Amending and Extending the Budget

Once the budget is prepared there should be some mechanism for its revision to reflect changing conditions. If sales increase, what effect does this have on per-unit cost? Does this increase in sales result in higher overtime costs, quantity discounts, additional storeroom requirements, etc.? The revision of the budget should be made in some formal fashion so that the total effect of a change can be determined.

In recent years there has been a tendency to realise the shortcomings of an annual budget. Consider a budget prepared in November 19.8 for the calendar year 19.9. On January 1st, 19.9, the next 12 months are budgeted. As each month goes by, the budget applies to shortening periods of future time until on November 1st, 19.9, only two months of future time are budgeted. As soon as the 19.0 calendar-year budget is prepared in November 19.9, there are 13 months of budgeted future time.

This deficiency in budgets has been met in part by use of a budget that is revised periodically (monthly or quarterly). In this way the amount of future budgeted time remains approximately the same, and any current changes are reflected over the extended budget time. Such procedure is called a rolling budget. Here again the value of the control and what it can mean to the company in terms of additional profits must be measured against costs.

Break-even Analysis

The information included in the budget can be reworked to provide some form of break-even analysis. Some of the items in a budget may be fixed, some may vary but not proportionately to output, and others may vary proportionately to output. If the expenses are classified on this basis it is possible to calculate and to display on a graph the costs for varying levels of output. At the same time the revenue expected from varying levels of sales can be estimated. If these are plotted on the same graph, the point where the two lines intersect is known as the break-even point. Above that level of output and sales, a profit is made; below that level the result is a loss.

The procedure can be illustrated from the data contained in the budget shown on page 136, which covers three items. It is necessary to assume that fluctuation in output and sales affect each item proportionately. This is the only basis on which a break-even graph can be prepared; otherwise an infinite range of possible combinations of output and sales for the three products would be possible.

The following additional information will be required:

Income: selling price constant over all levels of sales;
Direct Labour: proportionate to output;
Direct Materials: proportionate to output;
Production Overhead: £80,000 fixed,
£40,000 proportionate to output;
Selling Expenses: £5,000 fixed,
£15,000 proportionate to output;
Administrative Expenses: fixed;

The expenses can then be classified as follows:

	Fixed £	*Variable* £	*Total* £
Direct Labour		385,000	385,000
Direct Materials		180,000	180,000
Production Overhead	80,000	40,000	120,000
Selling Expenses	5,000	15,000	20,000
Administrative Expenses	25,000	—	25,000
	£110,000	£620,000	£730,000

The break-even chart can then be produced as follows:

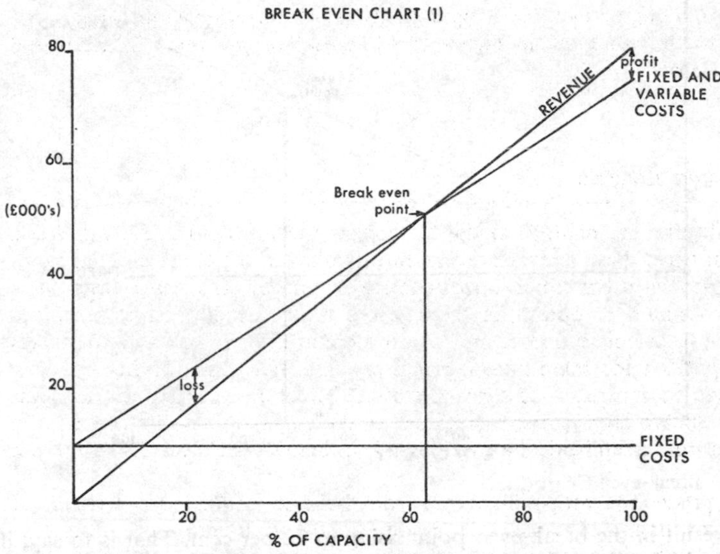

Fig. 4. Break-even Chart (1)

Let us assume that the possibility arises of introducing a greater degree of automation into the works, the effect of which will be to reduce the direct-labour cost but to increase substantially the fixed element of the production overhead, so that the position would become:

	Fixed	*Variable*	*Total*
	£	£	£
Direct Labour		190,000	190,000
Direct Materials		180,000	180,000
Production Overhead	240,000	40,000	280,000
Selling Expenses	5,000	15,000	20,000
Administrative Expenses	25,000	—	25,000
	£270,000	£425,000	£695,000

Before making a decision it would be necessary to consider the effect of these changes in cost, not only when the factory is working at full capacity, but also at other levels of output at which it might be necessary to operate if market conditions were to deteriorate. The break-even chart is perhaps the best method of giving a quick overall impression of the effect of the change as can be seen by comparing the new break-even chart (Fig. 5) with the one already prepared (Fig. 4).

It can readily be seen that, although the change would result in a larger profit being earned when the factory was working to capacity, it would

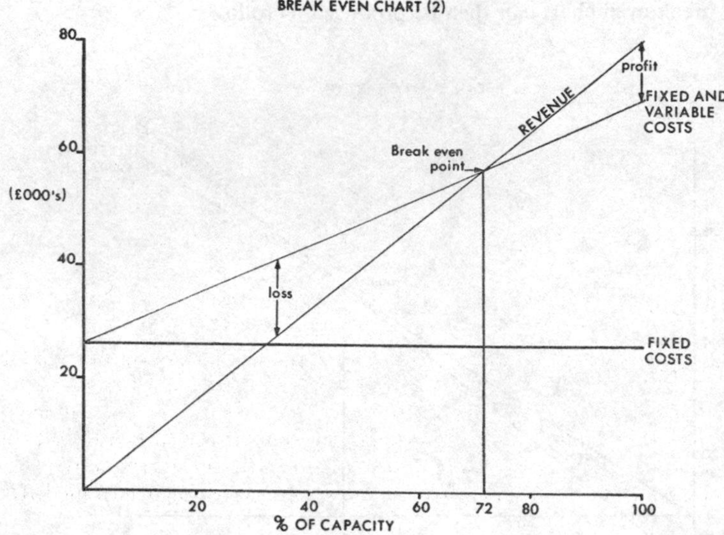

Fig. 5. Break-even Chart (2)

also result in the break-even point rising to 72 per cent. That is to say, if the level of activity fell below 72 per cent the firm would start making a loss. This compares with a break-even point of 61 per cent at present. Notice, too, that as production falls below the break-even point, the resultant loss will increase much more quickly after the change in production methods than before it.

The break-even point can be checked arithmetically by considering the contribution each 1 per cent of sales (by value in this case, but it might be physical units) makes towards the fixed costs and profits of the firm. In the second case considered above, each 1 per cent of sales means variable costs of £4,250 (£425,000 ÷ 100), leaving £3,750 as a contribution to fixed costs. The break-even point will be the point at which the total contribution from sales is equal to the total fixed costs (which in this case are £270,000).

The break-even point is given therefore by the following formula:

270,000 ÷ 3,750 = 72 per cent

A break-even chart is also a very quick way of considering the effect of anticipated or projected changes in costs or revenue on the prospects of the firm. It would be very easy to see the effect of, for instance, an increase of 10 per cent in direct-labour costs and an increase of 5 per cent in selling price.

12
Management Accounting: Cost Accounting

Cost accounting is the branch of accounting that has as its purpose the determination of costs of products, operations, processes or functions. In a trading business, the per-unit cost of an article sold can be determined by the invoice (perhaps with an adjustment for freight or returned items). But in a manufacturing plant, values are added as a result of productive effort which cannot be found on a vendor's invoice; it must be determined from the accounting records.

Function of Cost Accounting

The collection of data concerning production costs is the function of cost accounting. It requires an understanding of the production process, components of manufacturing cost, the establishment of a cost-gathering system, and the determination of total and per-unit cost.

The various production processes are too many to describe in detail here, but some general concepts of processes can be described. There are the chemical analytic processes (breaking down of water into hydrogen and oxygen) and synthesis processes (making nylon). There are the mechanical processes of drilling (drill press), turning (lathe), cutting (saw, planer, mill, or shear), and fastening (riveting, welding). There are annealing and tempering processes. There are sanding, painting, enamelling, and other finishing processes. There is the assembly process. Although these are but a few, a knowledge of them and their place in the production to be costed is necessary if good cost figures are to be developed.

The components of manufacturing cost are direct labour, direct materials and production overheads. These terms can be defined as follows:

Direct labour—the labour actually expended in producing the product. If we were to examine a chair, direct labour would include wages paid to the saw operator who cut the timber to size, the assembler who glued and screwed the pieces together, the assembler who attached the springs, and the upholsterer who fitted the padding and covered the chair with fabric.

Direct materials—those materials of which the product is made. If we examine the chair again, this category would include the wood, for the legs, rails, seat, and arms; glue, for the joints; nails and screws, for fastening the pieces together; the fabric, for covering; springs, for support; padding, for comfort; thread, for sewing; etc. For purposes of convenience in accounting, some of these items might not be considered (for example, the glue, nails, screws and thread).

Direct expenses—the costs, other than material or labour which can be identified with a specific product.

Production overhead—the cost of operating the factory other than the cost of direct labour and direct materials and direct expenses. Production overhead includes indirect labour (supervisors' salaries, salaries of stockroom and receiving clerks, etc.), indirect materials (repair and maintenance supplies, factory office supplies, etc.), rent, taxes (National Insurance contributions), depreciation, utilities (other than those used directly in the manufacturing process, like gas and electric ovens), water, heating, lighting, etc.

Labour—Direct and Indirect

The factory secures labour service from the local area on an individual basis and so each individual must be paid. The total amount of money earned by an individual is called his **gross pay**. This is computed by attendance or by work performance (number of pieces produced, etc.). In almost all cases attendance records are kept for other reasons than payroll-computation purposes, such as wage and hour legislation, control of workers and production, to assist in determination of missing persons in event of catastrophe, etc. The payroll consideration in this discussion is of paramount interest, and the other aspects of attendance recording will be ignored.

Time

When time is used as the basis for pay, the payroll department takes the time of attendance and multiplies it by the rate of pay to get gross wages. In the case of monthly or weekly employees, the gross pay is generally the same, period after period (except where a rate is increased), even though the employee may have been absent for a day or two. In the case of hourly employees, the number of hours shown on the time card is multiplied by the rate to get gross wages, and an employee must be in attendance to be paid (except for legal holidays, etc.).

The union contract may establish the time to be classified as overtime (for example, all hours over 40 in a week, or over eight in one day, etc.). The company may have established policies regarding overtime compensation. With respect to salaried employees, executive and supervisory personnel are generally not paid overtime, while the non-administrative salaried employees may be paid overtime or be given compensatory time off. Regarding hourly employees, there is generally an established work week of a stated number of hours and any time worked over the stated limit is paid for at premium rates. In some situations the employee may be paid a premium for any time over eight hours in one day, even though he may not work the stated hours in one week.

This gross wage is distributed between the direct-labour or indirect-labour accounts. Each of these accounts can be subdivided into more meaningful categories, and the following scheme might be developed:

Direct Labour		
Department 1	or	Job No. 1
Department 2	or	Job No. 2
etc.		etc.
Indirect Labour		
Department F1	or	Supervision
Department F2	or	Inspection
etc.		etc.

These amounts become the debits for the payroll entry. The credits are for taxes, deducted from the gross wages (National Insurance, PAYE, etc. as required by law), union dues (where applicable), pension fund, health or life insurance or similar deductions, and the net wage payable. The preparation of wages and salaries for a factory is the same as for a trading company in all respects, except that the debits are classified to suit the needs of factory accounting.

Production

When productive output is used as the basis for pay, it is necessary to relate the production to the time necessary to complete the task so that an equitable rate per piece completed can be established. The relationship can be established by having an operator complete the task and by measuring the units produced per hour.

The pieces completed per hour are related to the suggested wage rate per hour and determine the price per unit. For example, an employee works eight hours producing 400 units. His wage rate is £0.75 per hour. To determine the piecework rate for that particular employee or job, the following formulas are used:

$$\frac{400 \text{ units}}{8 \text{ hrs}} = 50 \text{ units/hr}$$

$$\frac{0.75/\text{hr}}{50 \text{ pieces/hr}} = £0.015$$

A more scientific method used for determining the number of pieces per time period is a systematic analysis of the production process, sometimes called a time-and-motion study. In the early days of time-and-motion study, the manager was accused of wanting to get continually greater production at no increase in cost, and there were even threats of physical violence against the industrial manager. Today time-and-motion studies are more acceptable and the manager can save money through the elimination of needless steps in the process, combining steps, etc. There is still cause for resentment when the piece-rate-per-hour standards are set too highly (so that few can complete the tasks in the time allowed) or too loosely (so the goal is easily achievable and the task becomes a 'plum').

Many systems have been devised using production as a basis for pay, but the details of each system will not be discussed here; it would be better to discuss the principles upon which the systems depend. One important principle is that the worker should be guaranteed a minimum wage regardless of the quantity produced. He has put in the time and is available for work and should be paid. The reasons why he cannot produce the quota may be that he is a new employee and is still in training; the machine might break down; goods delivered to the employee for his task might be defective. When the employee is guaranteed a wage he will perform better because the anxiety of not earning a steady wage is removed. If an employee continually fails to earn the minimum salary, then management must analyse the reasons and take corrective action. This corrective action may involve transfer to a different job, additional training, or, in extreme cases, dismissal.

Another important principle is that production in excess of the established goal reduces per-unit cost. Since the total of production is direct material, direct labour, and production overhead, the major source of total production cost increase is direct material and direct labour. Production overhead is relatively constant. Therefore, when production rises, the per-unit cost falls, and the company encourages the employee to produce more than the expected quantity per hour.

Another important principle is that employees will increase production over the expected amount if they will be paid more. Therefore, pay-incentive systems recognise the value of the additional units in reducing cost per unit. These systems may have a built-in sliding scale of incentive and are referred to as accelerating or differential piecework systems. This can be illustrated as follows:

For:	Employee is paid:
0–100 pieces	0.010 per piece or £0.8 per hour
101–110 pieces	0.011 per piece
111–120 pieces	0.013 per piece

Thus, a worker can achieve the guaranteed wage of £0.8 per hour by producing 80 pieces per hour. If he produces 100 pieces per hour his pay is £1.00 per hour. If he produces 110 pieces, his pay is £1.21 per hour, and if he produces 120 pieces, it is £1.56 per hour. To prevent careless work on the part of the worker, some notion of acceptable quality is tied to the production measurement.

After the gross pay is determined by the measure of production (or a guarantee, when it is operative), the debit and credit distributions are made as before.

The Payroll Entry:

	£	£
Work-in-Progress—Dept. 1	XX	
Work-in-Progress—Dept. 2	XX	
etc.		
Production Overhead—Dept. F1	XX	
Production Overhead—Dept. F2	XX	
etc.		
Income Tax (PAYE)		XX
National Insurance		XX
Other Deductions credited to appropriate accounts		XX

Notice that the debits may be made in total to Work-in-Progress and to Production Overhead and the details may be shown in subsidiary ledgers or account analyses. The Work-in-Progress debits may also be analysed by Job or Progress Orders as well as by Departments.

Non-payroll Labour Costs

The total cost of labour to an employer is not the total of the gross pay earned by employees during a period. Rather, it is the total of the gross pay earned by employees during a period *plus* all other costs the employer pays out for employees. These additional costs might be required by statute, by a union contract, or by an agreement between the employer and employee. The employer may be required by the union to make payments to a pension or welfare fund based on wages, hours worked, or production. The employer may institute a fringe-benefit programme under which he pays all or part of the employee's life-insurance or health-insurance premiums (to certain limits) or contributes to a pension plan, or matches employee's savings for share purchases, etc. Only when these additional items are considered, does the employer know his total labour cost. These non-payroll labour costs may be charged to production overhead, or an attempt may be made to allocate them to productive effort.

Materials—Direct and Indirect

The question of what should be produced is decided by the company before production begins. There is an assumption that materials will be received in a particular stage of completion to be combined with other materials and formed into a new product after going through some industrial process.

The factory secures materials from the market in whatever stage of completion production requires—iron may be purchased in ore form (by a steel mill) or in rolls of sheet steel (by a tin-can manufacturer).

The problems of purchasing in an industrial situation are the same as in a trading situation; that is, to get the proper amount of suitable material delivered when needed at the lowest cost per unit.

After the material is ordered and the vendor delivers it, a materials-handling and storage system is involved. The material is received and, if necessary, tested for quality. It is then stored until needed in production. At this stage it might be well for the company to ask itself whether a centralised storeroom or a number of decentralised storerooms should be used. There are arguments for and against each method, but the ultimate decision is in the hands of management.

As the material is required by a worker for his task, he prepares a storeroom requisition (Fig. 6) and presents it to the storekeeper. The storekeeper locates the material, reduces the stock as shown on the bin card, and gives the material to the worker.

In the accounting department, each item is priced out by LIFO, FIFO, average, or some other method discussed previously. The requisitions are recorded in a Materials Journal, or Materials Abstract, which shows the

STOREROOM REQUISITION

Req. No. 1-063-69

Storekeeper: Please furnish bearer with the following: Date January 15th 19 X9

Charge A/c No. 625-93 Dept. 4-Assembly Dept. No.

Quantity	Articles	Stock No.	Price	Amount	
10	Shanks	351	1·97	19	70
10	Spindles	338	2·15	21	50
10	Shank Bushings	413	3·27	32	70
20	Spindle Washers	341	0·02		40
				74	30

Charge Job No. 93	Entered on Stock Ledger A.S.	Entered on Recap AB	Signed C. W. Leary

Fig. 6. Storeroom requisition

date, requisition number, and job or department to be charged.

When the journal is cast an entry is made debiting the jobs or departments and crediting materials as follows:

		£	
Work-in-Progress—Job No. 1		XX	
Job No. 2		XX	
etc.			
Production Overhead—Department F1		XX	
Department F2		XX	
etc.			
Materials			£Total

Stock Security

Stock is often composed of low-volume, high-value items, or items with high personal utility, or some that may be crucial to the smooth flow of manufactured goods, and it is essential that there be a system of control. This will vary from minimum control over the coal stock (because one can see if there is enough coal, and the value of coal stolen by employees and others is negligible) to a maximum control over gold and jewels in a watch-manufacturing plant.

It is important to remember that not all items must be under the same degree of control. Each item must be reviewed to determine the degree of control that it merits. Remember that control costs money, and the cost of control must be measured against the savings resulting from the use of the controls.

Economic Order Quantity

In order to reduce the cost of material to the lowest possible price at point and time of use, a study should be made of the usage of stocks, the cost of ordering merchandise, and the costs of storing and holding merchandise. Ideally, a company would like each unit of material to arrive just before it is needed so that no storage costs are incurred, and it would like to be able to issue one purchase order for the requirements of materials for long periods of time. In practical terms, these two goals are opposed, and neither is absolutely attainable. The business must store materials, and purchase orders have to be processed to purchase new material. The problem then resolves itself into finding out how much to order and how often.

The total cost of material at the place and time of use is invoice price per unit plus ordering cost per unit plus storage cost per unit. The invoice cost is easily calculated. The ordering cost per *order* can be determined by ascertaining the number of purchase orders processed and dividing that number into the total purchasing-department expense for a period, adding the total receiving-department expense for the same period, and dividing by the number of shipments received. A similar analysis is performed for all elements of the expenses of ordering materials.

Let us assume that the order cost equals £60 per order. The larger the quantity ordered, the lower the cost per unit. This is shown in Fig. 7.

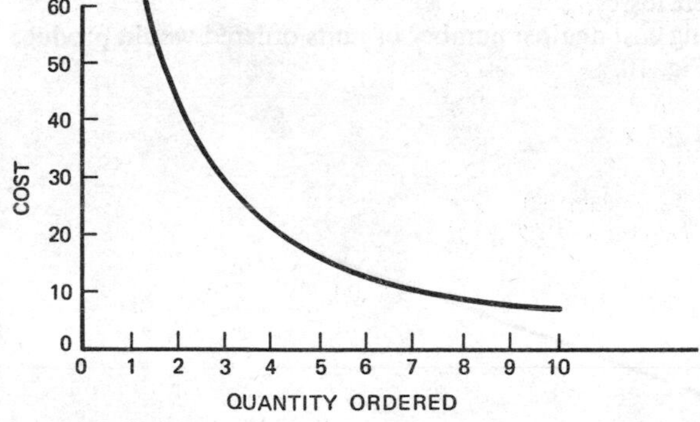

Fig. 7. Ordering-cost curve

Let us assume that a company orders 1,000 units, at a cost of £2 per unit, four times a year, and that the materials are used equally over the year and there are no days off. A graph of the usage pattern would show fluctuations in stock size as in Fig. 8.

The average stock would be 500 units (1,000 units × ½) worth £1,000 (500 units × £2/unit). There is storage space required for these 1,000 units

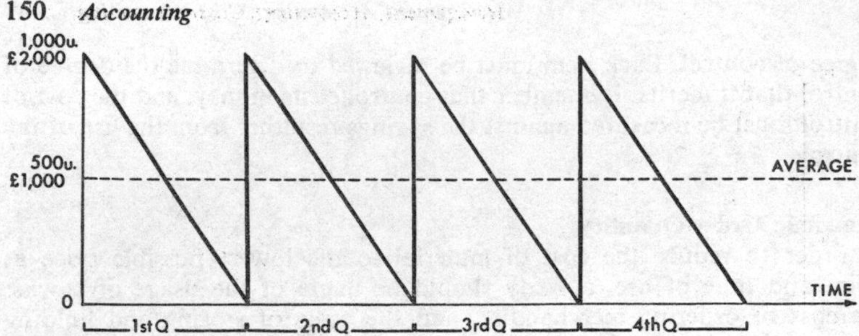

Fig. 8. Orders received four times a year

as well as warehousing costs (storekeepers' salaries), fire insurance, interest on the investment in stocks, and the possibility of deterioration, destruction, or theft. Collectively, these are called **holding costs**.

If, however, the company ordered 500 units per order, eight orders per year would be required. The graph of usage would appear as in Fig. 9.

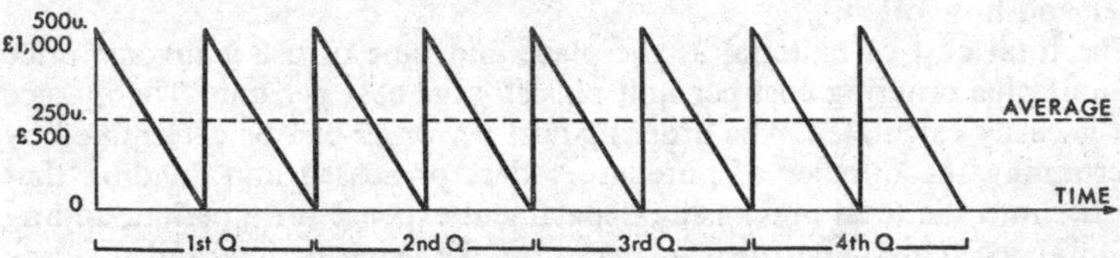

Fig. 9. Orders received eight times a year

The average stock would be 250 units (500 units × ½) worth £500 (250 units × £2/unit). The storage space required for the item, fire insurance, and interest on investment in stocks is cut in half. There is a reduction (although not necessarily by half) of warehousing costs and deterioration, destruction, and theft losses.

Plotting the holding cost against number of units ordered would produce a graph similar to Fig. 10.

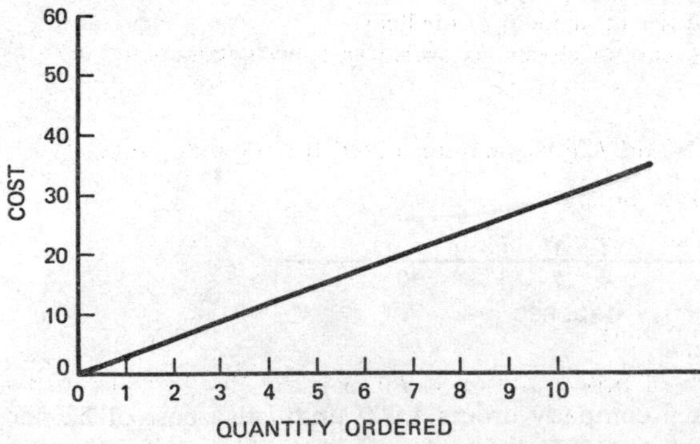

Fig. 10. Holding-cost curve

Superimposing the ordering-cost curve (Fig. 7) on the holding-cost curve (Fig. 10) produces a graph showing the two curves and a curve of total cost (Fig. 11).

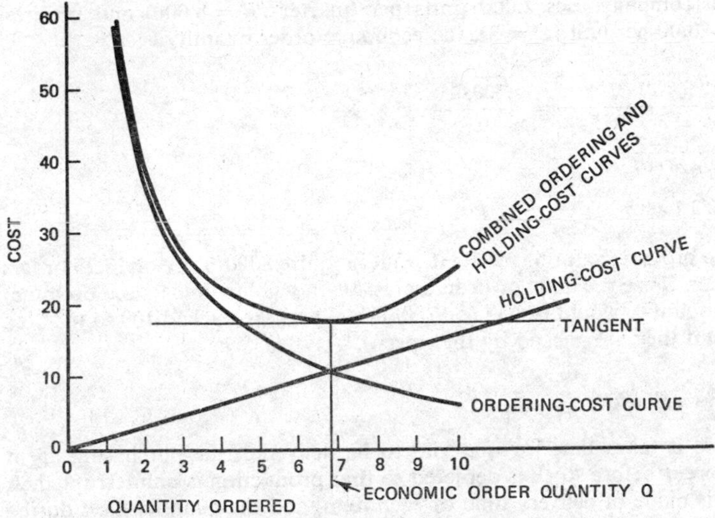

Fig. 11. Total-Cost Curve

Point Q would be the most economic quantity to order. To produce a graph for each item may prove to be quite a time-consuming job, so formulas have been developed to allow a more rapid calculation of the optimum size of order. One such formula is as follows:

$$Q = \sqrt{\frac{2 \times R \times P}{C \times I}}$$

where Q is the optimum order quantity
R is the annual requirement of the item in units
P is the cost of placing one order
C is the invoice price of one unit of the item
I is the holding cost of stocks, expressed as a percentage of the average stock.

To use the formula P and I must be determined for the company.

$$P = \frac{\text{total cost of ordering}}{\text{number of orders placed per year}}$$

$$\text{and } I = \frac{\text{total cost of holding stocks}}{\text{average inventory}}$$

Assume that the cost of processing an order (writing the purchase order, purchasing-department salaries and expenses, receiving-department salaries and expenses, and all other costs relative to purchasing) is £80,000 per year and 4,000 purchase orders are written. Then P = £20. Assume that holding costs (storeroom salaries and expenses, stock insurance, obsolescence, deterioration, theft) are £100,000, and the average stock is £400,000. Then I = 25 per cent.

If a company uses 2,000 units per quarter ($R = 8{,}000$) and material costs £3.00 per unit ($C = 3$), the economic order quantity is:

$$Q = \sqrt{\frac{2 \times 8{,}000 \times 20}{3 \times 0.25}} = \sqrt{\frac{320{,}000}{0.75}}$$

$$= \sqrt{426{,}667}$$

$$= 653.2 \text{ units}$$

If each order were for 653 units it would require 8000/653.2 or 12.25 orders per year. Since the units or orders must be in whole numbers the optimum order quantity would be 653 (or 700 if the items are packed 100 to the box, or 660 if they are packed by the dozen).

Minimum Stock

Because it takes time for material to be delivered, the purchasing agent must order before stock is depleted so that production is uninterrupted. A study is made of delivery time of each item, and the quantity used during this time is computed to establish the time of reorder in terms of quantity of material. This is shown in Fig. 12.

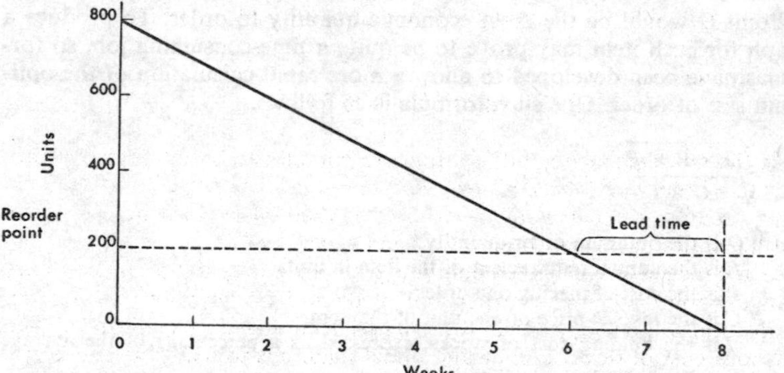

Fig. 12. Computing the time at which the stocks should be reordered

The optimum stock size is determined to be 800 units ordered every eight weeks (a usage of 100 per week). It takes two weeks between the time an order is placed and the time it is delivered. Therefore, the order is placed two weeks prior to the time the inventory will be depleted or when the quantity level is 200 units (2 weeks × 100 units/week). When the material arrives, two weeks after it is ordered, the stock is just reaching the depletion point. The time between the order date and the receiving date is called 'lead time'.

Defective Work

When some of the goods produced are inspected and found to be defective, the production department assesses whether the items are to be reworked into acceptable items or scrapped.

Reworking

If the defective items are to be reworked, they are separated from the acceptable items and moved along whatever line is necessary to convert them. The item may be dismantled, reworked, defective parts replaced, etc., until it is ready for stock.

These defective items are segregated from an accounting standpoint as well. The entry is easy enough to prepare except for the valuation of the defective items. Three approaches to the problem can be taken. The first is to assume that up to the point of separation all items in the group cost the same per unit. The second is to value the defective items at their present worth but increase the per-unit cost of the non-defective ones. The third is to value the defective items at their present worth but not increase the per-unit cost of the non-defective items. The results of these different treatments will be as follows.

(*a*) *All units up to point of separation cost the same*. Under this assumption it is an easy matter to determine the cost of the group of items and the number of items produced (good and defective) and obtain a per-unit cost. The entry made to separate the defective items from the acceptable ones is:

Work-in-Progress—Defective Goods	£280	
Work-in-Progress (7 units @ £40)		£280

As the non-defective goods continue to completion, additional costs are normally collected. The cost per unit of these completed goods will be approximately what it would have been if there were no defective goods and the entire batch had been completed as acceptable.

As the defective goods also continue to completion, additional costs are normally collected. The cost per unit of these defective goods brought to completion will be higher than if there had been no deficiences. The entries to record cost of direct labour and direct materials to defective goods is:

Work-in-Progress—Defective Goods	Debit	
Remainder of labour entries shown on page 146	Debits	Credits
Work-in-Progress—Defective Goods	Debit	
Remainder of materials entries shown on page 148	Debits	Credits

The objection to using this method is that the per-unit cost of finished goods is greater for the defective goods than for the non-defective ones.

(*b*) *Defective items are valued at their present worth, but the per-unit cost of the non-defective items will increase*. Under this assumption an analysis is made of how much, per unit, it would cost to complete the defective goods. Let us assume this cost is £65. Assume the unit cost to point of separation is £40, as used in the previous example, and the expected completion cost of a unit is £90. Then the present value must be £25 (£90 − £65), and the entry is:

Work-in-Progress—Defective Goods	£175	
Work-in-Progress (7 × £25)		£175

The objection to this treatment is that by only removing the present value of the defective goods the *total* cost of non-defective goods rose by £105, and the per-unit cost rose accordingly. The third approach overcomes this objection.

(*c*) *Defective items are valued at their present worth, but the per-unit cost of the non-defective items will not increase.* Under this assumption an analysis is made of how much, per unit, it would cost to complete the non-defective goods (say £50). An analysis is also made of how much, per unit, it would cost to complete the defective goods (say £65, as used in the previous example). If the per-unit cost to point of separation was £40 (as above), the expected completion cost per non-defective unit is £90, but the reworked defective items would cost £105 per unit. To equalise the per-unit cost of the defective and non-defective goods *at the end* of the productive effort, the defective goods are reduced in value now by the following entry:

Work-in-Progress—Defective Goods (7 × £25)	£175	
Production Overhead—Defective Goods (7 × £15)	105	
Work-in-Progress		£280

As the non-defective and defective goods continue to completion, the cost per unit of these completed goods will be approximately what it would have been if there were no defective goods and the entire batch of goods had been completed as acceptable.

Scrapping

If the defective items are not to be reworked, but instead are scrapped, they are separated from the acceptable items and put into bins or elsewhere for disposal.

The accountant should remove these defective items from the remainder of the batch, just as the goods were physically removed. Three methods can be used to calculate the value of the defective items. The first is to assume that up to the point of separation all items in the group cost the same per unit. The second is to value the scrap at its present market value and to increase the per-unit cost of the non-defective items. The third is to value scrap at its present market value and to maintain the per-unit cost of the non-defective items. These different treatments are discussed below.

(*a*) *All units up to the separation cost the same.* As explained before, a per-unit cost to point of separation is determined. The entry made to separate the scrap from the acceptable units is:

Scrap Inventory	£280	
Work-in-progress (7 units @ £40)		£280

The treatment for the non-defective goods is the same as explained in the section on 'Re-working'—they collect additional costs and at completion the unit cost approximates what it would have been had there been no scrap and the whole batch of goods had been completed as acceptable.

When the scrap is sold, an entry is made as follows:

	£	£
Cash (or Debtors)	XX	
Loss or Gain on Sales of Scrap (or Production Overhead)	XX or	XX
Scrap Inventory		280

The objection to this treatment is that in many cases the market value of the scrap may not be as great as the per-unit cost up to the point of separation. This method overstates scrap inventory, although the per-unit cost of the units remaining in production is equitable.

(*b*) *Scrap is valued at its present market value and the per-unit cost of the non-defective items is increased.* Under this method the market value of the scrap is obtained. The Scrap Inventory account is set up at this value, while Work-in-Progress is reduced by the same amount as follows:

	£	£
Scrap Inventory	75	
Work-in-Progress		75

When the scrap is sold, the entry is as follows:

Cash (or Debtors)	XX	
Loss or Gain on Sale of Scrap (or Production Overhead)	XX or	XX
Scrap Inventory		75

The objection to this treatment is that the per-unit cost of the non-defective goods up to the point of separation is increased. The way to overcome this objection is to use the third approach.

(*c*) *Scrap is valued at its present market value but the per-unit cost of the non-defective items remains the same.* Under this assumption the market value of scrap is determined, and Scrap Inventory is debited by this amount, but Work-in-Progress is credited with the per-unit cost to the point of separation. The difference in these two values is absorbed by Production Overhead as follows:

	£	£
Scrap Inventory	75	
Production Overhead—Scrap	205	
Work-in-Progress (7 × £40)		280

Alternatively the balance can be written off to the profit and loss account which avoids distorting the production overhead figure. When the scrap is sold, the entry prepared for the second treatment is used. We can see that this treatment establishes scrap at its conservative value and preserves the per-unit cost up to point of separation.

One of the purposes of the account records is to present facts on which management can act. The method to be used for recording the value of defective goods or scrap, and the per-unit cost of work-in-progress at the point of separation, should be chosen keeping in mind the use to be made by management of the additional information and the cost of collection *versus* the potential savings.

Production Overhead

Production overhead is the cost, other than direct labour and direct materials and direct expenses of operating the factory. Indeed it is common to refer to this group of charges as factory overhead but the term more current in the UK and recommended by the ICMA is production overhead which is therefore adopted here. The costs of the factory may come from goods and services purchased from outsiders, and goods and services previously purchased but now used up. The entries for these types of transaction are:

	£	£
Production Overhead—Indirect Labour	XXX	
(or Production Overhead—Dept. F1)		
etc.		
Remainder of payroll debits	XXX	
Wages		XXX
To record the payroll for the period. (This entry is prepared from the payroll summary. At the end of the period the normal accrued-wages is made.)		
Production Overhead—Materials	XXX	
(or Production Overhead—Dept. F1)		
etc.		
Remainder of materials debits	XXX	
Stocks		XXX
To record the materials usage for the period. (This entry is prepared from the Materials Journal.)		
Production Overhead—Telephone	XXX	
Production Overhead—Sundries	XXX	
Production Overhead—Rent	XXX	
etc.		
Vouchers (Accounts) Payable		XXX
To record invoices received for goods or services purchased for use. (At the end of the period the normal accrual entry is made.)		
Production Overhead—Insurance	XXX	
Production Overhead—Supplies	XXX	
etc.		
Various Prepaid Assets		XXX
To record the expired cost of the prepaid assets.		
Production Overhead—Depreciation of Factory Equipment	XXX	

Production Overhead—Depreciation of Factory Building, etc.	XXX	
Accumulated Depreciation—		
Factory Equipment		XXX
Factory Building		XXX
etc.		
To record depreciation expense determined by the depreciation schedules.		

If these charges were posted to the Production Overhead Account, it would appear as follows:

PRODUCTION OVERHEAD

Indirect Labour	
Indirect Materials	
Charges from the Voucher Register	
Expired Cost of Pre-paid Assets	
Depreciation Expense	

Production Overhead is one account, and the balance of this account is a cost applicable to all production during the period. To calculate total per-unit cost, the debit balance in this account must be allocated to the production of the period. The total in the account is not known until the end of the period.

Charges to Production—Burden or Overhead Absorption Rate

How can this debit balance be charged to production during the year when the total is not known until the end of the period? This process is variously termed overhead absorption, recovery or application of burden. In the following pages the term will be restricted to Absorption Rates. Cost accounting has developed a principle of overhead absorption. In manufacturing a product, direct labour and direct materials are used. In many cases there is a relationship between the productive output and direct-labour hours, direct labour cost, direct-material cost, or some other measurable factor. When this relationship exists, a way can be devised to absorb the production overhead.

First, the total production overhead must be estimated. This estimate can be determined by an analysis of last year's expense and productive process and the changes in costs since last year. Second, the **distribution basis** that can be measured and used for allocation is selected, and the portion of this basis to be used in the next period is estimated. This estimate can be obtained by use of the figures from the previous year and by analysis of the changes in the productive situation. (More than one basis may be used, but for purposes of illustration only one will be discussed now.) Third, the estimated production overhead is divided by the estimated number of units produced to get the production **absorption rate**. The absorption rate is expressed in either of two ways:

(*a*) Where the basis is expressed in money terms the absorption rate is expressed as some figure multiplied by the distribution basis (1.2 times direct-labour cost, for example) or by a percentage of the distribution basis (e.g., 120 per cent of direct-labour cost).

(*b*) Where the basis is expressed in units other than pounds, the absorption rate is expressed as some cost figure times the distribution basis (for example, £2.50 per direct-labour hour).

Once the absorption rate is determined, the distribution basis is measured as production progresses. When the company is ready to add overhead to work-in-progress (as when a job is completed or at the end of a financial period), the distribution basis for the production is multiplied by the absorption rate to obtain the total amount of the overhead charge to production.

Example of the Absorption Rate Calculation

It is estimated that the factory overhead for 19.0 will be £180,000, that direct-labour hours (dlh) best measure the productive effort, and that in 19.0 120,000 direct-labour hours will be used. The production overhead absorption rate is calculated as follows:

$$\text{Production rate} = \frac{\text{Estimated factory overhead}}{\text{Estimated number of distribution units to be used}}$$

$$= \frac{\text{£180,000}}{\text{120,000 hours}}$$

$$= \text{£1.50/direct-labour hour}$$

During January 19.0 direct labour was used as follows:

On product A—	2,000 direct-labour hours (dlh)
On product B—	6,000 dlh
On product C—	2,500 dlh
	10,500 dlh

The amount of production overhead to be allocated to each product would be:

Product A—£3,000	(2,000 dlh × £1.50/dlh)
Product B— 9,000	(6,000 dlh × 1.50/dlh)
Product C— 3,750	(2,500 dlh × 1.50/dlh)

and the entry would be:

Work-in-Progress—Product A	£3,000	
Work-in-Progress—Product B	9,000	
Work-in-Progress—Product C	3,750	
Production Overhead		£15,750

(In some instances an account called Production Overhead Absorbed or Applied is used as the credit. At the end of the period the Production Overhead and Production Overhead Absorbed Accounts are merged to give the same results as the entry above would give.)

Use of Different Bases for the Absorption of Production Overhead

In some manufacturing situations the use of a single base might not give intelligent results. For example, consider a situation in which all effort in one department is by machine (perhaps a mechanised spray-painting booth) and all labour in the next is by hand (hand rubbing of the finish). To use direct-labour hours would put all the overhead in the second department. To use material costs (the cost of the paint and the rubbing compound) would put most of the overhead in the first department. Either result does not reflect the facts—both departments probably contribute some relatively equal value to the finished product.

Therefore, to find a measurable factor to relate to productive effort, it might very well be that the use of two or more bases will result in a better and more plausible distribution of the production overhead. The total overhead is then allocated or apportioned on some bases and a series of overhead rates determined, one for each absorption method, so that the production overhead can be distributed according to the analysis of productive effort.

Direct Department Charges

Where the factory is large and there are many possible bases for the overhead rate absorption, a system is sometimes used of departmentalising all factory expense. Wherever possible, the individual charges for goods or services are broken down by department (on some basis such as, for telephone expense, the number of telephones in the department, etc.). Then the expense of the non-productive departments are allocated to the production department (on a basis such as heating capacity of boilers for the steam plant) until all production overhead is allocated. An overhead rate is determined for each production department and is used to allocate the department's overhead to its productive effort.

Variance Analysis

At the end of the period, after the actual expenses are posted and the distribution of overhead is made, the Production Overhead Account appears as follows:

PRODUCTION OVERHEAD ACCOUNT

Indirect Labour	Absorption of Overhead to Production (using absorption rate(s))
Indirect Materials	
Charges from the Voucher Register	
Expired Cost of Prepaid Assets	
Depreciation Expense	

There will almost always be a difference between the total debits and the total credits, although it may be relatively small. In such an event, the accountant prepares an entry to close the account to Cost of Goods Sold as follows:

(*a*) If the balance in the account is a debit:

Cost of Goods Manufactured	£XX	
Production Overhead		£XX

This increases the Cost of Goods Manufactured by the balance in the Production Overhead Account.

(*b*) If the balance in the account is a credit:

Production Overhead	£XX	
Cost of Goods Manufactured		£XX

This decreases the Cost of Goods Manufactured.

Even the difference is relatively small, there may be some areas of trouble or improvement, and the difference, called 'production overhead variance', should always be analysed. Let us consider again the components of the Production Overhead Account. The debits were actual costs. The credits were the charges to Work-in-Progress obtained by multiplying the actual distribution basis by the absorption rate. The absorption rate was the estimated factory overhead divided by the estimated number of distribution units. Implied in the estimated number of distribution units is the assumption that the firm operates at some percentage of capacity, because the distribution units will be greater or lesser as the capacity is greater or lesser.

In the analysis we can examine the following variances:

(*a*) *Expenditure or budget variance*. This is the difference between the estimated or budgeted overhead and the actual production overhead. A comparison of each item in the total may reveal significant areas.

(*b*) *Volume* (*or capacity*) *variance*. This is the difference between what the overhead is at the actual production capacity and what the estimated overhead was with the implied production capacity.

(*c*) *Efficiency variance*. This is the difference between the actual production overhead at the actual production capacity, and the estimated production overhead at the actual production capacity, assuming normal rate of efficiency.

These three variances individually may be great but may combine in such a fashion that the net variance is relatively small. Therefore, the relative size of the total variance cannot be relied on exclusively. The analysis will tell more.

Let us assume that a plant plans to operate at 80 per cent capacity. At this capacity, it is expected that there will be £96,000 of production overhead expense and 40,000 direct-labour hours which will be used as the distribution base. The absorption rate is set at £2.40 per direct-labour hour (i.e. £96,000 ÷ 40,000 hours). If the plant operates at 86 per cent capacity absorbing 44,000 direct-labour hours in production, and the total actual expense is £102,000, the Production Overhead Account is as follows:

PRODUCTION OVERHEAD ACCOUNT

Actual	£102,000	Absorbed 44,000 dlh × £2.40/dlh £105,600

The total variance is £3,600. In analysing this variance, however, we find some interesting data:

Budget variance: It was planned to spend £96,000 for overhead, but actually £102,000 was spent, an actual expenditure of £6,000 more than was planned.

Volume variance: It was planned to operate at 80 per cent of capacity, using 40,000 direct-labour hours (500 direct-labour hours per 1 per cent of capacity), but actually the capacity was 86 per cent (which would have been 43,000 direct-labour hours) or an actual expense of £7,200 more than was planned ((43,000 – 40,000) × £2.40).

Efficiency variance: Had the ratio of 500 direct-labour hours per 1 per cent capacity held constant, there would have been only 43,000 direct-labour hours, but actually there were 44,000, or an additional 1,000 direct-labour hours charged at £2.40 per direct-labour hour, or £2,400 more absorbed production overhead.

Now management is in a position to ask questions such as:

(*a*) Were the budgeted figures correct for 80 per cent capacity?

(*b*) Using the same data and methods as in the original budget, what would the budgeted figures for 86 per cent capacity have been?

(*c*) Does the direct-labour usage vary directly with percentage capacity, or is there some other relationship?

(*d*) Why is there a lowering of efficiency between 80 per cent and 86 per cent of capacity?

(*e*) Can figures be developed so that budgets can be amended during the operating cycle?

(*f*) Can any meaningful figures be extracted if the data does not distinguish between fixed and variable items of expense?

By analysing the variance intelligently, management can often discover areas for improvement. As these areas are reviewed and changes are made, the business becomes more profitable (because per-unit cost decreases) and we find that operating personnel start questioning areas of operation *before* the cost appears in the accounting records. An attitude of awareness and care becomes more prevalent, and the business improves its competitive position.

13
Management Accounting: Costing Methods

There are two basic methods for collecting cost-accounting data. The first is based on the **method of production** (job-order *vs* process costing). The second is based on the **cost price of labour, materials and overheads** (historical costing *vs* standard costing). These methods can be combined as follows:

		Based on Method of Production	
		Job-Order	Process
Based on Price of Labour, Materials and Overheads	Historical	Historical Job-Order	Historical Process
	Standard	Standard Job-Order	Standard Process

It is important to see the relationships of these methods, because the organisation of many cost-accounting texts has led readers to believe that there are three costing methods: job-order, process and standard.

Job-Order versus Process Methods

The job-order or specific order cost method keeps the costs of various jobs or contracts separate during their manufacture or construction. This method presupposes the possibility of physically identifying the jobs produced and of charging each with its own cost.

The process cost method consists of computing an average unit cost of production by dividing the total manufacturing cost by the total number of units produced in the factory over a specific period of time. This method is used when:

(*a*) products are not separately distinguishable from one another during one or more processes of manufacture;

(*b*) the product of one process becomes the material of the next process;

(*c*) different products, or even by-products, are produced by the same process.

There is no basic difference in the accounting treatment; the difference is in the processing. In both productive situations the elements of cost are direct labour, direct materials, and factory or production overhead. In both cases a productive operation is set in motion and then terminates at some future time.

Job-order Costing

If a job-order project is started and completed in the same financial period, the total cost of the job consists of direct labour, direct materials, and production overhead. The per-unit cost is the total cost divided by the actual number of units produced.

Assume that a job started in January and was completed in June in a company that has a calendar-year financial period. The direct labour charged to Work-in-Progress is £50,000; direct materials, £30,000; factory overhead, £20,000 (40 per cent of direct labour). The total is £100,000. If 50 units are produced, the per-unit cost is £2,000.

But what happens if a job-order project is started in one year and completed in the next? You can see that a problem of valuation of year-end Work-in-Progress arises, even though when the job is completed the total cost is the same.

Assume that a job started in October, 19.1 is completed in April, 19.2 in a company that operates on a calendar-year financial period. The direct labour charged to Work-in-Progress is £50,000 (£20,000 in 19.1 and £30,000 in 19.2); direct materials, £30,000 (£7,000 in 19.1 and £23,000 in 19.2); production overhead, £20,000 (40 per cent of direct labour, or £8,000 in 19.1 and £12,000 in 19.2). The total is £100,000. At December 31st, 19.1 the Work-in-Progress inventory is valued at £35,000 (charges in 19.1 of direct labour of £20,000; direct materials, £7,000; production overhead, £8,000). In 19.2 the additional £65,000 is spent to complete the job.

Process Costing

If a process project is started and completed in the same period, the total cost of the process consists of direct labour, direct materials, and production overhead. The per-unit cost is the total cost divided by the actual number of units produced. You can see that this is the same definition used for job-order costing when the project is started and completed in the same accounting period.

If, however, a process project is started in one period and is not completed by the end of the period, the situation is different from the job-order project started in one year and completed in the next. In the latter *none* of the project is completed, while in the process project some units may be completed. To illustrate, if a continuous process takes 60 days from start to completion, the item completed at the end of the period was begun 60 days before, but in the process line there are goods 59 days complete, 58 days complete, etc., down to items one day complete. And each day the unit begun 60 days ago is completed. The stage of completion is not the same throughout the process. The closing Work-in-Progress comprises the total cost of the uncompleted product, and the remaining cost of production for the period is established as completed stock.

Thus the original charges are to Work-in-Progress as described in Chapter 12 (page 143) for direct labour, direct materials, and production overhead. At the end of the period the total charges must be separated into those applicable to Finished Goods and those still remaining in Work-in-Progress. Total costs charged to production during the period equal the cost of goods finished during the period plus cost of goods unfinished at the end of the period:

Total costs charged to production = Finished Goods +
Closing Work-in-Progress

If there had been an opening Work-in-Progress inventory or stock (production uncompleted at the previous year end) the formula is changed to:

Opening Work-in-Progress + Total costs charged to production =
Finished Goods + Closing Work-in-Progress

The problem of valuing the closing Work-in-Progress inventory can be solved by calculating what has been done on the closing Work-in-Progress inventory and pricing out the production thus far. Subtracting that figure from the opening Work-in-Progress and total costs charged to production during the period gives the finished goods.

Assume that at December 31st, 19.1, the Work-in-Progress inventory is valued at £552,500 (direct labour, £292,500; direct materials, £162,500; and production overhead £97,500) and contains 325 units of saleable merchandise only partially complete. In 19.2 the 325 units are completed and an additional 540 units are started, of which 400 are completed. The effort made by the business in 19.2 can be summarised as follows:

(*a*) Effort needed to complete the 325 units, *plus*;
(*b*) Effort needed to begin and complete 400 units, *plus*;
(*c*) Effort needed to begin and bring 140 units up to their present stage of completion.

In any well-organised productive effort the amount of direct labour, direct materials, and production overhead needed to complete a project is fairly well known. Therefore one could say, with a fair degree of accuracy, that the Work-in-Progress is a certain percentage of direct-labour costs, another percentage of direct materials, and a third percentage of production overhead. The production can then be analysed in terms of **equivalent** full units of production.

In the illustration above, determining the amount of completion for the opening and closing stocks might produce a chart similar to the following:

	Labour	Material	Overhead
Opening Stock	30%	10%	10%
To complete the opening stock	70%	90%	90%
Completion of closing stock	20%	25%	15%

To determine how many completed items the direct-labour effort would have produced, the computation is as follows:

To complete opening stock (70% × 325)	227.5 equivalent units
To begin and complete new production	400.0
To begin and bring 140 units up to present completion (20% × 140)	28.0
Equivalent units of direct labour	655.5 eu

The total cost of direct labour used in the production of this item might be divided as follows:

$$\frac{227.5}{655.5} \text{ (or 34.7\%)}; \frac{400.0}{655.5} \text{ (or 61.0\%)}; \frac{28.0}{655.5} \text{ (or 4.3\%)}$$

The same type of computation would be made for direct materials as follows:

To complete opening stock (90% × 325)	292.5 eu
To begin and complete new production	400.0
To begin and bring 140 units up to present completion (25% × 140)	35.0
Equivalent production of direct materials	727.5 eu

The total cost of direct material used in the production of this item might be divided as follows:

$$\frac{292.5}{727.5} \text{ (or 40.2\%)}; \frac{400.0}{727.5} \text{ (or 55.0\%)}; \frac{35.0}{727.5} \text{ (or 4.8\%)}$$

The same type of computation would be made for production overhead as follows:

To complete opening stock (90% × 325)	292.5 eu
To begin and complete new production	400.0 eu
To begin and bring 140 units up to present completion (15% × 140)	21.0 eu
Equivalent production of production overhead	713.5 eu

The total cost of production overhead used in the production of this item might be divided as follows:

$$\frac{292.5}{713.5} \text{ (or 41.0\%)}; \frac{400.0}{713.5} \text{ (or 56.1\%)}; \frac{21.0}{713.5} \text{ (or 2.9\%)}$$

During 19.0 the following charges were made to Work-in-Progress for this item:

	£
Direct Labour	1,900,950
Direct Materials	3,710,250
Production Overhead	2,069,150

It is now possible to determine the cost of production and the closing stock as follows:

	Direct Labour	Direct Materials	Production Overhead	Total
	£	£	£	£
Opening Stock	292,500	162,500	97,500	552,500
Charges during year	1,900,950	3,710,250	2,069,150	7,680,350
Total Cost	£2,193,450	£3,872,750	£2,166,650	£8,232,850

Cost per unit is as follows:

$$\text{Direct labour/equivalent units} = \frac{£1,900,950}{655.5} = £2,900/\text{eu}$$

$$\text{Closing Stock} = 28.0 \text{ eu} \times £2,900/\text{eu} = £81,200$$

$$\text{Direct material/equivalent units} = \frac{£3,710,250}{727.5} = £5,100/\text{eu}$$

$$\text{Closing Stock} = 35.0 \text{ eu} \times £5,100/\text{eu} = £178,500$$

$$\text{Production overhead/equivalent units} = \frac{£2,069,150}{713.5} = £2,900/\text{eu}$$

$$\text{Closing Stock} = 21.\text{eu} \times £2,900/\text{eu} = £60,900$$

The transfer to finished goods inventory and the closing stock is as follows:

		£
Transferred to finished goods		7,912,250
Closing Stock (December 31st, 19.0)		
Direct labour	81,200	
Direct materials	178,500	
Factory overhead	60,900	320,600
Total charges to production		£8,232,850

Where the product of one process becomes the material of the next process, it is only a matter of making an analysis similar to the one above for each successive process through which an item in production passes. There may be an opening Work-in-Progress inventory in each process and a closing Work-in-Progress inventory in each process, but the effort within the process in the period under study can be broken down into equivalent units of direct labour, direct materials, and production overhead. Once the cost per equivalent unit of the production factors is determined, it is relatively simple to compute the value of the closing stock and the material transferred to the next department.

Cost Allocation or Apportionment

When two different products, or perhaps a main product and a by-product, are produced as the result of a single operation, the cost of the goods transferred out of the process (determined as shown above) must then be allocated between the products. Definitions of joint products and by-products may help in understanding the following discussion. If two or more products are produced together and each bears a significant value relationship to the other, the products are called **joint products**. If two or more products are produced together and one of them bears an insignificant value relationship to the others, that one is called a **by-product**. Because of the difference in relative significance, the accounting treatment varies somewhat.

Joint-product Treatment

The problem of cost allocation is one of giving to each product an equitable share of the cost up to the point of cost division (which may occur at the end of any process where the physical processing is separated). There are several methods of treatment, of which the following are examples.

(*a*) *Market value of the end product.* In this method the total sales value of the various products is determined, and the joint costs are divided between the joint products in like proportion. To illustrate assuming the joint costs to be allocated are £30,000:

Product	No. of Units Produced	Sale Value	Percentage	Joint Cost
		£		£
A	2,000	32,000	$66\frac{2}{3}$%	20,000
B	3,000	16,000	$33\frac{1}{3}$%	10,000
		£48,000	100%	£30,000

(*b*) *Market value of the end product less further conversion costs.* In this method the total sales price of the various products is determined, the cost to complete the product is determined and subtracted, and the joint costs are divided between the joint products in like proportion. To illustrate, assuming the joint costs to be allocated are £50,000 and conversion costs *post separation* are £25,000 for C and £15,000 for D.

Product	No. of Units Produced	Sale Value	Conversion Cost	Balance
		£	£	£
C	7,000	70,000	25,000	45,000
D	6,000	30,000	15,000	15,000
		£100,000	£40,000	£60,000

Then:

Balance	Percentage	Joint Cost
£		£
45,000	75%	37,500
15,000	25%	12,500
£60,000	100%	£50,000

(*c*) *Quantitative unit allocation.* At the point of separation, the products are measured in units which are used to allocate the costs. In pouring concrete into decorative moulds, for example, the allocation of cost can be made on the basis of weight of the decorative item.

(*d*) *Equivalent unit allocation.* If, at the point of separation, the units of measurement vary from product to product, it may be possible to assign relative weights to the end products so that an allocation can be made.

There are other methods for cost allocation of joint-product cost. The object here is not to exhaust them all but rather to give you an idea of some of the prevalent methods. If you are confronted with a joint-cost pricing situation at least you will be able to recognise it.

By-product Treatment

The problem that this treatment attempts to solve is the allocation of cost to the by-product which leaves the main product with an equitable share of the total production cost to date. The treatment is different from that used in joint-product costs because of the relative insignificance in value of the by-product with respect to the main product.

(*a*) *Sales price of the by-product is treated as income.* Where the by-product is sold, the sales price can be added to the sales price of the main product or it can be shown at the bottom of the Income Statement as Other Income.

	£
Sales (main product)	40,000
Sales (by-product)	2,000
Total Sales	£42,000
Cost of Sales (main product only because no cost is assigned to the by-product)	30,000
Gross Profit	12,000
Selling and General Expenses	8,000
Operating Profit	£4,000

An alternative form of presentation is:

Sales (main product)	£40,000
Cost of sales	30,000
Gross Profit	10,000
Selling and General Expenses	8,000
Operating Profit	2,000
Other Income (by-product sales)	2,000
Net Income	£4,000

(b) *Sales price of the by-product is treated as income but the costs of product completion, sales, and administration are allocated to the by-product.* When this treatment is used, the selling and general expenses are allocated between the main product and the by-product, and the costs necessary to complete the by-product are collected.

Using the facts above, the Income Statement might look as follows:

	Main Product	By-product	Total
	£	£	£
Sales	40,000	2,000	42,000
Cost of Sales	29,500	500	30,000
Gross Profit	10,500	1,500	12,000
Selling and General Expenses	7,400	600	8,000
Operating Profit	£3,100	£900	£4,000

Remember that the cost of sales of the by-product includes only the costs applicable to the by-product after separation from the main product.

(c) *Sales price of the by-product is deducted from the cost of sales of the main product.*

	£	£
Sales (main product)		40,000
Cost of Sales	30,000	
Less by-product sales	2,000	28,000
Gross Profit		12,000
Selling and General Expenses		8,000
Operating Profit		£4,000

(d) *Sales price of the by-product is deducted from production overhead.* Since the by-product is an unwanted result of the production of the main product, it can be treated as scrap (see Chapter 12): credit Production Overhead with the income from by-product sales. The Income Statement would not show the income from by-product sales as a separate item, but the Cost of Goods Manufactured Schedule would have a lower overhead cost than would be the case in the above examples.

(e) *By-product used in production is valued at its replacement cost.* When a by-product is separated from a main product somewhere in the productive process and then later used in the productive process, the company may assign to the by-product the value it would have had to pay to purchase it from an outside vendor. If the by-product is available on the open market, the problem of costing is simplified. The by-product is taken into stock, and the costs of the main product are reduced by a similar amount.

(f) *By-product is assigned a cost that will yield an estimated rate of gross profit return.* In this method the value of the finished by-product, the gross profit ratio, and the cost of completing the by-product are estimated. The value of the by-product is then the amount which, when added to the completion cost and the estimated gross profit, will equal sales.

Assume 1,000 units of a by-product can be sold for £5 each upon completion; it would take £2.75 to complete each item; and the gross profit ratio is estimated to be 20 per cent. The computation to determine the assigned value of the by-product is as follows:

	£
Sales (1,000 × £5)	5,000
Gross Profit (20%)	1,000
Cost of Sales	4,000
Completion costs (1,000 × £2.75)	2,750
Assigned Value of by-product	£1,250

Historical versus Standard Costing

It was pointed out earlier in the chapter that one of the costing alternatives is concerned with determining the prices that will be used, actual or standard. Regardless of which method is used, the actual costs must ultimately be charged to production. At this point we might recall that there are different methods of valuing stock, devised because of price fluctuations of the items in stock. The use of one method or another may yield different profits in any one year, but in the total life of the business the total profits must be the same.

Historical Costs

Historical costs are the costs of production which can be traced to an actual invoice or other document and which are used to establish price based on the actual expenditure. In this method, direct and indirect labour costs are determined from the Payroll voucher, and the exact amount of the credits in the Payroll entry are charged to Work-in-Progress or Production Overhead. Raw-materials costs are determined from invoices, and the exact amount of the credits to Cash or Trade Creditors are charged to Raw Materials Inventory. When the materials are used they are priced out at actual cost (using LIFO, FIFO, average, or some other pricing system).

The historical method might produce varied costs of goods manufactured, depending on the wage rate and skill of an individual performing a task, the pricing system used in charging inventory to production, and the quantity of material used. The increase of wage rates with increase of skills would tend to minimise the cost differences attributable to the use of different persons for performing a given task. Fluctuation in price levels would create some problems in costing materials, but we have already seen that methods have been devised to handle the problem.

If production costs can vary from year to year or period to period, management might like to know why. A superimposed analytic method might prove very costly; thus the standard-cost method was devised.

Standard Cost

In the standard-cost system, an assumption is made that a given volume of production requires definite units of direct labour and direct materials and that the prices of the direct labour and direct materials can be determined. This is sometimes called a 'budget of direct costs'.

How can the quantities and prices of direct labour and direct materials be determined? One method is to analyse what happened in the past; another method is to study analytically the production process and the present price structure; a third is to study analytically the production process and the changes that might be made; a fourth is to study the present price structure and possible price changes.

Once the hours of direct labour needed to complete a project and the wage rate per hour are determined, and once the quantities and costs of direct materials needed to complete a project are calculated, the direct costs of production can be determined. Any difference in expenditure between the standard and the 'actual' cost can be measured more quickly because the accounting system provides special accounts for variance measurement.

Let us assume that the production of 100 units of Tomred requires 40 hours of direct labour and two ingredients: 100 lb of A and 200 lb of B. It is estimated that labour costs £4/hr; that A costs £3/lb; and that B costs £1/lb. The estimated total direct cost of 100 units of Tomred would be:

Direct Labour (40 hrs × £4/hr)		£160
Direct Materials (100 lb A × £3/lb)	£300	
(200 lb B × £1/lb)	200	500
Total Direct Costs		£660

The entries to Work-in-Progress are as follows:

Work-in-Progress	£160	
Labour Summary		£160
To record direct labour used in production		
Work-in-Progress	£500	
Materials		£500
To record direct material used in production		

If, however, the number of hours spent on the project, or the wage rate per hour, varied from the estimate, there might be a variance in total direct-labour cost.

Assume that it took 41 hours at £4 per hour to complete the project. There is £164 of actual direct-labour charges. The entry for this would be:

Work-in-Progress (40 hrs × £4/hr)	£160	
Labour Hours Variance (1 hr × £4/hr)	4	
Labour Summary (actual wage)		£164
To record direct labour used in production		

This variance, being a debit, is an **unfavourable variance.**

Assume that it took 40 hours at £3.95 per hour to complete the project. There is £158 of actual direct-labour charges. The entry for this would be:

Work-in-Progress (40 hrs × £4/hr)	£160	
Labour Summary (actual wage)		£158
Wage Rate Variance (40 hrs × £0.05/hr)		2
To record direct labour used in production		

This variance, being a credit, is a **favourable variance.**

Thus, actual hours worked can be greater than, equal to, or less than those estimated; and the wage rate can be greater than, equal to, or less than what was estimated. There are nine conditions, then, for direct labour, shown graphically in Fig. 13.

If the actual hours are *less* than standard and the actual wage rate is *less* than standard, the hour and wage-rate variances are always favourable: the hour and wage-rate lines cross in area *A*. If the actual hours are *more* than standard and the actual wage rate is *more* than standard, the hour and wage rate variances are always unfavourable; the hour and wage-rate lines cross in area *B*. If the actual hours are *less* than standard but the actual wage rate is *more* than standard, the hour and wage-rate lines cross in area *C*; the wage-rate variance is unfavourable, but the hours variance is favourable. If the actual hours are *more* than standard but the actual wage rate is *less* than standard, the hour and wage rate is less than standard. The hour and wage-rate lines cross in area *D*; the wage-rate variance is favourable, but the hours variance is unfavourable. When the hour and wage-rate lines cross in areas *C* or *D*, the total direct-labour costs may be less than, equal to, or greater than the estimates, depending upon whether the favourable variance is more than, equal to, or less than the unfavourable variance.

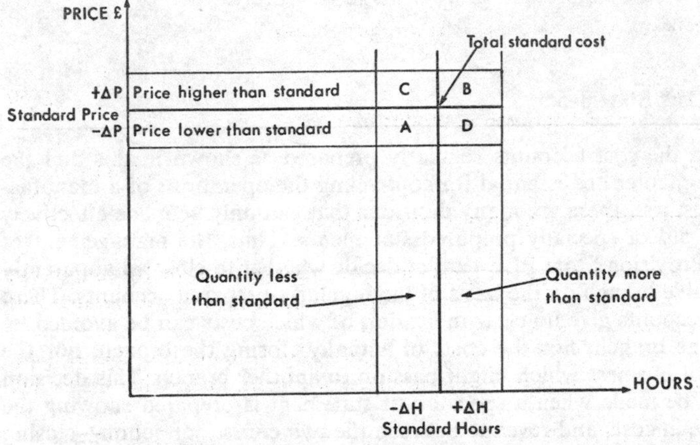

Fig. 13. The nine possible conditions for direct labour

A similar analysis can be made of materials when standard costs are used to determine the cost of work in progress. It is also acceptable to debit Work-in-Progress accounts with actual quantities and rates—the variance accounts then being entered via the Work-in-Progress accounts. Further if using absorption costing—overhead variances are extracted simultaneously, as described at the end of the previous chapter.

Absorption versus Direct (or Marginal) Costing

Within the last decade a new concept of costing has been proposed. It stems from the breakdown of overhead charges into fixed and variable overhead, and a greater emphasis on revenue-producing activity rather than production. This new costing method is called **direct costing** (some countries) or **Marginal Costing** (usually in UK) in contrast to **absorption costing**, the term given to the costing methods discussed previously in this chapter.

It is argued that fixed costs are not related to the quantity produced and therefore should be charged as an expense in the period in which they were incurred. Thus, depreciation on buildings and equipment, rates, factory administrative salaries, etc., are to be considered **period** costs.

The variable costs (direct labour, direct materials, and variable overhead) are production-related costs and should be included in inventories and Cost of Goods Sold.

The direct-costing system has merit because it concentrates attention on variable costs where management's cost-reduction efforts can be effective, and eliminates from the cost-reduction consideration those costs that are allocations of expenditures of past years (depreciation), costs determined by outside agencies (taxes), or costs determined by considerations of maintaining administrative continuity (salaries and wages).

Direct or marginal costing can be used with either job-order or process cost accounting or with either historic or standard costing methods. Direct costing has gained much acceptance in the past decade, and it is likely that it will be used by more and more firms in the future.

Special Cost Statements

Although the cost accounts regularly prepared as shown in this and the previous chapter are essential for controlling the operations of a manufacturing business, there are many decisions that can only be made effectively with the aid of specially prepared statements. Thus, the management of Central Provision Store PLC cannot decide whether to close an apparently unprofitable branch on the basis of the regularly-prepared accounts. These regular accounts give no clear indication of which costs can be avoided by closing the branch, nor the costs of actually closing the branch, nor the amount of business which might pass on to another branch. This decision can only be made when a special cost statement is prepared showing the difference in costs and revenue between the two courses of action—closing or not closing. It is unnecessary to consider any costs which are not influenced by the decision, and the statement will indicate the difference in profit in the two cases.

Let us look at the following details regarding one particular branch:

PROFIT AND LOSS ACCOUNT
(for year about to end)

	£	£	£
Sales		50,000	
Gross Profit (25% of Sales)			12,500
Less Wages	3,800		
Rent	2,500		
Sundry Expenses	1,200		
Overheads Allocated by Head Office	2,000		9,500
Net Profit			£3,000

Assume that if this branch is closed, 20 per cent of the sales will be transferred to other branches. The manager, earning £1,400 p.a., can be transferred at the same salary to another branch whose present manager is retiring. The remaining staff will have to be dismissed with two months' wages. If the lease is renewed the rent will rise to £4,500 p.a. The total overheads to be allocated between the branches will fall by £500.

If the branch is kept open the only change will be an increase in rent of £2,000 p.a., and the profit will fall to £1,000 p.a.

If the branch is closed down the changes will be as follows:

CHANGE IN PROFIT OF BUSINESS RESULTING FROM CLOSING A BRANCH

	£	£
Sales		(−) 40,000
Gross Profit		(−) 10,000
Wages		
(subject to redundancy payments of £400, i.e. ⅙th of (£3,800 − £1,400))	(−) 3,800	
Rent	(−) 4,500	
Sundry expenses	(−) 1,200	
Overheads	(−) 500	
		(−) 10,000
		£ —

It will be seen that by coincidence the profits of the company will be unchanged by the closing of this branch, apart from a once and for all payment of £400. The final decision would depend upon whether there were opportunities for opening more profitable branches elsewhere, in which case the capital released by closing the branch could well be used for that purpose.

This is a simple illustration of the approach which is necessary when considering any substantial change in the operation of a company.

Discounted Cash Flow

Many costing statements either do not take into account interest on the funds that are tied up in a project, or else introduce a very rough approximation. The technique of 'Discounted Cash Flow' enables the interest costs involved in a course of action to be calculated with precision.

The significance of this can be seen from the following simple example. A company has the option of buying a machine (type *A*) costing £8,000 with a life of 10 years and a scrap value of £1,000, or a machine (type *B*) costing £4,000, with the same capacity and running costs but having a life of five years and a scrap value of £500, followed by the purchase of a further machine of the same type at the end of five years.

Ignoring the interest element, both alternatives would cost the same:

	£
Type-*A* Machine	8,000
Less Scrap Value	1,000
Net Cost	£7,000

	£
Two Type-*B* Machines	8,000
Less Scrap Value (2 × £500)	1,000
Net Cost	£7,000

When we look at the time pattern of the expenditure in the two cases we see that it is quite different.

End of Year	*Type-A Machine*	*2 Type-B Machines*
	£	£
0	8,000	4,000
5	—	3,500
10	(−) 1,000	(−) 500

It is obvious that the second alternative will be decidedly cheaper as far as capital costs are concerned. In the first case £8,000 is required initially, gradually reducing to £1,000. In the second, never more than £4,000 is required. It can be better illustrated graphically, as in Fig. 14.

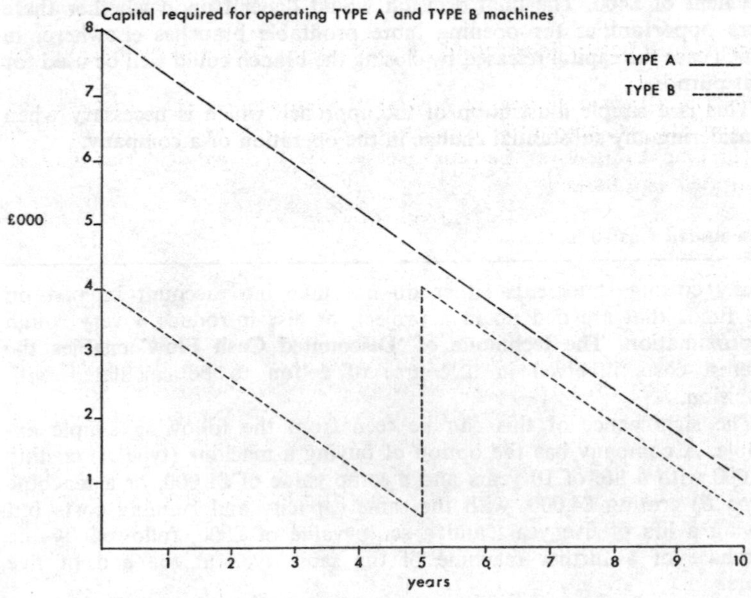

Fig. 14. Capital required for operating type-*A* and type-*B* machines

A decision becomes more difficult to make when the net cost of the type-*A* Machine is lower than the net cost of two type-*B* Machines. How much cheaper should it be to make it a more attractive proposition than two type-*B* Machines? We shall revert to this after examining the Discounted Cash Flow technique.

This technique concentrates on the cash flow and its pattern over time. The various items of cost and revenue which are spread over a period are reduced to a comparable basis by equating each of them to an equivalent amount either on a single date or on an annual basis. Thus any firm would prefer to receive revenue of £100 now rather than in one year's time, and would prefer to incur an expense payable in one year's time rather than now. The strength of these preferences depends upon the rate of interest. If the firm could borrow money freely at 6% per annum it would be a matter of indifference as to whether revenue of £100 were received now or £106 in one year's time. In those circumstances the present equivalent of £106 in one year's time would be £100. The concept is simple but the calculations become onerous where there are sums of money due on many different dates. To facilitate calculations, four tables of compound interest formulae are available. They are:

(*a*) *The Accumulation Factor*, or $(1 + i)^n$. This gives the amount to which 1 unit will amount after n periods by the addition of compound interest at the rate i per period. Taking n as 8, this may be illustrated as follows:

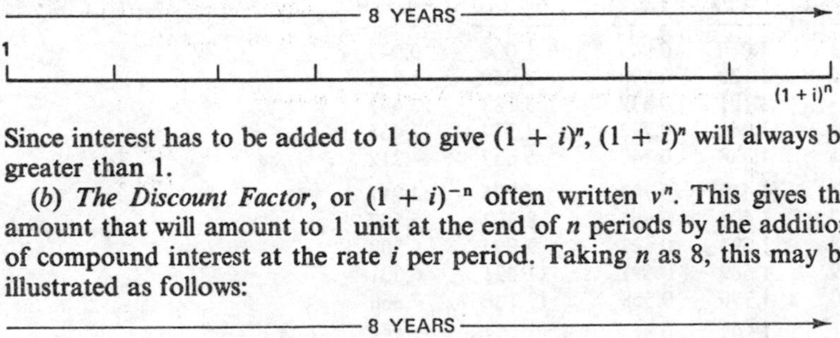

8 YEARS

1 $(1 + i)^n$

Since interest has to be added to 1 to give $(1 + i)^n$, $(1 + i)^n$ will always be greater than 1.

(*b*) *The Discount Factor*, or $(1 + i)^{-n}$ often written v^n. This gives the amount that will amount to 1 unit at the end of n periods by the addition of compound interest at the rate i per period. Taking n as 8, this may be illustrated as follows:

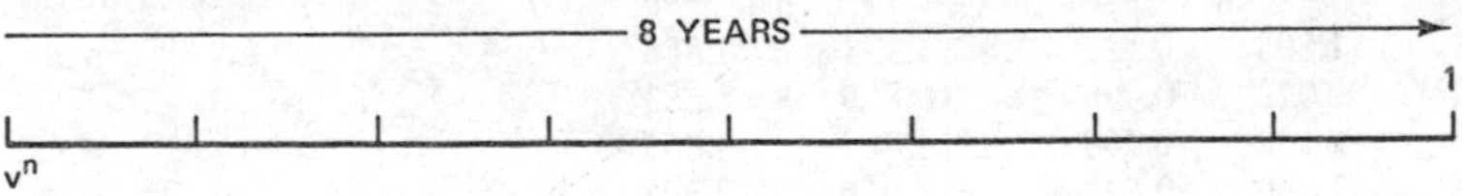

8 YEARS

v^n 1

Since interest has to be v^n to give 1, v^n will always be less than 1.

(*c*) *The Amount of an Annuity*, or $S_{\overline{n}|}$ (read as '*S* angle *n*'). An annuity is a series of periodic payments of equal amounts, in this instance each of 1 unit. The sum of an annuity is the amount to which 1 unit at the end of each of n periods will amount at the end of the n periods by the addition of compound interest on each payment from the time of the payment to the end of the period. Taking n as 8, this may be illustrated as follows:

8 YEARS

1 1 1 1 1 1 1 1

$S_{\overline{n}|}$

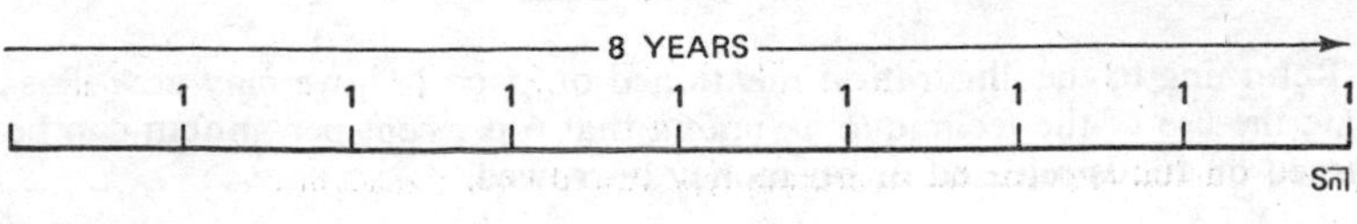

Since interest will be added to the n payments of 1 unit to give S_n, S_n will always be greater than n.

(*d*) *The Present Value of an Annuity*, or a_n (read as '*a* angle *n*'). This gives the equivalent at the beginning of n periods, of payments of 1 unit at the end of each of the n periods. It may alternatively be regarded as the amount which is necessary, allowing for interest that may be earned on the balance, to provide a payment of 1 unit at the end of each of n successive periods. If we assume n to be 8, it may be illustrated as follows:

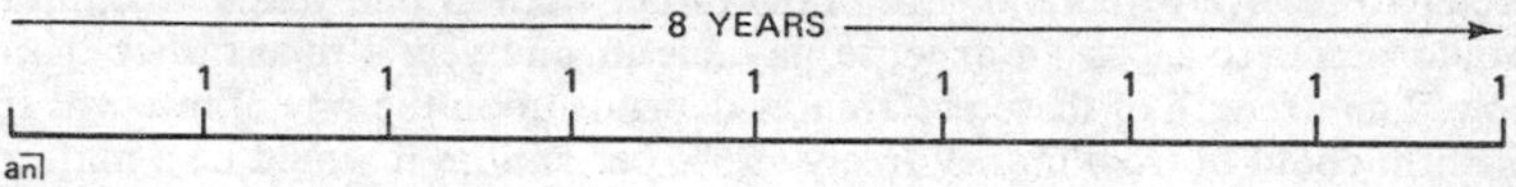

8 YEARS

1 1 1 1 1 1 1 1

$a_{\overline{n}|}$

Since interest will be added to the balance of $a_{\overline{n}|}$ not yet paid out, a_n will always be less than n.

These factors will obviously be different for different rates of interest. A limited number of values are given below on the basis of 6 per cent interest to enable the reader to understand the examples which follow.

Compound Interest Tables
6 per cent

n	$(1 + i)^n$	v^n	$s_{\overline{n}|}$	$a_{\overline{n}|}$
1	1.060	0.943	1.000	0.943
2	1.123	0.890	2.060	1.833
3	1.191	0.839	3.183	2.673
4	1.262	0.792	4.374	3.465
5	1.338	0.747	5.637	4.212
6	1.418	0.704	6.975	4.917
7	1.503	0.665	8.393	5.582
8	1.593	0.627	9.897	6.209
9	1.689	0.591	11.491	6.801
10	1.790	0.558	13.180	7.360
11	1.898	0.526	14.971	7.886
12	2.012	0.496	16.869	8.383
13	2.132	0.468	18.882	8.852
14	2.260	0.442	21.015	9.295
15	2.396	0.417	23.276	9.712
20	3.207	0.311	36.785	11.469
25	4.291	0.233	54.864	12.783
30	5.743	0.174	79.058	13.764
40	10.285	0.097	154.762	15.046
50	18.420	0.054	290.335	15.761

Returning to the illustration mentioned on page 175, we may now illustrate the use of the technique assuming that 6 per cent per annum can be earned on funds released or on money borrowed.

The present cost of the type-*A* machine is	£8,000
The present equivalent of the scrap value to be received in ten years is	
$1{,}000 \times v^{10} = 1{,}000 \times 0.558$	£ 558
The present cost is	£7,442

The present cost of the first type-*B* machine is	£4,000
The present cost of the second type-*B* machine after allowing for the scrap value of the first machine is	
$(4{,}000 - 500) \times v^{5} = 3{,}500 \times 0.747$	£2,614
	£6,614
The present equivalent of the scrap value to be recovered in ten years' time on the second machine is	
$500 \times v^{10} = 500 \times 0.558$	£ 279
The present cost is	£6,335

Such a calculation enables us to assess whether a type-*A* machine is sufficiently cheaper than two type-*B* machines to make it a better proposition.

A further illustration is the valuing of debentures or other loans. We may be asked on January 1st, 1979, at what price 8 per cent debentures may be purchased to give a return of 6 per cent per annum. They are repayable on December 31st, 1986 at par and interest is payable annually on December 31st.

The method is to obtain the present equivalent of the interest payments and the capital repayment separately and to add them together to give the appropriate price.

On December 31st, 1986, in exactly eight years £100 will be repaid for each nominal £100 of debentures held.	
The present value is $100 \times v^{8} = 100 \times 0.627$	£62.70
In the meantime £8.00 will be received at the end of each of the eight years. This is an annuity and the present equivalent is	
$8.00 \times a_{\overline{8}|} = 8.00 \times 6.209$	£49.67
The present equivalent on the basis of 6% p.a. is	£112.37

It will be noticed that although the debentures are nominally 8 per cent debentures, we are looking for a return of 6 per cent on our investment and consequently 6 per cent compound-interest tables are used.

In some cases it is necessary to reduce all costs and revenue to an annual basis. This must be done when we are comparing, for instance, machines or projects with a different life in order to obtain comparative costs.

We are presented with these alternatives: there is machine *X* costing £6,500 with a life of eight years and running costs of £2,150 per annum, and machine *Y* with the same capacity costing £4,500 with a life of five years and running costs of £2,100 per annum. Neither machine will have any scrap value. The necessary funds will be obtained by borrowing money at 6 per cent per annum, and we have to decide which is the better proposition.

The cost of machine X corresponds to an annual charge (really an annuity) of

$£6{,}500 \times \dfrac{1}{a_{\overline{8}|}} = 6{,}500 \div 6.209$	£1,047
The annual running costs are	£2,150
Capital and running costs on an annual basis	£3,197

The cost of machine Y corresponds to annual charge of

$£4{,}500 \times \dfrac{1}{a_{\overline{5}|}} = 4{,}500 \div 4.212$	£1,068
The annual running costs are	£2,100
Capital and running costs on an annual basis	£3,168

Thus machine Y is a marginally better proposition.

If the capacities of the machines were different it would be necessary to convert these annual costs to an annual cost per unit before making the comparison.

It must be emphasised that calculations such as these will not necessarily provide the last word when it comes to making the decision. The following points are among those which must also be taken into account.

(*a*) The effect of a changing price level. Will it be possible to buy machines later at present prices, and will annual running costs be affected?

(*b*) Are interest rates likely to change? The accuracy of the calculations depends in many cases on good correspondence between the rate of interest used in the calculations and the actual rate throughout the period concerned.

(*c*) How steady is the demand for the product? Operating below capacity may well have different effects on the level of costs with different machines.

(*d*) Is there a greater degree of uncertainty the further we look into the future? There is always some degree of uncertainty, but is there a serious risk that the demand for the product will disappear, or the equipment may become obsolete? If this is so, it will make the alternative with the shorter life the more attractive proposition, other things being equal.

(*e*) What is the effect of taxation? Generous taxation grants or allowances may affect considerably both the initial capital cost and the amount and timing of inward cash flows after taxation.

14
Published Company Accounts

We now reproduce the published accounts of the Transport Development Group PLC together with the notes which are relevant for our purpose.

The accounts are reproduced to give the reader some indication of a good style of presentation. Although greater conformity to a prescribed layout has been imposed by the latest legislation there is still an art in presenting data and the Institute of Chartered Accountants awards annual prizes for what are judged to be the best examples of this art.

The aim is to present a certain body of financial information, the contents of which are closely defined by laws and accounting practice in a form which is easily assimilated and pleasing (if such a term can be applied to company accounts).

It will be noticed that a considerable amount of statistical information is included in the accounts. Most of this is now required by law. We have not dealt with this in any detail as it does not present any accounting problems within the scope of this book. Similarly, although it will quickly date, the directors' report, notice of the meeting and financial calendar are included as examples of the type of statement of a year's activities most chairmen would be expected to produce.

The accounts are annotated with the pages on which particular items are referred to in previous chapters. This is designed to provide a handy index on the one hand and an essential guide for those readers who are primarily concerned with the understanding and interpretation of published accounts on the other.

Transport Development Group PLC Annual Report and Accounts (year ended December 31st. 1982)

The Year at a Glance

	1982 £000	*1981* *£000*
TURNOVER Chiffre d'affaires Omzet	347,786	*275,681*
PROFIT BEFORE TAX Resultats avant impôts Winst voor belasting	18,329	*15,166*
CAPITAL EMPLOYED Capitaux permanents Totaal vermogen	182,885	*167,263*
OPERATING PROFIT % OF TURNOVER Bénéfice d'exploitation par rapport au chiffre d'affaires en % Bedrijfswinst % van omzet	6.8%	*6.6%*
OPERATING PROFIT % OF CAPITAL EMPLOYED Bénéfice d'exploitation par rapport aux capitaux permanents en % Bedrijfswinst % van totaal vermogen	12.9%	*10.9%*
NET TANGIBLE ASSETS PER ORDINARY SHARE Actif net par action ordinaire Intrinsieke waarde per gewoon aandeel	95.7p	*91.1p*
EARNINGS PER ORDINARY SHARE Bénéfice net par action ordinaire Winst na belasting per gewoon aandeel	7.9p	*6.1p*
DIVIDENDS PER ORDINARY SHARE Dividende par action ordinaire Dividend per gewoon aandeel	4.45p	*4.25p*

Summary of Operating Results

FUNCTIONAL	£000	1982 %	*£000*	*1981 %*
TURNOVER *				
Road haulage	198,173	57.0	*161,179*	*58.5*
Storage	43,207	12.4	*38,579*	*14.0*
Plant hire and other transport services	22,499	6.5	*21,517*	*7.8*
Reinforcement and exhibitions	83,907	24.1	*54,406*	*19.7*
	347,786	100.0	*275,681*	*100.0*
PROFIT BEFORE TAX *				
Road haulage	11,613	49.3	*9,629*	*52.7*
Storage	8,311	35.3	*6,628*	*36.3*
Plant hire and other transport services	1,168	4.9	*1,143*	*6.2*
Reinforcement and exhibitions	2,476	10.5	*874*	*4.8*
	23,568	100.0	*18,274*	*100.0*
Net interest payable	5,239		*3,108*	
	18,329		*15,166*	

GEOGRAPHICAL				
TURNOVER *				
United Kingdom	212,001	61.0	*191,410*	*69.4*
Europe	63,447	18.2	*56,117*	*20.4*
Australia	20,870	6.0	*17,229*	*6.2*
North America	51,468	14.8	*10,925*	*4.0*
	347,786	100.0	*275,681*	*100.0*
PROFIT BEFORE TAX *				
United Kingdom	13,838	58.7	*11,079*	*60.6*
Europe	4,775	20.3	*4,992*	*27.3*
Australia	2,188	9.3	*1,538*	*8.4*
North America	2,767	11.7	*665*	*3.7*
	23,568	100.0	*18,274*	*100.0*
Net interest payable	5,239		*3,108*	
	18,329		*15,166*	
CAPITAL EMPLOYED				
United Kingdom	119,742	65.5	*115,820*	*69.2*
Europe	30,420	16.6	*27,084*	*16.2*
Australia	11,420	6.2	*10,997*	*6.6*
North America	21,303	11.7	*13,362*	*8.0*
	182,885	100.0	*167,263*	*100.0*

*** These sections form part of the audited accounts**

Report of the Directors (Year ended December 31st, 1982)

To make plans 'in case anything turned up' was a characteristic of Mr Micawber. It was widely shared in 1982. But, despite encouraging signs from time to time, very little has turned up. Certainly not the economy. For most companies it has been an aggressive hard slog to secure a modest increase in profits. That there is an increase is in considerable measure due to the hard work of the previous year in cutting costs and increasing efficiency. Profits are being made in the most adverse conditions.

Among Group executives no Micawbers remain, but, as things do turn up, profitability will rapidly increase.

Road Haulage in the United Kingdom

For road hauliers, the year started with appalling weather, the worst in living memory for some areas. Vehicle movements were hampered by treacherous roads, by freezing fuel, and by associated mechanical faults. Revenue fell and maintenance costs inevitably rose sharply during the period.

As the year progressed demand increased and this gave rise to some optimism. Neither the demand, nor the optimism, were long sustained. There has been some rise in traffic volume, but more is needed if laid up vehicles are to be restored to service and filled with traffic. Until that position is reached rates will not harden, and the haulier be able to secure the return on his investment which has for so long been lacking.

The fortunes of haulage companies are, in great measure, tied to those of their major customers. Movements of steel and heavy industrial products continued to decline, and companies dependent on such industries suffered. The decline was particularly marked in Scotland, and, towards the end of the year, Strathclyde Transport Services Limited was merged with McKelvie & Company (Transport) Limited. Tanker operations associated with the petro-chemical industry also had a hard time.

In the North of England Econofreight Transport Limited which, having moved away from its traditional steel traffic, now specialises in heavy haulage, made considerable progress. Two further hydraulic trailer units were added to its extensive range of specialised equipment. The company has been very active, and long term contract work has continued into the current year.

In the more specialised field of distribution much change and development is taking place. Operating companies have to be very alert and adaptable to such change in order to sustain profitability and enlarge market share, but there are many opportunities. Several small enterprises were acquired by Group subsidiaries during the year in order to extend distribution areas and provide additional depot accommodation. The contract hire fleets performed well.

At last the Government response to Armitage has reached the statute book and 38 tonne vehicles (provided they have five axles) may legally be operated from May 1st, 1983. Substantially increased excise duty is payable on these heavier lorries and operators may need some persuading to invest in expensive new equipment at the present time when a fair proportion of their existing fleets stand idle.

The report of the enquiry into the effects of restrictions on heavy lorries in London has been deferred until mid-1983. It is worth noting that in evidence to the enquiry, the Freight Transport Association stated that a ban by the GLC on all lorries over 16 tonnes gross would increase distribution costs in London by £780 million a year; if the ban were on lorries over 8½ tonnes gross the additional cost would be £2,100 million a year.

Storage in the United Kingdom

For most general warehouses low stock levels at the opening of the year had increased but little by the close. There was not much sign of the fall in interest rates persuading customers to invest in increased stocks. At the present time, warehouse managements face great difficulty in assessing likely future demand.

Distribution services for national companies were developed during the year by a number of subsidiaries. With a view to expansion in this sector of the market, J. A. Irving & Co. Limited, which operated warehouses in Warrington, Newton-le-Willows and Stretton, was absorbed in August by another subsidiary, Beck & Pollitzer Warehousing Limited which operates stores in London, Bristol and King's Lynn. The enlarged undertaking created by this merger is better able to handle demands for national distribution. The Beck & Pollitzer warehouses at Barking were extended during the year.

Other distribution companies are enlarging their operations. C. Albany & Sons Limited obtained Customs and Excise approval for storage of wines and spirits under bond at its Harlow warehouse and this facility has already attracted considerable interest among wine importers.

The new warehouse complex built by Storage & Haulage Limited on a 16 acre site at Grantham, to serve the distribution requirements of a major customer, was, despite much bad weather, completed on schedule in April. It is now operating twenty-four hours a day, seven days a week.

In December, London and Coastal Oil Wharves Limited purchased from the Receiver the assets and business of Thames Terminals Limited. The assets comprise 200,000 cubic metres of tankage on 35 acres of freehold land at Dagenham. The site, which has useful ancillary buildings, is adjacent to the Thames, and has a jetty able to accommodate vessels up to 35,000 dwt with 35 foot draught at low tide. This business is complementary to the existing business of London and Coastal and extends the range of services it is able to offer customers.

Though there were few indications at the start of the year, cold storage proved to be one of the major contributors to profits. Stocks at the beginning of the year were at an all time low, but, as the year progressed, large tonnages of EEC butter and New Zealand meat became available, and storage facilities were put under great pressure. Even the well publicised sale to the domestic market, towards the end of the year, of heavily subsidised butter from the EEC stock-pile so upset the sale of the current production that much of that tonnage had to be placed into store.

Increase in the profits of the cold storage companies has been achieved against a background of increasing costs, most notably in general and water rates and energy costs. With pressure on handling and storage rates still continuing, the results are attributable largely to the increase in stock levels and the attention given by executives to containing costs.

The new cold store at Newport, the opening of which was deferred last year, was brought into use as planned in March and, with traffic plentiful, profitable advantage was taken of this fine new facility.

The modernised ex-government cold store in Reading acquired by The Western Ice and Cold Storage Company Limited has been so successful that a major extension is now planned to meet demands from existing customers.

At the end of the year Yorkshire Cold Stores Limited bought a 10,195 cubic metre sub-zero cold store at Cannock near Wolverhampton so extending this company's spread of distribution stores.

For Freezing & Cold Store Services Limited which specialises in the freezing of vegetables, new arrangements for freezing root vegetables helped in what was a difficult year because of a shortfall in pea tonnage. This company has now established itself as a contract freezing plant of high calibre; its packing operations have been reorganised and re-equipped to good effect.

Plant Hire and Other Transport Services

Plant hire companies are traditionally dependent on the construction industry. After a poor start to the year, because of the bad weather, activity increased in the spring and raised hopes of continuing revival. As with road haulage, this did not last through the summer and there has since been little sign of revival.

Crane hire in particular suffered acutely from depressed hire rates. A large amount of surplus equipment overhangs the market. Even with a return to active conditions, it will be some years before all this equipment can hope to find active use. Crane hire facilities of Group subsidiaries are being concentrated in the London area.

It is increasingly obvious that small operating depots are uneconomic. A number of unprofitable outlets were closed during the year, and plant transferred to the larger profit centres.

Whilst the recession continues, capital projects remain scarce and plant hire companies have to be active and resourceful in seeking new markets, and in ensuring that their equipment programme anticipates change in demand. Their success in 1982 was shown by the fact that, despite all problems, profits were increased.

Industrial removal and engineering companies thrive during periods of high investment; they also benefit from factory closures and clearances; they suffer when industry stagnates. A major installation contract in Scotland, which began in 1981, continued throughout the year, and, as a result of supplementary work, has extended to March 1983. It has been of considerable help in a difficult period. One of the engineering depots in London has been closed and has since been sold. Considerable work was undertaken overseas with the installation of printing presses in Norway, Belgium, France, Italy, Spain and Egypt.

Trading was quiet for the freight forwarding and export packing companies and also for the French container service where rates were on very fine margins.

Reinforcement and Exhibitions

With a continuing weakness in United Kingdom demand for steel reinforcement, margins have been narrow and the market competitive. The difficulties were compounded by very cheap steel imports offered by overseas manufacturers. In spite of these difficulties, the Square Grip companies have so far continued to operate profitably, benefiting from stringent control of costs and the up-dating of automated equipment. The immediate prospects for the reinforcement industry are however somewhat bleak.

In October the old established business of J & A Binns was acquired. The company specialises in the production of high quality drawn wire and extends the range of wire products manufactured by Carrington Wire Limited. The two companies have now merged under one management and operate under the name of Carrington Binns Limited. It is an excellent foundation for further expansion in the wire industry.

For the exhibition companies, it can at least be said that the results were a considerable improvement on those of the previous year.

Beck & Pollitzer Contracts Limited were again appointed by the Society of British Aerospace Companies to carry out the main contract for stands at the biennial exhibition at Farnborough and the electrical division was appointed by the National Exhibition Centre to be the main electrical contractor for all exhibitions and events at the Centre for the next three years. Clements and Street Limited carried out a major contract for British Leyland, which was the largest exhibitor, at the Motor Show.

Since the end of the year, the 20 per cent interest which the Group held in Industrial and Trade Fairs Holdings Limited has been sold to Reed International PLC (which already owned 40 per cent) for a consideration of £780,000 in cash. The exhibition companies will continue to provide stand fitting and electrical services for the Industrial and Trade Fairs Group at the National Exhibition Centre and elsewhere in the UK and overseas as hitherto.

Europe

Despite difficult trading conditions in The Netherlands, profits for the Etom Group were only marginally below those of 1981. Companies transporting food and agricultural products prospered and some additional equipment was purchased. However, the deteriorating situation in the construction industry made life difficult for the heavy haulage and plant hire enterprises and, as in the United Kingdom, the depressed demands for chemical products affected the tank haulage companies.

The warehousing company at Leeuwarden in the north of Holland is extending its storage and container services and during the year purchased land adjacent to its existing premises to build a new warehouse.

The small contract hire company in Delft, International Transportbedrijf Kwaadland 'De Vrachttaxi' BV was sold to its chief executive, Mr J. C. Kwaadland, at its net asset value. The company had consistently failed to produce adequate profits; the size of the fleet has been steadily reduced; closure costs would have been high; there were no alternative buyers. It was a good solution for all concerned.

As a result of re-organisation and an increase in charges, the warehousing company in Belgium showed a significant improvement in results.

The political uncertainties for business in France increased during the year. The social policies of the government are leading to increased costs while price and wage controls interfere with normal market adjustments. Against this background the Ostra Group performed well.

In July, a warehousing and road haulage undertaking, Baillivet SA was acquired. Founded in 1964 the company specialises in long distance haulage between Lille, Paris and Rouen and it has modern warehouses in each of those cities. The head office is near Lille. The addition of these facilities in an area in France where industry and agriculture are highly developed has been most useful.

The distribution depot of Clergue Transports Frigorifiques SA which opened in Paris in 1981 has progressed well, and combined with a new depot at Toulouse opened in 1982, has enabled the company to extend its services.

Since the end of the year, Ostra has acquired Transports Liberatore, a haulage company based at Nancy. With a fleet of 25 vehicles, the company specialises in express delivery of paper, ink, books and materials connected with the printing and publishing industry in eastern France.

The Irish cold storage companies are heavily dependent on the levels of intervention stock and affected by changes in the Common Agricultural Policy. The active sales policy pursued by the intervention agency has reduced the storage time of beef stocks, and rental income suffered. However, towards the end of the year, there were signs that beef production was increasing and stocks should now rise.

Australia

The results of the Australian companies for the year to June 30th, which are those consolidated in Group results, were more than 30 per cent ahead of those of the previous year. This was largely due to a substantial increase in haulage profits. Margins showed a welcome increase and the buoyant conditions experienced by the car industry helped Arnolds Transport Pty. Limited whose principal activity is movement of new cars.

A record cotton crop helped to keep the Sydney warehouses filled to capacity, and a new store was built at Smithfield, New South Wales. Green McCandlish Limited also extended its warehousing activities at Brooklyn in Victoria by purchasing an adjacent site containing 5,600 square metres of warehouse space.

The demand for cold storage was somewhat lower than in the previous year. The crane hire company had a difficult time and produced lower profits.

Until the end of 1982, the Australian companies continued to trade well. But circumstances have materially changed with the declining economy. The early months of 1983 are proving exceptionally difficult for most companies, a position not made easier by the uncertainties following the election.

North America

In California, Willig Freight Lines Inc. has been obliged to come to terms both with recession (and it is the first year in which the impact has been significant on the west coast), and with the effects of de-regulation of the road transport industry. Many carriers are on the verge of bankruptcy and there have been a number of casualties. In this climate, Willig operated with its usual skill and efficiency, and although earnings were below projection, the results were satisfactory. There has been continued growth of business on the new routes to Arizona and Nevada with profits frequently exceeding targets.

There remain many opportunities for expansion in the western states, both in road transport and also in warehousing and cold storage.

Hausman Steel Corporation completed and commissioned its new plant in Denver, Colorado for the production of fabricated reinforcing bars and structural steel. At the year end a plant was under construction at Grand Rapids, Ohio, for the production, under licence, of epoxy coated reinforcing bars. The market for this latter product continues to grow in spite of the downturn in the construction industry for it has been found to be the best material to combat the problems of corrosion prevalent in many substructures of buildings, highways and bridges. Production has now begun.

In Canada, both Raymond Steel Limited and Rhodes-Vaughan Reinforcing Limited increased their turnover and earnings. Raymond Steel established a new manufacturing plant in Halifax, Nova Scotia, in order to meet the growing demand in the Maritimes. The plant commenced operation in 1983 and has a full order book for some months ahead.

However, overall in North America, market conditions for the reinforcement businesses are extremely difficult and competitive. It needs a pick up in the economy to restore a measure of life to the construction industry. The new 'nickel on the gallon' tax which provides specific funds for road building and repair may well be a stimulus in that direction.

Accounts

Group turnover has increased from £276 million to £348 million. After adjusting for the substantial acquisitions made in 1981, the increase over the previous year, on a like for like basis, is one of £36 million, or 13 per cent. Operating profit represented 6.8 per cent of turnover compared with 6.6 per cent in 1981. Return on capital employed was 12.9 per cent compared with 10.9 per cent.

Welcome though these increases may be, present trading conditions are holding margins considerably below those consistently attained in previous years, an indication of the profit potential of the Group as trading conditions return to a more normal basis.

The foundations of the Group are strong. Strength comes from the range and spread of activities, with more than 40 per cent of operating profit now being earned overseas, and from the basic financial position; cash flow in 1982 was £31 million, 24 per cent greater than in 1981.

In these days of volatile exchange rates, international companies can be exposed to considerable exchange risks. For the Group these risks are minimised; investment in overseas territories is, so far as practicable, matched by borrowing in the territories in which the investment takes place.

Net borrowings during the year increased from £36.1 million to £44.7 million and it is the intention, as soon as market conditions are appropriate, to arrange further long-term fixed rate borrowing by means of an issue of loan stock.

The accounts this year have been prepared to satisfy the requirements of the Companies Act, 1981, with comparative figures for 1981 being re-stated accordingly. The Act follows EEC demands for accounting uniformity within the Community. The result, in the initial stages at least, is to introduce a rigidity and complexity which is both uncomfortable and confusing.

The Company has always sought to produce accounts in a simple and clear manner and to give information beyond the statutory requirement where it appeared helpful. It was one of the early providers of accounting information adjusted for the effects of inflation, and has consistently provided such information since 1974.

However, the increasing complexity of accounts is now creating a situation where, for the general user the wood cannot be seen because of the trees. Relevence is concealed behind a mass of detail and trivia. In particular, the directors feel that the volume of current cost information required by Statement of Standard Accounting Practice No. 16 is out of all proportion to the benefit conferred, particularly when one bears in mind the somewhat arbitrary and subjective nature of some of the contents.

For that reason, the Board has included (on page 212) summarised current cost information only. Shareholders will see that any reader requiring a set of current cost accounts to SSAP 16 standards can obtain a copy on request to the Company Secretary.

In view of the record of the Company in accounting for inflation over the past eight years, the directors hope that the step taken will be seen as a positive rather than a negative contribution. They are wholly in favour of continuing efforts to find a practical system for determining 'real' profits. Current cost accounts may point in that direction, but are far from the last word. Unfortunately, the formality of their presentation in accordance with SSAP 16 vests them quite unjustifiably with an authority they do not, and should not, have.

Dividend

Because of the difficult trading conditions of recent years there has been no increase in dividend since 1979. In the light of the considerably improved results for 1982, both in current cost and historical cost terms, the directors now propose an increase. A final dividend on the Ordinary shares of 3.0p per share, making a total for the year of 4.45p (1981 4.25p), is recommended for payment on May 13th, 1983 to shareholders registered on April 8th, 1983.

Share Option Scheme

In 1973 shareholders approved a share option scheme, and a number of options under the scheme were granted to directors and managers throughout the Group in 1978. In May 1982 it was decided to grant further options (within the limits already authorised by shareholders) to existing participants, and to managers recruited or promoted since the first issue was made. In all, options to subscribe for a total of 652,500 shares at 82½p per share were granted. Such options, like the options previously granted, are exercisable under the terms of the scheme only after four years and not later than seven years from the date of grant. At the present time a total of 1,690,000 shares are under option.

Annual General Meeting

The annual general meeting will be held at Glaziers Hall, 9 Montague Close, London Bridge, London, SE1 9DD, on Friday April 29th, 1983 at 12 noon. This is a new location for the meeting and a location map accompanies the notice of meeting.

The director to retire by rotation is Mr C. J. Palmer who is aged 63. Mr Palmer was an executive of the Group for more than 30 years until his retirement in 1979, but is now a non-executive director and has no contract of service. Being eligible, he offers himself for re-election.

A resolution proposing the re-appointment of Dearden Farrow as auditors for the ensuing year will be put to the meeting.

It will be seen from the notice that there are two items of special business. These two items merely repeat resolutions passed last year, and, as explained then, are designed to give the directors a limited freedom of action in the issue and allotment of shares during the coming year.

Thanks to Employees

In hard times particularly, the support energy and loyalty of employees is paramount to success. Throughout the Group, every effort is made to see that exceptional contribution is recognised and well rewarded and that continuity of employment is secured so far as practicable. Thanks are due to many individuals throughout the Group for the contribution they have made to the results for the year.

Outlook for 1983

In the United Kingdom profits to date are ahead of the previous year, helped by the generally mild weather.

Overseas the pattern is mixed and the outlook more uncertain, particularly in the case of the North American reinforcement companies, but most executives remain optimistic.

On behalf of the Board.

James Duncan

Chairman.

March 14th, 1983

Appendix to the Report of the Directors

Directors' Interests

The following were directors of the company during the year; they and their families had interests in shares of the company and of its subsidiary Transport Development Australia Limted (TDA) as shown below:

	At January 1st, 1982	At December 31st, 1982
Sir James Duncan		
Ordinary shares	36,597	37,214
Ordinary share options	50,000	75,000
Ordinary shares of 50 cents of TDA	4,875	5,850
J. D. Lockhart		
Ordinary shares	20,978	20,978
Ordinary share options	40,000	60,000
Ordinary shares of 50 cents of TDA	5,452	6,542
C. J. Palmer		
Ordinary shares	22,990	22,990
Ordinary shares of 50 cents of TDA	1,089	1,306
J. Wishart		
Ordinary shares	13,279	13,279
Ordinary share options	35,000	52,500
Ordinary shares of 50 cents of TDA	1,874	2,248
D. S. Horner		
Ordinary shares	6,242	6,242
Ordinary shares (non-beneficial interest)	4,435	4,435
Ordinary share options	35,000	52,500
Ordinary shares of 50 cents of TDA	879	2,114
J. G. Lithiby		
Ordinary shares	400	400

There was no change in the interest of any director in the shares of the company or of its subsidiaries between the end of the year and March 14th, 1983.

Political and Charitable Contributions

	£
Aims of Industry	500
Centre for Policy Studies	2,000
Conservative Party	2,500
Economic League	800
Charitable contributions	10,905

Ownership of Ordinary Share Capital at December 31st

Category of holding	1982 %	1981 %
Banks and nominees	33.3	31.2
Insurance companies	21.9	21.4
Pension funds and charities	16.9	17.2
Investment trusts	5.2	5.4
Other holders	22.7	24.8
	100.0	100.0

Size of holding	1982 %	1981 %
1– 1,000 shares	2.8	3.1
1,001– 5,000 shares	9.2	9.9
5,001–10,000 shares	3.2	3.5
10,001 shares upwards	84.8	83.5
	100.0	100.0

Throughout the financial year the close company provisions of the Income and Corporation Taxes Act, 1970 did not apply to the company and no one person held or, so far as the company was aware, was beneficially interested in any substantial part of the share capital of the company. There was no change in the position at March 14th, 1983.

Consolidated Profit and Loss Account (Year ended December 31st, 1982)

	Notes	1982 £000	*1981 £000*
TURNOVER (pp. 13 and 184)	*2*	347,786	*275,681*
OPERATING EXPENSES (p. 13)	*3*	324,218	*257,407*
OPERATING PROFIT (p. 13)		23,568	*18,274*
Net interest payable (p. 31)	*4*	5,239	*3,108*
PROFIT ON ORDINARY ACTIVITIES BEFORE TAX	*2*	18,329	*15,166*
Tax (p. 129)	*5*	7,338	*6,659*
PROFIT AFTER TAX		10,991	*8,507*
Minority interests (p. 48)		480	*346*
		10,511	*8,161*
Extraordinary items	*6*	136	*760*
PROFIT AVAILABLE FOR APPROPRIATION		10,375	*7,401*
Dividends paid and proposed (p. 28)	*7*	5,973	*5,707*
TRANSFER TO RESERVES (p. 28)	*17*	4,402	*1,694*
EARNINGS PER ORDINARY SHARE (before extraordinary items)	*8*		
On attributable earnings		7.87p	*6.10p*
On pre-tax basis		13.16p	*10.99p*

Consolidated Balance Sheet (December 31st, 1982)

	Notes	£000	1982 £000	*£000*	*1981* *£000*
FIXED ASSETS (p. 79)	*9*				
Tangible assets (p. 95)			166,581		*158,143*
Investments (p. 115)			801		*805*
			167,382		*158,948*
CURRENT ASSETS (p. 2)					
Stocks (p. 87)	*10*	14,110		*14,308*	
Debtors (p. 72)	*12*	66,011		*58,578*	
Short term investments and deposits (p. 115)	*13*	7,212		*12,931*	
Cash at bank and in hand		1,167		*1,318*	
		88,500		*87,135*	
CREDITORS: DUE WITHIN ONE YEAR (p. 117)	*14*	82,601		*82,525*	
NET CURRENT ASSETS			5,899		*4,610*
TOTAL ASSETS LESS CURRENT LIABILITIES			173,281		*163,558*
CREDITORS: DUE AFTER ONE YEAR (p. 125)	*15*	36,620		*34,454*	
PROVISIONS FOR LIABILITIES (p. 125)	*16*	3,902		*3,005*	
INVESTMENT GRANTS		1,099		*914*	
			41,621		*38,373*
			131,660		*125,185*
CAPITAL AND RESERVES					
Called up share capital (p. 37)	*18*		34,617		*34,617*
Revaluation reserve (p. 111)			10,406		*10,406*
Other reserves (p. 39)	*17*		83,563		*77,431*
			128,586		*122,454*
MINORITY INTERESTS (p. 48)			3,074		*2,731*
			131,660		*125,185*

Parent Company Balance Sheet (December 31st, 1982)

	Notes	£000	1982 £000	£000	*1981 £000*
FIXED ASSETS (p. 79)	*11*		122,419		*119,172*
CURRENT ASSETS (p. 2)					
ACT recoverable after one year (p. 129)		1,711		*1,595*	
Debtors (p. 72)	*12*	531		*588*	
Short term investments and deposits (p. 115)	*13*	2,984		*1,000*	
Cash at bank and in hand		36		*72*	
		5,262		*3,255*	
CREDITORS: DUE WITHIN ONE YEAR (p. 117)	*14*	22,803		*19,376*	
NET CURRENT LIABILITIES			17,541		*16,121*
TOTAL ASSETS LESS CURRENT LIABILITIES			104,878		*103,051*
CREDITORS: DUE AFTER ONE YEAR (p. 125)	*15*		25,073		*23,278*
			79,805		*79,773*
CAPITAL AND RESERVES					
Called up share capital (p. 20)	*18*		34,617		*34,617*
Revaluation reserve (p. 111)			10,611		*10,611*
Other reserves (p. 39)	*17*		34,577		*34,545*
			79,805		*79,773*

The accounts were approved by the Board of Directors on March 14th, 1983.

JAMES DUNCAN J. D. LOCKHART

Notes on the Accounts

1. Accounting Policies

Basis of accounting

The accounts have been prepared under the historical cost basis of accounting as modified by the revaluation of certain assets.

Basis of consolidation

The accounts consolidate those of the company and its subsidiaries. The accounts are made up to December 31st, except that for administrative reasons the accounts of the subsidiaries on the mainland of Europe and in North America are made up to September 30th and those in Australia to June 30th.

The premium or discount on consolidation, being the difference between the value of attributable net tangible assets at the date of acquisition and the cost of shares acquired, is taken to reserves in the year of acquisition.

All amounts denominated in overseas currencies have been translated into sterling at the rates ruling at December 31st.

Differences arising on the translation of the net tangible assets of overseas subsidiaries at the beginning of the year and of foreign currency borrowings of the parent company to finance overseas assets are taken direct to reserves. All other currency differences are dealt with through the profit and loss account.

Depreciation

Freehold and long leasehold land is not depreciated.

Depreciation is provided on the cost or subsequent valuation of other tangible assets over their estimated useful lives on a straight line basis as follows:

Freehold and long leasehold buildings	20–50 years
Short leaseholds (less than 40 years to run)	Amortised over remaining life of lease
Motor vehicles	4–6 years
Trailers	8 years
Cranes, plant and furniture	4–10 years
Insulation and refrigeration plant	10–20 years

Investment grants are credited to revenue in equal annual amounts over the expected life of the asset.

Deferred tax

Deferred tax is provided when it is expected that the potential tax liability will be payable in the foreseeable future.

Stocks

Stocks and work in progress are stated at the lower of cost and net realisable value. The cost of work in progress includes a proportion of overhead.

Pensions

Group companies contribute to a variety of pension schemes and arrangements appropriate to the circumstances and countries in which they operate. The funds of the principal schemes are administered by trustees and are completely separate from the funds of the companies concerned. The schemes are reviewed every three years by independent actuaries and were fully funded at the last review; contributions paid in the light of such actuarial advice are charged as incurred against profits. Pensions in the course of payment are regularly reviewed.

2. Turnover and Profit before Tax

Turnover is based on the invoiced value of services and goods provided to external customers. VAT, similar sales related taxes and customs duties are excluded.

The analysis of turnover and profit by function and geographical location is set out (on page 184) and forms part of the accounts.

3. Operating Expenses

	1982	*1981*
	£000	*£000*
Hire of plant	1,686	*1,126*
Leasing charges	178	*31*
Raw materials consumables and other external charges	144,464	*109,337*
Staff costs	117,009	*94,984*
Redundancy costs	712	*852*
Depreciation (p. 100)	21,287	*17,749*
Auditors' remuneration	552	*484*
Other operating charges	38,575	*33,052*
	324,463	*257,615*
Release of investment grants	(161)	*(132)*
Income from:		
Listed investments (p. 115)	(15)	*(23)*
Unlisted investments	(69)	*(53)*
	324,218	*257,407*
Staff costs amounted to:		
Wages and salaries	99,917	*81,242*
Social security costs	14,724	*11,815*
Other pension costs	2,368	*1,927*
	117,009	*94,984*

The average weekly number of employees in the group during the year was made up as follows:

	1982 Number	*1981 Number*
Road haulage	5,745	*5,370*
Storage	1,505	*1,659*
Plant hire and other transport services	646	*707*
Reinforcement and exhibitions	1,097	*1,102*
Office and management	3,002	*2,939*
	11,995	*11,777*

At December 31st, 1982 one officer had a loan outstanding of £10,227.

	1982 £000	*1981 £000*
Directors' remuneration comprised:		
Management salaries	210	*197*
Pension contributions	76	*59*
Fees	13	*13*
Past director's pension	4	*4*
	303	*273*

The emoluments, excluding pension contributions, of the directors of the company and of employees of the group in the UK were within the following ranges:

	Directors 1982	Directors 1981	Employees 1982	Employees *1981*
£1– £5,000	1	1		
£10,001–£15,000	1	1		
£30,001–£35,000	—	—	7	*6*
£35,001–£40,000	—	1	4	*4*
£40,001–£45,000	1	1	2	*1*
£45,001–£50,000	1	—	—	—
£50,001–£55,000	1	1	—	—
£60,001–£65,000	—	1	—	—
£65,001–£70,000	1	—	—	—

The emoluments of the Chairman were £65,021 (1981 £61,532)

As stated in the 1981 accounts, the option which the company and Sir James Duncan each had to acquire the other's interest in a leasehold flat was terminated during 1982.

	1982 £000	*1981 £000*
Depreciation comprised:		
Provision for year	22,296	*19,487*
Amounts over provided in previous years	(1,009)	*(1,738)*
	21,287	*17,749*

4. Net Interest Payable

	1982 £000	*1981 £000*
Interest payable on:		
Short term borrowings and bank overdrafts	2,527	*999*
Loan capital:		
Repayable within 5 years	1,382	*1,741*
Repayable after 5 years	3,022	*1,702*
	6,931	*4,442*
Less:		
Short term interest receivable	1,692	*1,334*
	5,239	*3,108*

5. Tax

	1982 £000	*1981 £000*
The tax charge based on the profit on ordinary activities for the year is made up as follows:		
Corporation tax at 52% (p. 129)	3,942	*4,631*
Double tax relief	(38)	*(79)*
	3,904	*4,552*
Overseas tax (p. 134)	2,986	*1,743*
Deferred tax	448	*364*
	7,338	*6,659*

If full deferred tax had been provided the tax charge for the year would have been £8,513,000 (1981 £5,970,000).

6. Extraordinary Items

	1982 £000	*1981 £000*
Loss/(profit) on sale of properties (p. 108)	102	*(1)*
Closure costs (p. 174)	95	*905*
Other items	(12)	*348*
	185	*1,252*
Tax relief	49	*492*
	136	*760*

7. Dividends Paid and Proposed (p. 28)

	1982 p per share	1982 £000	*1981 p per share*	*1981 £000*
Ordinary shares:				
Interim	1.45	1,927	*1.45*	*1,927*
Proposed final	3.00	3,987	*2.80*	*3,721*
	4.45	5,914	*4.25*	*5,648*
Preference shares		59		*59*
		5,973		*5,707*

8. Earnings per Ordinary Share (p. 28)

	1982 £000	*1981 £000*
Earnings per ordinary share are based on the group profit before extraordinary items and after minority interests and preference dividends.		
On attributable earnings	10,452	*8,102*
On pre-tax basis (after minority interests of £782,000; 1981 £501,000)	17,488	*14,606*

Ordinary shares in issue ranking for dividend totalled 132,892,000. There is no material dilution of earnings per share as a result of the existence of the shares under option.

Fixed assets—Group

	TANGIBLE ASSETS					INVESTMENTS
	Freehold land & buildings £000	*Leasehold land & buildings* £000	*Vehicles* £000	*Plant & equipment* £000	*Total* £000	£000
Cost or valuation (p. 96):						
At beginning of year	79,171	11,495	101,029	48,023	239,718	805
Exchange rate adjustment	1,474	272	2,576	730	5,052	3
Companies acquired during year	2,209	—	1,262	1,160	4,631	15
Purchases	4,820	356	16,306	6,209	27,691	14
Sales	(2,391)	(34)	(9,277)	(3,238)	(14,940)	(36)
Cost or valuation at December 31st, 1982	85,283	12,089	111,896	52,884	262,152	801
Depreciation (p. 100):						
At beginning of year	4,341	966	52,497	23,771	81,575	—
Exchange rate adjustment	54	13	1,183	364	1,614	—
Companies acquired during year	—	—	462	113	575	—
Provision for year	1,517	358	15,348	5,073	22,296	—
Relating to sales	(188)	(25)	(7,780)	(2,496)	(10,489)	—
Depreciation at December 31st, 1982	5,724	1,312	61,710	26,825	95,571	—
Book-value at December 31st, 1982 (p. 96)	79,559	10,777	50,186	26,059	166,581	801
Cost or valuation at December 31st, 1982 includes assets valued at January 1st, 1978 (p. 111)	54,362	7,877	—	—	62,239	—

The book-value of leasehold property at December 31st, 1982 includes £4,918,000 (1981 £2,955,000) in respect of leases with less than 50 years to run from the balance sheet date.

It is not practical to identify the original cost to the group of those assets which are included at valuation at January 1st, 1978.

Investments at cost at December 31st, 1982 comprise listed investments of £426,000 (1981 £457,000) with a market value of £343,000 (1981 £272,000) and unlisted investments of £375,000 (1981 £348,000). The unlisted investments include a 20 per cent interest in Industrial and Trade Fairs Holdings Ltd at a cost of £216,000. This investment has been sold subsequent to the balance sheet date for an amount of £780,000.

10. Stocks (p. 91)

	1982 £000	*1981 £000*
Raw materials	7,410	*8,431*
Work in progress	1,267	*1,352*
Finished goods	1,108	*1,134*
Consumable supplies	4,879	*4,513*
	14,664	*15,430*
Receipts on account of work in progress	554	*1,122*
	14,110	*14,308*
Reinforcement steel	8,636	*9,653*
Transport and others	5,474	*4,655*
	14,110	*14,308*

11. Fixed Assets—Parent Company

	Tangible assets £000	*Invest-ments in subsidi-aries* £000	*Invest-ments* £000	*Total* £000
At beginning of year (p. 96):				
Cost	366	9,777	459	10,602
Valuation at January 1st, 1978	—	25,051	—	25,051
Purchases	61	6	—	67
Sales	(37)	—	(36)	(73)
At December 31st, 1982	390	34,834	423	35,647
Depreciation (p. 100):				
At beginning of year	115	—	—	115
Provision for year	43	—	—	43
Relating to sales	(29)	—	—	(29)
At December 31st, 1982	129	—	—	129
	261	34,834	423	35,518
Amounts due from subsidiaries (p. 46)	—	92,025	—	92,025
Amounts due to subsidiaries	—	(5,124)	—	(5,124)
Book-value at December 31st, 1982	261	121,735	423	122,419
Book-value at December 31st, 1981	251	118,462	459	119,172

The investments are listed and at December 31st, 1982 had a market value of £339,000 (1981 £266,000).

The original cost of the investments in subsidiary companies at December 31st, 1982 amounted to £21,992,000. Details of subsidiaries are set out on pages 216 to 220.

12. Debtors (p. 72)

	1982		*1981*	
	Group £000	Parent £000	*Group £000*	*Parent £000*
Trade debtors	56,530	—	*50,075*	—
Other debtors	1,748	185	*1,884*	*375*
Prepayments and accrued income	7,733	346	*6,619*	*213*
	66,011	531	*58,578*	*588*

13. Short Term Investments and Deposits (p. 115)

	1982		*1981*	
	Group £000	Parent £000	*Group £000*	*Parent £000*
Government securities	1,984	1,984	—	—
Certificates of tax deposit	1,000	1,000	*1,000*	*1,000*
Deposits	4,228	—	*11,931*	—
	7,212	2,984	*12,931*	*1,000*

The market value of the government securities is £1,997,000 (1981—nil).

14. Creditors: due within one year (p. 117)

	1982		*1981*	
	Group £000	Parent £000	*Group £000*	*Parent £000*
Current instalments due on loan capital	3,878	824	*2,191*	*1,663*
Unsecured bank overdrafts and short term loans	14,105	12,057	*15,763*	*6,557*
	17,983	12,881	*17,954*	*8,220*
Trade creditors	26,780	—	*23,474*	—
Corporate tax	6,783	4,461	*7,770*	*6,055*
Other creditors	18,023	1,340	*20,911*	*1,248*
Payroll taxes and social security	9,045	134	*8,695*	*132*
Proposed ordinary dividend	3,987	3,987	*3,721*	*3,721*
	82,601	22,803	*82,525*	*19,376*

In 1981 £1,377,000 of the bank overdrafts and short term loans of the group were secured.

15. Creditors: due after one year (p. 125)

	1982 Group £000	1982 Parent £000	*1981 Group £000*	*1981 Parent £000*
Loan capital	35,070	24,701	*32,378*	*22,575*
Corporate tax	1,550	372	*2,076*	*703*
	36,620	25,073	*34,454*	*23,278*

Loan capital comprises:			1982 £000	*1981 £000*
Unsecured				
Parent company:				
Currency	Rate %	Term		
£	7	1983–87	150	*151*
£	6¾	1989–94	2,346	*2,346*
£	8¼	1993–98	1,215	*1,252*
£	9¼	1995–2000	5,000	*5,000*
£	Variable	1991	5,000	*5,000*
Dfl	9½	1983	824	*1,489*
DM	10¾	1987	1,169	*1,049*
FFr	13½	1982	—	*919*
C$	Variable	1988	854	*749*
US$	Variable	1988–91	8,967	*6,283*
			25,525	*24,238*
Overseas subsidiaries:				
Currency	Rate %	Term		
Dfl	8⅛–10¼	1983–89	5,764	*5,213*
FFr	Variable	1983–90	3,042	*1,699*
BFr	Variable	1983–84	243	*306*
Ir£	Variable	1987	819	*785*
A$	Variable	1983–87	1,818	*1,035*
			37,211	*33,276*
Secured on tangible assets				
Overseas subsidiaries:				
Currency	Rate %	Term		
Dfl	5½–8½	1983–94	66	*68*
FFr	Variable	1983–92	1,142	*740*
US$	8½–10	1983–92	529	*485*
			1,737	*1,293*
			38,948	*34,569*
Less: Loan capital repayments due within 1 year			3,878	*2,191*
			35,070	*32,378*

	1982 Group £000	1982 Parent £000	*1981 Group £000*	*1981 Parent £000*
Repayable as follows:				
Between 1 and 2 years	2,980	—	*3,419*	*745*
Between 2 and 5 years	5,462	1,319	*4,073*	—
After 5 years	26,628	23,382	*24,886*	*21,830*
	35,070	24,701	*32,378*	*22,575*

£2,674,000 (1981 £2,448,000) of the loans of overseas subsidiary companies have been guaranteed by the parent company.

The total net borrowings of the group comprise:

	£000	1982 £000	*£000*	*1981 £000*
Loan capital:				
Repayments due within one year		3,878		*2,191*
Repayments due after one year		35,070		*32,378*
Bank overdrafts and short term loans		14,105		*15,763*
		53,053		*50,332*
Short term investments and deposits	7,212		*12,931*	
Cash at bank and in hand	1,167	8,379	*1,318*	*14,249*
		44,674		*36,083*

16. Provisions for Liabilities (p. 124)

	Deferred tax £000	*Overseas pension provision* £000	*Total* £000
At beginning of year	4,085	515	4,600
Exchange rate adjustment	295	93	388
Companies acquired	260	—	260
Transfer for the year	413	113	526
Payments made during year	—	(161)	(161)
	5,053	560	5,613
Advance corporation tax recoverable (1981 £1,595,000)	(1,711)	—	(1,711)
At December 31st, 1982	3,342	560	3,902

	1982 £000	*1981 £000*
No provision has been made for:		
Tax deferred principally by capital allowances	25,730	*24,545*
Tax deferred on properties sold	1,180	*958*
	26,910	*25,503*

It is not practical to quantify the notional tax liability which might arise if all the properties were sold at their book value. No provision has been made for any tax which may be payable on the distribution of reserves by overseas subsidiaries.

17. Other Reserves (pp. 26, 37)

	Group £000	Parent £000
At beginning of year	77,431	34,545
Exchange rate adjustment	1,203	(1,016)
Discount arising on consolidation	527	—
Surplus of the year retained	4,402	1,048
At December 31st, 1982	83,563	34,577

Reserves include a capital redemption reserve of £435,000 (1981 £435,000). The profit dealt with in the accounts of the parent company was £7,021,000 (1981 £6,329,000).

18. Called-up Share Capital (p. 26)

	Auth-orised £000	1982 issued called up & fully paid £000	*Auth-orised £000*	*1981 issued called up & fully paid £000*
Shares of 25p each	49,056	33,223	*45,000*	*33,223*
4.55 % Redeemable cumulative preference shares of £1 each	—	—	*450*	—
4.2 per cent cumulative preference shares of £1 each	1,394	1,394	*1,394*	*1,394*
Second preference shares of £1 each	—	—	*3,606*	—
	50,450	34,617	*50,450*	*34,617*

Under the 1973 share option scheme there are options, exercisable between 1983 and 1989, to purchase 1,690,000 ordinary shares at 82½p per share.

The unissued authorised preference shares were converted to unclassified shares of 25p each by a resolution dated April 30th, 1982.

19. Capital Commitments (p. 124)

	1982 £000	*1981 £000*
Outstanding contracts for capital expenditure	4,225	*4,837*
Capital expenditure authorised but not contracted for	11,935	*8,966*
	16,160	*13,803*

20. Exchange Rates (p. 124)

Assets, liabilities and profits of the year in overseas currencies have been translated into sterling at rates ruling at December 31st. The principal exchange rates used were:

	1982	*1981*
American dollar	1.62	*1.91*
Australian dollar	1.65	*1.69*
Canadian dollar	1.99	*2.27*
French franc	10.90	*10.93*
Dutch guilder	4.25	*4.70*

21. Companies Act, 1981

The accounts have been prepared in accordance with the requirements of the Companies Act, 1981 and comparative figures have been restated accordingly.

Source and Use of Funds (p. 53)

	1978 *£000*	*1979* *£000*	*1980* *£000*	*1981* *£000*	*1982* *£000*
SOURCE OF FUNDS					
Profit before tax	19,785	22,256	21,373	15,166	18,329
Deduct					
Tax paid	4,158	4,812	5,150	7,787	8,335
	15,627	17,444	16,223	7,379	9,994
Depreciation	12,436	14,488	16,285	17,749	21,287
Generated from trading operations	28,063	31,932	32,508	25,128	31,281
Sale proceeds/(cost) of investments	(245)	2,729	(546)	67	34
Net movements on investment grants and pension provision	214	225	256	203	80
Closure costs	—	—	—	(905)	(95)
	(31)	2,954	(290)	(635)	19
	28,032	34,886	32,218	24,493	31,300
USE OF FUNDS					
Net expenditure on tangible assets	21,467	22,993	22,987	21,053	22,333
Subsidiaries acquired	2,023	563	4,728	14,511	3,373
Minority interests acquired	109	—	865	—	93
Redemption of preference shares	—	—	—	456	—
Dividends paid:					
to minority and preference shareholders	189	240	190	222	187
to ordinary shareholders	4,403	5,051	5,648	5,648	5,648
	28,191	28,847	34,418	41,890	31,634
Increase/(decrease) in working capital					
Stocks	601	1,661	(1,448)	960	(1,280)
Debtors	4,941	9,947	(4,531)	4,725	4,992
Creditors	(4,340)	(7,708)	1,575	(6,142)	1,103
	1,202	3,900	(4,404)	(457)	4,815
	29,393	32,747	30,014	41,433	36,449
(Increase)/decrease in net borrowings	(1,361)	2,139	2,204	(16,940)	(5,149)
	28,032	34,886	32,218	24,493	31,300

The movement of funds during 1982 may be reconciled with the opening and closing balance sheets as follows:

	Balance sheet movement	*Acquisitions*	*Exchange*	*Extra-ordinary items*	*Movement of funds*
	£000	*£000*	*£000*	*£000*	*£000*
Tangible assets	29,725	(4,056)	(3,438)	102	22,333
Investments	(4)	(15)	(3)	(12)	(34)
Stocks	(198)	(26)	(1,056)	—	(1,280)
Debtors	7,433	(796)	(1,645)		4,992
Creditors	(768)	164	1,707		1,103
Investment grants and pension provision	(230)	—	150		(80)
Net borrowings	(8,591)	954	2,488		(5,149)
Other liabilities		116	594		
Discount on acquisition		286	—		
		(3,373)	(1,203)		

Current Cost Information (p. 111)

	1982	*1981*
	£000	*£000*
HISTORICAL COST OPERATING PROFIT	23,568	*18,274*
Deduct adjustments:		
Additional depreciation	6,632	*8,057*
Cost of sales	(66)	*438*
Monetary working capital	588	*599*
	7,154	*9,094*
CURRENT COST OPERATING PROFIT	16,414	*9,180*
Interest on net borrowings	5,239	*3,108*
Less: Gearing adjustment	1,872	*1,646*
	3,367	*1,462*
CURRENT COST PROFIT BEFORE TAX	13,047	*7,718*
	7,338	*6,659*
CURRENT COST PROFIT AFTER TAX	5,709	*1,059*
Minority interests and preference dividends	386	*237*
Extraordinary items	5,323	*822*
	776	*701*
CURRENT COST PROFIT ATTRIBUTABLE TO ORDINARY SHAREHOLDERS	4,547	*121*
CURRENT COST EARNINGS PER ORDINARY SHARE (BEFORE EXTRAORDINARY ITEMS)	4.01p	*0.62p*
CURRENT COST NET TANGIBLE ASSETS PER ORDINARY SHARE	131.2p	*124.5p*

Current cost accounts in accordance with Statement of Standard Accounting Practice No. 16 for the year to December 31st, 1982 have been prepared and audited, and will be supplied by the Company on request. Set out above is a summarised version of the current cost profit and loss account. The full accounts have not been reproduced for the reasons stated in the Report of the Directors (on p. 191).

Report of the Auditors

To the members of Transport Development Group PLC

We have audited the accounts (on page 184 and on pages 195–211) in accordance with approved Auditing Standards.

In our opinion the accounts, which have been prepared under the historical cost convention as modified by the revaluation of certain assets, give a true and fair view of the state of affairs of the company and the group at December 31st, 1982 and of the profit and source and use of funds of the group for the year then ended and comply with the Companies Acts 1948 to 1981.

The accounts do not contain sufficient current cost information to comply with Statement of Standard Accounting Practice No. 16.

The current cost information on page 111 is extracted from supplementary abridged current cost accounts upon which we have reported separately. Our report on those accounts states that, in our opinion, they have been properly prepared in accordance with the accounting policies and methods described in the notes thereon and give the information required by Statement of Standard Accounting Practice No. 16.

DEARDEN FARROW

Chartered Accountants, London, March 14th, 1983.

Statement of Value Added (p. 58)

	1978	*1979*	*1980*	*1981*	*1982*
	£000	*£000*	*£000*	*£000*	*£000*
TURNOVER	219,448	248,246	263,682	275,681	347,786
Deduct					
Cost of services and materials purchased	113,339	127,823	134,414	143,822	185,210
VALUE ADDED	106,109	120,423	129,268	131,859	162,576
Applied as follows:					
EMPLOYEES	71,316	80,436	89,033	95,836	117,721
GOVERNMENTS (CORPORATE TAX)	5,694	7,506	6,810	6,659	7,338
PROVIDERS OF CAPITAL:					
Net interest payable	2,572	3,243	2,577	3,108	5,239
Minority and preference shareholders	396	350	453	405	539
Ordinary shareholders	4,786	5,648	5,648	5,648	5,914
REINVESTMENT IN THE BUSINESS:					
Depreciation	12,436	14,488	16,285	17,749	21,287
Profit retained (excluding extraordinary items)	8,909	8,752	8,462	2,454	4,538
	106,109	120,423	129,268	131,859	162,576

The above figures showing the application of value added may be expressed in percentage terms as follows:

	%	%	%	%	%
Employees	67.2	66.8	68.9	72.7	72.4
Governments	5.4	6.2	5.3	5.1	4.5
Providers of capital	7.3	7.7	6.7	6.9	7.2
Reinvestment in the business	20.1	19.3	19.1	15.3	15.9
	100.0	100.0	100.0	100.0	100.0

Five-year Record (p. 15)

	1978	*1979*	*1980*	*1981*	*1982*
	£000	*£000*	*£000*	*£000*	*£000*
TURNOVER	219,448	248,246	263,682	275,681	347,786
Operating profit	22,357	25,499	23,950	18,274	23,568
Net interest payable	2,572	3,243	2,577	3,108	5,239
PROFIT BEFORE TAX	19,785	22,256	21,373	15,166	18,329
Tangible assets	127,682	134,634	141,527	158,143	166,581
Investments	1,735	671	1,190	805	801
Net current assets (excluding cash and short term borrowings)	7,172	9,784	3,645	8,315	15,503
NET ASSETS EMPLOYED	136,589	145,089	146,362	167,263	182,885
Ordinary shareholders' funds	102,051	110,824	117,571	121,060	127,192
Preference share capital	1,829	1,829	1,829	1,394	1,394
Minority interests	2,727	2,604	2,123	2,731	3,074
Deferred liabilities and provisions	4,057	6,463	5,778	5,995	6,551
Net borrowings	25,925	23,369	19,061	36,083	44,674
CAPITAL EMPLOYED	136,589	145,089	146,362	167,263	182,885
	%	%	%	%	%
Operating profit as a percentage of capital employed	16.4	17.6	16.4	10.9	12.9
	p	*p*	*p*	*p*	*p*
Earnings per ordinary share on attributable earnings	10.3	10.8	10.6	6.1	7.9
Dividends gross per ordinary share	5.2	6.1	6.1	6.1	6.4
Net tangible assets per ordinary share	76.8	83.4	88.5	91.1	95.7

List of Subsidiary Companies and their Activities

Unless stated otherwise subsidiary companies:

(i) Have a share capital consisting solely of ordinary shares wholly owned by Transport Development Group PLC.
(ii) Are incorporated in Great Britain and registered in England.
(iii) Operate principally in the country in which they are incorporated.

Subsidiaries whose shares are held directly are marked *; in all other cases the shares are held by intermediate subsidiaries.

Subsidiaries marked † are audited by the parent company's auditors Dearden Farrow and comprise the main UK holding companies and a significant proportion of trading subsidiaries based in southern England. In view of the number and geographical spread of the trading subsidiaries, it is the policy of the company to appoint auditors on a regional basis.

The statement includes the principal subsidiaries at December 31st, 1982.

Southern Area Transport Group Ltd *†
'A non-trading holding company.'

C. Albany & Sons Ltd †
Haulage, warehousing, distribution.

Beck & Pollitzer Engineering Ltd
Contract engineering, factory removals.

Beck & Pollitzer Packing & Shipping Ltd
Packing, forwarding, exhibition transportation.

Beck & Pollitzer Warehousing Ltd
Distribution and warehousing.

Becks Industrial Contracts Ltd
Machinery removals, haulage, lifting services.

Collings & Stevenson (Contracts) Ltd
Haulage, contract hire.

Contract Hire (Commercial Vehicles) Ltd †
Contract hire.

Cousins Transport Ltd †
Haulage, commercial vehicle repairs.

Crow Carrying Company Ltd †
Bulk haulage of liquids.

Dallas (Kingston) Ltd †
Heavy haulage, machinery removals, contract hire and warehousing.

The Erith and Dartford Lighterage Co. Ltd †
Lighterage, wharfage, warehousing, haulage.

Hatfield Warehousing and Distribution Ltd †
Storage and distribution.

LBS Cold Stores Ltd †
Cold storage.

London and Coastal Oil Wharves Ltd †
Oil and chemical storage, oil and solvent recycling.

Molo Transport Ltd †
Refrigerated and general haulage, commercial vehicle repairs.

Plymouth Cold Stores Ltd †
Cold storage at Plymouth and Exeter.

J. Spurling Ltd †
Haulage, contract hire, warehousing.

Transcontainer Express Ltd †
Container services to and from Europe.

Welsh Cold Stores Ltd †
Cold storage at Cardiff, Newport, Swansea.

The Western Ice and Cold Storage Co. Ltd †
Cold storage and refrigerated distribution.

Western Transport Ltd †
Haulage, warehousing, distribution.

Midpeak Holdings Ltd *†
A non-trading holding company.

Beck & Pollitzer Manchester Ltd †
Contract engineering services.

Blyth Cold Stores Ltd
Cold storage at Retford and Derby.

Cleveland Tankers Ltd
Haulage of liquids.

DMT Transport Ltd
Haulage, contract hire, storage, distribution.

Econofreight Transport Ltd
Heavy haulage, project management, forwarding.

Flowers Transport Ltd
Haulage, warehousing and distribution.

Freezing & Cold Store Services Ltd
Cold storage, freezing and packaging.

Gilyott and Scott Ltd
Lighterage, warehousing, haulage, shipping and forwarding.

Hereford Transport Ltd †
Haulage, warehousing and open storage.

Midlands Storage Ltd
Warehousing and distribution.

R. Rankin & Sons Ltd
Haulage of liquids, general haulage.

J. Stirland Ltd
Haulage, warehousing.

Storage & Haulage Ltd
Storage and distribution, haulage.

Tuffnells of Sheffield Ltd
Storage, express parcels service.

A. M. Walker Ltd
Haulage, powder tankers, contract hire.

Williams Bros (Wales) Ltd
Haulage, distribution, warehousing.

Williams Cold Storage (Thetford) Ltd †
Freezing, cold storage, haulage.

Yorkshire Cold Stores Ltd
Cold storage.

Freight Transport Holdings Ltd *†
A non-trading holding company.

Autozero Ltd
Cold storage, blast freezing.
Incorporated in the Republic of Ireland.

Buckley Tankers Ltd
Haulage of liquids.

William Harper & Sons Ltd
Haulage, commercial vehicle engineering.

Harris Road Services Ltd
Haulage, warehousing, distribution.

Harris Warehousing & Distribution Ltd
Storage and distribution.

Liverpool Cold Stores Ltd
Cold and cool air storage, refrigerated distribution.

The Liverpool Warehousing Company Ltd
Bonded and free warehousing, distribution, forwarding.

Manchester Haulage & Warehousing Ltd
Haulage, warehousing, cool storage.

Old Hall Estates Ltd
Commercial premises, building services

Parker's Transport Ltd †
General and contract haulage.

Reliance Tankers Ltd
International haulage of liquids and powders.

W. & J. Riding Ltd
Haulage, bulk powder transport.

Runcorn Transport Services Ltd
Haulage, road-rail services, warehousing.

Smiths of Eccles Ltd
Haulage, plant installation, warehousing, contract hire.

Trafford Park Cold Storage Ltd
Cold storage, ice manufacture, haulage.

Waterford Cold Stores Ltd
Cold storage, blast freezing.
Incorporated in the Republic of Ireland.

Westinghouse Cool Storage Ltd
Cool storage, distribution, transport.

Cairngorm Holdings Ltd *†
A non-trading holding company.

All companies in this section are registered in Scotland.

Aberdeen Ice Company Ltd
Ice manufacture, cold storage, freezing.

Carfin Bonded Warehouses Ltd
Bonded warehousing and blending.

Charles Alexander and Partners (Transport) Ltd
Haulage.

Connal & Company Ltd
Warehousing and distribution, haulage.

Glasgow Hiring Company Ltd
Distribution, warehousing, transport.

Highland Haulage Ltd
Haulage, warehousing and distribution.

Inter-City Transport & Trading Co. Ltd
Haulage, warehousing and distribution.

McKelvie & Company (Transport) Ltd
Haulage, warehousing, contract hire.

McPhersons' Transport (Aberlour) Ltd
Haulage, storage, vehicle repairs.

James Paterson Transport Ltd
Haulage, warehousing and distribution.

Russell of Bathgate Ltd
Haulage, storage.

John Russell (Grangemouth) Ltd
Haulage and warehousing.

Thomas Smith Jnr (Newhaven) Ltd
Haulage, storage and warehousing.

Sutherlands of Peterhead (Road Hauliers) Ltd
Haulage, warehousing, heated storage.

Square Grip Ltd *†
A non-trading holding company.

Carrington Binns Ltd
Manufacture of wire.

Jones Reinforcement Ltd †
Manufacture of steel reinforcement.

Square Grip (Eastleigh) Ltd †
Manufacture of steel reinforcement.

Square Grip International Ltd †
Export of steel reinforcement.

Square Grip (London) Ltd †
Manufacture of steel reinforcement.

Square Grip (Midlands) Ltd
Manufacture of steel reinforcement.

Square Grip (Northern) Ltd
Manufacture of steel reinforcement.

Square Grip Reinforcement (Scotland) Ltd
Manufacture of steel reinforcement.

Square Grip (Western) Ltd †
Manufacture of steel reinforcement.

Weldgrip Ltd
Manufacture of steel reinforcement.

Betonijzerbuigcentrale en Handelmaatschappij BV (90%)
Manufacture of steel reinforcement.
Incorporated in The Netherlands.

Hausman Steel Corporation
Manufacture of steel reinforcement.
Incorporated in Delaware USA

Raymond Steel Ltd (70%)
Manufacture of steel reinforcement.
Incorporated in Ontario, Canada.

Rhodes–Vaughan Reinforcing Ltd (70%)*
Manufacture of steel reinforcement.
Incorporated in Canada.

Exhibition Developments Ltd *†
A non-trading holding company.

Beck & Pollitzer Contracts Ltd
Worldwide exhibition construction.

Clements and Street Ltd
Exhibition stands, showrooms and displays.

Priestley Studios Ltd
Screen-printing, industrial printing, displays.

Gielissen's Bedrijven BV
Exhibition stands, storefitting.
Incorporated in The Netherlands.

H. Cox & Sons (Plant Hire) Ltd*
A non-trading holding company.

Beck & Pollitzer Crane & Transport Ltd
Crane and fork lift hire, heavy haulage.

Cox Plant Hire London Ltd
Crane, plane and portable accommodation hire, compressed air rental.

Cox Plant Hire Midlands Ltd
Plant and portable accommodation hire.

Cox Plant Hire Northern Ltd
Plant and portable accommodation hire.

Mansfield Plant Hire Ltd
Plant and tool hire.

Omnium de Stockage et de Transport (OSTRA) SA
A non-trading holding company.

All companies in this section are incorporated in France.

Baillivet SA
Haulage, distribution and warehousing.

Clergue Transports Frigorifiques SA (85%)
Refrigerated transport, cold storage.

Eurotex SARL
Heavy haulage.

Frimeyz SARL (80%)
Cold storage and distribution.

Royer et Cie SA
Long distance haulage.

Société de Messagerie et d'Affrètement (SOMAF) SARL
Parcel deliveries and forwarding.

Translittoral SARL
Contract hire and long distance haulage.

Transports A. Berthet et Cie SA
Parcels and distribution services.

Transports Liberatore SA
Haulage, distribution and warehousing.

Transports Marye SA
General haulage, warehousing.

Transunionvrac SARL
Contract hire and long distance haulage.

Europa Transport Ontwikkelings Maatschappij 'ETOM' NV
A non-trading holding company.

Companies in this section are incorporated in The Netherlands unless stated otherwise.

Internationaal Transportbedrijf Gebr Althuisius BV
Haulage, warehousing, bulk transport.

Gebr van den Bos Transporten BV
Haulage of flowers and vegetables.

Adr van Daalen & Zn BV
Haulage of fruit and vegetables.

Internationaal Transportbedrijf E. J. van Dijk BV
Haulage, industrial removals, cranes.

International Transportbedrijf E. J. van Dijk Belgium NV
National and international haulage.
Incorporated in Belgium.

Jawico BV
National and international tank haulage.

BV Internationaal Transportbedrijf KLMV (68%)
Haulage, warehousing.

König Transport BV
Haulage, ferry services.

Priems BV
Haulage of concrete and indivisible loads.

Rombouts Internationale Transporten BV
General and refrigerated haulage.

Jos Schreurs NV
Haulage, warehousing and distribution.
Incorporated in Belgium.

Vereinigte Spediteure GmbH
Haulage, warehousing and distribution.
Incorporated in W Germany.

Verenigd Veembedrijf BV
Warehousing, cold storage.

Handels-en Transportbedrijf Joh de Waal BV
Haulage, heavy haulage.

The reinforcement companies in N America are listed in the Square Grip section on page 218.

Transport Holdings Inc.
A non-trading holding company.
Incorporated in Delaware, USA.

Willig Freight Lines Inc.
Common carrier.
Incorporated in California, USA.

Transport Development Australia Ltd
A non-trading holding company.

All companies in this section are incorporated in Australia, and are 70 per cent owned.

Arnolds Transport Pty Ltd
Haulage of cars, containers, general freight.

De Julia Transport Pty Ltd
General warehousing.

Footscray Mobile Cranes & Transport Pty Ltd
Crane hire, machinery installation, cartage.

Green McCandlish Ltd
Cartage, storage, machinery removals.

Greenway's Refrigerated Transport (Vic) Pty Ltd
Refrigerated haulage.

McInnes Transport Pty Ltd
Cartage, storage, industrial removals.

John Pinnell Cold Stores Pty Ltd
Cold storage, freezing, refrigerated transport.

Vales Cold Stores Pty Ltd
Cold storage, refrigerated transport.

Overseas financial holding companies.

T. D. Holdings BV*
Incorporated in The Netherlands.

T. D. Finance BV*
Incorporated in The Netherlands.

TDG-USA Inc.
Incorporated in Delaware, USA.

Transport Development Holdings Ltd
Incorporated in Australia.

Notice of Meeting

Notice is hereby given that the thirty-fourth annual general meeting of Transport Development Group PLC will be held at Glaziers Hall, 9 Montague Close, London Bridge SE1 9DD on Friday April 29th, 1983 at twelve noon for the following purposes:

1. To consider the accounts for the year ended December 31st, 1982 and the reports of the directors and auditors thereon.

2. To declare a dividend on the ordinary shares.

3. To elect a director.

4. To appoint auditors.

5. To authorise the directors to fix the remuneration of the auditors.

As special business to consider and if thought fit pass the following ordinary and special resolutions.

Ordinary resolution

6. That the Board be and it is hereby generally and unconditionally authorised to exercise all powers of the Company to allot relevant securities (within the meaning of Section 14 of the Companies Act, 1980) up to an aggregate nominal amount of £10 million provided that this authority shall expire on the date of the next annual general meeting of the Company after the passing of this resolution save that the Company may before such expiry make an offer or agreement which would or might require relevant securities to be allotted after such expiry and the Board may allot relevant securities in pursuance of such offer or agreement as if the authority conferred hereby had not expired.

Special resolution

7. That subject to the passing of the previous resolution the Board be and it is hereby empowered to allot equity securities pursuant to the authority conferred by the previous resolution as if sub-section (1) of Section 17 of the Companies Act, 1980 did not apply to any such allotment provided that this power shall be limited.

(*a*) to the allotment of equity securities in connection with a rights issue in favour of ordinary shareholders where the equity securities respectively attributable to the interests of all ordinary shareholders are proportionate (as nearly as may be) to the respective numbers of ordinary shares held by them, and;

(*b*) to the allotment (otherwise than pursuant to sub-paragraph (*a*) above) of equity securities up to an aggregate nominal value of £2.45 million.

and shall expire on the date of the next annual general meeting of the Company after the passing of this resolution save that the Company may before such expiry make an offer or agreement which would or might require equity securities to be allotted after such expiry and the Board may allot equity securities in pursuance of such an offer or agreement as if the power conferred hereby had not expired.

Any member of the Company entitled to attend and vote at the meeting is entitled to appoint one or more proxies to attend and vote instead of him. A proxy need not be a member.

By order of the Board.

R. D. GARWOOD, *Secretary*.

Kingsgate House,
66/74 Victoria Street, London SW1E 6SR
April 5th, 1983.

Copies of the contracts of service of the directors are available for inspection at the registered office of the Company during usual business hours and also at the place of meeting from 11.45 a.m. until its conclusion.

Financial calendar

Final ordinary dividend payable on May 13th, 1983 to shareholders registered on April 8th, 1983.

Half-year results expected to be announced on August 15th, 1983.

Interim ordinary dividend normally payable in the first week of November.

Exercises—First Series

Examples from Chapter 1 (Answers on page 316)

No. 1

Certain mistakes have been made in drawing up the following Balance Sheet of M. Rose:

BALANCE SHEET
(as at December 31st, 19. .)

	£	£		£
Capital Account:			Freehold Premises	3,000
Jan. 1st, 19. .	6,000		Stock, Dec. 31st, 19. .	2,845
Add Loan Received from H. Glass	1,000		Plant and Machinery	2,560
		7,000	Cash in Hand	78
Net Profit for Year	1,368		M. Rose, Drawings	702
Sundry Debtors	1,412		Bank Overdraft	349
Stock, Jan. 1st, 19. .	1,634		Sundry Creditors	1,880
	£11,414			£11,414

Show the Balance Sheet as it should be.

Examples from Chapter 2 (Answers on page 316)

No. 2

From the following trial balance and the account 'Wilkinson, Capital', prepare a Balance Sheet, Statement of Proprietor's Capital, and Profit and Loss Account for the Golden Gate Landscaping Company.

GOLDEN GATE LANDSCAPING COMPANY

TRIAL BALANCE
(December 31st, 19..)

	£	£
Cash	562	
Debtors	2,116	
Garden Supplies	402	
Lorry	2,100	
Accumulated Depreciation—Lorry		560
Gardening Tools	317	
Prepaid Insurance	109	
Creditors		107
Contracts Payable (11 payments @ £60/mo.)		660
Wilkinson, Capital		4,500
Wilkinson, Drawings	3,600	
Income From Landscaping		7,350
Telephone	50	
Garden Supplies Used	2,516	
Depreciation—Lorry	560	
Petrol and Oil	373	
Office Supplies	27	
Insurance	207	
Sundry Expenses	238	
	£13,177	£13,177

WILKINSON, CAPITAL

	19..	£
	Jan. 1st Balance	3,500
	May 6th Cash	1,000

No. 3

Using the same data as in the previous example show only the liabilities and owner's equity sections of the Balance Sheet when no separate Statement of Proprietor's Capital is used.

No. 4

From the following trial balance of Santini & Casey, Insurance Brokers, and the two capital accounts shown, prepare a Balance Sheet (showing a detailed equity section) and an Income Statement.

SANTINI & CASEY, INSURANCE BROKERS

TRIAL BALANCE
(As at December 31st, 19.8)

	£	£
Cash	4,015	
Debtors	700	
Commissions Receivable	5,603	
Office Supplies	1,210	
Office Furniture	9,315	

Accumulated Depreciation— Office Furniture		3,702
Motor Vehicles	7,600	
Accumulated Depreciation— Motor Vehicles		3,300
Prepaid Insurance	570	
Prepaid Rent	600	
Premiums Payable		2,950
Creditors		111
M. Santini, Capital		10,000
M. Santini, Drawings	5,200	
W. Casey, Capital		10,000
W. Casey, Drawings	5,200	
Commissions Income		29,585
Wages	9,050	
Rent	2,400	
Telephone	1,100	
Office Supplies Used	560	
Insurance	210	
Vehicle Running Expenses	2,300	
Depreciation— Office Equipment	955	
Depreciation— Motor Vehicles	2,010	
Sundry Expenses	1,050	
	£59,648	£59,648

M. SANTINI, CAPITAL

	19.8			
				£
	Jan.	1st	Balance	8,000
	March	3rd	Cash	2,000

W. CASEY, CAPITAL

	19.8			
				£
	Jan.	1st	Balance	10,000

No. 5

From the data given in the previous example prepare a separate Statement of Partners' Capital and show how the liability and equity sections of the Balance Sheet would appear.

No. 6

The partnership agreement between Messrs Brick, Bat and Rubble contained the following provisions:

	Brick	*Bat*	*Rubble*
Fixed Capital	£16,000	£12,000	£10,000
Salaries	—	£1,000	£900
Interest on Fixed Capital	7%	7%	7%
Profit-sharing Ratio	3 :	2 :	2
Current-Account Balance, at Jan. 1st	£500	£400	£450
Drawings during Year	£2,000	£1,400	£1,100

The year's profits of the partnership before charging items included above was £7,430.

Show the Profit and Loss Appropriation Account and the Current Accounts of the partners for the year in question.

Examples from Chapter 3 (Answers on page 321)

No. 7

The following is the Balance Sheet of Messrs Hit and Miss, who share profits in the ratio of 3:2.

BALANCE SHEET

	£	£		£
Capital: Hit	8,000		Assets	20,000
Miss	5,000			
		13,000		
Liabilities		7,000		
		£20,000		£20,000

The business has been valued and the net worth is £18,000. It is decided to introduce a new partner, Target, who has £6,000 to contribute. The profits are to be shared in the ratio of 4:3:3.

(*a*) Show the Balance Sheet after goodwill has been entered in the accounts, and Target has been introduced into the partnership.

(*b*) Show the Balance Sheet when the goodwill has been eliminated after the admission of Target.

(*c*) Show the Balance Sheet and the payment made to the other partners if Target pays a premium for admission to the partnership.

No. 8

From the information contained in the following two Balance Sheets, prepare a Consolidated Balance Sheet of Shark Ltd and its subsidiary as at December 31st.

SHARK LTD

BALANCE SHEET
(as at December 31st, 19..)

	£		£
Share Capital	150,000	Fixed Assets	120,000
Reserves	40,000	30,000 shares in Minnow Ltd (acquired on Jan. 1st)	45,000
Liabilities	75,000	Current Assets	100,000
	£265,000		£265,000

MINNOW LTD

BALANCE SHEET

(as at December 31st, 19..)

	£		£
Share Capital		Fixed Assets	40,000
40,000 £ shares	40,000	Current Assets	33,000
Reserves at Jan. 1st	12,000		
Profit for Year	6,000		
Liabilities	15,000		
	£73,000		£73,000

No. 9

From the information contained in the following two Balance Sheets prepare a Consolidated Balance Sheet of House Ltd and its subsidiary Hut Ltd as at December 31st.

HOUSE LTD

BALANCE SHEET

(as at December 31st, 19..)

	£		£
Share Capital	200,000	Fixed Assets	160,000
Reserves	50,000	40,000 shares in Hut Ltd	
Liabilities	60,000	(acquired on Jan. 1st)	54,000
		Loan to Hut Ltd	6,000
		Current Assets	90,000
	£310,000		£310,000

BALANCE SHEET OF HUT LTD

(as at December 31st, 19..)

	£		£
Share Capital			
50,000 £ shares	50,000	Fixed Assets	50,000
Reserves at Jan. 1st	5,000	Stock bought from House	
Profit for Year	7,500	Ltd for £750	1,000
Loan from House Ltd	6,000	Other Current Assets	51,500
Other Liabilities	34,000		
	£102,500		£102,500

Examples from Chapter 4 (Answers on page 324)

No. 10

Trunk Ltd opened a branch at Southend on January 1st. All merchandise is provided by the head office and is invoiced to the branch at selling price. The following is a summary of the transactions for the first year:

		£
Goods from Head Office	(cost price)	6,000
" " " "	(selling price)	8,000
Goods returned to Head Office	(cost price)	600
" " " " "	(selling price)	800
Proceeds from cash sales remitted to Head Office		6,500
Stock-in-hand, December 31st, 19. .	(selling price)	600
Stock-on-hand, December 31st, 19. .	(cost price)	450

Show in summary form the entries that would appear in the Head Office books if the selling price entries were treated as memorandum entries.

No. 11

From the information in the previous example, prepare the summarised entries if the goods were transferred at selling price, and the selling price were recorded in the Branch Account. Include the adjustments necessary at the end of the year.

No. 12

100 units were consigned by Senders Ltd to Sellers Ltd at £10 each. Expenses amounting to £180 were paid by Senders Ltd, and £250 by the consignee, Sellers Ltd. 70 units have been sold by Sellers Ltd for £1,800, their commission being 10 per cent on sales. £1,000 has been remitted back to Senders Ltd.

Show the entries in the books of Senders Ltd and balance the Consignment Account.

No. 13

From the details in the previous example, show the entries in the books of Sellers Ltd.

Examples from Chapter 5 (Answers on page 327)

No. 14

The total sales of Departmentalised Stores Ltd for the financial year ended March 31st, 19.9, are £360,000 from the following sources:

	£
Dept. 1	85,000
Dept. 2	72,000
Dept. 3	93,000
Dept. 4	110,000

The opening stock in each department is:

	£
Dept. 1	7,000
Dept. 2	6,000
Dept. 3	7,000
Dept. 4	11,000

The net purchases in each department are:

	£
Dept. 1	74,000
Dept. 2	68,000
Dept. 3	81,000
Dept. 4	99,000

The closing stock in each department is:

	£
Dept. 1	6,000
Dept. 2	7,000
Dept. 3	8,000
Dept. 4	10,000

The selling expenses in each department are:

	£
Dept. 1	7,000
Dept. 2	4,000
Dept. 3	6,000
Dept. 4	4,000

The total administrative expense is £8,000.

Prepare a departmentalised Trading and Profit and Loss Account with percentages.

Examples from Chapter 6 (Answers on page 328)

No. 15

An abbreviated Profit and Loss Statement for REMCO Ltd, follows:

	£
Sales	200,000
Cost of Goods Sold	170,000
Gross Profit	30,000
Operating Expenses	12,000
Net Profit	£18,000

The business is contacted by a credit-card company with a proposal to redeem all credit-card sales slips at 6 per cent discount. It is estimated that sales will increase by 25 per cent but that 20 per cent of the current business will convert to credit-card sales. The gross-profit percentage would remain the same but operating expenses (excluding credit-card discounts) would increase by 5 per cent of new sales.

Should REMCO Ltd, make credit-card sales? Why?

No. 16

What factors might a company selling on credit in the following circumstances look at?

(*a*) Houses
(*b*) Cars
(*c*) Mail order
(*d*) General retail goods (department store)

No. 17

The auditor for DERINI Products finds the following after an analysis of trade debtors:

Age of Account	Amount
	£
0–30 days	170,000
31–60 days	80,000
61–90 days	40,000
over 90 days	30,000

On analysis of past experience it is found that the loss ratios for overdue accounts are as follows:

31–60 days	2 per cent
61–90 days	5 per cent
over 90 days	10 per cent

(*a*) What should be the balance in the Provision for Bad Debts Account?

(*b*) If the balance in the Provision for Bad Debts Account is £2,200 prior to the calculations made in (*a*) above, prepare the journal entry required.

No. 18

It is decided to sell the trade debtors to our bank at a discount of 4 per cent with no recourse. Under this plan we give £200,000 of debts to the bank.

Prepare the required journal entry.

No. 19

Under an arrangement with Factors Ltd we pledge £150,000 of trade debtors as security for a loan of £100,000. The accounts are to be collected by us and are to be maintained at our office. At the end of each month a photostat is to be made of each account on which a collection has been made and these copies are to be forwarded to Factors Ltd with a cheque for the amounts collected and interest on the loan balance at the beginning of the month at 5 per cent.

(*a*) Prepare the entry (entries) required on transfer of the accounts to Factors Ltd on February 1st.

(*b*) In February £20,000 is collected. Prepare the required February 28th entry (entries).

(*c*) In March £50,000 is collected. Prepare the required March 31st entry (entries).

(*d*) In April £30,000 is collected. Prepare the required April 30th entry (entries).

No. 20

Goods costing £300,000 are sold for £500,000 on instalment contracts in 19.8. Prepare the required entry (entries).

No. 21

In 19.8, collections on the goods sold in the previous example amounted to £70,000. Prepare the necessary entry (entries).

No. 22

In 19.9, collections on the goods sold in Example No. 20 amounted to £180,000. Prepare the necessary entry (entries).

No. 23

At the beginning of 19.9 there are credit balances in these accounts:

Gross Profit on Instalment Sales—19.6: £20,000
Gross Profit on Instalment Sales—19.7: £160,000
Gross Profit on Instalment Sales—19.8: £500,000

The gross profit percentages in these years were as follows:

19.6: 32 per cent
19.7: 37 per cent
19.8: 35 per cent

The balances in the accounts at the end of 19.9 are:

Gross Profit on Instalment Sales—19.6: 0
Gross Profit on Instalment Sales—19.7: £30,000
Gross Profit on Instalment Sales—19.8: £220,000

What were the collections on the 19.6, 19.7, and 19.8 instalment sales? Answer to the nearest pound.

No. 24

A customer wants to trade in a used machine for a new one priced at £15,000 that cost £13,000. The salesman allows £3,000 on the used machine and accepts an instalment contract for £12,500. The used machine can be sold for £4,500 after spending £800 to recondition it. The mark-up for used equipment is 20 per cent of the selling price.

(*a*) Prepare a schedule showing the value of the trade-in merchandise.
(*b*) Prepare the entry (entries) for the sale.

No. 25

A machine selling for £10,000 (costing £7,000) is sold on the instalment basis in 19.8. The customer pays £1,000 down and gives an instalment note of £9,720. After making £2,160 in payments, the customer defaults and the merchandise is repossessed. It would cost £1,000 to recondition the machine, which could then be sold for £8,000. The normal gross profit ratio on used-machine sales is 15 per cent of sales price.

(*a*) Prepare the entry (entries) for the sale.
(*b*) Prepare the entry (entries) for the payments received (assume that interest earnings are prorated).
(*c*) Compute the stock value of the machine when repossessed.
(*d*) Prepare the entry to record the repossession.

Examples from Chapter 7 (Answers on page 335)

No. 26

Mention (*a*) some advantages, and (*b*) some disadvantages of using the periodic inventory method.

No. 27

From the following partially adjusted trial balance of Traders Ltd, prepare a Cost of Goods Sold Statement for the year 19.9:

	£	£
Stock	150,000	
Stock	130,000	150,000
Purchases	1,600,000	
Purchase Returns and Allowances		30,000
Purchase Discounts		31,000
Carriage Inwards	21,000	

No. 28

When the re-order point for Item 3XB is reached, the count of the items shows 150 units but the perpetual inventory card shows 140 units. The unit price is £1.25. Prepare the adjusting entry.

No. 29

A sale is made for cash (200 units costing £1.50 each are sold for £2 each). The periodic inventory method is used.

(*a*) Prepare the Sales entry.
(*b*) Prepare the Cost of Sales entry.

No. 30

A count is made of Item 66–329B, and 297 units are counted. The perpetual inventory card shows 325 units. The unit price of the item is £1.60. Prepare the adjusting entry.

No. 31

Concerning the perpetual inventory method:

(*a*) Mention some advantages of using this method.
(*b*) Mention some disadvantages of using this method.

No. 32

A sale is made for cash (300 units costing £4 each are sold for £5 each). The perpetual inventory method is used.

(*a*) Prepare the Sales entry.
(*b*) Prepare the Cost of Sales entry.

No. 33

The following information is taken from the perpetual inventory card for Item 49–3B127:

Balance, Jan. 1st, 19..	1,000 units	£5.70 each
Received, Jan. 31st	2,000 units	£6.20 each
Received, Feb. 15th	2,000 units	£6.40 each
Received, March 18th	2,000 units	£6.60 each
Sold, April 20th	3,000 units	£7.40 each
Sold, May 15th	1,500 units	£8.00 each

Complete the following table:

	LIFO	Average	FIFO
Sales			
Cost of Goods Sold			
Gross Profit			
Stock, May 31st			

No. 34

Below is a table of items showing the invoice price and current market price for each item. What is the value of the stocks using Cost or Market, whichever is lower?

Item		*Invoice price*	*Cost price*
		£	£
A1	100 units	60	67
A2	120 units	120	110
A3	600 units	210	200
A4	210 units	300	290
B1	430 units	400	410
B2	10 units	75	72
B3	25 units	450	430
C1	900 units	790	810
C2	42 units	575	560
C3	150 units	815	804
C4	200 units	615	627

No. 35

From the figures: cost = £4 each and selling price = £5 each, what is the gross profit:

(*a*) as a percentage of the selling price?
(*b*) as a percentage of the cost?

Examples from Chapter 8 (Answers on page 338)

No. 36

The Smith Products Company bought land consisting of a site and an old building. The entry to record the purchase of the property was:

Land	£27,457	
Prepaid Rates	200	
Cash		£7,657
Mortgage Loan Payable		20,000

No allocation of cost between land and building was made because the building is to be removed to make room for a warehouse. The company investigated the removal of the building, and two methods were suggested and bids secured. The best bids under the two methods were as follows:

(*a*) Liverpool Demolition Company Ltd will remove the building in two months, salvaging timber, piping, fixtures, etc., and will pay Smith Products Company £3,900.

(*b*) Speedy Demolition Ltd will demolish the building in seven working days and remove all debris so that the land is level. This will cost Smith Products Company £1,750.

Disregarding decisions of time involved in the proposals above, prepare a journal entry to reflect the signing of a contract with:

(*a*) Liverpool Demolition Company Ltd
(*b*) Speedy Demolition Ltd

No. 37

Northern Aero-Space Ltd decides to open a London office. It eventually finds and buys a suitable property in one of the inner suburbs. The cost is charged as follows:

Land	£18,972
Building	£113,832

Before moving, management decides that certain repairs and improvements should be made. The cost of these repairs and improvements are:

	£
Architect's fees	1,000
Construction costs	20,000
Repaint exterior	900
Fire escapes	2,500
Repair roof	1,000
Replace broken windows	200

(*a*) Prepare the entry for the above. (Credit sundry creditors)
(*b*) What is the total cost of the building?

No. 38

Five years later (see previous example) Northern Aero-Space, Ltd, remodels the second floor and repaints the exterior of the building. The costs are as follows:

	£
Architect's fees	300
Construction costs	5,000
Repaint exterior	900

(*a*) Prepare the entry for the above. (Credit sundry creditors)
(*b*) Is there any difference in the treatment between the journal entry in Example No. 37 and this one? If so, explain.

No. 39

A machine costing £5,000 is purchased and shipped to the San Antonio plant of Penexco. The freight charges are £105, insurance while the machine is in transit is £75, and installation charges are £200. What is the total cost of the machine?

No. 40

A machine costs £10,600 installed and ready to use. Bay Machine Co. pays

£2,000 down and agrees to assume contract obligations to pay £400 per month for 24 months. Prepare the journal entry for this transaction.

No. 41

A machine costing £9,800 is installed on January 2nd. It is intended to be used for eight years and will have a scrap value of £200. What is the yearly amount of depreciation charge using the straight-line method?

No. 42

A machine costing £15,000 is installed on January 2nd, 19.8, and is used for special jobs on an intermittent basis. It will have a scrap value of £1,000 after 2,000 hours of use. Time records of machine usage are kept as follows:

19.7	175 hours
19.8	62 hours

(*a*) What is the hourly depreciation rate?

(*b*) What amount should be charged to depreciation expense in the calendar years 19.7 and 19.8?

No. 43

A company buys a machine costing £40,000 on January 2nd, 19... It has an expected life of eight years. Assuming a scrap value of £400, determine the yearly depreciation expense using the Sum-of-the-Years-Digits Method.

No. 44

On July 1st, 19.0, a business buys a machine costing £25,200 having an estimated life of ten years and a scrap value of £1,200. Management depreciates the machine on a straight-line basis. The accumulated depreciation at December 31st, 19.7 was £18,000. On October 1st, 19.8, the company part-exchanges the asset for a new and larger machine of the same type. This asset costs £30,000 and the dealer agrees to allow a trade-in of £1,800 for the old machine if it is used as a down payment on the new one. Management decides to depreciate the new asset on the Sum-of-the-Years-Digits Method, assuming a scrap value of £1,100 and an estimated life of ten years.

(*a*) Prepare the entry to record the depreciation of the machine to October 1st, 19.8.

(*b*) Prepare the entry to record the purchase of the new machine on October 1st, 19.8.

(*c*) Prepare the entry to record the depreciation expense of the new machine to December 31st, 19.8, using the straight-line method. Assume a scrap value of £1,600 and an eight-year life.

No. 45

Mr Overstreet, the owner of an apartment house that cost £75,000 and has now depreciated to a book value of £32,000, wants to present a statement to the bank to secure credit. The building has a current value of £125,000 and is insured for £90,000. The balance owing on the mortgage is £60,000. What entry should be made to present the facts of current value to the bank?

Examples from Chapter 9 (Answers on page 340)

No. 46

A business purchases merchandise on account. The amount of the invoice is £6,742.90. Terms are 2 per cent/10 days; net 30 days.

(*a*) Prepare the entry for the purchase. (Debit Merchandise Purchases.)
(*b*) Prepare the entry for payment made during the discount period.
(*c*) Prepare the entry for payment made after the discount period.

No. 47

In reviewing shipments of merchandise and the invoices covering these shipments, the following are found:

(*a*) Goods shipped FOB shipping point on December 28th, 19.8, arrive on January 5th, 19.9. The invoice for £8,200 is received on January 6th, 19.9, and is recorded on that date.

(*b*) Goods shipped FOB destination on December 28th, 19.8, arrive on January 5th, 19.9. The invoice for £3,500 is received on January 6th, 19.9, and is recorded on that date.

Prepare any entry (entries) required in 19.8.

No. 48

Better Living Review has subscription rates of one year for £2.40, two years for £3.60, and five years for £7.20. An analysis of the Prepaid Subscription Received in 19.8 account shows the following:

Month	*Number of Subscriptions*			*Prepaid Subscriptions*		
	1 yr.	*2 yrs.*	*5 yrs.*	*1 yr.*	*2 yrs.*	*5 yrs.*
				£	£	£
Jan.	100	175	130	240.00	630.00	936.00
Feb.	75	162	205	180.00	583.20	1,476.00
March	83	181	197	199.20	651.60	1,418.40
April	97	135	188	232.80	486.00	1,353.60
May	105	166	142	252.00	597.60	1,022.40
June	82	175	155	196.80	630.00	1,116.00
July	56	185	187	134.40	666.00	1,346.40
Aug.	71	119	193	170.40	428.40	1,389.60
Sept.	89	122	167	213.60	439.20	1,202.40
Oct.	43	163	152	103.20	586.80	1,094.40
Nov.	52	180	193	124.80	648.00	1,389.60
Dec.	60	205	215	144.00	738.00	1,548.00
TOTAL	913	1,968	2,124	£2,191.20	£7,084.80	£15,292.80

(*a*) How much of the subscriptions was earned in 19.8?
(*b*) How much of the subscriptions was unearned at December 31st, 19.8?
(*c*) What is the adjusting entry needed at December 31st, 19.8?
(*d*) How much of the subscriptions will be earned in 19.9?

Examples from Chapter 11 (Answers on page 342)

No. 49

The Income Statement for the year 19.8 of the Progressive Company is shown below:

	£	£
Sales		200,000
Cost of Goods Sold		
Labour	80,000	
Materials	46,000	
Overhead	14,000	140,000
Gross Profit		60,000
Selling Expenses	25,000	
Administrative Expenses	20,000	45,000
		£15,000

Prepare a budget for 19.9, assuming:

(*a*) sales increase 20 per cent
(*b*) labour increases 15 per cent
(*c*) materials increase 20 per cent
(*d*) selling expenses increase 15 per cent
(*e*) administrative expenses increase 10 per cent
(*f*) overhead maintains the same ratio to sales.

No. 50

From the following information for producing 60,000 units, prepare a break-even chart and check by calculating the break-even point.

	Variable £	*Fixed* £	*Total* £
Direct Labour	13,000	—	13,000
Direct Materials	12,000	—	12,000
Factory Overhead	4,000	7,000	11,000
Selling Expenses	6,000	3,000	9,000
Administration Expenses	—	5,000	5,000
Total	£35,000	£15,000	£50,000

The price per unit is £1 irrespective of the level of sales.

No. 51

Prepare a second break-even chart to show the effect of the following changes in the information given in the previous example:

(*a*) An increase of 10 per cent in direct labour cost.
(*b*) An increase of 2 per cent in all other variable costs.
(*c*) An increase of £3,260 in fixed costs.
(*d*) An increase of 5 per cent in selling price.

Examples from Chapter 12 (Answers on page 343)

No. 52

The time analysis for Department 1 is:

	Mon.	Tues.	Wed.	Thurs.	Fri.
Jones	8	8	8	8	8
Smith	7	9	8	8	8
Blue	8	8	7	7	9
Green	8	9	9	6	10
Acme	3	11	8	6	10

The hourly rates of pay are as follows:

Jones	£1.75
Smith	£2.10
Blue	£2.05
Green	£1.95
Acme	£1.52

Compute gross pay, assuming:

(*a*) Overtime of 50 per cent is paid for all hours over 40 worked in one week.

(*b*) Overtime of 50 per cent is paid for all hours over eight worked in one day.

No. 53

The piecework rate for Part 632 is:

First 100 pieces	17½p each
Next 50 pieces	18p each
All over 150 pieces	19p each

Jones produces 70 pieces; Smith, 110 pieces; Blue, 180 pieces. Compute the week's wages for each worker.

No. 54

Would any of the answers to the previous example have been different if the minimum weekly wage was £16?

No. 55

What would the week's wages be if the piece rate in Example No. 53 had read:

0–100 pieces	17½p each
0–150 pieces	18p each
over 150 pieces	19p each

No. 56

In analysing storeroom requisitions, the following is found:

Storeroom Requisition Number	Total	Job 16	Job 19	Job 22	Dept. A	Dept. B
	£	£	£	£	£	£
615	19.20	19.20				
616	42.50		20.50	12.00		10.00
617	53.15				53.15	
618	109.30	19.00	80.00	10.30		
619	41.70					41.70

Prepare an entry to record the above data. (Assume that the departments mentioned are service departments.)

No. 57

Using the formula given on page 151, determine the economic order quantity for Item 335, given:

Annual requirement	2,000 units
Cost per unit	£6.40
Inventory holding cost	30 per cent
Ordering cost per order	£14.00

No. 58

Assuming 250 working days a year, how often must Item 335 (in the previous example) be ordered?

No. 59

Determine the minimum stock for Item XB–222, given the following:

Daily usage	30 units
Lead time	2 calendar weeks

The plant is on a five-day-per-week schedule.

No. 60

A batch of 700 units in production is inspected. Twenty units are found to be defective. The cost sheet up to the point of inspection shows:

Labour	£2,114
Materials	£4,228
Overhead	£1,057

How much is the cost of defective items, assuming:

(*a*) Defective goods and accepted goods should be valued the same at point of separation?

(*b*) Defective goods are valued at present worth (assume completed value to be £18.00; it costs £9.75 to complete) with all costs chargeable to Work-in-Progress?

(*c*) Defective goods priced at present worth and accepted goods priced at cost to point of inspection?

No. 61

Prepare entries for parts (*a*), (*b*), and (*c*) of the previous example.

No. 62

To the Production Overhead Account post data from the following facts:

(*a*) An analysis of the payroll summary shows Work-in-Progress £18,629; Production Overhead £2,302; Sales Salaries £5,621; Office Salaries £8,897.

(*b*) An analysis of the Materials Requisition shows:

	£
Work-in-Progress	42,915
Plant Maintenance	297
Equipment Repair Orders	623
Production Office Supplies	105

(*c*) The Ledger shows purchases as follows:

	£	
Materials	62,336	
Telephone	128	50% sales 30% office 20% factory
Sundry Expenses	215	10% sales 10% office 80% factory
Rent	1,450	5% sales 5% office 90% factory

(*d*) An analysis of the prepaid accounts shows:

	Opening Balance	Additions	Closing Balance
	£	£	£
Insurance	3,900	9,000	3,600
Production supplies	4,200	5,000	4,800

70 per cent of insurance expenses chargeable to production.

(*e*) The depreciation is computed to be £15,320.

No. 63

The 19.8 production overhead is £152,310. It is estimated that in 19.9 this will increase 10 per cent. Determine the various overheads:

(*a*) per direct-labour hours (assuming 16,750 direct-labour hours in 19.9).
(*b*) per direct-labour pounds (assuming an average of £0.75 per hour).

No. 64

In 19.7 it was determined that 19.9 plant production would involve 42,700 direct-labour hours, that factory overhead would be £623,950, and that the plant would operate at 80 per cent of capacity. However, the plant operated at 85 per cent capacity, using 45,000 direct-labour hours. The actual production overhead was £651,259. Determine the total variance.

No. 65

Analyse the variance determined in the previous example as to:

(*a*) Budget variance
(*b*) Volume variance
(*c*) Efficiency variance

Examples from Chapter 13 (Answers on page 346)

No. 66

Part of the debit side of the Payroll entry for November 19.8 is:

Work-in-Progress—	Job 16	£7,387
	Job 17	7,622
	Job 20	9,468
	Job 21	763

Part of the debit side of the Payroll entry for December 19.8 is:

Work-in-Progress—	Job 17	£7,341
	Job 20	2,901
	Job 21	2,538
	Job 22	806

Part of the debit side of the Payroll entry for January 19.9 is:

Work-in-Progress—	Job 20	£203
	Job 21	4,742
	Job 23	1,542

Part of the debit side of the Materials Requisition analysis entry for November 19.8 is:

Work-in-Progress—	Job 16	£6,802
	Job 17	2,121
	Job 20	2,253
	Job 21	968

Part of the debit side of the Materials Requisition analysis entry for December 19.8 is:

Work-in-Progress—	Job 17	£8,591
	Job 20	905
	Job 21	6,437
	Job 22	8,807

Part of the debit side of the Materials Requisition analysis entry for January 19.9 is:

Work-in-Progress—	Job 20	£347
	Job 21	8,642
	Job 23	3,763

The overhead rate is computed anew each month based on the performance of the two previous months:

November:	47 per cent of direct-labour pounds
December:	44 per cent of direct-labour pounds
January:	46 per cent of direct-labour pounds

Job 20 is completed in January 19.9. What is the value of Job 20 on:

(*a*) November 30th, 19.8?
(*b*) December 31st, 19.8?
(*c*) January 31st, 19.9? (Before transfer to Finished Goods Stock)

No. 67

In a situation where process cost accounting is used, the following facts are determined:

3,000 lb of Material A and 2,000 lb of Material B have been put into production at the beginning of the job. Material A costs £3/lb; B costs £15/lb. Direct labour expended in processing this material is £18,400. Overhead burden is 1.4 times direct labour. No shrinkage of material is involved in the process. At the end of the month 4,000 lb of the end product are completely finished and 1,000 lb are 60 per cent complete as to direct labour (100 per cent complete as to material).

Determine the value of:

(*a*) Completed production.
(*b*) Work-in-progress at the end of the month.

No. 68.

In a process situation there is an opening inventory whose cost for completion to the present stage is:

	£
Direct labour	6,000
Direct materials	14,000
Overhead	12,000

To complete this inventory would take £9,000 of direct labour. (The overhead is expressed as a percentage of labour, and this percentage has not changed.) How much will the completed inventory cost?

No. 69

In Department 6 there is both opening and closing inventory for January 19. .. Details concerning the status of production in the department are as follows:

		Percentage Completion	
	Units	Direct Labour and Overhead	Direct Materials
Opening inventory	300	50%	75%
Started in production	2,000		
Closing inventory	500	60%	100%

Determine the equivalent units of production for labour, materials and overhead. (Check your answer before going on to Example No. 70.)

No. 70

The value of the opening inventory in Example No. 69 is as follows:

	£
Direct labour	£1,050
Direct materials	2,250
Overhead	2,100

The value of additions to production during the month is as follows:

	£
Direct labour	£13,845
Direct materials	20,542
Overhead	27,495

Determine the value of the equivalent units of production.

No. 71

In a joint production situation, it costs £40,000 to manufacture Products A and B to point of separation. When completed, the sales value of A and B will be £60,000 and £40,000 respectively. It will cost £10,000 and £20,000 respectively to complete A and B. Determine the valuation of A and B at point of separation, using:

(*a*) Market value of the end product.
(*b*) Market value of the end product less further conversion.

No. 72

In a company using a standard costing system, the following facts are found:

The standard labour rate for drilling is £2 per hour.

The standard labour time required to complete 100 units of Part X34B is 7 hours.

The actual time it took to complete 100 units of Part X34B was 7.1 hours and the pay rate of the operator was £2.10 per hour.

(*a*) How much was the actual cost of direct labour to produce the 100 units of Part X34B?

(*b*) How much was the standard cost of direct labour to produce the 100 units of Part X34B?

(*c*) Analyse any variance.

No. 73

There are two types of machine available to a firm. The details are as follows:

	Machine A	*Machine B*
Output per year	6,000 units	8,000 units
Cost	£75,000	£60,000
Scrap value	£5,000	£5,000
Life	8 years	6 years
Annual running costs	£3,430	£8,610

The annual output required is 24,000 units. Disregarding the effect of any change in the price level, and assuming that the funds required will be borrowed at 6% per annum, indicate which type of machine the firm should purchase.

Exercises—Second Series

Examples from Chapter 1

No. 101

Timber Chests Ltd is a public company and its shares are quoted on the London Stock Exchange. Its most recent results are as follows:

BALANCE SHEET
(as at March 31st, 19.9)

	£000	£000		£000	£000
Ordinary Share Capital			*Fixed Assets*		
Authorised			Land and Buildings at Cost		26,700
Issued, and Fully Paid		38,600	Plant and Machinery at Cost	51,000	
Capital Reserves		11,900	*Less* Depreciation	26,600	
Profit and Loss Account		13,600			24,400
		64,100			51,100
6% Debentures		15,000			
Future Taxation		1,500	*Trade Investments* at Cost		3,700
Current Liabilities			*Current Assets*		
Creditors	23,700		Stocks	34,300	
Current Taxation	5,600		Debtors	17,800	
Proposed Dividends	1,900		Quoted Investments	2,400	
		31,200	Cash at Bank	2,500	
					57,000
		£111,800			£111,800

PROFIT AND LOSS ACCOUNT
(for the year ended March 31st, 19.9)

	£000	£000
Trading Profit		15,850
Less Directors' Emoluments	150	
Depreciation	4,600	
Debenture Interest	900	
		5,650
Profit before Taxation		10,200
Less Taxation		4,900
Profit after Taxation		5,300
Less Ordinary Dividend, paid and proposed (gross)		4,600
		700
Add Balance as at April 1st, 19.8		12,900
		£13,600

Required: Define and calculate, from the figures in these accounts, the five accounting ratios which you think would be most helpful to a prospective investor in the company. Explain the significance and limitations of each.

No. 102

You are the treasurer of the Polecon Cricket Club, whose latest annual accounts are set out below. The club is planning to build a new pavilion at an estimated cost of £5,000. Recently you received the following letter from the chairman of the committee:

Dear—,

I see from the club's Balance Sheet that we have £1,200 in the General Fund, £2,000 in the Building Reserve, £1,900 in Investments and £125 in the bank: that makes £5,225 in all, £225 more than we need for the new pavilion. I suggest that we place the contract at once. What is your opinion?

Yours sincerely,

J. Bowler.

POLECON CRICKET CLUB
BALANCE SHEET
(as at March 31st, 19.9)

Claims	£	*Assets*	£	£
General Fund	1,200	Cricket Ground: at Cost		6,500
Building Reserve	2,000	Equipment: Cost	750	
Mortgage Loan	5,400	Accumulated Depreciation	675	
				75
		Investments: at Cost (Note: market value £1,450)		1,900
		Cash at Bank		125
	£8,600			£8,600

INCOME AND EXPENDITURE ACCOUNT
(for the year ended March 31st, 19.9)

	£	£
Subscriptions		490
Less General Expenses	400	
Depreciation of Equipment	75	
		475
Surplus carried to General Fund		£15

Required: Your reply to the chairman's letter.

No. 103

Holt's accounts for 19.8 were as follows:

PROFIT AND LOSS ACCOUNT

	£	£
Sales		5,000
Less Cost of Goods Sold		4,000
Gross Profit		1,000
Less General Expenses	200	
Depreciation	500	
		700
Net Profit		£300

BALANCE SHEET
(at December 31st, 19.8)

	£		£	£
Capital	4,000	*Fixed Assets*	5,000	
Creditors (for Goods)	500	*Less* Depreciation	2,000	
				3,000
		Current Assets		
		Stock	500	
		Debtors	800	
		Cash	200	
				1,500
	£4,500			£4,500

During 19.9:

(i) Sales increased by 20 per cent.
(ii) The gross profit rate was 30 per cent of sales.
(iii) General expenses (all paid in cash) were £250.
(iv) Depreciation was the same as in 19.8.
(v) The average length of credit allowed to debtors was 2 months.
(vi) The stock turnover rate was 7 times per year.
(vii) The creditors turnover rate was 11 times per year.

The stock turnover rate, creditors turnover rate, and length of credit allowed to debtors are calculated using the average of the opening and closing figures for stock, creditors, and debtors respectively.

All sales and purchases of goods were on credit.

Required:

(*a*) Profit and Loss Account for 19.9.
(*b*) Balance Sheet at the end of 19.9.

No. 104

Write brief notes on each of the following to show that you understand what is meant by them:

(*a*) appropriation account;
(*b*) working capital;
(*c*) control account;
(*d*) receipts and payments account, and
(*e*) account sales.

(SCCA)

No. 105

The following account relates to the Comma Social Club.

RECEIPTS AND PAYMENTS ACCOUNT
(for the year ended December 31st, 1982)

	£		£
Balances b/f:		Rent	300
Deposit A/c	500	Printing, postage and	
Current A/c	250	stationery	150
Cash	15	Secretary's expenses	50
Donations	20	Sports equipment	400
Subscriptions	2,400	Sports competition fees	800
Interest on deposit account	58	Sports prizes	120
Sports entry fees paid by		Refreshments bought	400
members	300	Raffle prizes	60
Sale of refreshments	550	Donations to charity	200
Raffle takings	350	Balances c/f:	
		Deposit A/c	1,800
		Current A/c	150
		Cash	13
	£4,443		£4,443

The club has 250 members who pay £10 p.a. subscription. All subscriptions had been paid by the end of 1981 and at that date no other amounts were outstanding. It is the policy of the club to take credit for all subscriptions due, whether paid or not. At December 31st, 1982 there was a printing bill for £20 outstanding and the secretary was owed £30 for his expenses. The sports equipment consisted of items which were expected to last for four years.

You are required to prepare the Income and Expenditure Account for the club for the year ended December 31st, 1982 showing the results of each activity clearly *in the account.*

(SCCA)

No. 106

Song Ltd has operated for many years and the financial statements for 1981 and 1982 were as follows:

BALANCE SHEET
(as at March 31st)

		1981		1982
		M$000		M$000
Share Capital and Reserves				
Ordinary Shares		1,200		1,200
Retained Earnings		720		726
		1,920		1,926
Long Term Loan		—		600
	M$000		M$000	
Current Liabilities				
Creditors	420		468	
Proposed Dividend	60		6	
Bank	—	480	600	1,074
		2,400		3,600
Fixed Assets				
Cost		3,600		4,320
Less Depreciation		1,800		2,082
		1,800		2,238
Current Assets				
Stock	150		462	
Debtors	300		900	
Bank	150	600	—	1,362
		2,400		3,600

REVENUE ACCOUNT
(year to March 31st)

	1981	1982
	M$000	M$000
Sales (all on credit)	1,200	1,800
Less Cost of Goods sold	900	1,386
Gross Profit	300	414

	M$000		M$000	
Less Admin. Expenses	60		108	
Selling Expenses	120		216	
Bank Interest	—		18	
Loan Interest	—	180	60	402
Net Profit		120		12
Less Proposed Dividend		60		6
Addition to Retained Earnings		60		6

Required:

(i) Using appropriate ratios, compare the profitability and liquidity of Song Ltd for the years ended March 31st, 1981 and March 31st, 1982. You should calculate at least *eight* ratios in respect of each year.

(ii) Discuss the limitations of comparing one year with another when assessing a company's performance and suggest any alternative standards of comparison with which you are familiar.

(LCC)

No. 107

Galvin Ltd commenced business on January 1st, 1981. The following ratios were extracted from the information contained in the first year's accounts.

Share capital:	
36,000 £1 ordinary shares, issued and fully paid	
Working capital	£6,000
Ratio of turnover to capital employed (at end of year)	2 to 1
Ratio of turnover to stock	12 to 1
Current ratio	1.6 to 1
Liquid (or acid test) ratio	1.1 to 1
Ratio of debtors to sales	0.075 to 1
Ratio of general expenses to sales	0.2 to 1

Notes

(1) Current assets are made up of stock (unchanged throughout the year), debtors and cash.

(2) Capital employed is share capital plus revenue reserve.

(3) Ignore depreciation and profit appropriations.

You are required to prepare, as far as is possible from the above figures—

(*a*) a trading and profit and loss account for the year ended December 31st, 1981, and

(*b*) a balance sheet as at December 31st, 1981.

(SCCA)

No. 108

Falco, the manager of a small grocery shop owned by Perryman Ltd, decided to go into business on his own account, and agreed to buy from the company the goodwill, fixtures and fittings of the branch shop for £5,000, plus stock at valuation.

The fixtures and fittings were valued at £500. Falco arranged a new lease with the owner of the premises for seven years at £800 per annum, payable quarterly in arrear.

Falco opened a business bank account with £12,000, paid Perryman Ltd the agreed amount including the stock, and opened for business on April 1st, 1981.

He failed to keep proper records. A cash payments notebook showed the following details for the year:

	£
Drawings	1,248
Cash purchases for resale	316
Wages and national insurance	1,194
Sundry shop expenses	208

A summary of his bank account for the year showed—

		£
Deposits	Cash introduced	12,000
	Takings banked	24,100
Withdrawals	Perryman Ltd	7,500
	Purchases for resale	20,000
	Rent	600
	Rates	196
	Electricity	98
	Additional fixtures (April 1st, 1981).	200

At March 31st, 1982 stock valued at cost was £2,912, cash on hand £224, trade creditors £534 and electricity £34.

Depreciation on fixtures is to be provided at 10 per cent.

You are required to prepare—

(*a*) a trading and profit and loss account for the year ended March 31st, 1982

(*b*) a balance sheet as at that date.

(SCCA)

No. 109

The following balances are left in the books of Swain Ltd at June 30th, 1982, after the Trading Account has been prepared:

	£
Authorised and issued share capital:	
120,000 ordinary shares of 50p each	60,000
40,000 6% £1 preference shares	40,000
Stock at June 30th, 1982	43,794
Debtors	13,600
Trade creditors	7,034
Bank balance	6,842
10% Debentures	10,000
General reserve	22,000

Bad debts	230
Wages and salaries	15,630
Gross profit for the period	52,682
Insurance	830
Postage and telephone	320
Heating and lighting	946
Debenture interest (half-year to December 31st, 1981)	500
General expenses	2,626
Directors' fees	3,500
Vehicles (cost £9,800)	3,400
Office furniture (cost £22,320)	13,720
Land and buildings at cost	70,000
Goodwill	30,000
Profit and loss account as at July 1st, 1981	14,222

The following information should be taken into account.

(*a*) Office furniture is to be depreciated at 15 per cent on cost, and vehicles at 20 per cent of written down value.

(*b*) An electricity bill for £274 remains unpaid.

(*c*) Included in the figure for insurance is £150 for fire cover for the year to December 31st, 1982.

(*d*) Provision is to be made for the following: (1) directors' fees £3,500; (2) audit fee £1,200, and (3) debenture interest outstanding.

(*e*) The directors have recommended that £16,000 be transferred to General Reserve, the preference dividend and an ordinary dividend of 10 per cent be paid.

You are required to prepare—

(*a*) the profit and loss account for the year ended June 30th, 1982, and
(*b*) the balance sheet as at that date.

Ignore taxation.

(SCCA)

No. 110

Answer *either* (*a*) *or* (*b*), *but not both.*

(*a*) Accountants are sometimes accused of misleading by producing a precise figure for the profit of a business when, in arriving at that figure, they use other figures which are imprecise, such as the provisions for depreciation and doubtful debts.

Explain this statement and say to what extent you agree with this criticism.

(*b*) Ratio analysis is an important technique in the understanding of company accounts. (i) What is ratio analysis? (ii) What standards can be used to compare ratios? (iii) What are the problems involved in producing useful and meaningful ratios? (iv) Give one example of—(*a*) a liquidity ratio; (*b*) a profitability ratio, and (*c*) an investment ratio, and show how each is calculated.

(SCCA)

No. 111

The Water Born Anglers Club did not keep their account books up to date. When the club's auditors called on May 31st, 1982 to count the stock and bar floats for the preparation of the annual accounts to that date, it was found that the club treasurer had disappeared and there were no cash floats.

The bank account for the year was summarized as follows:

	£		£
Balance, June 1st, 1981	728	Rent and rates	1,000
Deposits	86,432	Bar purchases	72,897
		Telephone	320
		Miscellaneous	600
		Insurance	94
		Cash from bank	11,764
		Balance, May 31st, 1982	485
	£87,160		£87,160

Other information available.

(*a*) Balances at 31st May were—

	1981	*1982*
	£	£
Rent due	94	126
Insurance in advance	36	44
Telephone accrued	80	94
Bar stock	6,432	7,112
Rates prepaid	64	76

(*b*) The barman lodges intact all the takings into the bank night safe. His paying-in slips came to £82,124 for the year. The treasurer did not have access to the bar stock or takings.

(*c*) Counterfoils in the subscription receipts book totalled £8,200.

(*d*) Cash payments were listed, and the yearly figures were wages £6,011, bar replacements £2,742 and sundries £520.

You are required to prepare—

(*a*) a calculation of the amount of money missing at May 31st, 1982, and

(*b*) an income and Expenditure Account for the year.

(SCCA)

No. 112

On January 1st, 1981 Jackett started in business as a small trader, opening a bank account with his initial capital of £3,000. He has kept no proper records of his business transactions and in April 1983 he received a large, estimated tax demand. This has made him seek help in preparing some accounts, and he has now produced the following information:

	1981	*1982*
	£	£
Cash sales, all banked	14,630	16,970
Cheque payments, analysed:		
Stock purchases	7,292	8,896
Sundry expenses	2,649	2,982
Drawings	3,000	3,500
Fixtures and fittings	1,000	300
Stock at December 31st	3,790	5,740
Stock taken for private use	520	780
Trade creditors at December 31st	1,980	2,100

You are required to prepare—

(*a*) trading and profit and loss accounts for 1981 and 1982, and
(*b*) balance sheets as at 31st December 1981 and 1982.

Ignore depreciation. Show all calculations.

(SCCA)

Examples from Chapter 2

No. 113

Mr Green started in business as a retail grocer on January 1st. He opened a bank account for his business and paid into it £500, borrowed from Mr White, and £1,000, drawn from his personal bank account; the bank agreed that he might borrow up to £500 on overdraft to help finance his trading stock requirements. He immediately purchased a delivery van for £300 and initial trading stock for £1,476.

You are given the following additional information:

(1) On December 31st, Mr Green's trading stock had a value, at cost prices, of £2,204. Included in this sum was £143, the cost of 3,000 tins of corned beef, purchased some months ago in response to a special offer; this product has not been selling well and so all 3,000 tins will have to be sold for £75.

(2) Several customers have weekly accounts with Mr Green and, on December 31st, they owed him £86.

(3) On December 31st, the business bank account is overdrawn by £196 and trade creditors are owed £876 for goods supplied.

(4) The delivery van has a market value of £220 at December 31st. Mr Green believes that his best policy will be to keep the van for another two years, after which time he expects to be able to sell it for £120.

(5) Mr Green receives all his takings in cash. From these, he meets small business expenses and his own 'wages' of £15 per week. He pays the remainder into his business bank account.

(6) However at one time during the year, the business bank account had

reached the allowed overdraft limit and so Mr Green had to pay £94, a wholesaler's account for groceries supplied, from his personal bank account. He has not subsequently made any adjustment for this item.

(7) During the year, Mr Green repaid £150 to Mr White, by cheque drawn on his business account.

Required: Calculation of Mr Green's profit for the year ended December 31st, 19.., according to normal accounting conventions.

No. 114

Below is a very rough draft of the Balance Sheet of Moon & Son Ltd, as at November 30th, prepared by an unskilled book-keeper. The company has an authorised share capital of £40,000.

	£		£
Trade Debtors	6,473	Creditors	3,972
Plant and Machinery at Cost	16,320	6% Debentures	8,500
Stocks	10,348	Profit and Loss Account	13,763
Preliminary Expenses	4,550	Expenses paid in advance	475
Freehold Property at Cost	25,500	24,000 Ordinary Shares of £1 each	24,000
Quoted Investments	5,853	Depreciation of Plant and Machinery	6,420
Share Premium Account	9,000		
	£78,044		£57,130

All the entries in the firm's books have been checked and found to be correct: and the *amounts* listed in the above Balance Sheet agree with the balances in the books, except that the bank overdraft has been omitted.

No adjustments have been made for:

(*a*) Depreciation of Plant and Machinery for the year ended November 30th, at 10 per cent of cost.

(*b*) Accrued expenses £870.

(*c*) A bonus issue, of one new ordinary share for every four previously held, made during the year. Part of the share premium account is to be applied in issuing these shares as fully paid.

(*d*) A bad debt of £236, included in trade debtors.

(*e*) The directors' proposal to pay a final dividend of 10 per cent on the ordinary capital (as increased by the bonus issue).

(*f*) The market value of the quoted investments, £6,213.

Ignore tax.

Required: The Balance Sheet of Moon & Son Ltd as at November 30th, 19.., in good style and according to normal accounting conventions.

No. 115

You are the accountant of Gabriel Ltd, a rough draft of whose accounts is shown below. At the directors' meeting to consider the 19.8 results, the following questions are put to you by directors with little accounting knowledge:

(*a*) 'You remember that extra store we bought from Michael in June at a price of £50,000? I thought we paid him in new shares. How have you shown the transaction?'

(*b*) 'Should we be worried about the fall in cash, or do all those reserves keep us liquid?'

(*c*) 'Now tell me this. Reserves and profits are good things, provisions for tax and so on are bad. So how can they all be classed together on the same side of the balance sheet?'

(*d*) 'I don't like showing shareholders that £2,750 written off our government stocks. Can't we leave them at cost?'

(*e*) 'Why are you writing down the goodwill so savagely when we're getting more popular every day?'

Briefly answer *any four* of the questions in non-technical language, trying to clarify any issues at stake.

No. 116

Annual accounts of GABRIEL LTD

BALANCE SHEETS

(as at December 31st, 19.7 and 19.8)

	19.7 £	19.8 £		19.7 £	19.8 £
Ordinary Shares of £1	280,000	320,000	Goodwill	34,000	22,000
Contingency Reserves	100,000	115,000	Land and Buildings (Freehold), Cost	53,400	103,400
Unappropriated profits	25,600	38,620	Fittings, etc., Cost	80,000	94,600
Reserve—Premium on Shares		10,000	Government Securities	30,200	8,650
6% Debentures, see (*d*)	20,000	20,000	Stocks	44,300	47,300
Accrued Expenses	4,600	2,300	Trade Investments, Cost	225,200	300,100
Trade Creditors	30,400	32,900	Debtors	20,800	27,000
Provisions for:			Bank	34,300	7,800
Tax	35,900	39,100			
Depreciation on Fittings	25,700	32,300			
Doubtful Debts		630			
	£522,200	£610,850		£522,200	£610,850

From the figures for Gabriel shown above and on page 258, work out the following:

(*a*) Turnover rate (to nearest month) of average stock in 19.8.

(*b*) 'Acid test' ratio at close of 19.8 (to two decimal places).

(*c*) Debtors' ledger control account for 19.8. (Use your imagination for data not stated in the accounts.)

(*d*) Current market value of £100 of debentures. Assume that the market yield on such securities is now 5 per cent p.a., that the debentures were issued exactly 7 years ago at 95 and will be redeemed at par in exactly 20 years, and that interest is payable yearly (the next instalment being due 12 months hence).

PROFIT AND LOSS ACCOUNT
(for the year ended December 31st, 19.8)

	£		£
Cost of Goods Sold	72,200	Sales (credit)	173,200
Trading Expenses	26,000	Income from:	
Depreciation	8,400	Government Stocks (gross)	900
Directors' Salaries	6,700	Trade Investments (gross)	22,700
Debenture Interest (gross)	600	Balance from 19.7	25,600
Loss on Sales of Government Stocks	3,800		
Amount written off Government Stocks still held	2,750		
Bad Debts written off	1,350		
Doubtful Debt Provision	630		
Amount written off Goodwill	12,000		
General Reserve	15,000		
Corporation Tax on Profits of Year	22,600		
Ordinary Dividend Paid on December 31st, 19.8 (net)	11,750		
Balance c/f	38,620		
	£222,400		£222,400

No. 117

Summarised accounts of Cornucopia Ltd, for 1978 are shown below:

CORNUCOPIA LTD
Accounts for year ended December 31st, 1978

INCOME STATEMENT

	£000	*£000*
Operating Profit		53
Less Debenture Interest		6
		47
Less Corporation Tax		21
		26
Less Ordinary Dividend (gross)	15	
Transfer to Reserve	10	
		25
Increase in Carry Forward		£1

BALANCE SHEET

	£000		£000
Ordinary Shares of £1	200	Fixed Assets—Cost	430
Reserve	150	*Less* Depreciation	53
Profits Undistributed	18		
6% Debenture Stock, 1984	100		377
Creditors, etc.	120	Stocks	126
		Debtors	64
		Cash	21
	£588		£588

Required: Calculate *any five* of the following from the given data:

(*a*) Balance sheet value of £1 ordinary share of Cornucopia.

(*b*) Market value of a £1 ordinary share, on the basis that the price: earnings ratio of similar shares is 11.

(*c*) Market value of a £1 ordinary share, on the basis that the current dividend yield on similar shares is 6 per cent.

(*d*) Market value of £100 debenture stock *ex div*, if the appropriate yield is 7 per cent and this stock is redeemable at par in exactly 6 years. (Interest is paid on December 31st each year.)

(*e*) The company's liquid asset ratio.

(*f*) The annual instalment of a sinking fund at 7 per cent, to redeem the debentures at December 31st, 1984, (the first instalment being invested at December 31st, 1978, and the last set aside on December 31st, 1984).

No. 118

(*a*) For a small business man, what are the advantages and disadvantages of taking a business partner?

(*b*) For a partnership, what are the advantages and disadvantages of converting into a limited company?

(SCCA)

No. 119

R. Jenkins was a sole trader, running a small manufacturing business. She prepared the following balance sheet of the business as at May 31st, 1982:

	£	£		£	£
Capital account,			Fixed assets:		
June 1st, 1981	22,260		Premises	7,500	
Profit for the year	5,980		Machinery	8,000	
					15,500
	28,240		Current assets:		
Drawings	6,400		Stock	4,760	
		21,840	Debtors	12,165	
Trade creditors	4,860		Cash	265	
Expenses	440				17,190
		5,300			
Bank overdraft		5,550			
		£32,690			£32,690

You have been asked to redraft the final accounts, and find the following matters need to be taken into consideration.

(*a*) An examination of the debtors' list shows that £340 should be written off, and a provision of 4 per cent raised.

(*b*) Machinery is shown at the written down value at June 1st, 1981. The original cost of £14,500 includes machinery bought at £2,500, now fully depreciated. Depreciation should be calculated at 5 per cent.

(*c*) £1,120 has been omitted from the closing stock figure, which is at cost.

(*d*) Creditors include £350 for goods returned to suppliers during May, for which no credit notes have been received.

(*e*) Insurance of £360 for the year to November 30th, 1982 has been paid.

(*f*) £226 is owing for electricity at the end of the year.

(*g*) Jenkins has taken goods costing £300 for her own use.

You are required to prepare—

(1) a summary of the necessary adjustments to the profit for the year, and

(2) a revised balance sheet as at May 31st, 1982.

(SCCA)

No. 120

Ho Ltd present you with the following summarised Balance Sheet as at March 31st, 1982.

	M$		*M$*
Ordinary share capital		Land (at cost)	100,000
M$I Ordinary shares		Sundry depreciable	
(fully paid)	95,000	assets (net)	59,800
Retained earnings	77,000	Stocks	36,000
		Investments (at cost)	30,000
	172,000	Debtors and	
10% Debentures	33,000	prepayments	55,600
Creditors and accruals	47,600		
Bank	24,500		
Suspense account	4,300		
	281,400		281,400

The Suspense Account represented a difference on the Trial Balance taken out prior to preparing the annual accounting statements. No control accounts are maintained.

On examining the books and other records, you discover the following errors:

(1) A total in the purchase day book had been carried forward as M$11,950 instead of M$11,590.

(2) Ho Ltd operates a periodic inventory system and has under-added the stock sheets by M$1,000 at the end of the year.

(3) A page in the sales day book totalling M$2,850 had been omitted from the amount posted to sales account.

(4) No account had been taken of a liability of M$250 for accrued rent.

(5) An invoice for M$1,290, though entered in the purchase day book had not been posted to the purchase ledger.

(6) An item in the sales day book of M$700 had been posted in the sales ledger as M$900.

(7) A report from expert valuers revaluing the land at M$120,000 had not yet been taken into consideration.

(8) The figure for Bank was the balance appearing on the company's bank statement on March 31st, 1982. According to the bank reconciliation statement, unpresented cheques amounted to M$3,800, and a deposit of M$4,200 was un-recorded at that date.

(9) Included under investments were M$15,000 (nominal value) of the company's own debentures purchased (after adjusting for accrued interest) for M$12,000.

Required:

Show:

(i) The suspense account;

(ii) Your calculation of the corrected balance of retained earnings at March 31st, 1982;

(iii) The corrected summarised balance sheet at March 31st, 1982.

(LCC)

No. 121

On April 1st, 1982 the directors of Blissett PLC issued 60,000 £1 ordinary shares at £1.25 a share, 50p payable on application (including the premium), 30p on allotment, 20p on November 1st, 1982 and the balance on January 1st, 1983.

By April 9th, 1982, when the lists were closed, applications for 90,000 shares had been received. It was decided to reject completely the applications for 10,000 shares, and to allot the shares to the other applicants in proportion to their application. On April 15th cash was returned to the rejected applicants, but the other oversubscription money was carried forward to be set off against the allotment. The shares were issued.

The balance due on allotment was received in full on April 28th.

All shareholders, with the exception of the holder of 1,000 shares, paid the first call. The unpaid shares were declared forfeit in December 1982, but had not been reissued by the time of the balance sheet date, December 31st.

You are required—

(*a*) to prepare journal entries, including those for cash, to record these transactions, and

(*b*) to show the relevant entries in the company's balance sheet as at December 31st, 1982.

(SCCA)

Examples from Chapter 3

No. 122

Old and Middle are partners. They share all profits in the ratio 3:2 (but get no salaries or interest). Their 19.8 accounts run:

BALANCE SHEET
(as at December 31st, 19.8)

	£		£
Old, Capital	12,000	Net Tangible Assets	19,000
Middle, Capital	7,000		
	£19,000		£19,000

PROFIT AND LOSS ACCOUNT
(year ended December 31st, 19.8)

	£		£
Workshop Expenses	8,000	Sales	14,000
Bad Debts	500		
Profit: Old	3,300		
Middle	2,200		
	£14,000		£14,000

Old retires at December 31st, 19.8. The agreement provides that, on the death or retiral of either partner, assets are to be revalued at current figures, and 'goodwill' is to be calculated at two years' purchase of the average profits ('to be computed by an independent expert in accordance with normal accounting practice') of the last three years. You find that:

(i) Profits before adjustment were shown in the firm's accounts for 19.6, 19.7, and 19.8 as £4,800, £5,200, and £5,500.

(ii) Actual bad debts charged against profits were £300, £700, and £500.

(iii) In 19.6, a £1,700 loss due to fire was charged against profit.

(iv) In 19.7, an £800 loss on realisation of property was charged against profit.

(v) The net tangible assets have a current value of £20,000.

Required:

(*a*) Calculate the sum due to Old.

(*b*) Advise Young, a potential new partner not at present connected with the firm, what capital and premium he should pay for a one-quarter share of profits.

No. 123

(*a*) A company's Balance Sheet runs:

	£		£
Ordinary Shares of £1:		Net Assets	4,000
Mr *A*	1,000		
Mr *B*	3,000		
	£4,000		£4,000

A and *B* are directors, each getting a salary of £2,400 p.a. Profit is £1,200 p.a.

A retires. He sells all his shares to *C* for £2,400 (their full market value). *C* becomes a director, with a salary (at his current market rate) of only £2,000 p.a., so that profit rises to £1,600 p.a.

Required: Table showing the Balance Sheets, before and after the sale, on the alternative assumptions that:

(i) book-values of assets are written up (and bonus shares issued) just before the sale, to reflect the shares' full market value; and

(ii) the old book-values are instead retained.

(*b*) Suppose instead that the firm is a partnership, owned again by *A* and *B* with capitals of £1,000 and £3,000, and sharing profits 1:3 after crediting salaries of £2,400 each. *C* buys out *A* in return for a direct private payment of £2,400, and agrees with *B* that profits be shared:

B—60%
C—40%

(no salaries being allowed).
Otherwise the facts resemble those in (*a*) as closely as possible.

Required: Extension to the table under (*a*) to show the firm's post-sale balance sheets at (i) full values, (ii) the old values.

No. 124

The latest annual accounts for Wholesalers Ltd are:

WHOLESALERS LTD

BALANCE SHEET

(as at December 31st, 19.8)

	£	£		£	£
Claims			*Assets*		
Capital			*Fixed Assets*		
Share Capital 20,000			Motor Vans: Cost	5,000	
Shares of £1	20,000		Accumulated		
Profit and Loss A/c	2,500		Depreciation	3,000	
		22,500			2,000
Current Liabilities			*Current Assets*		
Trade Creditors		9,000	Trade Debtors	10,000	
			Stock	18,000	
			Prepaid Rent	1,000	
			Cash at Bank	500	
					29,500
		£31,500			£31,500

PROFIT AND LOSS ACCOUNT FOR 19.8

	£	£
Sales		100,000
Less Cost of Goods Sold		90,000
Gross Profit		10,000
Less Expenses		
Rent of Warehouse	4,000	
Depreciation of Motor Vans	1,000	
Wages and General Expenses	4,000	
		9,000
Net profit		£1,000

You are given the following information about the company's plans for 19.9:

(i) The lease on the present warehouse will expire on March 31st, 19.9. In its place the company will purchase a freehold warehouse currently under construction that is due to be completed late in March. It will cost £15,000 payable on completion.

(ii) In order to finance the purchase, the company will issue for cash 15,000 £1 ordinary shares at par.

(iii) Sales in 19.9 are expected to be 30 per cent higher than in 19.8.

(iv) The gross profit margin (as a percentage of sales) in 19.9 will be double that of 19.8.

(v) In 19.9 the following expenses, depreciation of motor vans, wages and general expenses, will be the same absolute amount as in 19.8.

(vi) In all other respects the same pattern of trading that the company experienced in 19.8 will be repeated in 19.9.

Required:

(*a*) State, giving your reasons, what you would expect the level of stock, trade debtors, and trade creditors to be at December 31st, 19.9.

(*b*) Prepare for Wholesalers Ltd,

(i) the budgeted Profit and Loss Account for 19.9, and
(ii) the budgeted Balance Sheet at December 31st, 19.9.

Note: Ignore tax.

No. 125

Below is a very rough draft of the Balance Sheet of Shaky Grounds Ltd, at December 31st, 19.8:

	£		£
Creditors	9,000	Plant—Cost	26,600
5½% Debentures	12,000	Depreciation	6,000
General Reserve	2,500		
Unappropriated Profit	1,560		20,000
Bank	2,250	Debtors	10,510
Tax Due Immediately	1,200	Patents, at Cost Less Amounts w/o	5,000
Capital:		Stocks	17,000
10,000 6% Preference Shares of £1	10,000		
14,000 Ordinary Shares of £1	14,000		
	£52,510		£52,510

The preference shares have priority for both dividends and repayment at winding up. No dividends have been declared for 19.8. No adjustments have so far been made for:

(i) A bad debt of £320.
(ii) Accrued charges of £1,500.

Required:

(*a*) Redraft the Balance Sheet in good style.

(*b*) Suppose that (as the patents have been superseded and the company's main product will no longer sell) the company is liquidated at the start of 19.9. The assets realize £34,450 in cash. Draw up a statement to show how much in the £ each class of creditors, shareholders, etc. will receive.

No. 126

The Balance Sheet of the ESBA Bookshop at the start of 19.8 was as follows:

ESBA BOOKSHOP

BALANCE SHEET

(as at January 1st, 19.8)

Claims	£	*Assets*	£	£
Ownership Interest	2,600	Shop Fittings: Cost	1,500	
Trade Creditors	850	Accumulated		
Rent Owing	250	Depreciation	450	
Bank Overdraft	750			1,050
		Stock of Books		2,600
		Trade Debtors		800
	£4,450			£4,450

Transactions for 19.8 were:

	£
(i) Sale of books	10,000
(ii) Cost of books sold	7,000
(iii) Wages and general expenses	850
(iv) Depreciation of shop fittings	150
(v) Payment to landlord for rent (see note)	1,500
(vi) Withdrawal of capital by owners	500

At December 31st, 19.8 the values of certain items in the Balance Sheet were:

(i) Stock of books	2,300
(ii) Trade debtors	650
(iii) Trade creditors	1,200

Note: Rental payment: The annual rent of the bookshop is £1,000. This payment represented rent for the period from October 1st, 19.7 to March 31st, 19.9.

Required:

(*a*) Prepare for the firm for the year 19.8

(i) Profit and Loss report, and

(ii) Flow of funds statement giving the causes of the change in the cash balance over the year.

(*b*) Indicate briefly the use which the firm's management might make of (*a*(i)) and (*a*(ii)), distinguishing between the function of each report.

No. 127

Dixon is considering purchasing a retail newsagent's business offered for sale by its owner, Evans. The most recent accounts for the business are given below, Dixon has asked you to advise him on the maximum price that he should offer for the business.

Required:

(*a*) State the principles that you would follow in calculating the maximum price that Dixon should offer.

(*b*) State, with reasons, what further information you would require before you could perform the calculation.

PROFIT AND LOSS ACCOUNT
(for the year ended May 31st, 19.9)

Sales of newspapers, etc.	25,503
Less Cost of Sales	21,352
	4,151
Less Overhead Expenses	279
Net Profit	£3,872

BALANCE SHEET
(as at May 31st, 19.9)

	£	£
Fixed Assets: at Cost		
Goodwill	3,750	
Freehold Shop	6,225	
Equipment	1,530	
		11,505
Current Assets:		
Stock of Goods for Resale	103	
Debtors	15	
Cash	1	
	119	
Less Creditors	52	
		67
		£11,572
Capital:	£	£
As at June 1st, 19.8		10,651
Profit for 19.8–9	3,872	
Less Drawings	2,951	
		921
		£11,572

No. 128

Look through the information given below about Scallions Ltd. Then answer *any three* of sub-questions (*a*), (*b*), (*c*), (*d*) and (*e*) below, from that information. Ignore tax.

(*a*) The figures for the 'shareholders' interest' section of the 19.8 Balance Sheet are not complete. Draft a statement showing, in detail, all the figures that should go in this section. (You can assume that all figures already shown in the Balance Sheet are correct.)

(*b*) Show the 19.8 Appropriation Account as it would appear in order to be consistent with the Balance Sheets. (The directors take the view that goodwill should be written off as far as possible, but regard any such amounts written off as 'appropriations of profit', not as 'business expenses'.)

(*c*) Explain to what extent, and how, the bonus issue in 19.8 will be of advantage to the shareholders.

(*d*) Suppose that the debentures must be redeemed at par by annual instalments over a period of 17 years, beginning on January 1st, 19.0. The amount of money to be used in redemption each year is the annual instalment of a sinking fund (which is assumed to earn interest at 4 per cent *per annum*) plus the annual interest added to the fund. What is the amount of the annual instalment?

(*e*) A prospective purchaser of all the ordinary shares in Scallions requires a valuation per share as at December 31st, 19.9. It is agreed that:

(i) the asset values shown in the Balance Sheet are good approximations of the saleable value of the assets (the figure for goodwill being excepted), and

(ii) if a stock market quotation were obtained for the ordinary shares they would be quoted on the basis of a 5 per cent dividend yield (dividend/price ratio) applied to the 19.8 dividend.

What is the maximum price that could reasonably be offered, *per ordinary share*? Show your calculations.

SCALLIONS LTD

Simplified Balance Sheets, at December 31st

	19.7 £	19.8 £		19.7 £	19.8 £
Shareholders' Interest			*Fixed Assets*		
Ordinary Shares of £1	20,000		Goodwill—Cost, *Less* written off	5,370	3,000
7% Preference Shares of £1	14,000		Plant and Buildings—Cost	36,800	51,800
Revenue Reserves	19,087	9,570	*Less* Depreciation	14,350	17,600
				22,450	34,200
	53,087				
6% Debentures	10,000	10,000			
Current Liabilities			*Current Assets*		
Dividends Payable to Shareholders	3,980	5,180	Stocks	17,415	17,900
Creditors	9,173	7,830	Debtors	18,585	19,415
	13,153	13,010	Bank	12,420	17,065
				48,420	54,380
	76,240	91,580		76,240	91,580

In January 19.8:

A one-for-two bonus issue was made to the ordinary shareholders by capitalising reserves.

In February 19.8:

The plant of a retiring competitor was bought, and the full price of £15,000 was added to 'plant and buildings' (and was met by the issue to him of 12,000 ordinary shares, then valued at £1.25).

In December 19.8:

The directors decided to recommend the payment of the whole year's dividends (i.e. the preference dividend and a dividend on all ordinary shares at £0.10 per share); this is already allowed for in the Balance Sheet above.

19.8 trading results:

Sales revenue £55,000 Net profit £8,033 (against £6,500 in 19.7)

In a liquidation the preference shares and debentures are repayable at par.

No. 129

Suppose that Scallions Ltd (see Example 128) is suspected of monopolistic practices. Do you consider that the information supplied supports this suspicion? State:

(*a*) what figures might reasonably be used to support or refute your conclusion?

(*b*) what qualifications, if any, would you place on such a conclusion?

No. 130

You are in the chair at the directors' meeting that discusses the company's annual accounts (for publication to shareholders). Some of your colleagues (experienced on the engineering side rather than accounting) put the following points:

(*a*) 'With such a big bank overdraft, there must have been quite a lot of interest due at the year end. How have we allowed for this accrued cost?'

(*b*) 'What about the payment for that new hydraulic press that we bought during the year? Is it included in the charge for maintenance?'

(*c*) 'Isn't it a bit silly of us, when we've got a big general reserve, not to use it to pay off that expensive overdraft?'

(*d*) 'Why don't we show the sales? I feel rather proud of them.'

(*e*) 'A chap was telling me all about cash flow. How would one find the figure for our company?'

Required: Suitable answers to *any four* of these questions. (Aim to give a clear picture to laymen, rather than to show your mastery of technical subtleties.)

No. 131

At March 31st, 19.. the balances in the ledger of the London and Hampstead Bank Ltd, are:

	£
Premises	49,000
Capital (4,800 shares of £10, fully paid)	48,000
Advances	293,000
Deposits, etc.	1,030,000
Reserves	30,000
Cash	315,000
Bills discounted	22,000
Money at call	75,000
Profits	3,000
Investments	357,000

These balances require adjustment for certain last-minute transactions:

(*a*) New premises have been bought for £24,000, the price being met by the issue of 1,600 new shares of £10 at an agreed market value of £15 each.

(*b*) 'Deposits etc. . . . £1,030,000' is in fact the aggregate of deposits by the public (£970,000) and a secret 'reserve for contingencies' (£60,000). £7,000 of the reserve is now to be brought back and credited to profit.

(*c*) The bank has subscribed for £40,000 of a new government loan at par.

Required: Balance sheet in conventional form.

No. 132

The accounts for a company's first two years (up to December 31st last), have been put before the directors (by an unskilled book-keeper) in this form:

INCOME ACCOUNTS

	Year I	*Year II*
	£	£
Materials Used	7,200	8,400
Factory Wages	11,400	13,200
Factory Expenses (including Rent)	4,600	4,900
Depreciation Reserve	520	750
Office Expenses	2,300	2,600
Contingency Reserve	280	180
General Reserve	—	3,000
Dividend Reserve	—	600
Net Profit for the Year	1,800	470
Sales	£28,100	£34,100

BALANCE SHEETS

	£	£
Cash	4,300	2,200
Debtors	2,800	4,600
Stock	1,900	2,500
Plant—Cost	5,200	7,500
	£14,200	£16,800

Creditors	5,600	3,200
Reserves: General	—	3,000
Depreciation	520	1,270
Contingency	280	460
Dividend	—	600
Profit	1,800	2,270
Capital (6,000 ordinary shares of £1)	6,000	6,000
	£14,200	£16,800

No dividend was paid for Year I. The directors have tentatively decided to pay a dividend of £0.10 per share for Year II (hence the reserve in the above accounts). Some of them now oppose the payment, on the ground that 'the revenue account shows profit to be falling' and 'if cash goes on sinking at this rate, we'll need every penny'.

Required: Submit a brief formal report to the directors on this matter. Include, as an appendix or otherwise, a revised balance sheet in 'narrative' form, and such other figures as seem helpful. Ignore tax. You find that the 'contingency reserve' is for doubtful debts, and is fully justified by delays in payment.

No. 133

On January 1st, 19.8 *Pyramid Ltd* acquired 100 per cent of the equity capital of *Y Ltd* and 70 per cent of the equity capital of *Z Ltd.* The accountant of *Pyramid Ltd* is unable to determine the appropriate treatment in the accounts of the company and the group for the year ending December 31st, 19.8 of certain items arising in connection with the subsidiaries, viz.:

(*a*) Cash remitted by *Y Ltd* in December 19.8 was received and recorded by *Pyramid Ltd* in January 19.9.

(*b*) On January 1st, 19.8 *Y Ltd* had a debit balance on Profit and Loss Account. (The accountant reminds you of the normal accounting convention of conservatism in writing off losses.)

(*c*) *Pyramid Ltd* paid for the shares in *Y Ltd* more than the book value of the net assets acquired. (The accountant hesitates to record a cost for 'goodwill' on purchase of a company with accumulated losses.)

(*d*) During 19.8 *Z Ltd* paid a dividend out of profits earned in 19.7.

(*e*) During 19.8 *Pyramid Ltd* has sold goods to *Z Ltd* at cost plus 25 per cent. *Z Ltd* has resold most of these goods, but some are still in stock at December 31st, 19.8, and are recorded in the books of *Z Ltd* at the cost to that company.

Required: In respect of each item, a clear statement of the accounting problems involved, and a recommendation, with reasons, as to their most appropriate solution.

No. 134

Winter and Felton are partners sharing all profits in the ratio 2:1. Their Balance Sheet at May 31st, 19.. ran:

	£		£
Creditors	1,373	Cash	58
Capital: Winter	2,300	Debtors	705
Fenton	1,590	Premises	4,500
	£5,263		£5,263

Business has been poor, and the partners accept an offer from Buckingham Stores Ltd, to take over all their assets (save cash) and the creditors, on June 1st. The price is £3,700 (£1,400 in cash plus 2,000 new ordinary shares issued by Buckingham Stores and valued at £1.15).

Closing expenses are £33, borne by the partnership and paid in cash. On June 10th, the price is paid, the partners each take 1,000 shares, and the partnership is wound up.

Required:

(*a*) The accounts in the partners' ledger needed to show the dissolution.
(*b*) Journal entry in the company's books to record the purchase (the old book-values being retained, save that the premises are revalued at £4,390).

No. 135

Singh and Pereira are in partnership sharing profits equally, their accounting year end being December 31st. On March 1st, 1982, a company (SP Ltd) was incorporated in order to take over the trading activities of the partnership as from January 1st, 1982. The purchase consideration was settled by the issue to the partnership of 420,000 M$1 Ordinary Shares in exchange for the following assets: goodwill, land and buildings, plant and machinery, and stocks.

The business was carried on by the partnership on behalf of the new company from January 1st, 1982 to March 31st, 1982 and no recognition of the change in ownership appeared in the accounting records during this period.

The following trial balance was extracted from the partnership books as at March 31st, 1982:

	M$	*M$*
Goodwill	54,000	
Land and buildings	150,000	
Plant and machinery	132,000	
Stock (January 1st, 1982)	30,000	
Debtors and creditors	48,000	33,000
Purchases and sales	138,000	273,000
Wages and salaries	105,000	
Discounts allowed and discounts received	3,600	1,800
Directors' remuneration	3,000	
Other expenses	13,200	
Company formation expenses	11,000	
Bank	4,000	
Capital accounts: Singh		223,800
Pereira		160,200
	691,800	691,800

Stocks on March 31st, 1982 were valued at M$21,000 and all revenues and expenses accrued evenly over the three month period. Depreciation is to be ignored.

It had been agreed that the partnership would be responsible for collecting money from customers, and paying suppliers, in respect of the period ending February 28th, 1982. During March 1982 all sales and purchases were made under the company name. The debtors and creditors above include M$24,000 and M$18,000 respectively relating to March 1982.

Required:

(i) Prepare the Trading and Profit and Loss Account of SP Ltd for the three months ending March 31st, 1982, distinguishing between the pre- and post-incorporations profits (or losses).

(ii) Prepare the account of SP Ltd in the books of the partnership for the three months ending March 31st, 1982.

(iii) Prepare the Balance Sheet of the partnership at March 31st, 1982.

(LCC)

No. 136

The following balance sheet was prepared for the partnership of Ardiles and Villa, who shared profits in the ratio of 2 to 1, as at March 31st, 1982:

	£	£		£	£
Capital accounts			*Fixed assets*		14,130
Ardiles	16,000		*Current assets*		
Villa	6,000		Stock	8,400	
		22,000	Debtors	13,770	
Current accounts			Bank	2,290	
Ardiles	4,036				24,460
Villa	3,054				
		7,090			
Loan account					
Ardiles		2,000			
Creditors		7,500			
		£38,590			£38,590

Included in the fixed assets were two cars, having book values of £1,800 and £2,500.

Burkinshaw Ltd made an offer to buy the stock and fixed assets, other than the cars, of the partnership for £21,000, and the partners, wishing to retire from business, accepted. The consideration was satisfied by allotting to the partners 3,000 preference shares and 18,000 ordinary shares in the company.

The debtors were settled for £12,690, and the creditors paid off in full. The partners agreed the closing distribution as follows:

(*a*) Ardiles to take one car for £1,870, and Villa the other for £2,450;

(*b*) Ardiles to take preference shares to the value of his loan, the balance to Villa;

(*c*) the ordinary shares to be allocated according to their profit sharing ratio, and

(*d*) the balance to be settled in cash.

You are required to prepare:

(*a*) the realisation account;
(*b*) the bank account, and
(*c*) the partners' capital accounts.

(SCCA)

No. 137

T. Jones and H. Higgins were partners in a manufacturing business trading under the provisions of the Partnership Act, 1890.

Trial Balance at September 30th, 1982

	£	£
Stocks October 1st, 1981: Raw materials	8,000	
WIP	16,000	
Finished goods	14,000	
Capital: T. Jones		28,000
H. Higgins		40,640
Drawings: T. Jones	14,800	
H. Higgins	12,000	
Creditors		7,600
Debtors	20,800	
Sales of finished goods		210,500
Purchases of raw materials	80,000	
Factory wages	50,000	
Office salaries	9,850	
Rent and rates (factory $\frac{2}{3}$, office $\frac{1}{3}$)	15,000	
Factory power	6,000	
Heat and light (factory $\frac{3}{5}$, office $\frac{2}{5}$)	5,000	
Returns outwards	500	
Salesmen's commission	2,100	
Delivery expenses	4,000	
Postage, stationery, printing	1,800	
Bank charges and interest	800	
Advertising	500	
Plant and equipment (cost)	50,000	
Provision for depreciation		20,000
Office furniture (cost)	5,000	
Provision for depreciation		3,000
Office machinery (cost)	3,000	
Provision for depreciation		1,800
Insurance	390	
Bank		20,000
Factory manager's salary	12,000	
	£331,540	£331,540

Additional information

(1) Stocks on hand September 30th, 1982:

Finished goods	£16,000
Raw materials	£12,000
Work in progress	£18,000

(2) At the end of the year the following adjustments have to be made: factory wages due £2,000; office wages due £150, and insurance prepaid £40.

(3) During the year Mr Jones had taken finished goods for his personal use valued, at cost, at £200.

(4) Depreciation is to be provided as follows:

Plant and equipment	10 per cent	on cost
Office furniture	5 per cent	on cost
Office machinery	20 per cent	on cost

(5) A bad debt provision equal to 5 per cent sundry debtors is to be provided.

From the trial balance and additional information provided, you are required to prepare the Manufacturing Account, the Trading and Appropriation Account for the year ended September 30th, 1982 and a Balance Sheet as at that date.

(SCCA)

No. 138

Mr Wong, the owner of a furniture store, submits the following Balance Sheet to you soon after March 31st, 1982, the end of his first year of trading:

	S$		S$
Wong: Capital Account		Fixtures and fittings	
		(cost S$10,000)	9,000
Introduced April 1st, 1981	20,000	Motor vehicle (cost S$4,800)	3,600
Net profit for the year	8,500	Stock on premises, at cost	7,700
	28,500	Debtors for goods sold	5,210
Drawings	6,900		
	21,600		
Creditors and accrued expenses	2,900		
Bank	1,010		
	25,510		25,510

On investigation you discover the following:

(1) All the fixed assets were acquired on April 1st, 1981 and the depreciation policy adopted (straight-line, ignoring residual value, with

annual rates of 10 per cent on fixtures and 25 per cent on vehicles) appears reasonable. However, a fixture costing S$800 had been sold on January 1st, 1982 for S$690 and Wong had recorded this by debiting bank and crediting the proceeds to Sales Account. No other entry had been made in respect of this sale.

(2) Included in the stock of S$7,700 was an item costing S$700 which Wong estimates will be saleable for between S$300 and S$400 if further advertising expenditure of S$45 is incurred.

(3) Goods costing S$750 had been sent to a customer on sale or return in March for which he had been invoiced at S$1,000. The full amount was in fact paid in April.

(4) Another customer had bought a suite of furniture in February for cash but soon afterwards complained that it was faulty. After much argument the customer kept the suite but in April Wong paid him S$60 as an allowance in settlement of his claim.

(5) On March 31st, 1982 Wong had received an invoice for S$150 from his insurance company for fire insurance for the year ended March 31st, 1983. Since it was payable immediately Wong included it in accrued expenses.

(6) In all other respects you consider the amounts appearing in the Balance Sheet to be satisfactory.

Required:

(i) A revised Balance Sheet at March 31st, 1982, in good style, prepared in accordance with recognised concepts, showing clearly the revised net profit figure.

(ii) Explain the concepts which you have applied in respect of items (2), (3), (4) and (5) above.

(LCC)

No. 139

Ang, Boon and Chan had traded as partners for many years, sharing profits and losses in proportion to their fixed capitals. Their Balance Sheet at March 31st, 1982 was as follows:

	Ang	*Boon*	*Chan*	*Total*			
	S$	*S$*	*S$*	*S$*			*S$*
Capital accounts	30,000	30,000	20,000	80,000	Fixed assets (net of depreciation):		
					Motor vehicles		16,800
Current accounts	1,100	2,100	900	4,100	Others		51,000
							67,800
Trade creditors				12,800		S$	
Bank overdraft				2,900	Stock		18,500
					Debtors	15,000	
					Less provision	1,500	13,500
				99,800			99,800

On April 1st 1982 it was agreed that Chan should retire and that Tan should be admitted to the partnership. The following terms were agreed:

(1) The assets were to be revalued, and the new valuations were to appear in the books, as follows:

	S$
Motor vehicles	20,000
Other fixed assets	60,000
Stock	16,400

The doubtful debts provision was to be reduced *to* S$800.

(2) Goodwill was valued at S$24,000: no goodwill account was to appear in the books, any necessary adjustments being made through the partners' *current* accounts.

(3) Chan was to take one of the motor vehicles (at its revised value of S$2,000) and the balance due to him in cash.

(4) Tan was to contribute, in cash, S$30,000 as capital and S$8,000 for his one-third share of goodwill. Future profits and losses were to be shared equally by Ang, Boon and Tan.

The above transactions all took place on April 1st, 1982.

Required:

(i) Journal entries to record the above transactions.

(ii) The Balance Sheet of the new partnership immediately afterwards.

(LCC)

No. 140

On January 1st, 1982 the Balance Sheet of Able Ltd, was as follows:

	£		£
100,000 Issued		Freehold premises	35,000
50p Ordinary Shares, fully paid	40,000	Plant and machinery	20,000
		Motor vehicles	5,000
Revenue reserves	10,900	Stock	6,700
		Debtors	7,800
Creditors	13,800	Bank	200
	£74,700		£74,700

At the same date the Balance Sheet of Mr Baker, a sole trader, was:

	£		£
Capital	10,000	Leasehold premises	4,500
Bank overdraft	600	Plant and machinery	1,800
Creditors	1,700	Motor vehicles	1,200
		Stock	3,300
		Debtors	1,500
	£12,300		£12,300

Baker agreed to the immediate transfer of his business assets and liabilities (except the overdraft) to Able Ltd, for a total consideration of £12,500. For this purpose, the following revised values were decided upon:

Leasehold premises	£5,000
Plant and machinery	£1,500
Motor vehicles	£900
Stock	£3,200
Debtors	£1,300
Creditors	£1,600

In full satisfaction, Baker was given £10,000 cash and 4,000 Ordinary Shares in Able Ltd. Able Ltd raised cash by issuing to existing shareholders a further 10,000 Ordinary Shares at the same price as those issued to Baker and by issuing £4,000 10 per cent Debentures at a discount of 2½ per cent.

Required:

(i) In the books of Baker, the realisation account and the account of Able Ltd.

(ii) The Balance Sheet of Able Ltd, after the transactions were completed.

Note:
Assume that all transactions took place on January 1st, 1982, and that there were no other transactions.

(LCC)

No. 141

Shah Ltd has the following long term capital structure:

	M$000
Share Capital (issued and fully paid)	
Ordinary shares of M$1 each	600
12% Redeemable preference Shares	300
Reserves	
Share premium account	60
Retained earnings	250
Loan Capital	
10% Debentures	100
	1,310

The company's directors now propose the following actions:

(1) Redeem the preference shares at a premium of 8 per cent.

(2) Finance (1) above by: making a rights issue of ordinary shares (one new share for every five existing shares at a premium of 15 per cent); issuing M$150,000 of 10 per cent debentures at a discount of 4 per cent; arranging for the company's bank overdraft limit to be extended.

(3) Make a bonus (capitalisation) issue of ordinary shares on the basis of two shares for every five held before the rights issue in (2) above.

The directors of Shah Ltd are also anxious to minimise any restriction on their power to recommend dividends in future years.

Required:

(i) Show, by drafting the relevant ledger accounts, how the long-term capital structure of Shah Ltd will appear, after the directors' proposals have been carried out.

(ii) In relation to the redemption of redeemable preference shares, discuss the following statement: 'It is a firm principle of company law that share capital cannot be repaid.'

(LCC)

No. 142

Your colleague, Stanley, has passed to you the following Trial Balance of Zebra Ltd, after provisionally completing the Profit and Loss Account for the year ended April 30th, 1982:

	£	£
210,000 Authorised and issued £1 ordinary shares		210,000
Preliminary expenses	1,200	
Freehold land at cost	112,000	
Plant and machinery at cost	64,000	
Depreciation provisions:		
Plant and machinery		28,000
Motor vehicles		2,200
Motor vehicles at cost	7,800	
Work in progress	48,000	
Finished goods	27,600	
Raw materials	9,300	
Creditors and accruals		15,700
Debtors and prepayments	14,620	
Bank	180	
Profit & Loss		17,800
Share premium		11,000
	£284,700	£284,700

He seeks your assistance in preparing the company's Balance Sheet, but first would like to know if any revisions are necessary in respect of the following items:

(1) The legal costs of buying the land, amounting to £5,000, are included in the freehold land at cost account balance.

(2) The bank balance was in accordance with the company's books, but a bank statement received in May 1982 shows two other payments made in April 1982 as follows:

Bank charges—£220
Insurance premium in respect of fire insurance for the year commencing May 1st, 1982—£185.

(3) The plant and machinery was bought in May 1980. Acting on instructions, Stanley has provided £12,000 this year for its depreciation.

(4) The company has signed a contract to buy a further machine for £30,000 for delivery in June 1982.

(5) Stanley has forgotten to deal with the preliminary expenses. He was instructed to do so, without affecting the Profit and Loss Account balance.

(6) The directors are recommending a dividend of 5p per share.

(7) The values of work in progress and finished goods stock include an allocation of fixed manufacturing overhead, amounting to £10,000.

Required:

(i) Journal entries (including those relating to cash) in respect of those items where adjustments are necessary. (Narrations are not required.) Where no entry is necessary, briefly give your reasoning.

(ii) The Balance Sheet of Zebra Ltd, in good style, at April 30th, 1982.

Note:
Ignore taxation.

(LCC)

No. 143

The draft Balance Sheet of Stroke Ltd at September 30th, 1981 was presented to you in the following form:

	£		£
Share capital authorised issued and fully paid ordinary shares of £1 each	500,000	Property at valuation	250,000
Profit and Loss Account	160,000	Plant and machinery at book value	184,000
12% Debentures	140,000	Investments at cost	188,000
Creditors	180,000	Stocks	152,000
Corporation tax	64,000	Debtors	270,000
	1,044,000		1,044,000

You subsequently discover that:

(1) The property valuation had been made by an expert during the financial year. The original cost was £196,000 and the surplus on revaluation had been credited to the Profit and Loss Account.

(2) The accumulated depreciation in respect of plant and machinery was £88,000.

(3) Stocks have been valued at the lower of cost or net realisable value but include goods at branches at the cost to the branches of £48,000. Goods are invoiced by head office to branches at cost plus 50 per cent.

(4) The debtors figure includes £15,000 owed by the managing director and a short term loan to an employee of £6,000.

(5) Stroke Ltd originally issued debentures with a nominal value of £300,000 but has subsequently reduced the company's long term indebtedness by purchasing them on the open market. During the last financial year £20,000 at par value were so purchased at a discount of 5 per cent. These have been included (at cost) in investments at cost. *All* debentures purchased are available for reissue.

(6) The remaining investments comprise: shares costing £46,000 currently listed on a recognised stock exchange and having a market value of £41,000; shares purchased several years ago for £123,000 in an unlisted company in which Stroke Ltd both owns more than 20 per cent of the equity share capital and over whose policies Stroke Ltd exercises considerable influence. The unlisted shares are considered by the directors to be worth £160,000.

(7) Creditors include net indebtedness to the company's bankers of £25,000. According to Stroke Ltd's accounting records, the overdraft at North Bank was £40,000, whereas it had a balance in hand at South Bank of £15,000.

(8) The corporation tax figure comprises £28,000 payable January 1st, 1982 and £36,000 due January 1st, 1983.

Required: In so far as you are able, from the data available, prepare a revised Balance Sheet for Stroke Ltd at September 30th, 1981 in a form suitable for publication.

(LCC)

No. 144

The following items appeared (among others) in the Trial Balance of Gee Ltd, a company without subsidiaries, on June 30th, 1982.

	£000	£000
Trading profit for the year ended June 30th, 1982		140
Debenture interest	36	
Dividend on preference shares: half year to December 31st, 1981	7	
Share Capital: authorised, issued and fully paid		
200,000 7% preference shares of £1 each		200
700,000 ordinary shares of £1 each		700
12% Debentures		300
Retained profits at July 1st, 1981		59
Freehold land, at cost	220	
Freehold buildings, at cost	100	

In addition:

(1) Trading profit for the year is *after* charging:

	£000
Depreciation on machinery	65
Audit fee	3
Bank interest	6
Discounts allowed	19
Directors' salaries	83
Pension to former director	8
Loss on closure of overseas branch	28

(2) At June 30th, 1982 the directors resolve:

(*a*) To include freehold land in the accounts at its market value of £300,000.

(*b*) To provide depreciation at the rate of 2 per cent per annum on the cost of freehold buildings as from the date of purchase. The buildings were purchased on July 1st, 1978 and have not previously been depreciated.

(*c*) To provide for directors' fees of £10,000, and for bad debts of £8,000.

(*d*) To recommend the payment of the half-year's preference dividend to June 30th, 1982, and of an ordinary dividend of 8 pence (£0.08) per ordinary share.

Required: Prepare, in so far as the data permit, and in accordance with the requirements of the Companies Acts and of any relevant Statements of Standard Accounting Practice, a Profit and Loss Account (including Appropriation Account) for the year ended June 30th, 1982.

Note:
Ignore taxation.

(LCC)

No. 145

Xanthus Ltd's latest Balance Sheet, in summary form, was as follows:

Xanthus Ltd—Balance Sheet at 30th June, 1982

		£000
Share capital (authorised £2,000,000), issued and fully paid:		
7% Redeemable preference shares of £1 each		
(redeemable at par on July 1st, 1982)		600
Ordinary shares of £1 each		1,000
		1,600
Reserves:	£000	
Share premium account	100	
Retained profits	500	600
Sundry net assets		2,200

The redeemable preference shareholders were offered the following options with regard to the redemption of their shares (as specified in the original terms of issue):

Either: (1) accept 100 new ordinary shares of £1 each, fully paid, in exchange for each 150 preference shares,
Or: (2) accept £100 of 12 per cent unsecured loan stock, at par, in exchange for each 100 preference shares.

Holders of 330,000 redeemable preference shar[illegible]
shares, the remainder accepted loan stock. Both th[illegible]
loan stock were issued on July 1st, 1982, on which dat[illegible]
shares were redeemed.

Required:

(i) Journal entries to record the above transactions.

(ii) Xanthus Ltd's Balance Sheet, immediately after the transactions had occurred.

(iii) Explain briefly:

(*a*) the purpose of creating a Capital Redemption Reserve Fund;

(*b*) the use(s) to which it can be put, as compared with a Share Premium Account.

(LCC)

No. 146

The following balances appeared in the books of Poon Ltd and Sing Ltd at December 31st, 1981 after the Trading and Profit and Loss Accounts for the year had been prepared.

	Poon Ltd		*Sing Ltd*	
	Dr	*Cr*	*Dr*	*Cr*
	S$000	*S$000*	*S$000*	*S$000*
Trading profit for the year 1981		160		100
Retained profits at January 1st, 1981		58		90
Ordinary Shares of S$1 each		920		400
Current liabilities		180		254
Fixed assets (net of depreciation)	470		312	
Investment in Sing Ltd at cost	400			
Current assets	448		532	
	1,318	1,318	844	844

Notes:

(1) The investment in Sing Ltd comprises 320,000 shares acquired on January 1st, 1978 when Sing Ltd had a *credit* balance of S$40,000 on Retained Profits Account.

(2) At December 31st, 1981:

(*a*) The directors of Poon Ltd proposed a dividend of S$184,000.

(*b*) The directors of Sing Ltd proposed a dividend of S$50,000.

Required: Prepare for Poon Ltd and its subsidiary Sing Ltd:

(i) Consolidated Profit and Loss Account for the year ended December 31st, 1981.

(ii) Consolidated Balance Sheet at December 31st, 1981.

(LCC)

No. 147

The following balance sheet extracts relate to the business of Essence Ltd. You are required to prepare a Funds Flow Statement for the year ended December 31st, 1981.

		£	December 31st 1980 £	£	December 31st 1981 £
Capital (£1 ordinary shares)			1,000		1,000
Reserves			2,000		3,000
10% Debentures			1,000		—
Creditors			3,000		3,500
Bank overdraft			—		500
			£7,000		£8,000
Fixed Assets					
Fixtures and Fittings	Cost.	2,000		3,000	
	Depn.	500		1,000	
			1,500		2,000
Equipment	Cost	3,000		4,000	
	Depn.	1,500		2,000	
			1,500		2,000
			3,000		4,000
Current Assets					
Stock			2,500		2,800
Debtors			1,300		1,200
Bank			200		—
			£7,000		£8,000

(SCCA)

No. 148

Martin Ltd agreed to buy all the shares of Norman Ltd and Oracle Ltd on April 1st, 1982 for a total consideration of 270,000 ordinary £1 shares in Martin Ltd to be divided in proportion to the agreed net asset values. The Balance Sheets of the three companies at that date were as follows:

	Martin Ltd £000	*Norman Ltd* £000	*Oracle Ltd* £000
Ordinary shares of £1 each	300	150	45
Share premium	60	20	8
Retained profits	90	10	7
Creditor: Norman Ltd	—	—	18
Other current liabilities	75	57	54
	525	237	132
Fixed assets	375	150	90
Debtor: Oracle Ltd	—	18	—
Other current assets	150	69	42
	525	237	132

For the purposes of the takeover it was agreed that:

(1) The fixed assets and 'other current assets' of Norman Ltd and Oracle Ltd should be revalued at:

	Norman Ltd	*Oracle Ltd*
	£000	*£000*
Fixed assets	164	104
Other current assets	77	39

(2) Goodwill should be valued at four years' purchase of the average trading profits of the past three years after deducting, for each year, 'normal profit' equal to 15 per cent of the equity shareholders' interest at 1st April, 1982 as shown by the Balance Sheets of Norman Ltd and Oracle Ltd. *before* the revaluations mentioned above had taken place.

Trading profits have been:

	Norman Ltd	*Oracle Ltd*
	£000	*£000*
Year ended March 31st, 1980	31	18
" " " " 1981	38	20
" " " " 1982	45	28

Required:

(i) Explain what you understand by 'equity shareholders' interest'; calculate the goodwill of Norman Ltd and Oracle Ltd, and calculate the *number* of shares to be issued by Martin Ltd to the shareholders of Norman Ltd and Oracle Ltd respectively in exchange for their existing shares.

(ii) Prepare a summarised Balance Sheet of Martin Ltd immediately after the takeover.

(LCC)

No. 149

John, a friend of yours who knows that you are studying accounting, asks you to help in understanding the accounts of Lim Ltd, a company in which he holds a lot of shares, and which for the last few years has paid an annual dividend of S$60,000 on its share capital of S$300,000. However, no dividend is being proposed for 1981; according to the Chairman's statement accompanying the annual accounts, this is because of a shortage of cash. John finds this difficult to understand. He says:

According to the Flow of Funds Statement for 1981, sources of funds during the year included S$80,000 net profit, S$92,000 depreciation written off and a loss of S$30,000 on old machinery which was sold for S$78,000. Also, in the Balance Sheet at the end of the year total depreciation was S$180,000.

I don't understand how a loss on sale can be a source of funds, but if it is, and if the company has so much depreciation money set aside, why can't they afford to pay a dividend?

On examining the Balance Sheets at December 31st, 1980 and 1981 you see the following:

	1980	*1981*
	S$000	S$000
Machinery at cost	384	495
Less accumulated depreciation	210	180
	174	315

The company has no fixed assets except machinery.

Required:

(i) Draft the ledger accounts relating to machinery for the year ending December 31st, 1981 and state the amount spent on new machinery during the year.

(ii) Write a letter to John, explaining in simple language those features of Lim Ltd's results which are puzzling him.

(LCC)

No. 150

The Balance Sheets of T. Caddy's business at October 31st, 1980 and October 31st, 1981 are summarised below:

	1980	*1981*		*1980*	*1981*
	£	£		£	£
Opening capital	39,100	46,700	Equipment (at cost)	51,200	47,740
Profit (Loss) for year	16,440	(19,280)	*Less* Depreciation	17,600	14,400
	55,540	27,420		33,600	33,340
Drawings	8,840	7,720	Stock	19,000	12,640
	46,700	19,700	Debtors	9,900	14,940
Loan 12% (repayable December 31st, 1983)	—	15,000	Bank	—	180
Creditors	12,940	26,400			
Bank	2,860	—			
	62,500	61,100		62,500	61,100

You are given the following additional information:

(1) On May 1st, 1981, equipment costing £15,000 was sold for £6,900. The profit of £900 has been credited to Caddy's Profit and Loss Account.

(2) Caddy's loss during the year ended October 31st, 1981 reflects the fact that he had to cease trading for several weeks while the equipment sold was dismantled and replaced.

Required:

(i) Calculate the depreciation expense in respect of the year to October 31st, 1981.

(ii) Prepare a Sources and Uses of Funds Statement for T. Caddy in respect of the year to October 31st, 1981 in such a way as to explain the change in his bank balance over that year.

(iii) Calculate two liquidity ratios from each of the above Balance Sheets and comment briefly on T. Caddy's financial position at October 31st. 1981.

(LCC)

No. 151

Mr and Mrs Hardy are the only directors and shareholders of Hardy Ltd, a company which sells and repairs television sets. The directors work full-time in the business. Summarised Balance Sheets and Revenue Accounts for 1980 and 1981 are given below.

BALANCE SHEETS
(as at December 31st)

	1980	*1980*		*1980*	*1981*
	£	£		£	£
Issued share capital	56,000	56,000	Freehold premises (at cost or valuation)	64,000	86,000
Capital reserve arising on property revaluation	—	22,000	Equipment (cost *Less* depreciation)	24,000	28,320
Retained profits	10,000	19,000			
10% Mortgage (repayable 1984)	32,000	32,000	Stock	12,500	19,680
Trade creditors	8,000	9,800	Debtors	7,500	3,900
Bank overdraft	2,000	—	Bank	—	900
	108,000	138,800		108,000	138,800

REVENUE ACCOUNTS

	1980	*1981*
	£	£
Cost of goods sold	100,000	116,000
Wages and salaries	12,000	17,700
Depreciation of equipment	4,800	6,400
General expenses	24,000	31,700
Mortgage interest	3,200	3,200
Directors' remuneration	8,000	8,000
Net profit	8,000	9,000
Sales	£160,000	£192,000

No dividends were paid or proposed in either year.

During April 1981, some equipment, which had a net book value of

£1,980 on December 31st, 1980, was sold for £1,750. The loss was included in 'general expenses'. In the same month other equipment was bought, but there were no movements in property during 1981.

Required:

(i) A Statement of Sources and Applications of Funds for 1981, in good style.

(ii) A brief written report, comparing the company's performance in 1981 with 1980. Your report should include, and comment upon, the following ratios for both years:

1. Working Capital ratio.
2. The 'Acid Test' ratio.
3. Gross profit to sales percentage.
4. Net profit to sales percentage.
5. Return on Capital employed.

Note:
Ignore dividends.

(LCC)

No. 152

The following are the summarised Balance Sheets of Quorn Ltd, a company without subsidiaries, at December 31st, 1980 and December 31st, 1981:

	1980	*1981*
	£000	*£000*
Ordinary shares of £1 each	50	80
Share premium	10	25
Surplus on revaluation of freehold land	—	28
Retained profits	25	29
Mortgage loan	17	15
Creditors	13	19
Proposed dividend	5	9
Bank	9	—
	129	205

	£000	*£000*	*£000*	*£000*
Freehold land		25		68
Fixtures and vehicles: cost	32		41	
Fixtures and vehicles: accumulated depreciation	16	16	19	22
Investments, at cost	—	18	—	27
Stocks		43		41
Debtors		27		45
Bank		—		2
		129		205

In addition:

(1) A bonus (capitalisation) issue of 10,000 shares (at par) had been made out of retained profits during the year.

(2) Fixtures and vehicles originally costing £13,000 (book value at date of sale £5,000) had been sold during the year for £4,000. No other fixed assets had been sold.

(3) No interim dividends had been paid during the year.

(4) No investments had been sold during the year.

Required:

(i) What do you understand by the 'net liquid funds' of a company? How would you decide whether Quorn Ltd's 'investments' were part of 'net liquid funds'?

(ii) Calculate the net profit for 1981 and the total funds generated from operations during 1981.

(iii) Prepare, in accordance with Standard Accounting Practice, a Statement of Source and Application of Funds for the year 1981.

Assume, for this part of the answer, that 'investments' are long-term assets.

Note:
Ignore taxation.

(LCC)

Examples from Chapter 4

No. 153

Hotspur Ltd, whose head office was in London, opened a branch in Newcastle on January 1st, 1981. Head office kept all the books, except for local debtor records. All purchases were made by head office and transferred to branch for sale on credit as required, the transfer price being cost plus 25 per cent.

During 1981—

	£
Goods sent to Newcastle (at cost to head office)	34,000
Returns to London (at invoice price to branch)	1,660
Branch sales, all on credit	36,780
Cash received from branch debtors and remitted to head office	31,240
Debtor balances written off as bad	1,470

Stock of goods held at the branch on December 31st, 1981, at invoiced price to branch, totalled £3,535.

The branch manager agreed to accept personal responsibility for all pilferages at the branch over and above an allowance of 1 per cent of goods received.

You are required to write up the following ledger accounts as they would appear in head office books for the year ended December 31st, 1981:

(*a*) goods to branch account;
(*b*) branch stock account;
(*c*) branch adjustment account, and
(*d*) branch debtors account.

(SCCA)

No. 154

(*a*) The Birmstol Trading Co. Ltd has a head office in London and a branch in Surrey. All books are kept at head office and goods are invoiced to the branch at cost.

From the following information you are required to write up the Branch Stock Account.

	£
At January 1st, 1982	
Stock at branch	8,000
Debtors of branch	2,000
Imprest balance	100
Cost of goods sent to branch	28,000
Cash sales made by branch	31,000
Cash paid by branch debtors	6,000
Credit sales made by branch	5,000
Return of faulty goods to head office	100
At December 31st, 1982	
Stock at branch	10,000
Debtors of branch	1,000
Cash imprest at branch	100

(*b*) The company prices its products to achieve a gross profit margin of 25 per cent on selling prices.

What could account for the discrepancy between the actual results achieved by the branch and the normal, anticipated results?

(SCCA)

Examples from Chapter 5

No. 155

Messrs E. Crouch and C. Cook run a retail newsagents and tobacconist business. They do not have a partnership agreement and do not maintain current accounts, but are content to work within the provisions of the Partnership Act of 1890. In the past they have not separated the results of the different activities of their business, but this year they wish the accounts to show the profit margin made on tobacco sales separately from that made on newspaper sales, and the percentage profit margins are also to be shown. The partners inform you that tobacco purchases and sales are consistently three times greater than the amounts for newspapers, but the stock figures relate exclusively to tobacco.

From the following trial balance and notes you are required to prepare the Trading and Profit and Loss Accounts for the year ended December 31st, 1981, in the form requested by the partners, together with a Balance Sheet as at that date.

Trial Balance as at December 31st, 1981

	£	£
Capital accounts: E. Crouch		25,200
C. Cook		42,000
Drawings accounts: E. Crouch	3,500	
C. Cook	4,600	
Leasehold premises	60,000	
Stock	14,800	
Purchases	300,000	
Fixtures and fittings	20,000	
Motor vehicles	15,000	
Debtors and creditors	28,000	20,000
Interest paid	1,000	
Cash	500	
Loan at 10% (repayable in 8 years from January 1st, 1981)		20,000
Sales		356,000
Motor expenses	2,000	
Heat and light	3,000	
Miscellaneous expenses	2,000	
Wages and salaries	4,400	
Rates and insurance	4,400	
	£463,200	£463,200

Further information:

(1) Closing stock was valued at £30,000.

(2) A general provision for bad debts should be made, equal to 10 per cent of sundry debtors.

(3) Depreciation should be provided as follows:

Leasehold Premises	20%
Fixtures and Fittings	25%
Motor Vehicles	20%

(4) The following amounts were due but were not paid as at December 31st, 1981:

	£
Motor Expenses	400
Wages and Salaries	600
Interest on loan	1,000

(5) Rates and insurance were prepaid by £400 at the end of the year.

(SCCA)

No. 156

Slice and Hook entered into a joint venture in order to purchase, and resell, the stock of a company in liquidation. This was acquired on September 1st, for £35,000 of which Slice contributed £20,000 and Hook contributed £15,000.

They agreed that profits (or losses) of the venture should be shared equally after charging interest equal to 5 per cent of the amount each had contributed initially (regardless of the length of time the venture existed) and a commission of 10 per cent in respect of each party's sales. All sales were to be on a cash basis.

Relevant transactions were as follows:

September 2nd	Hook purchased a delivery van for £2,300.
September 5th	Slice incurred advertising expenses £130.
September 7th	Slice collected £6,000, and Hook collected £9,000 in respect of sales.
September 11th	Hook hired a market stall for £160.
September 14th	Slice collected £20,000, and Hook collected £7,500, in respect of sales.
September 17th	Hook paid £430 in respect of van repairs.
September 24th	Slice collected £2,500, and Hook collected £4,200, in respect of sales.
September 30th	Hook took over the delivery van for his own use at an agreed value of £2,000 and Slice took over the small amount of stock remaining unsold at an agreed value of £600 in the hope of selling it on his own behalf. Debts between them were then settled in cash.

Required:

(i) Show in Slice's books—joint venture with Hook account;
(ii) Show in Hook's books—joint venture with Slice account;
(iii) Show the memorandum joint venture account;
(iv) Briefly outline the advantages (and disadvantages) of such arrangements as compared with more formal partnership agreements.

(LCC)

Examples from Chapter 6

No. 157

Clemence was in the transport business. His accounts were made up to

December 31st each year. His depreciation policy was to provide for 20 per cent per annum on a straight line basis, charging a full year in the year of purchase but none in the year of sale.

On February 15th, 1979 he bought two lorries for £4,300 each. He paid a deposit of 10 per cent and took out an agreement with a hire-purchase company to pay the balance, plus total interest of £2,160, over a period of 36 months, starting on the last day of the month following the month of purchase. Clemence could terminate the agreement at any time by payment of the capital amount owing, plus a penalty of £100. Interest is deemed to accrue evenly over the life of the agreement.

On January 1st, 1981 one of the lorries became involved in an accident, and was written off as a total loss. Clemence immediately terminated the agreement with the hire-purchase company on that lorry. On January 27th he received £2,100 from his insurance company.

You are required to write up the following ledger accounts for the period from February 15th, 1979 to December 31st, 1981:

(*a*) lorry account;
(*b*) hire-purchase company account;
(*c*) depreciation account, and
(*d*) disposal account.

(SCCA)

No. 158

Regis acted as agent for Batson Ltd, an exporter of bicycles, for a commission of 10 per cent of gross sales.

On May 1st, 1982 Batson Ltd despatched 90 bicycles, costing £80 each, to Regis, invoiced pro forma at £100 each. The company paid freight and insurance of £450 on the same day.

Only 82 bicycles arrived and £750 was received from the insurers two months later.

On November 11th, 1982 Batson Ltd received an account sales from Regis, showing the position at October 31st, 1982. 67 bicycles had been sold for a total of £7,620. Regis had paid warehouse charges of £180 and carriage of £90. With the account sales was a sight draft for the balance due, on which Regis had paid bank charges of £15. He estimated that repairs to machines unsold would be £160.

You are required to write up the following three ledger accounts in the books of Batson Ltd to record the above transactions:

(*a*) goods on consignment account;
(*b*) consignment to Regis' account, and
(*c*) Regis' account.

(SCCA)

No. 159

Statham designed a new football boot, with a special protective pad for the heel, and granted a licence to Regis Ltd for the manufacture and sale of these boots.

Under the terms of the agreement the company were to pay Statham a royalty of 50p for each pair sold up to 9,000 in any one year, with 40p for each pair sold above this number, subject to a minimum payment of £4,000 per annum. In any year that royalties came to less than the minimum of payment, the deficiency could be set off against excess royalties in either of the next two, succeeding years.

Payment was to be made at the end of the company's financial year, on March 31st.

The number of pairs of boots sold in the first four years of the agreement was as follows:

Year to March 31st, 1979	3,000
,, ,, ,, ,, 1980	9,200
,, ,, ,, ,, 1981	11,000
,, ,, ,, ,, 1982	17,000

Royalty payments were made on the correct day.

You are required to record the entries for the above transactions in the ledger accounts of Regis Ltd.

(SCCA)

No. 160

Write brief notes on any *five* of the following:

(*a*) Sales ledger adjustment account;
(*b*) Retained earnings;
(*c*) Appropriation account;
(*d*) Reserves;
(*e*) Account sales;
(*f*) Statement of affairs;
(*g*) Memorandum joint venture account;
(*h*) Del Credere agent.

(SCCA)

Examples from Chapter 7

No. 161

Mr Nova and his wife own all the shares in the Widget Manufacturing Corporation Ltd, a business which they started just over a year ago. You have prepared the accounts for the first year and they run as follows:

PROFIT AND LOSS ACCOUNT

	£
Direct Manufacturing Costs:	
Materials	54,000
Labour	72,000
Cost of 2,000 Widgets	126,000
Less Stock of 1,000 Finished Widgets	63,000
	63,000
Depreciation of Plant and Machinery	55,000
Other Factory Overheads	34,000
General Overheads	21,000
Research and Development Expenditure written off	17,000
	190,000
Sales—1,000 units @ £130	130,000
Net Loss for the Year	£60,000

BALANCE SHEET

	£		£
Ordinary Shares	500,000	Plant and Machinery—Cost	500,000
Less Profit and Loss Account	60,000	*Less* Depreciation	55,000
			445,000
	440,000	Stocks	63,000
Creditors, etc.	29,000	Debtors	26,000
Bank Overdraft	65,000		
	£534,000		£534,000

Depreciation is provided at 11 per cent p.a. by the reducing-balance method. This rate will reduce the book-value of the plant approximately to £50,000, its residual value, at the end of its life of 20 years.

Mr Nova writes the following letter to you:

Dear Sir,

Thank you for sending me the accounts.

I was very surprised to see that these showed a loss of £60,000 for things seem to have been going rather well. I had planned to produce many more widgets than I could sell in the first year. At maximum capacity, I can only produce 3,000 widgets per annum with this plant and I expect to be able to sell a larger number once my product becomes known. In fact the sales of 1,000 widgets during the first year were slightly better than I expected. In addition, the research department have been working on an improved model with excellent results. It should be possible to produce this soon and make a much higher profit per unit than with the current model.

At the end of the first year, someone offered to buy all the shares of my wife and myself in the company for £750,000. Since we only invested £500,000 in the business, this proves that we have made a profit.

A friend of mine has suggested three alterations which might improve the accounts of the first year:

(*a*) Production overheads (including depreciation) should be included as a cost of production in the valuation of stock.

(*b*) Depreciation of Plant and Machinery should be on a straight-line basis.

(*c*) Research and Development expenditure should be treated as an asset.

Please let me know what profit (or loss) would be shown if these adjustments were made and whether you agree that they are desirable.

Yours faithfully,
S. Nova.

Required: Your reply.

No. 162

The transactions of Rebus Ltd, are:

			£
Year 1.	Jan. 1st	Capital received in cash	1,000
	Jan. 1st	Cash purchase of 100 tons stock at £9	900
Year 2.	June 30th	Cash sale of above stock at £15	1,500
		Cash purchase of 90 tons of same kind of stock at £12	1,080

The general price index stood at 100 on January 1st of Year 1, rose smoothly to 110 during Year 1, and stayed at 110 thereafter.

Required: Table comparing the income accounts and balance sheets for Year 2, drafted according to:

(*a*) Conventional accounting principles (stock valued by FIFO); and

(*b*) As (*a*) (stock valued by LIFO); and

(*c*) Revised principles, based on £s of constant purchasing power. (Use the £ at the close of Year 2.)

No. 163

Moonshine Ltd, manufacturer of plastic name-plates, operates a job costing system in which actual costs incurred on jobs are recorded and accumulated daily on job cards from source documents. Batch totals of the various source documents are posted monthly to the Work-in-Progress and other Control Accounts. On the day a job is completed and transferred to Finished Goods Stock the accumulated cost on the job card is posted to the detail Stock Ledger Account but the total of all transfers is not posted to the Nominal Ledger Control Accounts until the end of the month.

On April 30th, 19. . Moonshine Ltd made a routine quarterly physical stock check at which all jobs actually found to be in progress in the factory were listed on stock sheets and then valued by the accountant at the accumulated cost shown on the individual job cards as at April 30th. The stock sheets for uncompleted jobs were totalled as £6,320 for 148 kg. The balance shown by the Work-in-Progress Control Account (WIPCA) was £6,598 for 158 kg.

When the difference was investigated only the following discrepancies came to light:

(i) 5 kg of Raw Materials in excess of requirements and valued at £155 had been returned to stores by production departments. The transfers had been recorded on the job cards but omitted from the batch totals posted to the control accounts.

(ii) There was an over-addition of £30 in the stock sheet total for uncompleted jobs at April 30th.

(iii) Job No. 253 had been in progress on January 31st but was still not finished at April 30th. Although included in the April stocksheet total the job had been completely overlooked at stocktaking on January 31st and therefore excluded from the adjusted opening balance on the WIPCA for February 1st even though there was an accumulated cost of £92 for 2 kg on the job card.

(iv) Direct costs of £68, correctly charged to WIPCA in April for Job No. 371, were not recorded on the Job Card until May 4th.

(v) On April 10th direct labour of £18 had been incorrectly charged against Job No. 310 which was still in progress at stocktaking when it should have been charged against Job No. 311 which had been transferred to Finished Goods Stock on April 26th but had not been sold at the end of the month.

(vi) Job No. 298 with an accumulated cost of £250 for 5 kg had been totally destroyed in a fire in March. The insurers agreed to meet a claim for £300 in respect of the job but the appropriate entries had not been made in the WIPCA.

(vii) The total of £460 for a batch of documents recording scrap material arising in production and deducted individually from job costs was incorrectly posted as £640 in the Scrap Stock Account and WIPCA.

It is the policy of the company to adjust the WIPCA balance to agree with the corrected total sheet total if there is any difference between the two.

Required:

(*a*) A statement showing the quantity and value of Work-in-Progress which should appear in the Balance Sheet at April 30th, 19. . .

(*b*) The reconciliation of this value with the figures shown in the Work-in-Progress Control Account (£6,598) and Stocksheets (£6,320) before the errors were corrected.

No. 164

Hooks & Crooks Ltd make one type of power bicycle. You find the following figures for the year 19. .

	£
Raw Materials, January 1st	25,000
" " purchased	125,000
Finished Goods, January 1st, 3,200 Bicycles at £30	96,000
Direct Labour	165,000
Manufacturing Expenses (including Foremen's Wages £19,000)	46,000
Selling Costs	240,000
Depreciation, Plant, and Machinery	11,000
Administration (including Depreciation on Office Equipment (£950)	80,000
Bad Debts	16,000
Sales, 12,000 Bicycles	1,080,000
Raw Materials, December 31st	8,000
Finished Bicycles, December 31st, numbered 1,600.	

Required: Suitable income statement. Show also (in extra columns, or separate notes)

(*a*) The number of bicycles manufactured.
(*b*) The manufacturing cost per bicycle (on FIFO assumptions).

No. 165

At the end of its first year of business a manufacturing company's accounts include the following ledger balances:

	£	£
Raw Materials Stock	11,000	
Work-in-Progress Stock	15,600	
Finished Goods Stock	18,900	
Cost of Goods Sold	65,700	
Sales		88,000
Office and Selling Expenses	6,000	

The Work-in-Progress Account has, throughout the year, been debited with the direct-labour cost, the direct-material cost, and the general expenses of the factory. These amounted in total to:

	£
Direct-labour Cost	40,200
Direct-material Cost	26,600
Production Overhead	33,400

The balances of work-in-progress and finished goods at the end of the year contain these three cost components in the same proportion.

Required:

(*a*) Accounting report showing the profit for the year.
(*b*) The same report if, instead of valuing work-in-progress and finished goods on the above basis, they had been valued at prime cost (direct labour and material cost only) throughout the year, cost of sales being computed accordingly.
(*c*) The end-year Balance Sheet values of stocks on the same assumption as in (*b*). Show calculations.

No. 166

On August 2nd, 1982 a fire occurred on the premises of Taylor Ltd which destroyed most of the company's stock. The eventual salvage value proved to be £2,897. The books and records had not been damaged, and showed the following details:

	£
Sales for the year to March 31st, 1982	122,000
Sales for the period to August 2nd, 1982	47,200
Purchases for the year to March 31st, 1982	83,080
Purchases for the period to August 2nd, 1982	29,880
Stock at cost, April 1st, 1981	35,440
Stock as per balance sheet, March 31st, 1982	30,040

The stock figure in the March 1982 balance sheet was valued at cost, except for one item which cost £8,300 and was written down to £4,000. This was finally sold on April 20th, 1982 for £8,073. Otherwise, the rate of gross profit was constant.

You are required to compute the amount to be claimed on insurance for loss of stock.

(SCCA)

Examples from Chapter 8

No. 167

The One-shot Company Ltd owns the freehold interest in a plot of land which it may develop.

The plot was purchased five years ago for £5,000. Its market value has now appreciated to £10,000. A development scheme has been prepared by an architect: his fee, 1,000 guineas, is payable forthwith. The scheme requires the demolition of a building on the site, at a current cost of £2,000 (payable at the commencement of the development). Building costs, at current prices, would amount to £20,000, payable in equal instalments on the first and second anniversaries of the commencement. The development would be completed on the second anniversary and it is expected that the finished building and land could be sold in two years' time for £40,000. The company's cost-of-capital is 7 per cent p.a.

If the commencement were delayed for one year:

(*a*) It would be necessary to spend £500 at once to make the site safe and tidy during the interim.

(*b*) Each payment for demolition and building would be 5 per cent higher and

(*c*) The sale price would increase by 10 per cent.

There are three possibilities worth considering:

(i) the undeveloped site could be sold immediately,
(ii) the site could be developed immediately, and
(iii) the site could be developed, commencing in one year's time.

There is no advantage in selling the undeveloped site at a future date or in delaying the development by more than one year. The directors have ruled out the possibility of an immediate development followed by a delayed sale because they believe that the building would deteriorate if it were unoccupied for a year or more.

Required:
Calculation showing whether the development should be commenced immediately.

No. 168

A firm buys a lorry for £10,000. The expected costs, etc. are:

Year	*1*	*2*	*3*	*4*	*5*	*6*
	£	£	£	£	£	£
Maintenance during year		100	800	500	1,000	1,200
Scrap value, end of year	7,000	5,300	3,200	2,400	1,000	200
Miles run during year	10,000	30,000	30,000	20,000	10,000	10,000

Required:
(*a*) Calculation of optimum life.
(*b*) On the assumption that actual mileages prove to be the same as those in the budget, draft ledger accounts (over the optimum life) for

(i) The asset; and
(ii) Depreciation provision,

using the service-unit method of depreciation.
Ignore tax and interest.

No. 169

(*a*) In relation to stock evaluation a business man nearly always has to make certain assumptions about the movement of stock.

(i) Why does he have to do this?
(ii) Describe the assumptions that can be made, and explain the effect that each would have on the final accounts of a business.

(*b*) 'Accounting for depreciation is a process of allocation, and not of valuation.'

(i) What does this statement mean?
(ii) Do you agree with it?
(iii) Give four methods which can be used for the calculation of depreciation.

(SCCA)

Examples from Chapter 9

No. 170

Among the items appearing in the Balance Sheet of Wan Ltd at March 31st, 1982 are the following:

	S$000
Share premium account	80
Capital redemption reserve fund	200
Debenture redemption reserve	100

Explain the nature of each of the above items, describing how and why they arise, and the purpose for which each may be used.

(LCC)

No. 171

The following items appear on a limited liability company's balance sheet:

(i) Goodwill
(ii) Capital Redemption Reserve Fund
(iii) Profit and Loss Account (Debit Balance).

In respect of each of these suggest:

(*a*) Circumstances in which the balance might have arisen.
(*b*) Circumstances in which the balance might be reduced or eliminated.

(LCC)

No. 172

Giving illustrations where appropriate, distinguish carefully between each of the following:

(i) Current liabilities and long term liabilities;
(ii) Liabilities and reserves;
(iii) Reserves and provisions;
(iv) Provisions and contingent liabilities.

(LCC)

No. 173

On January 1st, 1981 Jones and Co. drew a bill of exchange upon DJ Traders for £2,000 at 2 months for goods supplied. The bill was accepted and then immediately discounted by Jones and Co. at a cost of £15. At maturity the bill was dishonoured and Jones and Co. agreed to accept £500 in cash and another bill of exchange for £1,600 at 3 months from DJ Traders, which amount included interest charged by Jones and Co. This bill was not discounted and was duly met at maturity.

You are required to record these transactions in the books of Jones and Co.

(SCCA)

No. 174

What do you understand by the term 'bonus issue' of shares (sometimes known as a capitalisation or scrip issue)?

Explain why companies make such issues, and their possible advantages and disadvantages to shareholders.

(LCC)

Examples from Chapter 11

No. 175

(*a*) The master budget of Mercanti Ltd, for the year ending September 30th, 19.., runs as follows:

		£000
Direct Costs:	Materials	80
	Labour	70
		150
Production Overhead		60
	Total Works Cost	210
General Overhead		70
	Total Cost	280
Sales		315
	Profit	35

After this budget has been drawn up, Mercanti Ltd is offered an additional job, a special contract to manufacture military equipment for the government of Ruritania. The government agrees that the price of the contract is to be found by:

(i) Calculating the total production cost of the job by adding to its direct costs a percentage to cover production overheads;
(ii) Calculating the total cost of the job by adding to its total production cost a percentage to cover general overheads; and
(iii) Adding a profit margin equal to 12½ per cent of total cost.

The overhead absorption rates are to be found from the corresponding total figures in the above master budget. The equipment would require £9,500 of direct materials and £12,000 of direct labour.

Required: Calculation of the price which Mercanti Ltd would receive if it accepted the contract.

(*b*) The direct materials cost of the contract includes £2,750, the cost of 100 units of Part QX 9, already in stock. These parts are not likely to be required for any other future jobs. However if £75 were spent on conversion, they could be used as substitutes for 100 parts of ML 9 which would otherwise have to be bought in at a cost of £22 each. Or they could be sold (without conversion) for £19 each. The direct materials cost of the contract also includes £1,500, the cost of the required quantity of material PX 8, which is also in stock. This material is used frequently by the company and, because it is in short supply, its current cost has risen to £1,800. All other direct costs of the contract would arise in cash during the coming year.

The general overhead expenditure will be the same whether the contract is accepted or not, but acceptance of the contract would increase production overhead expenditure by £3,250 (for additional supervisory labour, fuel and power etc.).

Required: Calculation showing whether acceptance of the project is worthwhile and by how much.

No. 176

Mr Planet will commence business, manufacturing Elektraps, on January 1st. His plans for the first six months are as follows:

(i) He will manufacture 1,000 units per month.

(ii) He will purchase machinery costing £300,000 on January 1st: an initial payment of £210,000 is to be made on January 1st and the balance will be paid in 12 monthly instalments, the first on January 31st. This machinery has the capacity to produce up to 3,000 units per month. Depreciation is to be provided at the rate of £30,000 p.a.

(iii) Each man employed in the factory can produce 10 units per month, and will require a wage of £80 per month. The minimum number of men required for the planned output will be employed.

(iv) Each unit requires 1 lb of material @ £4 per lb. An initial stock of material of 250 lb will be purchased and paid for on January 1st. Subsequently material will be replaced immediately it is used and paid for in the following month.

(v) Factory rent will amount to £6,000 p.a. and it will be payable by the firm, quarterly in advance, on January 1st, etc.

(vi) Other overhead expenditure will require payments of £3,000 per month.

(vii) Sales will be 600 units per month for the first 3 months and 1,000 units per month for the second 3 months, at the price of £25 per unit. Customers will pay in the second month after receiving the goods.

(viii) Mr Planet has been offered a bank overdraft of £30,000.

(ix) Stocks are to be valued at direct cost (labour plus materials).

Required:

(*a*) Budget showing the minimum amount of cash that Mr Planet mush pay into his business bank account in order just to keep within the agreed bank overdraft during the first six months of operation (assume that Mr Planet will draw no cash for his personal use): and (*b*) budgeted Balance Sheet at June 30th, assuming that this sum is paid in as capital.

No. 177

For 19. ., the master budget of Quasar Supplies, Ltd, ran thus:

		£000
Direct Costs:	Materials	180
	Labour (120,000 hours)	75
		255
Production Overhead (all fixed)		60
	Total Production Cost	315
General Overhead (all fixed)		63
	Total Cost	378
Sales		410
	Profit	32

Required:

(*a*) Statements showing the costs and results of Job 79, on the alternative assumptions that the costing system is based on:

(i) Direct costing; and instead;

(ii) Full allocation of overheads ('direct-labour hour' method, for production overhead, and 'percentage of production cost' method for general overhead).

Job 79 used £3,600 of direct material and £1,400 of direct wages (2,600 hours). The price was £7,800.

(*b*) A conventional break-even chart on graph paper, with sales on the *OX*-axis. From your chart, state:

(i) The break-even point; and

(ii) Profit if sales reach £500,000.

No. 178

In the year ended April 30th, 1982, on sales of £228,000, Oliver made £72,000 gross profit and £5,840 net profit. His expenses included discount allowed £3,120, and depreciation calculated at 20 per cent on the cost of his fixed assets.

His balance sheet as at April 30th, 1982 was:

	£		£	£
Capital	60,200	Fixed assets at cost	56,000	
		Less depreciation	22,400	33,600
Creditors	26,000	Stock		18,800
		Debtors		19,000
		Bank		14,800
	£86,200			£86,200

His monthly sales were constant throughout the financial year, and his creditors, debtors and stock totals at the end of each month were approximately the same as the Balance Sheet figures.

During May 1982, he intends to spend £15,000 on advertising, and to purchase enough stock to double his month-end stock, in preparation for the expected increase in his sales from June 1st onwards. Thereafter, his monthly purchases will be sufficient to maintain this level. All his purchases are on credit, and he will continue to pay his creditors as quickly as previously.

He has advised his customers that no discounts will be given on sales made after May 1st, 1982, and, as a result, expects that all debts arising from subsequent sales will take twice as long to collect as before.

He anticipates that his monthly sales will remain as previously in May 1982, but will increase by 50 per cent from June 1st, 1982, without altering his gross profit percentage.

From June 1st, expenses—excluding discounts, advertising and depreciation—will rise by 33⅓ per cent. As before, they will be paid in the month in which they are incurred, at the monthly rate of one-twelfth of the annual total.

Oliver does not expect to buy or sell any fixed assets during the coming year, or to change his method of calculating depreciation.

Required:

(i) Oliver's budgeted Trading and Profit and Loss Account for the year ending April 30th, 1983.

(ii) His cash budget for each of the months May, June and July 1982.

(LCC)

No. 179

Your company is considering plans to improve its turnover by a combination of increased advertising and a reduction in the selling price of its product. In 1981 one million units were sold at £1 each and a net profit of £30,000 was made. It is estimated that if £50,000 were spent on advertising and the unit selling price were reduced to 90p, the number of units sold would be doubled. Stock levels are expected to increase in direct proportion to unit sales, whilst debtors are expected to increase to an average of two months sales. With an anticipated bank balance of £20,000 at the end of the year the current ratio is expected to be 2:1. The fixed assets will be written down to £220,000 by the end of the year. The balance sheet as at December 31st, 1981 is given below:

	£		£	£
Capital	385,000	Fixed Assets (net		
Profit for year	30,000	after depreciation		230,000
		Current Assets		
	415,000	Stock	200,000	
Creditors	185,000	Debtors	120,000	
		Bank	50,000	
				370,000
	£600,000			£600,000

You are required to prepare the forecast balance sheet as at December 31st, 1982 based upon the above estimates, showing the net profit for the year as a separate figure in the balance sheet

(SCCA)

No. 180

F. Driver intends to start a manufacturing business on January 1st, 1983. This will involve the following:

(1) Paying £1,000 each month for the rent of factory premises; paying wages and other manufacturing expenses of £4,000 each month; paying office salaries and other office expenses of £1,500 each month; making personal drawings of £500 in cash each month.

(2) Buying machinery for delivery on January 1st, 1983, costing £24,000 payable on March 31st, 1983. This machinery will last at least ten years and have a negligible scrap value at the end of that period.

(3) A sales pattern for the year (in units each selling for £20) as follows:

January	0	April	500	July	1,200	October	1,000
February	0	May	800	August	1,500	November	800
March	300	June	900	September	1,300	December	800

(4) Half the sales revenues of any month will be received (net of a cash discount of 5 per cent) in the following month and the remainder (with no cash discount) in the month after that.

(5) Raw materials will cost £10 per unit of output and will be paid for in the month following purchase. Sufficient for two months' pro-

duction will be purchased in January 1983 and one month's supply each month thereafter. Production will be 800 units per month starting in January 1983.

(6) A special advertising campaign paid for in February will cost £2,200.

Required:

(i) Calculate by means of a monthly cash budget up to and including July 1983, the minimum capital F. Driver would have to introduce on January 1st, 1983 in order to have at least £7,000 in his bank account after all monthly deficits have been covered.

(ii) Assuming that finished goods stocks are to be valued at their materials cost only, prepare F. Driver's budgeted trading and profit and loss account for the year ending December 31st, 1983.

(iii) Calculate what the net profit in (ii) above would have been, had F. Driver valued finished goods stocks at their manufacturing cost.

(LCC)

No. 181

The trading account of Reggie Countant Ltd for the year ended December 31st, 1982 is given below:

	£		£
Stock	5,000	Sales	28,000
Purchases	20,000		
	25,000		
Less: Closing stock	4,000		
Cost of stock sold	21,000		
Gross profit	7,000		
	£28,000		£28,000

In an attempt to increase the profits and turnover for the coming year, the directors decide to spend more money on advertising, to reduce the unit selling price of the product and to introduce a one per cent commission payment to their salesmen. The commission is calculated on sales value and is to be included in the trading account as part of the cost of stock sold.

It is estimated that if the unit price of the product is reduced by 10 per cent, with the combination of advertising and commission incentives the number of units sold will double. The increased level of business would enable the goods to be bought more economically. It is estimated that a quantity discount would be offered of 2 per cent. The closing stock will be kept at the same value as presently held.

You are required to prepare the forecast trading account for 1983 assuming that all estimates are fulfilled.

(SCCA)

Examples from Chapter 13

No. 182

Planrite Ltd is considering what products to manufacture during the coming year. The available products are *A*, *B*, *C*, *D* and *E*; there is a complete flexibility as regards mix. The following table (showing costs, etc. *per unit* of each product) has been drawn up by the firm's accountant to assist management in their decision:

Available Products:	*A*	*B*	*C*	*D*	*E*
Skilled Labour Hours Required	10	8	8	6	4
Unskilled Labour Hours Required	4	20	8	16	12
Selling Price	£28	£38	£37	£42	£29
Direct Costs:					
Materials	8	11	12	15	7
Skilled Labour	5	4	4	3	2
Unskilled Labour	1	5	2	4	3
	14	20	18	22	12
Overhead Expenditure—50% of Direct Cost	7	10	9	11	6
	£21	£30	£27	£33	£18
Profit per Unit	£7	£8	£10	£9	£11
Net Profit per £1 spent on Labour	£1.17	£0.89	£1.67	£1.29	£2.20
Estimated demand for the year (units)	500	600	300	200	400

Overhead expenses will be the same regardless of what combination of products is manufactured. The firm can employ up to 5 skilled men and 8 unskilled men; each man works for 2,000 hours per annum.

Required: Criticise the accountant's statement as a basis for management's deciding what to produce in the coming year. If you think some other calculation would be more appropriate, describe the method and include a formation of the problem: a numerical solution is *not* required.

Add a short note on factors which might influence the decision but would not be reflected in your calculations.

No. 183

Summarised accounts for Beaver Enterprises Ltd, for 19.9 are shown on page 309:

BEAVER ENTERPRISES LTD

PROFIT AND LOSS ACCOUNT

(for the year ended December 31st, 19.9)

	£000
Operating Profit	97
Less Debenture Interest	10
	87
Less Corporation Tax	32
Net Profit after Taxation	55
Balance brought forward from last year	178
	233
Less Dividend	45
	£188

BALANCE SHEET

(as at December 31st, 19.9)

	£000		£000
Ordinary Share of £1	180	Fixed Assets—Cost	538
Capital Reserve	72	*Less* Depreciation	114
Profit and Loss Account	188		
5% Debenture Stock	200		424
Creditors, etc.	96	Stocks	191
		Debtors	89
		Cash	32
	£736		£736

Required:

(*a*) Calculate the following from the given data:

(i) Balance Sheet Value of £1 Ordinary Share of Beaver Enterprises.

(ii) Market Value of a £1 Ordinary Share on the basis that the current dividend yield on similar shares is 8 per cent.

(iii) Ratio of net profit after taxation to ordinary shareholders interest.

(iv) Market Value of £100 debenture stock, *ex div*, if the appropriate gross redemption yield is 7 per cent and this stock is redeemable at par in exactly 10 years. (Interest is paid on December 31st each year.)

(*b*) Discuss shortly the usefulness and limitations of the ratio in (iii) above as a measure of the efficiency of management.

No. 184

Mini-Motors Ltd, is drawing up its production plan for the coming year. It deals in four types of motor vehicle: the 'Mouse' and the 'Rat' are saloon cars, and the 'Beatle' and the 'Bee' are vans. There is complete flexibility as regards product mix. The selling price of each model has been set having regard to competitive considerations, and it will be maintained whatever the level of output of the model. The firm can buy all the parts which are required for its vehicles in sufficient quantities for any likely needs.

The firm has two divisions; in one the vehicles are assembled, and in the other they are sprayed. Next year, whatever the volume or mix of production, the costs of the assembly division are likely to be labour £100,000 and overheads £50,000, and 200,000 man-hours will be worked: the costs of the spraying division are likely to be labour £60,000 and overhead £45,000 and 120,000 man-hours will be worked. General overhead expenses of the firm are likely to be £51,000.

The accountant has prepared the following statement to assist management in deciding what products to manufacture:

	Mouse	*Rat*	*Beatle*	*Bee*
Estimated demand for the year (units)	900	1,600	1,900	1,100
Number of man-hours to process one vehicle:				
in assembly division	100	66	34	50
in spraying division	32	20	36	28
Profit per unit sold				
Costs of assembly division:	£	£	£	£
labour	50	33	17	25
overheads—50% of labour cost (say)	25	16	8	12
Cost of spraying division:				
labour	16	10	18	14
overheads—75% of labour cost (say)	12	8	14	11
Total Divisional Costs	103	67	57	62
General Overheads—20% of divisional cost (say)	21	13	11	12
	124	80	68	74
Cost of parts and materials	220	197	172	188
Total Costs	344	277	240	262
Selling Price	410	340	280	310
Profit	£66	£63	£40	£48
Ranking	1	2	4	3

Required

Criticise the accountant's statement as a basis for management's deciding what to produce in the coming year. If you think some other calculations would be more appropriate, describe the method and include a formulation of the problem; a numerical solution is not required.

No. 185

I am planning to build a motel with 100 double bedrooms.

(*a*) The initial costs are:

	£
Land	20,000
Architect's and other fees	15,000
Construction	220,000
Furnishing	70,000

I can borrow the needed funds at 7 per cent p.a. by mortgaging this and other property.

(*b*) Running costs (less the net contribution from bars and dining rooms, etc.) will come to some £65,000 p.a. This includes maintenance of buildings, but excludes their depreciation: it also includes renewals of furniture.

(*c*) I expect a room to be let for about 220 nights a year, on average with one and a half persons per room.

Required:

(*a*) Calculate the minimum room charge per person per night to break even on the alternative assumptions that

(i) the building will have a life of 30 years with residual site value £40,000;

(ii) the building will have an indefinitely long life.

(*b*) If inflation raises the net running costs, and enables me to put up charges (above the amount calculated in (ii)), by 2½ per cent p.a., what will be my profit p.a. at the end of 20 years on the assumption that the building will have an indefinitely long life?

No. 186

Tertium Ltd makes one product. It has a standard costing system based on the following:

Each unit of product needs 1 lb of material (normally costing £0.15 a lb) and one hour of labour (paid £0.40 per hour). Overheads (fixed, for any likely output) are budgeted at £200 per month. Sale price is £0.80. The firm carries no stocks.

The production budget for July calls for 2,000 articles. But the actual results run:

	£	£
Sales (1,600 units at £0.80)		1,280
Cost of Sales:		
Materials: 1,000 lb at £0.15	150	
720 lb at £0.16½ approx.	120	
	270	
Wages: 1,650 hours at £0.40	660	
Overheads	184	
		1,114
Profit		166

Required:

(*a*) Statement showing standard cost per unit.
(*b*) Budget of expected total revenue and total cost for July.
(*c*) Revised operating statement showing standards and variances.

No. 187

Chapman had been offered the exclusive agency for the sale of the ESBA transistor radio in England. The manufacturer would supply him with radios at £4 each, paying all freight charges and allowing one month's credit. Chapman would resell the radios at £6 each and allow his customers two months' credit. He has £3,000 cash available for investment in the business and would have to give up his present job (annual salary £1,400). He plans to start trading on January 1st. Chapman makes the following calculations:

(i) A suitably equipped office and warehouse can be rented for £1,400 a year payable quarterly in advance.
(ii) He expects sales in the first year to be:

January	50 radios
February	150 „
March	250 „
April	300 „
May and each following month	350 „

In the following years he expects sales to be at the rate of 400 radios a month.

(iii) A stock of 400 radios would be maintained at all times.
(iv) All other business expenses (e.g. wages, advertising, etc.) are estimated at £120 per month payable in cash as and when incurred.

Required: A report to Chapman stating whether it is worthwhile, and on what assumptions, for him to accept the agency.
Show all calculations clearly. Ignore tax.

No. 188

Biggs commenced business as a plumber on January 1st, 19.8, when he deposited £500 in a special bank account. At first trade was very slack, so in June 19.8 he introduced a new form of contract for customers: in return for a fee of £10 payable in advance he undertook to repair a customer's water system at no extra charge any time during the contract period, which ran from July 1st, 19.8 to June 30th, 19.9. This scheme was a great success and by July 19.8, 87 people had joined the scheme paying a total of £870 in advance. The only other cash received by Biggs in 19.8 was £160 for work done for customers who had not joined the scheme.
Other information:

(*a*) On April 1st, 19.8 Biggs purchased for cash a motor van for £405.

He expects to use it until the end of the following three years when it will have a scrap value of £30. Van running expenses paid out in cash (petrol, repairs, etc.) have averaged £5 per month.

(*b*) Payments for materials (pipes, solder, etc.) in 19.8 totalled £112. In addition at December 31st, 19.8 there was an unpaid bill of £27 for pipes. Stock of unused materials at that date was worth £5.

(*c*) At December 31st, 19.8 Biggs' bank account was overdrawn by £7. There was no cash in hand and the only debtors and creditors were those mentioned previously.

Required: Draft an accounting report in the form of a Profit and Loss Account for 19.8 and Balance Sheet as at December 31st, 19.8 using generally accepted conventions and presenting the figures in as clear a way as possible for Biggs.

Ignore tax. Show all calculations clearly.

No. 189

Caucus Ltd makes several products. Six years ago, it set up a department to deal with a new contract—for 1,000 units p.a. of product *K*, for £15,000 p.a. This contract has still four more years to run, and the chief engineer now suggests that a reorganisation of the department (methods, materials, and plant) will cut working costs.

The cost accountant drafts the following statement to enable the directors to decide on the proposal:

		Account for year 6	*Annual budget years 7–10 (If proposals adopted)*	*Remarks*
		£	£	
Costs:				
1. Materials: Type	X	1,000	900	Less waste.
	Y	2,000		Discontinued.
	Z		1,600	Substitute for Y.
2. Labour		6,000	4,200	Less needed.
3. Departmental Expense		3,000	2,100	50% of direct labour.
4. Depreciation: Machine	A	450	315	Straight-line (10 years).
	B		550	Straight-line (4 years).
		12,450	9,665	
Gain by new plan			2,785	
		12,450	12,450	

Note

(i) *Materials*

X & Z: bought as and when needed. None have so far been ordered.

Y: there is a firm contract to buy this quantity each year till the end of year 10, for £2,000 p.a. If not used in this department, the material can be used in other departments as a substitute for materials costing £1,750 p.a. Or it can be sold for £2,160 p.a.

(ii) *Labour* can be varied readily.

(iii) *Departmental expense*

The total for the firm is not likely to be affected by the change.

(iv) *Depreciation*

Under the plan, A will be scrapped at once; it would still (start of year 7) fetch £540 if sold, but will fetch nothing by the end of year 10. It will be replaced by a new machine, B (cost £2,350, scrap value £150 after year 10).

(v) *Interest*

Assume, for simplicity, that interest can be ignored.

Required:
Statement to assist decision, in form of alternative budgets of net cash flow (total for years 7–10) if:

(*a*) Old plan is retained, and
(*b*) New plan is adopted.

Ignore tax.

No. 190

Five years ago, you bought machine *A* (with a life of ten years) for £1,000. Its scrap value will be £100 at the end of its life; it has been depreciated on the straight-line basis, and so now has a book-value of £550. Its scrap value now is £200. Its annual running costs are £300.

An improved machine, *B*, could do the same job as *A* for running costs of only £213 a year. Its price is £500, and it will last five years and then have a scrap value of £20, so its yearly depreciation will add a further £96 to book costs.

Required: Show whether it is in your interest to replace *A*. Ignore tax, and assume that running costs arise at the year's end and the cost of capital is 5 per cent p.a.

No. 191

A firm plans to install a new machine—either of type *A* or of type *B*. The cost of purchase and installation would be £6,000 (type *A*) and £8,000 (type *B*). The output capacity of the two types is the same and will remain constant over the life of each machine. *A* has an effective life of 10 years, and *B* of 12. *A*'s running cost at the level of use expected is £1,000 p.a., and *B*'s £900 p.a. Final scrap values of both are *nil*. Funds can be borrowed readily at 7 per cent.

Required:
(*a*) A calculation of annual costs, based on the given data.
(*b*) Justify your method of solution, writing as for a layman.
Ignore tax.

No. 192

The following figures are taken from the books of Welkin Ltd:

		£
Stock-on-Hand at January 1st, 19.8:	Raw Materials	700
	Work-in-Progress	1,300
	Finished Goods	500
Materials Purchased		3,000
Wages: Direct		2,000
Indirect		400
Direct Expenses		300
Rent, Lighting, etc.: Factory		650
Office and Administrative		400
Salaries (General Office)		600
Depreciation, Factory Plant		450
Selling Value of Completed Contracts invoiced during Year		8,000
Stock-on-Hand at December 31st, 19.8:	Raw Materials	800
	Work-in-Progress	1,000
	Finished Goods	1,500

Required:

(*a*) Draw up an income account for the year, in a form suitable for use in costing. Work-in-Progress and finished goods are valued at works cost.

(*b*) Prepare a cost estimate for a contract in respect of which it is computed that material will cost £300, direct wages £400, and direct expenses £60. Assume that the 'direct wages' basis is in use for allocating production overhead, and apply the rate found from (*a*). Select your own method for allocating other cost and profit.

(*c*) Comment briefly on the theoretical and practical justifications for the use of the method of cost estimating in (*b*).

Answers to Exercises—First Series

No. 1

BALANCE SHEET
(as at December 31st, 19. .)

	£	£		£	£
Capital as at Jan. 1st		6,000	Fixed Assets:		
Add Net Profit for Year	1,368		Freehold Premises	3,000	
Less Drawings	702		Plant & Machinery	2,560	
					5,560
		6,666	Current Assets:		
Loan from H. Glass		1,000	Stock	2,845	
			Sundry Deptors	1,412	
			Cash	78	
				4,335	
			Less Current Liabilities:		
			Sundry Creditors	1,880	
			Bank Overdraft	349	
				2,229	
					2,106
		£7,666			£7,666

No. 2

GOLDEN GATE LANDSCAPING COMPANY

BALANCE SHEET
(as at December 31st, 19. .)

ASSETS

	£	£	£
Fixed Assets:			
Lorry	2,100		
Less Accumulated Depreciation	560		
		1,540	
Gardening Tools		317	
Total Plant Assets			1,857

	£	£
Current Assets:		
Cash	562	
Debtors	2,116	
Garden Supplies	402	
Prepaid Insurance	109	
Total Current Assets		3,189
TOTAL ASSETS		£5,046

LIABILITIES AND OWNERS' EQUITY

	£	£
Current Liabilities:		
Creditors	107	
Contracts Payable	660	
Total Liabilities		767
Wilkinson, Capital		4,279
TOTAL LIABILITIES AND OWNERS' EQUITY		£5,046

GOLDEN GATE LANDSCAPING COMPANY

STATEMENT OF PROPRIETOR'S CAPITAL

(Year Ended December 31st, 19..)

	£	£
Capital, January 1st		3,500
Capital introduced in May		1,000
		4,500
Add Profit for Year	3,379	
Less Drawings During Year	3,600	
		−221
CAPITAL, DECEMBER 31st		£4,279

GOLDEN GATE LANDSCAPING COMPANY

PROFIT AND LOSS STATEMENT

(Year Ended December 31st, 19..)

	£	£
Sales		7,350
Expenses:		
Gardening Supplies	2,516	
Depreciation—Lorry	560	
Petrol and Oil	373	
Telephone	50	
Office Supplies	27	
Insurance	207	
Sundry Expenses	238	
Total Expenses		3,971
NET PROFIT		£3,379

No. 3

LIABILITIES AND OWNER'S EQUITY

	£	£	£
Current Liabilities:			
Creditors		107	
Contracts Payable		660	
TOTAL LIABILITIES			767
Wilkinson, Capital:			
Balance, January 1st		3,500	
Cash introduced in May		1,000	
		4,500	
Add Profit for Year	3,379		
Less Drawings During Year	3,600		
		−221	
Capital, December 31st			4,279
TOTAL LIABILITIES AND OWNERS' EQUITY			£5,046

No. 4

SANTINI & CASEY, INSURANCE BROKERS

BALANCE SHEET

(as at December 31st, 19..)

ASSETS

Fixed Assets	£	£	£
Office Furniture	9,315		
Less Accumulated Depreciation	3,702	5,613	
Motor Vehicles	7,600		
Less Accumulated Depreciation	3,300	4,300	
Total Fixed Assets			9,913
Current Assets:			
Cash		4,015	
Debtors		700	
Commissions Receivable		5,603	
Office Supplies		1,210	
Prepaid Insurance		570	
Prepaid Rent		600	
Total Current Assets			12,698
TOTAL ASSETS			£22,611

LIABILITIES AND PARTNERS' EQUITY

Partners' Capital:	£ M. Santini	£ W. Casey	
Balance 1/1/.8	£8,000	£10,000	
Cash introduced 3/3/.8	2,000	—	
	£10,000	£10,000	
Add Profit for Year 19.8	4,975	4,975	
	£14,975	£14,975	
Less Drawings for Year 19.8	5,200	5,200	
Current Liabilities:			
Premiums Payable			2,950
Creditors			111
TOTAL LIABILITIES			3,061
TOTAL CAPITAL DECEMBER 31st, 19.8	£9,775	£9,775	19,550
TOTAL LIABILITIES AND PARTNERS' CAPITAL			£22,611

SANTINI & CASEY, INSURANCE BROKERS—INCOME STATEMENT
(Year Ended December 31st, 19.8)

	£	£
Commissions Income		29,585
Expenses:		
Wages	9,050	
Rent	2,400	
Motor Vehicles	2,300	
Telephone	1,100	
Office Supplies	560	
Insurance	210	
Depreciation—Office Equipment	955	
Depreciation—Motor Vehicles	2,010	
Sundry Expenses	1,050	
Total Expenses		19,635
PROFIT FOR THE YEAR 19.8		£9,950
Distribution of Profit		
M. Santini		4,975
W. Casey		4,975
TOTAL PROFIT FOR THE YEAR 19.8		£9,950

No. 5

SANTINI & CASEY, INSURANCE BROKERS—STATEMENT OF PARTNERS' CAPITAL
(Year Ended December 31st, 19.8)

	M. Santini	W. Casey	Total
Balance, January 1st, 19.8	£8,000	£10,000	£18,000
Cash introduced March 3rd, 19.8	2,000	—	2,000
	£10,000	£10,000	£20,000
Add Profit for Year 19.8	4,975	4,975	9,950
	£14,975	£14,975	£29,950
Less Withdrawals for Year 19.8	5,200	5,200	10,400
TOTAL CAPITAL, DECEMBER 31st, 19.8	£9,775	£9,775	£19,550

LIABILITIES AND PARTNERS' EQUITY

	£	£
Current Liabilities:		
Premiums Payable	2,950	
Creditors	111	
Total Liabilities		3,061
Partners' Capital:		
M. Santini	9,775	
W. Casey	9,775	
Total Partners' Equity		19,550
TOTAL LIABILITIES AND PARTNERS' CAPITAL		£22,611

No. 6

PROFIT AND LOSS APPROPRIATION ACCOUNT
(for the year ended December 31st, 19..)

	£	£		£
Salaries: Bat	1,000		Net Profit	7,430
Rubble	900			
		1,900		
Interest: Brick	1,120			
Bat	840			
Rubble	700			
		2,660		
Profit: Brick	1,230			
Bat	820			
Rubble	820			
		2,870		
		£7,430		£7,430

CURRENT ACCOUNT—BRICK

	£		£
Drawings	2,000	Balance B/f	500
Balance c/f	850	Interest on Capital	1,120
		Profit	1,230
	£2,850		£2,850
		Balance, B/f	£850

CURRENT ACCOUNT—BAT

	£		£
Drawings	1,400	Balance B/f	400
Balace c/f	1,660	Salary	1,000
		Interest	840
		Profit	820
	£3,060		£3,060
		Balance B/f	£1,660

CURRENT ACCOUNT—RUBBLE

	£		£
Drawings	1,100	Balance B/f	450
Balance c/f	1,770	Salary	900
		Interest	700
		Profit	820
	£2,870		£2,870
		Balance B/f	£1,770

No. 7

(*a*)

	£
Valuation of business	18,000
Net Worth (assets—liabilities)	13,000
Goodwill	£5,000

BALANCE SHEET

	£	£	£		£	£
Capital: Hit	8,000			Goodwill		5,000
	3,000			Assets	20,000	
		11,000		Target's Cash	6,000	
Miss	5,000					26,000
	2,000					
		7,000				
Target		6,000				
Liabilities			24,000			
			7,000			
			£31,000			£31,000

(*b*)

BALANCE SHEET

	£	£		£
Capital: Hit	11,000		Assets	26,000
	2,000			
		9,000		
Miss	7,000			
	1,500			
		5,500		
Target	6,000			
	1,500			
		4,500		
Liabilities		7,000		
		£26,000		£26,000

(*c*) Purchase of three-tenths of goodwill

$\frac{3}{10} \times £5{,}000 = £1{,}500$

Payable as premium to: Hit (three-fifths)	900
Miss (two-fifths)	600
	£1,500

BALANCE SHEET

	£	£	£		£	£
Capital:				Assets	20,000	
Hit		8,000		Balance of Target's		
Miss		5,000		Cash	4,500	
Target	6,000					24,500
Premium	1,500					
		4,500				
			17,500			
Liabilities			7,000			
			£24,500			£24,500

No. 8

	£
Capital and Reserves of Minnow Ltd at date of acquisition	52,000
One-quarter minority interest	13,000
Three-quarter interest acquired	39,000
Cost of acquiring shares	45,000
Cost of control, or goodwill on consolidation	£6,000

CONSOLIDATED BALANCE SHEET OF SHARK LTD AND SUBSIDIARY
(as at December 31st, 19. .)

		£	£	£
Fixed Assets				
Intangible Assets				
Cost of Control			6,000	
Tangible Assets				
Fixed Assets	Shark	120,000		
	Minnow	40,000		
			160,000	
				166,000
Current Assets	Shark	100,000		
	Minnow	33,000		
			133,000	
Liabilities (Assumed under one year)	Shark	75,000		
	Minnow	15,000		
			90,000	
Net current assets				43,000
				209,000
Capital and Reserves				
Called up Share Capital				150,000
Reserves			40,000	
			4,500	
				44,500
				194,500
Minority Interest			13,000	
			1,500	
				14,500
				209,000

No. 9

	£
Capital and Reserves of Hut Ltd at date of acquisition	55,000
One-fifth minority interest	11,000
Four-fifths interest acquired	44,000
Cost of acquisition of shares	54,000
Cost of control, or goodwill on consolidation	10,000

	£
Profit for year on Hut Ltd	7,500
One-fifth minority interest	1,500
Four-fifths interest	6,000
Less profit on goods not yet sold by the group $\frac{4}{5}$ of (£1,000–£750)	200
Added to Group Reserves	£5,800

CONSOLIDATED BALANCE SHEET OF HOUSE LTD AND SUBSIDIARY
(as at December 31st, 19..)

	£	£	£
Fixed Assets			
Intangible Assets			
Cost of Control		10,000	
Tangible Assets			
Fixed Assets	160,000		
	50,000		
		210,000	
			220,000
Current Assets	90,000		
	51,500		
	800		
		142,300	
Liabilities (Assumed under one year)	60,000		
	34,000		
		94,000	
Net current assets			48,300
			268,300
Capital and Reserves			
Called up Share Capital			200,000
Reserves		50,000	
		5,800	
			55,800
			255,800
Minority Interest		11,000	
		1,500	
			12,500
			268,300

No. 10

GOODS SENT TO BRANCHES ACCOUNT

	£		£
Southend Branch Account	600	Southend Branch Account	6,000
Purchases or Trading Account	5,400		
	£6,000		£6,000

SOUTHEND BRANCH ACCOUNT

	Selling Price £	£		Selling Price £	£
Goods sent to branches	8,000	6,000	Goods sent to branches	800	600
Gross Profit transferred to Profit and Loss Account		1,550	Cash Sales	6,500	6,500
			Balance (Stock)	600	450
			Shortage	100*	
	£8,000	£7,550		£8,000	£7,550
Balance (Stock)	£600	£450			

*This is a memorandum entry required for assessing the efficiency of the management of the branch.

No.11

GOODS SENT TO BRANCHES ACCOUNT

	£		£
Southend Branch Adjustment Account	2,000	Southend Branch Account	8,000
Southend Branch Account	800	Southend Branch Adjustment Account	200
Purchases or Trading Account	5,400		
	£8,200		£8,200

SOUTHEND BRANCH ACCOUNT

	£		£
Goods sent to branches	8,000	Goods sent to branches	800
		Cash Sales	6,500
		Balance c/f (Stock-on-Hand)	600
		Shortage transferred to Profit and Loss Account or Branch Adjustment Account	100
	£8,000		£8,000
Balance b/f (Stock-on-hand)	£600		

SOUTHEND BRANCH ADJUSTMENT ACCOUNT

	£		£
Goods sent to branches	200	Goods sent to branches	2,000
Profit and Loss Account	1,650*		
Balance c/f (Loading on stock-on-hand)	150		
	£2,000		£2,000
		Balance b/f (Loading on stock-on-hand)	£150

*This figure would be reduced by £100 if the shortage were transferred to the Branch Adjustment Account.

No. 12

GOODS ON CONSIGNMENT ACCOUNT

	£		£
Purchases or Trading A/c	1,000	Goods to Sellers Ltd	1,000

CONSIGNMENT TO SELLERS LTD ACCOUNT

	£		£
Goods on consignment	1,000	Sales—Sellers Ltd	1,800
Cash—expenses	180	Balance c/d	429*
Sellers Ltd—expenses	250		
Sellers Ltd—commission	180		
Profit transferred to Profit and Loss Account	619		
	£2,229		£2,229
Balance B/d	£429		

*This represents the value of 30 units still unsold.

Cost 30 @ £10 each			£300
Expenses	£180		
	250		
		£430	
Three-tenths of £430			£129
Total			£429

SELLERS LTD

	£		£
Sales	1,800	Expenses	250
		Commission	180
		Cash	1,000
		Balance c/d	370
	£1,800		£1,800
Balance b/d	370		

CASH ACCOUNT

	£		£
Sellers Ltd	1,000	Expenses	180

No. 14

	Department 1		*Department 2*		*Department 3*		*Department 4*		*Total*	
	£	%	£	%	£	%	£	%	£	%
Total Sales	85,000	100.0	72,000	100.0	93,000	100.0	110,000	100.0	360,000	100.0
Opening Stock	7,000		6,000		7,000		11,000		31,000	
Net Purchases	74,000		68,000		81,000		99,000		322,000	
	81,000		74,000		88,000		110,000		353,000	
Closing Stock	6,000		7,000		8,000		10,000		31,000	
Cost of Sales	75,000	88.2	67,000	93.1	80,000	86.0	100,000	90.9	322,000	89.5
Gross Profit on Sales	10,000	11.8	5,000	6.9	13,000	14.0	10,000	9.1	38,000	10.5
Selling Expenses	7,000	8.3	4,000	5.5	6,000	6.5	4,000	3.6	21,000	5.8
Departmental Income	£3,000	3.5	£1,000	1.4	£7,000	7.5	£6,000	5.5	17,000	4.7
Administrative Expenses									8,000	2.2
Net Operating Profit									£9,000	2.5

No. 13

SENDERS LTD

Cash—Expenses	250	Cash—Sales	1,800
Commission Receivable	180		
Cash	1,000		
Balance c/d	370		
	£1,800		£1,800
		Balance b/d	£370

COMMISSION RECEIVABLE

			£
		Senders Ltd	180

CASH ACCOUNT

	£		£
Sales—Goods on Consignment	1,800	Expenses—Goods on Consignment	250
		Cash—Senders Ltd	1,000

Note

There will be a memorandum record to show that 30 of the 100 units received on consignment are still in stock.

No. 14 see page 327

No. 15

REMCO LTD

Analysis of proposed credit card plan

		Present (Actual)	*% of sales*	*Proposed* *Total*	*At present basis*	*Credit card basis*
Sales		200,000	100			
25% Increase in Sales				250,000		
Loss of 20% of Current Cash					160,000	
Sales Increase + 20% of old basis						90,000
Cost of Goods Sold		170,000	85	212,500		
Gross Profit		30,000	15	37,500		
Operating Expenses		12,000				
Plus 5% of New Sales	2,500					
Plus 6% of Credit Sales	5,400			19,900		
Net Profit		£18,000		£17,600		

The analysis indicates that increasing sales by £50,000 will result in a loss of profit of £400, and on that basis the proposed plan should be rejected. But since there is such a small drop in profit it might be worthwhile to re-examine some of the assumptions.

(*a*) Will operating expenses increase at the rate of 5 per cent for new sales? If they increase by only 4 per cent, the proposed plan would increase profits by £100 and should be adopted.

(*b*) Will 20 per cent of present customers change to credit card buying? If only 15 per cent change, the proposed plan would increase profits by £200 and should be adopted.

It seems advisable, therefore, to study the proposed plan again in order to review the fact-gathering assumptions and methods.

No. 16

(*a*) Ability and willingness to repay obligation; borrower's income vs outgoings (not more than 30 per cent of net income should be necessary to amortise the loan); willingness is determined by means of a credit report; recorded deed of trust so property can be taken over if payments are not made.

(*b*) Sufficient down payment (different for new and used cars); steady employment (two years); two years' residence in the area; 'good credit' (Retail Credit Association check); evidence of comprehensive insurance.

(*c*) Stability in employment and home address; good credit background (calls to the stores where accounts are now open); bank references.

(*d*) Length of time employed; type of job; other credit accounts; bank accounts; own or rent home; credit rating (Retail Credit Association check).

No. 17

(*a*)

DERINI PRODUCTS

Computation of Balance in Provision for Bad Debts

Age of Account	Amount	Loss Ratio	Estimated Allowance
31–60 days	£80,000	2%	£1,600
61–90 days	40,000	5%	2,000
over 90 days	30,000	10%	3,000
			£6,600

	£	£
(*b*) Bad Debts	4,400	
Provision for bad debts		4,400
To increase provision from £2,200 to £6,600		

No. 18

Cash	192,000	
Collection Charges	8,000	
Trade Debtors		200,000
To record sale of £200,000 of trade debtors for £192,000		

No. 19

(*a*) Debtors		
Pledged	150,000	
Sundry Debtors		150,000
To separate pledged debtors from sundry debtors		
Cash	100,000	
Notes Payable		100,000
To record receipt of cash from the note payable under the pledging contract		

(*b*) Cash	20,000	
Debtors—Pledged		20,000
To record receipt of cash in February on debtors pledged		
Notes Payable	20,000	
Interest Payable (£100,000 × 5% ÷ 12)	417	
Cash		20,417
To record payment on loan plus interest on £100,000 for February		

(*c*) Cash	50,000	
Debtors—Pledged		50,000
To record receipt of cash in March on debtors pledged		
Notes Payable	50,000	
Interest Payable (£80,000 × 5% ÷ 12)	333	
Cash		50,333
To record payment on loan plus interest on £80,000 for March		

(*d*) Cash	30,000	
Debtors—Pledged		30,000
To record receipt of cash in April on debtors pledged		
Notes Payable	30,000	
Interest Payable (£30,000 × 5% ÷ 12)	125	
Cash		30,125
To record payment on loan plus interest on £30,000 for April		
Sundry Debtors	50,000	
Debtors—Pledged		50,000
To return Debtors pledged to the Sundry Debtors now that the loan is paid		

No. 20

	£	£
Instalment Contracts Receivable	500,000	
Instalments Sales		500,000
Sales on instalment		
Cost of Instalment Sales	300,000	
Inventory		300,000
Cost of instalment sales		
Instalment Sales	500,000	
Cost of Instalment Sales		300,000
Unrealised Gross Profit on Instalment Sales—19.8		200,000
Close out Instalment Sales and Cost of Instalment Sales accounts and set up deferred profit. (Gross profit is 40%)		

No. 21

	£	£
Cash	70,000	
Instalment Contracts Receivable		70,000
Received moneys on instalment sales		
Gross Profit on Instalment Sales—19.8	28,000	
Instalment Sales Gross Profits Realised		28,000
Record gross profits realised on 19.8 instalment sales collected. (£70,000 × 40%)		

No. 22

	£	£
Cash	180,000	
Instalment Contracts Receivable		180,000
Received moneys on instalment sales contracts		
Gross Profit on Instalment Sales—19.8	72,000	
Instalment Sales Gross Profit Realised		72,000
Record gross profits realised on 19.8 instalment contract collections. (£180,000 × 40%)		

No. 23

$$19.6: \frac{£20{,}000}{£0.32} = £62{,}500$$

$$19.7: \frac{£160{,}000 - £30{,}000}{£0.37} = \frac{£130{,}000}{£0.37} = £351{,}351$$

$$19.8: \frac{£500{,}000 - £220{,}000}{£0.35} = \frac{£280{,}000}{£0.35} = £800{,}000$$

No. 24

	£	£
(*a*) Selling price of used machine	4,500	
Mark-up on selling price (20%)	900	
	3,600	
Less Reconditioning cost	800	
	2,800	

	£	£
(*b*) Trade-in Inventory	2,800	
Instalment Contracts Receivable	12,500	
Instalment Sales		14,800
Unearned Interest Income [12,500—(15,000 − 3,000)]		500
Sale on instalment Customer traded in used machine		
Cost of Instalment Sales	13,000	
Inventory		13,000
Cost of instalment sales		
Instalment Sales	14,800	
Cost of Instalment Sales		13,000
Unrealised Gross Profit on Instalment Sales—19.8		1,800
Close out Instalment Sales and Cost of Instalment Sales accounts, and set up deferred profit. (Gross profit ratio is 12.2%)		

No. 25

	£	£
(*a*) Instalment Contracts Receivable	9,720	
Cash	1,000	
Instalment Sales		10,000
Unearned Interest Income		720
Sale of goods on an instalment contract with £720 interest and carrying charges		
Cost of Instalment Sales	7,000	
Inventory		7,000
Cost of goods sold on instalment		
Instalment Sales	10,000	
Cost of Instalment Sales		7,000
Unrealised Gross Profit on Instalment Sales—19.8		3,000
Close out Instalment Sales and Cost of Instalment Sales accounts and set up gross profit deferred. (Gross profit ratio is 30%)		
(*b*) Cash	2,160	
Instalment Contracts Receivable		2,160
Receipts of cash on instalments receivable		
Unrealised Gross Profit on Instalment Sales—19.8	900	
Gross Profit on Instalment Sales Realised		900
Record realised portion of profit on receipt of instalment sales payments		

	%	Original Contract £	Paid on Contract £
Sale	100	9,000	2,000
Charges	8	720	160
Total	108	£9,720	£2,160

(£1,000 down payment + £2,000 payments × 30% = £900)

	£	£
Unearned Interest Income	160	
Interest Income		160
Record interest earned ($\frac{2}{9}$ × £720 = £160). See schedule above		

(This is not asked for in the question but is shown to explain the answers to (*c*) and (*d*) which follow.)

Instalment Contracts Receivable

£9,720	2,160
7,560 Balance	

Unrealised Gross Profit on Instalment Sales—19.8

£900	£3,000
	Balance 2,100

Unearned Interest Income

£160	£720
	Balance 560

(*c*) £5,000 × 1.15 = £5,750
Less reconditioning = 1,000

£4,750

	£	£
(*d*) Repossessed Stock	4,750	
Unrealised Gross Profit on Instalment Sales—19.8	2,100	
Unearned Interest Income	560	
Loss on Repossessions	150	
Instalment Contracts Receivable		7,560

Record termination of instalment contract due to default on payments, set up repossessed stock and recognise loss on repossessions

	Balance Due
108%	£7,560
100%	7,000 × 30 % = 2,100
8%	560

No. 26

(*a*) Advantages: 1. Inexpensive because no detailed inventory cards must be kept. 2. Cost of Goods Sold can be determined by formula.

(*b*) Disadvantages: 1. Lack of control because the quantity on hand cannot be determined readily. 2. Counting must be done when the plant is shut down or at night or at week-ends.

No. 27

TRADERS LTD

Cost of Goods Sold Statement
Financial Year Ended March 31st, 19.9

	£	£	£
Opening Stock, April 1st, 19.8			130,000
Purchases		1,600,000	
Add Carriage Inward		21,000	
		1,621,000	
Less Purchase Returns and Allowances	30,000		
Purchase Discounts	31,000		
		61,000	
			1,551,000
			1,681,000
Less Stock, March 31st, 19.9			150,000
Cost of Goods Sold			£1,531,000

No. 28

Stock (10 units @ £1.25 each)	£12.50	
Stock discrepancy		£12.50
To record overage of material		

No. 29

(*a*) Cash	£400	
Sales		£400
To record sale of 200 units @ £2 each.		

(*b*) In the periodic inventory method no Cost of Goods Sold entry is made when the goods are sold.

No. 30

Stock Discrepancy	£44.80	
Stock (28 units @ £1.60 each)		£44.80
To record shortage of material.		

No. 31

(*a*) Advantages: 1. Affords greater control over inventory quantity of low-volume high-value items (e.g. diamonds and watches); in items of great personal utility (e.g. hand tools and whisky); in situations of operating complexity (e.g. motor-car manufacture); in items of changing consumer demand (e.g. women's fashions). 2. Affords an immediate costing of sales.

(*b*) Disadvantages: 1. Requires an investment in filing equipment and cards. 2. Maintaining current records is expensive.

No. 33

			LIFO	*Average*	*FIFO*
		£	£	£	£
Sales: 3,000 @ 7.40 ea.		22,200			
1,500 @ 8.00 ea.		12,000			
4,500			34,200	34,200	34,200
Cost of Goods Sold					
LIFO: 2,000 @ 6.6 ea.		13,200			
2,000 @ 6.4 ea.		12,800			
500 @ 6.2 ea.		3,100	29,100		
4,500					
Average: 1,000 @ 5.7 ea.		5,700			
2,000 @ 6.2 ea.		12,400			
2,000 @ 6.4 ea.		12,800			
2,000 @ 6.6 ea.		13,200			
7,000		44,100			
4,500 @ 6.3 ea.				28,350	
FIFO: 1,000 @ 5.7 ea.		5,700			
2,000 @ 6.2 ea.		12,400			
1,500 @ 6.4 ea.		9,600			27,700
4,500					
Gross Profit			£5,100	£5,850	£6,500
Stock, May 31st					
LIFO: 1,500 @ 6.2 ea.		9,300			
1,000 @ 5.7 ea.		5,700	15,000		
2,500					
Average: 2,500 @ 6.3 ea.				15,750	
FIFO: 500 @ 6.4 ea.		3,200			
2,000 @ 6.6 ea.		13,200			16,400
2,500					
Proof:					
Cost of Goods Sold	4,500		29,100	28,350	27,700
Stock	2,500		15,000	15,750	16,400
Total Goods	7,000		£44,100	£44,100	£44,100

No. 32

	£	£
(*a*) Cash	1,500	
Sales		1,500
To record sale of 300 units @ £5 each		
(*b*) Cost of Sales	1,200	
Inventory		1,200
To record reduction in stock due to sale (300 units @ £4 each)		

No. 33 see page 336

No. 34

Item	*No. of units*	*Cost*	*Market*	*Stock value*
		£	£	£
A1	100	60	67	6,000
A2	120	120	110	13,200
A3	600	210	200	120,000
A4	210	300	290	60,900
B1	430	400	410	172,000
B2	10	75	72	720
B3	25	450	430	10,750
C1	900	790	810	711,000
C2	42	575	560	23,520
C3	150	815	804	120,600
C4	200	615	627	123,000
				£1,361,690

No. 35

Selling Price	£5.00
Cost	4.00
Gross Profit	£1.00

Gross Profit as a percentage of sales:

$$\frac{£1.00}{£5.00} = 20\%$$

Gross Profit as a percentage of cost:

$$\frac{£1.00}{£4.00} = 25\%$$

Notice that as the base changes, the percentage changes.

No. 36

	£	£
(*a*) Cash	3,900	
Land		3,900
To record money received from Liverpool Demolition Company Ltd to remove old building		
(*b*) Land	1,750	
Cash		1,750
To record money paid to Speedy Demolition Ltd to remove debris and level land		

No. 37

	£	£
(*a*) Building	25,600	
Creditors		25,600
To record remodelling cost		

The total cost of the building is £139,432 (£113,832 + £25,600)

No. 38

	£	£
(*a*) Building	5,300	
Repairs and Maintenance	900	
Creditors		6,200
To record costs of remodelling and repainting building		

(*b*) Yes. Although in both cases the exterior is painted, in Example 37 the painting was done as part of the work necessary to prepare the building for occupation. In Example 38 the painting is unrelated to the interior remodelling and is therefore in the nature of repairs.

No. 39

	£
Machine	5,000
Freight	105
Insurance in transit	75
Installation Cost	200
Total Cost	£5,380

No. 40

	£	£
Machinery	10,600	
Deferred Interest	1,000	
Cash		2,000
Contracts Payable		9,600
To record purchase of machine under an instalment contract		

No. 41

$$\frac{£9{,}800 - £200}{8 \text{ years}} = \frac{£9{,}600}{8 \text{ years}} = £1{,}200/\text{year}$$

No. 42

(*a*)

$$\frac{£15{,}000 - £1{,}000}{2{,}000 \text{ hours}} = \frac{£14{,}000}{2{,}000 \text{ hours}} = £7/\text{hour}$$

(*b*) 19.7: 175 hours × £7/hour = £1,225
19.8: 62 hours × £7/hour = £434

No. 43

8 + 7 + 6 + 5 + 4 + 3 + 2 + 1 = 36

To determine 1/36th:

$$\frac{£40{,}000 - £400}{36} = \frac{£39{,}600}{36} = £1{,}100$$

			£	£
Depreciation:	1st Year	8 ×	1,100 =	8,800
	2nd Year	7 ×	1,100 =	7,700
	3rd Year	6 ×	1,100 =	6,600
	4th Year	5 ×	1,100 =	5,500
	5th Year	4 ×	1,100 =	4,400
	6th Year	3 ×	1,100 =	3,300
	7th Year	2 ×	1,100 =	2,200
	8th Year	1 ×	1,100 =	1,100
		36		£39,600

No. 44

(*a*)

$$\frac{£25{,}200 - £1{,}200}{10 \text{ years}} = \frac{£24{,}000}{10 \text{ years}} = £2{,}400/\text{year}$$

9 months' depreciation = 9/12 × £2,400 = £1,800

Depreciation Expense—Machinery	£1,800	
Accumulated Depreciation—Machinery		£1,800
To record 9 months' depreciation		

(*b*) Accumulated Depreciation—		
Machinery (£18,000 + £1,800)	£19,800	
Machinery (new)	33,600	
Cash (£30,000 − £1,800)		£28,200
Machinery (old)		25,200
To record trade of old machinery for new machinery		

(*c*) $\frac{£33{,}600 - £1{,}600}{8 \text{ years}} = \frac{£32{,}000}{8 \text{ years}} = £4{,}000/\text{year}$

3 months' depreciation = 3/12 × £4,000 = £1,000

Depreciation Expense—Machinery	£1,000	
Accumulated Depreciation—Machinery		£1,000
To record 3 months' depreciation		

No. 45

Increase in Asset Value	£93,000	
Overstreet, Capital		£93,000
To record increase in value of building to reflect current market value:		

Current Value	£125,000
Book Value	32,000
	£93,000

No. 46

(*a*) Merchandise Purchases	£6,742.90	
Creditors or Purchases Ledger Control Account		£6,742.90
To record purchase of merchandise for sale		
(*b*) Creditors or Purchases Ledger Control Account	£6,742.90	
Cash		£6,608.04
Purchase Discounts		134.86
To record payments during discount period		
(*c*) Creditors or Purchases Ledgers Control Account	£6,742.90	
Cash		£6,742.90
To record payments after discount period		

No. 47

(*a*) Merchandise Purchases (or Merchandise Inventory	£8,200	
Creditors or Purchases Ledger Control Account		£8,200
To record merchandise purchased in 19.8		

(*b*) No entry is required because goods were shipped FOB destination and they did not arrive until January 5th, 19.9.

No. 48

Month Factor	*1-year Subscriptions*		*2-year Subscriptions*		*5-year Subscriptions*	
	Number	*Total Months*	*Number*	*Total Months*	*Number*	*Total Months*
12	100	1,200	175	2,100	130	1,560
11	75	825	162	1,782	205	2,255
10	83	830	181	1,810	197	1,970
9	97	873	135	1,215	188	1,692
8	105	840	166	1,328	142	1,136
7	82	574	175	1,225	155	1,085
6	56	336	185	1,110	187	1,122
5	71	355	119	595	193	965
4	89	356	122	488	167	668
3	43	129	163	489	152	456
2	52	104	180	360	193	386
1	60	60	205	205	215	215
TOTAL	913	6,482	1,968	12,707	2,124	13,510

	1-year	2-year	5-year
	$\frac{£2.40}{12}$ = 20p/mo.	$\frac{£3.60}{24}$ = 15p/mo.	$\frac{£7.20}{60}$ = 12p/mo.
(*a*) 19.8 Income	£1,296.40	£1,906.05	£1,621.20
(*b*) Unearned at Dec. 31st, 19.8	£894.80	£5,178.75	£13,671.60

(*c*) Prepaid Subscriptions Received in 19.8	£4,823.65	
Subscription Income		£4,823.65

To record subscriptions earned in 19.8

1 year = £1,296.40
2 year = 1,906.05
5 year = 1,621.20

£4,823.65

(*d*) Subscriptions received in 19.8 and earned in 19.9 (assuming no cancellations):

	£
1 year	894.80
2 year (1,968 × 12 mos. × 15p/mo.)	3,542.40
5 year (2,124 × 12 mos. × 12p/mo.)	3,058.56
	£7,495.76

No. 49

	Actual 19.8		Budget 19.9	
	£	£	£	£
Sales		200,000		240,000
Cost of Goods Sold				
Labour	80,000		92,000	
Materials	46,000		55,200	
Overhead	14,000		16,800	
		140,000		164,000
Gross Profit		60,000		76,000
Selling Expenses	25,000		28,750	
Administrative Expenses	20,000		22,000	
		45,000		50,750
Net Profit		£15,000		£25,250

No. 50

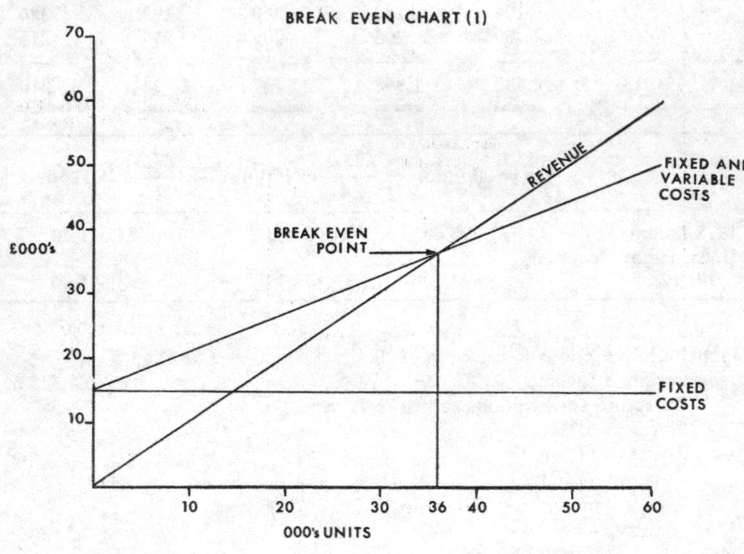

	£	£
Revenue from 60,000 units		60,000
Variable Costs:		
Direct Labour	13,000	
Direct Material	12,000	
Factory Overheads	4,000	
Selling Expenses	6,000	
		35,000
Total contribution to Fixed Expenses and Profit		25,000

Contribution per unit = 25,000 ÷ 60,000
Total contribution required for break-even point = £15,000
Break-even point = 15,000 ÷ (25,000 ÷ 60,000) units
= 36,000 units

No. 51

	Variable	Fixed	Total
	£	£	£
Total costs as stated in Example 50	35,000	15,000	50,000
Add 10% of Direct Labour	1,300		1,300
2% of other Variable Costs	440		440
Increase in Fixed Costs		3,260	3,260
	£36,740	£18,260	£55,000

Revenue 60,000 units @ £1.05 £63,000

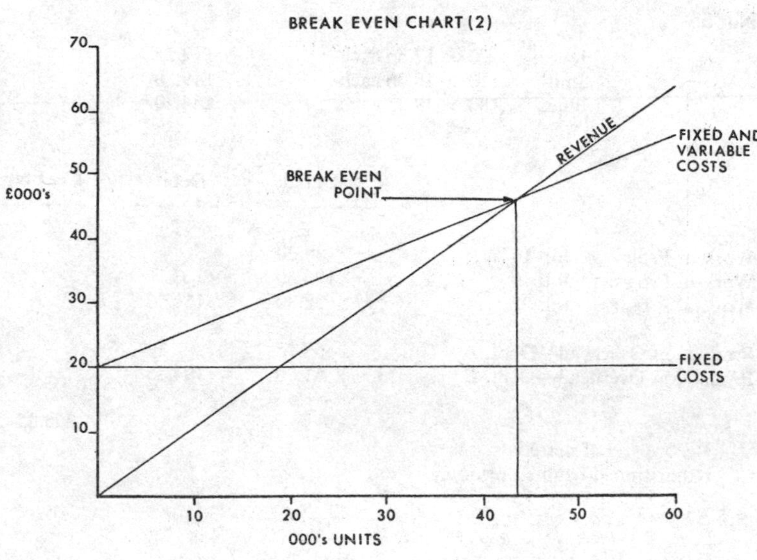

No. 52

	Regular Hours	Overtime Hours	Total Hours	Rate Per Hour	Gross Pay
(*a*) Jones	40	—	40	£1.75	£70.00
Smith	40	—	40	2.10	84.00
Blue	39	—	39	2.05	79.95
Green	40	2	42	1.95	83.85
Acme	38	—	38	1.52	57.76

	Regular Hours	Overtime Hours	Total Hours	Rate Per Hour	Gross Pay
(*b*) Jones	40	—	40	1.75	70.00
Smith	39	1	40	2.10	85.05
Blue	38	1	39	2.05	80.98
Green	38	4	42	1.95	85.80
Acme	33	5	38	1.52	61.56

No. 53

Jones:	70 × 17.5p each		£12.25
Smith:	100 × 17.5p each	£17.50	
	10 × 18.0p each	£ 1.80	£19.30
Blue:	100 × 17.5p each	£17.50	
	50 × 18.0p each	£ 9.00	
	30 × 19.0p each	£ 5.70	£32.20

No. 54

Yes, Jones would have earned £16.

No. 55

Jones:	70 × 17.5p each	£12.25
Smith:	110 × 18.0p each	£19.80
Blue:	180 × 19.0p each	£34.20

No. 56

	Details	Debits	Credits
	£	£	£
Work-in-Progress—Job 16	38.20		
Work-in-Progress—Job 19	100.50		
Work-in-Progress—Job 22	22.30	161.00	
Production Overhead—Dept. A	53.15		
Production Overhead—Debt. B	51.70	104.85	
Inventory Record use of materials requisitioned from storeroom.			265.85

No. 57

$$Q = \sqrt{\frac{2 \times R \times P}{C \times I}}$$

$$= \sqrt{\frac{2 \times 2{,}000 \times £14.00}{£6.40 \times 0.30}}$$

$$= 171$$

No. 58

$$\frac{2{,}000}{171} = 11.8 \text{ orders/year}$$

$$\frac{250}{11.8} = 21.2 \text{ days}$$

Order must be placed every 20 and 21 days alternately.

No. 59

2 calendar weeks = 10 days
30 units per day usage × 10 days = 300 units minimum stock

No. 60

(*a*) Total cost = £7,399.00

$$\text{Average cost} = \frac{£7{,}399.00}{700} = £10.57 \text{ each}$$

(*b*) £18.00 − £9.75 = £8.25 each

(*c*) £8.25 each

No. 61

	£	£
(*a*) Work-in-Progress—Defective Goods	211.40	
Work-in-Progress		211.40
Record cost of defective units @ £10.57 each		
(*b*) Work-in-Progress—Defective Goods	165.00	
Work-in-Progress		165.00
Record cost of defective units @ £8.25 each		
(*c*) Work-in-Progress—Defective Goods	165.00	
Production Overhead—Defective Goods	46.40	
Work-in-Progress		211.40
Record cost of defective units @ £8.25 each but relieve Work-in-Progress for 20 units @ £10.57 each		

No. 62

Production Overhead

	£	
Payroll Summary	2,302.00	
Materials Requisition	1,025.00	
Administration	1,347.80	
Insurance Expense	6,510.00	
Factory Supplies	4,400.00	
Depreciation	15,320.00	

No. 63

£152,310 × 1.10 = £167,541

(*a*) $\frac{£167{,}541}{16{,}750 \text{ dlh}} = £10/\text{direct-labour hour}$

(*b*) $\frac{£10/\text{dlh}}{£0.75/\text{hr}} = 13.3/\text{direct-labour pound}$

No. 64

Production Overhead

Actual	£651,259	Applied (45,000 dlh × £14.612/dlh)	£657,540

Total Variance: £651,259 − £657,540 = £6,281

No. 65

Budget Variance: £623,950 − £651,259 = £27,309 Unfavourable
Volume Variance:

$$\frac{42{,}700 \text{ dlh}}{80\%} = 5{,}337.5 \text{ dlh}/1\% \text{ capacity}$$

85% × 5,337.5 = 45,368.75 dlh
(45,368.75 − 42,700) dlh × £14.612/dlh
= £38,996 Favourable

Efficiency Variance:
(45,368.75 − 45,000) dlh × £14.612/dlh
= £5,388 Unfavourable

£6,299 Favourable

(The difference between the answer to Example 64 [£6,281] and this answer is due to rounding.)

No. 66

Work-in-Progress—Job 20

19.8			
Nov. 30th	Labour	£9,468	
	Materials	2,253	
	Overhead	4,450	
	Balance	16,171	
Dec. 31st	Labour	2,901	
	Materials	905	
	Overhead	1,276	
	Balance	21,253	
19.9			
Jan. 31st	Labour	203	
	Materials	347	
	Overhead	93	
	Balance	21,896	

No. 67

CALCULATIONS:

Material:		
3,000# A @ £3.00/lb		£9,000
2,000# B @ £15.00/lb		30,000
5,000# Total Material		£39,000
4,000# completed (80%)		£31,200
1,000# in process (20%)		7,800
5,000#		£39,000
Labour:		
4,000# (of end product) × 100%	4,000 eu	£16,000
1,000# (of end product) × 60%	600 eu	2,400
	4,600 eu	£18,400
Overhead		
£16,000 × 1.4		£22,400
£2,400 × 1.4		3,360
		£25,760

ANSWERS:

	Part (*a*)	Part (*b*)	Total
Material	£31,200	£7,800	£39,000
Labour	16,000	2,400	18,400
Overhead	22,400	3,360	25,760
Total	£69,600	£13,560	£83,160

No. 68

	Cost to Date	Cost to Complete	Total
Direct Labour	£6,000	£9,000	£15,000
Direct Materials	14,000	—	14,000
Overhead	12,000	18,000	30,000
Total	£32,000	£27,000	£59,000

No. 69

Direct Labour	300 × 50% = 150	
	1,500 × 100% = 1,500	
	500 × 60% = 300	1,950 eu
Direct Materials	300 × 25% = 75	
	1,500 × 100% = 1,500	
	500 × 100% = 500	2,075 eu
Overhead	300 × 50% = 150	
	1,500 × 100% = 1,500	
	500 × 60% = 300	1,950 eu

No. 70

Direct Labour $\frac{£13,845}{1,950 \text{ eu}} = £\ 7.10/\text{eu}$

Direct Materials $\frac{£20,542}{2,075 \text{ eu}} = £\ 9.90/\text{eu}$

Overhead $\frac{£27,495}{1,950 \text{ eu}} = £14.10/\text{eu}$

No. 71

	Sales Price	Percentages	Cost to Separation
(*a*) Product A	£60,000	60%	£24,000
Product B	40,000	40	16,000
	£100,000	100%	£40,000

	Sales Price Less Added Conversion	Percentages	Cost to Separation
(*b*) Product A	£50,000	83.33%	£33,333
Product B	10,000	16.67	6,667
	£60,000	100.00%	£40,000

No. 72

(*a*) 7.1 hours × £2.10/hr	=	£14.91
(*b*) 7.0 hours × £2.00/hr	=	14.00
Variance	=	£0.91

(*c*) Excess time (0.1 hr) × £2.00/hr	=	£0.20
Excess rate (£0.10) × 7.1 hr	=	0.71
		£0.91
or		
Excess rate (£0.10) × 7.0 hr	=	0.70
Excess time (0.1 hr) × £2.10/hr	=	0.21
		£0.91

No. 73

MACHINE A:	£
Cost	75,000
Present equivalent of scrap value 5,000 × v^8 = 5,000 × 0.627	3,135
	£71,865
Equivalent to an annual charge of 71,865 ÷ $a_{\overline{8}|}$ = 71,865 ÷ 6.209	11,570
Annual running costs	3,430
Total annual charge	£15,000
Cost per unit (£15,000 ÷ 6,000)	2.5

MACHINE B:	£
Cost	60,000
Present equivalent of scrap value 5,000 × v^6 = 5,000 × 0.704	3,520
	£56,480
Equivalent to an annual charge of 56,480 ÷ $a_{\overline{6}|}$ = 56,480 ÷ 4.917	12,990
Annual running costs	8,610
Total annual charge	£21,600
Cost per unit (£21,600 ÷ 8,000)	2.7

Therefore, on the basis of the information given, four type-A machines should be purchased.

Appendix—Compound Interest Tables

1 per cent

n	$(1 + i)^n$	v^n	$S_{\overline{n}\mid}$	$a_{\overline{n}\mid}$
1	1.0100	0.9901	1.000	0.990
2	1.0201	0.9803	2.101	1.970
3	1.0303	0.9706	3.030	2.941
4	1.0406	0.9610	4.060	3.902
5	1.0510	0.9515	5.101	4.853
6	1.0615	0.9420	6.152	5.795
7	1,0721	0.9327	7.214	6.728
8	1.0829	0.9235	8.286	7.652
9	1.0937	0.9143	9.369	8.566
10	1.1046	0.9053	10.462	9.471
11	1.1157	0.8963	11.567	10.368
12	1.1268	0.8874	12.683	11.255
13	1.1381	0.8787	13.809	12.134
14	1.1495	0.8700	14.947	13.004
15	1.1610	0.8613	16.097	13.865
16	1.1726	0.8528	17.258	14.718
17	1.1843	0.8444	18.430	15.562
18	1.1961	0.8360	19.615	16.398
19	1.2081	0.8277	20.811	17.226
20	1.2202	0.8195	22.019	18.046
21	1.2324	0.8114	23.239	18.857
22	1.2447	8.8034	24.472	19.660
23	1.2572	0.7954	25.716	20.456
24	1.2697	0.7876	26.973	21.243
25	1.2824	0.7798	28.243	22.023
26	1.2953	0.7720	29.526	22.795
27	1.3082	0.7644	30.821	23.560
28	1.3213	0.7568	32.129	24.316
29	1.3345	0.7493	33.450	25.066
30	1.3478	0.7419	34.785	25.808
31	1.3613	0.7346	36.133	26.542
32	1.3749	0.7273	37.494	27.270
33	1.3887	0.7201	38.869	27.990
34	1.4026	0.7130	40.258	28.703
35	1.4166	0.7059	41.660	29.409
36	1.4308	0.6989	43.077	30.108
37	1.4451	0.6920	44.508	30.800
38	1.4595	0.6852	45.953	31.485
39	1.4741	0.6784	47.412	32.163
40	1.4889	0.6717	48.886	32.835

$1\frac{1}{2}$ per cent

n	$(1 \times i)^n$	v^n	$S_{\overline{n}\rceil}$	$a_{\overline{n}\rceil}$
1	1.0150	0.9852	1.000	0.985
2	1.0302	0.9707	2.015	1.956
3	1.0457	0.9563	3.045	2.912
4	1.0614	0.9422	4.091	3.854
5	1.0773	0.9283	5.152	4.783
6	1.0934	0.9145	6.230	5.697
7	1.1098	0.9010	7.323	6.598
8	1.1265	0.8877	8.433	7.486
9	1.1434	0.8746	9.559	8.361
10	1.1605	0.8617	10.703	9.222
11	1.1779	0.8489	11.863	10.071
12	1.1956	0.8364	13.041	10.908
13	1.2136	0.8240	14.237	11.732
14	1.2318	0.8118	15.450	12.543
15	1.2502	0.7999	16.682	13.343
16	1.2690	0.7880	17.932	14.131
17	1.2880	0.7764	19.201	14.908
18	1.3073	0.7649	20.489	15.673
19	1.3269	0.7536	21.797	16.426
20	1.3469	0.7425	23.124	17.169
21	1.3671	0.7315	24.471	17.900
22	1.3876	0.7207	25.838	18.621
23	1.4084	0.7100	27.225	19.331
24	1.4295	0.6995	28.633	20.030
25	1.4509	0.6892	30.063	20.720
26	1.4727	0.6790	31.514	21.399
27	1.4948	0.6690	32.987	22.068
28	1.5172	0.6591	34.481	22.727
29	1.5400	0.6494	35.999	23.376
30	1.5631	0.6398	37.539	24.016
31	1.5865	0.6303	39.102	24.646
32	1.6103	0.6210	40.688	25.267
33	1.6345	0.6118	42.299	25.879
34	1.6590	0.6028	43.933	26.482
35	1.6839	0.5939	45.592	27.076
36	1.7091	0.5851	47.276	27.661
37	1.7348	0.5764	48.985	28.237
38	1.7608	0.5679	50.720	28.805
39	1.7872	0.5595	52.481	29.365
40	1.8140	0.5513	54.268	29.916

2 per cent

n	$(1 + i)^n$	v^n	$S_{\overline{n}\rceil}$	$a_{\overline{n}\rceil}$
1	1.0200	0.9804	1.000	0.980
2	1.0404	0.9612	2.020	1.942
3	1.0612	0.9423	3.060	2.884
4	1.0824	0.9238	4.122	3.808
5	1.1041	0.9057	5.204	4.713
6	1.1261	0.8880	6.308	5.601
7	1.1487	0.8706	7.434	6.472
8	1.1717	0.8535	8.583	7.325
9	1.1951	0.8368	9.755	8.162
10	1.2190	0.8203	10.950	8.983
11	1.2434	0.8043	12.169	9.787
12	1.2682	0.7885	13.412	10.575
13	1.2936	0.7730	14.680	11.348
14	1.3195	0.7579	15.974	12.106
15	1.3459	0.7430	17.293	12.849
16	1.3728	0.7284	18.639	13.578
17	1.4002	0.7142	20.012	14.292
18	1.4282	0.7002	21.412	14.992
19	1.4568	0.6864	22.841	15.678
20	1.4859	0.6730	24.297	16.351
21	1.5157	0.6598	25.783	17.011
22	1.5460	0.6468	27.299	17.658
23	1.5769	0.6342	28.845	18.292
24	1.6084	0.6217	30.422	18.914
25	1.6406	0.6095	32.030	19.523
26	1.6734	0.5976	33.671	20.121
27	1.7069	0.5859	35.344	20.707
28	1.7410	0.5744	37.051	21.281
29	1.7758	0.5631	38.792	21.844
30	1.8114	0.5521	40.568	22.396
31	1.8476	0.5412	42.379	22.938
32	1.8845	0.5306	44.227	23.468
33	1.9222	0.5202	46.112	23.989
34	1.9607	0.5100	48.034	24.499
35	1.9999	0.5000	49.994	24.999
36	2.0399	0.4902	51.994	25.489
37	2.0807	0.4806	54.034	25.969
38	2.1223	0.4712	56.115	26.441
39	2.1647	0.4619	58.237	26.903
40	2.2080	0.4529	60.402	27.355

$2\frac{1}{2}$ per cent

n	$(1 + i)^n$	v^n	$S_{\overline{n}\vert}$	$a_{\overline{n}\vert}$
1	1.0250	0.9756	1.000	0.976
2	1.0506	0.9518	2.025	1.927
3	1.0769	0.9286	3.076	2.856
4	1.1038	0.9060	4.153	3.762
5	1.1314	0.8839	5.256	4.646
6	1.1597	0.8623	6.388	5.508
7	1.1887	0.8413	7.547	6.349
8	1.2184	0.8207	8.736	7.170
9	1.2489	0.8007	9.955	7.971
10	1.2801	0.7812	11.203	8.752
11	1.3121	0.7621	12.483	9.514
12	1.3449	0.7436	13.796	10.258
13	1.3785	0.7254	15.140	10.983
14	1.4130	0.7077	16.519	11.691
15	1.4483	0.6905	17.932	12.381
16	1.4845	0.6736	19.380	13.055
17	1.5216	0.6572	20.865	13.712
18	1.5597	0.6412	22.386	14.353
19	1.5986	0.6255	23.946	14.979
20	1.6386	0.6103	25.545	15.589
21	1.6796	0.5954	27.183	16.185
22	1.7216	0.5809	28.863	16.765
23	1.7646	0.5667	30.584	17.332
24	1.8087	0.5529	32.349	17.885
25	1.8539	0.5394	34.158	18.424
26	1.9003	0.5262	36.012	18.951
27	1.9478	0.5134	37.912	19.464
28	1.9965	0.5009	39.860	19.965
29	2.0464	0.4887	41.856	20.454
30	2.0976	0.4767	43.903	20.930
31	2.1500	0.4651	46.000	21.395
32	2.2038	0.4538	48.150	21.849
33	2.2588	0.4427	50.354	22.292
34	2.3153	0.4319	52.613	22.724
35	2.3732	0.4214	54.928	23.145
36	2.4325	0.4111	57.301	23.556
37	2.4933	0.4011	59.734	23.957
38	2.5557	0.3913	62,227	24.349
39	2.6196	0.3817	64.783	24.730
40	2.6851	0.3724	67.403	25.103

3 per cent

n	$(1 + i)^n$	v^n	$S_{\overline{n}\rceil}$	$a_{\overline{n}\rceil}$
1	1.0300	0.9709	1.000	0.971
2	1.0609	0.9426	2.030	1.913
3	1.0927	0.9151	3.091	2.829
4	1.1255	0.8885	4.184	3.717
5	1.1593	0.8626	5.309	4.580
6	1.1941	0.8375	6.468	5.417
7	1.2299	0.8131	7.662	6.230
8	1.2668	0.7894	8.892	7.020
9	1.3048	0.7664	10.159	7.786
10	1.3439	0.7441	11.464	8.530
11	1.3842	0.7224	12.808	9.253
12	1.4258	0.7014	14.192	9.954
13	1.4685	0.6810	15.618	10.635
14	1.5126	0.6611	17.086	11.296
15	1.5580	0.6419	18.599	11.938
16	1.6047	0.6232	20.157	12.561
17	1.6528	0.6050	21.762	13.166
18	1.7024	0.5874	23.414	13.754
19	1.7535	0.5703	25.117	14.324
20	1.8061	0.5537	26.870	14.877
21	1.8603	0.5375	28.676	15.415
22	1.9161	0.5219	30.537	15.937
23	1.9736	0.5067	32.453	16.444
24	2.0328	0.4919	34.426	16.936
25	2.0938	0.4776	36.459	17.413
26	2.1566	0.4637	38.553	17.877
27	2.2213	0.4502	40.710	18.327
28	2.2879	0.4371	42.931	18.764
29	2.3566	0.4243	45.219	19.188
30	2.4273	0.4120	47.575	19.600
31	2.5001	0.4000	50.003	20.000
32	2.5751	0.3883	52.503	20.389
33	2.6523	0.3770	55.078	20.766
34	2.7319	0.3660	57.730	21.132
35	2.8139	0.3554	60.462	21.487
36	2.8983	0.3450	63.276	21.832
37	2.9852	0.3350	66.174	22.167
38	3.0748	0.3252	69.159	22.492
39	3.1670	0.3158	72.234	22.808
40	3.2620	0.3066	75.401	23.115

$3\frac{1}{2}$ per cent

n	$(1 + i)^n$	v^n	$s_{\overline{n}\rceil}$	$a_{\overline{n}\rceil}$
1	1.0350	0.9662	1.000	0.966
2	1.0712	0.9335	2.035	1.900
3	1.1087	0.9019	3.106	2.802
4	1.1475	0.8714	4.215	3.673
5	1.1877	0.8420	5.362	4.515
6	1.2293	0.8135	6.550	5.329
7	1.2723	0.7860	7.779	6.115
8	1.3168	0.7594	9.052	6.874
9	1.3629	0.7337	10.368	7.608
10	1.4106	0.7089	11.731	8.317
11	1.4600	0.6849	13.142	9.002
12	1.5111	0.6618	14.602	9.663
13	1.5640	0.6394	16.113	10.303
14	1.6187	0.6178	17.677	10.921
15	1.6753	0.5969	19.296	11.517
16	1.7340	0.5767	20.971	12.094
17	1.7947	0.5572	22.705	12.651
18	1.8575	0.5384	24.500	13.190
19	1.9225	0.5202	26.357	13.710
20	1.9898	0.5026	28.280	14.212
21	2.0594	0.4856	30.269	14.698
22	2.1315	0.4692	32.329	15.167
23	2.2061	0.4533	34.460	15.620
24	2.2833	0.4380	36.667	16.058
25	2.3632	0.4231	38.950	16.482
26	2.4460	0.4088	41.313	16.890
27	2.5316	0.3950	43.759	17.285
28	2.6202	0.3817	46.291	17.667
29	2.7119	0.3687	48.911	18.036
30	2.8068	0.3563	51.623	18.392
31	2.9050	0.3442	54.429	18.736
32	3.0067	0.3326	57.334	19.069
33	3.1119	0.3213	60.341	19.390
34	3.2209	0.3105	63.453	19.701
35	3.3336	0.3000	66.674	20.001
36	3.4503	0.2989	70.008	20.290
37	3.5710	0.2800	73.458	20.571
38	3.6960	0.2706	77.029	20.841
39	3.8254	0.2614	80.725	21.102
40	3.9593	0.2526	84.550	21.355

4 per cent

n	$(1+i)^n$	v^n	$S_{\overline{n}\rceil}$	$a_{\overline{n}\rceil}$
1	1.0400	0.9615	1.000	0.962
2	1.0816	0.9246	2.040	1.886
3	1.1249	0.8890	3.122	2.775
4	1.1699	0.8548	4.246	3.630
5	1.2167	0.8219	5.416	4.452
6	1.2653	0.7903	6.633	5.242
7	1.3159	0.7599	7.898	6.002
8	1.3686	0.7307	9.214	6.733
9	1.4233	0.7026	10.583	7.435
10	1.4802	0.6756	12.006	8.111
11	1.5395	0.6496	13.486	8.760
12	1.6010	0.6246	15.026	9.385
13	1.6651	0.6006	16.627	9.986
14	1.7317	0.5775	18.292	10.563
15	1.8009	0.5553	20.024	11.118
16	1.8730	0.5339	21.825	11.652
17	1.9479	0.5134	23.698	12.166
18	2.0258	0.4936	25.645	12.659
19	2.1068	0.4746	27.671	13.134
20	2.1911	0.4564	29.778	13.590
21	2.2788	0.4388	31.969	14.029
22	2.3699	0.4220	34.248	14.451
23	2.4647	0.4057	36.618	14.857
24	2.5633	0.3901	39.083	15.247
25	2.6658	0.3751	41.646	15.622
26	2.7725	0.3607	44.312	15.983
27	2.8834	0.3468	47.084	16.330
28	2.9987	0.3335	49.968	16.663
29	3.1186	0.3207	52.966	16.984
30	3.2434	0.3083	56.085	17.292
31	3.3731	0.2965	59.328	17.588
32	3.5081	0.2851	62.701	17.874
33	3.6484	0.2741	66.209	18.148
34	3.7943	0.2636	69.858	18.411
35	3.9461	0.2534	73.652	18.665
36	4.1039	0.2437	77.598	18.908
37	4.2681	0.2343	81.702	19.143
38	4.4388	0.2253	85.970	19.368
39	4.6164	0.2166	90.409	19.584
40	4.8010	0.2083	95.025	19.793

4½ per cent

n	$(1+i)^n$	v^n	$S_{\overline{n}\vert}$	$a_{\overline{n}\vert}$
1	1.0450	0.9569	1.000	0.957
2	1.0920	0.9157	2.045	1.873
3	1.1412	0.8763	3.137	2.749
4	1.1925	0.8386	4.278	3.588
5	1.2462	0.8025	5.471	4.390
6	1.3023	0.7679	6.717	5.158
7	1.3609	0.7348	8.019	5.893
8	1.4221	0.7032	9.380	6.596
9	1.4861	0.6729	10.802	7.269
10	1.5530	0.6439	12.288	7.913
11	1.6229	0.6162	13.841	8.529
12	1.6959	0.5897	15.464	9.119
13	1.7722	0.5643	17.160	9.683
14	1.8519	0.5400	18.932	10.223
15	1.9353	0.5167	20.784	10.740
16	2.0224	0.4945	22.719	11.234
17	2.1134	0.4732	24.742	11.707
18	2.2085	0.4528	26.855	12.160
19	2.3079	0.4333	29.064	12.593
20	2.4117	0.4146	31.371	13.008
21	2.5202	0.3968	33.783	13.405
22	2.6337	0.3797	36.303	13.784
23	2.7522	0.3634	38.937	14.148
24	2.8760	0.3477	41.689	14.495
25	3.0054	0.3327	44.565	14.828
26	3.1407	0.3184	47.571	15.147
27	3.2820	0.3047	50.711	15.451
28	3.4297	0.2916	53.993	15.743
29	3.5840	0.2790	57.423	16.022
30	3.7453	0.2670	61.007	16.289
31	3.9139	0.2555	64.752	16.544
32	4.0900	0.2445	68.666	16.789
33	4.2740	0.2340	72.756	17.023
34	4.4664	0.2239	77.030	17.247
35	4.6673	0.2143	81.497	17.461
36	4.8774	0.2050	86.164	17.666
37	5.0969	0.1962	91.041	17.862
38	5.3262	0.1878	96.138	18.050
39	5.5659	0.1797	101.464	18.230
40	5.8164	0.1719	107.030	18.402

5 per cent

n	$(1 + i)^n$	v^n	$S_{\overline{n\rceil}}$	$a_{\overline{n\rceil}}$
1	1.0500	0.9524	1.000	0.952
2	1.1025	0.9070	2.050	1.859
3	1.1576	0.8638	3.153	2.723
4	1.2155	0.8227	4.310	3.546
5	1.2763	0.7835	5.526	4.329
6	1.3401	0.7462	6.802	5.076
7	1.4071	0.7107	8.142	5.786
8	1.4775	0.6768	9.549	6.463
9	1.5513	0.6446	11.027	7.108
10	1.6289	0.6139	12.578	7.722
11	1.7103	0.5847	14.207	8.306
12	1.7959	0.5568	15.917	8.863
13	1.8856	0.5303	17.713	9.394
14	1.9799	0.5051	19.599	9.899
15	2.0789	0.4810	21.579	10.380
16	2.1829	0.4581	23.657	10.838
17	2.2920	0.4363	25.840	11.274
18	2.4066	0.4155	28.132	11.690
19	2.5269	0.3957	30.539	12.085
20	2.6533	0.3769	33.066	12.462
21	2.7860	0.3589	35.719	12.821
22	2.9253	0.3419	38.505	13.163
23	3.0715	0.3256	41.430	13.489
24	3.2251	0.3101	44.502	13.799
25	3.3864	0.2953	47.727	14.094
26	3.5557	0.2812	51.113	14.375
27	3.7335	0.2678	54.669	14.643
28	3.9201	0.2551	58.403	14.898
29	4.1161	0.2429	62.323	15.141
30	4.3219	0.2314	66.439	15.372
31	4.5380	0.2204	70.761	15.593
32	4.7649	0.2099	75.299	15.803
33	5.0032	0.1999	80.064	16.003
34	5.2533	0.1904	85.067	16.193
35	5.5160	0.1813	90.320	16.374
36	5.7918	0.1727	95.836	16.547
37	6.0814	0.1644	101.628	16.711
38	6.3855	0.1566	107.709	16.868
39	6.7047	0.1491	114.095	17.017
40	7.0400	0.1420	120.800	17.159

6 per cent

n	$(1+i)^n$	v^n	$S_{\overline{n}\rceil}$	$a_{\overline{n}\rceil}$
1	1.0600	0.9434	1.000	0.943
2	1.1236	0.8900	2.060	1.833
3	1.1910	0.8396	3.184	2.673
4	1.2625	0.7921	4.375	3.465
5	1.3382	0.7473	5.637	4.212
6	1.4185	0.7050	6.975	4.917
7	1.5036	0.6651	8.394	5.582
8	1.5938	0.6274	9.897	6.210
9	1.6895	0.5919	11.491	6.802
10	1.7908	0.5584	13.181	7.360
11	1.8983	0.5268	14.972	7.887
12	2.0122	0.4970	16.870	8.384
13	2.1329	0.4688	18.882	8.853
14	2.2609	0.4423	21.015	9.295
15	2.3966	0.4173	23.276	9.712
16	2.5405	0.3936	25.673	10.106
17	2.6928	0.3714	28.213	10.477
18	2.8543	0.3503	30.906	10.828
19	3.0256	0.3305	33.760	11.158
20	3.2071	0.3118	36.786	11.470
21	3.3996	0.2942	39.993	11.764
22	3.6035	0.2775	43.392	12.042
23	3.8197	0.2618	46.996	12.303
24	4.0489	0.2470	50.816	12.550
25	4.2919	0.2330	54.864	12.783
26	4.5494	0.2198	59.156	13.003
27	4.8223	0.2074	63.706	13.211
28	5.1117	0.1956	68.528	13.406
29	5.4184	0.1846	73.640	13.591
30	5.7435	0.1741	79.058	13.765
31	6.0881	0.1643	84.802	13.929
32	6.4534	0.1550	90.890	14.084
33	6.8406	0.1462	97.343	14.230
34	7.2510	0.1379	104.184	14.368
35	7.6861	0.1301	111.435	14.498
36	8.1472	0.1227	119.121	14.621
37	8.6361	0.1158	127.268	14.737
38	9.1542	0.1092	135.904	14.846
39	9.7035	0.1031	145.058	14.949
40	10.2857	0.0972	154.762	15.046

7 per cent

n	$(1+i)^n$	v^n	$S_{\overline{n}\rvert}$	$a_{\overline{n}\rvert}$
1	1.0700	0.9346	1.000	0.935
2	1.1449	0.8734	2.070	1.808
3	1.2250	0.8163	3.215	2.624
4	1.3108	0.7629	4.440	3.387
5	1.4026	0.7130	5.751	4.100
6	1.5007	0.6663	7.153	4.767
7	1.6058	0.6227	8.654	5.389
8	1.7182	0.5820	10.260	5.971
9	1.8385	0.5439	11.978	6.515
10	1.9672	0.5083	13.816	7.024
11	2.1049	0.4751	15.784	7.499
12	2.2522	0.4440	17.888	7.943
13	2.4098	0.4150	20.141	8.358
14	2.5785	0.3878	22.550	8.745
15	2.7590	0.3624	25.129	9.108
16	2.9522	0.3387	27.888	9.447
17	3.1588	0.3166	30.840	9.763
18	3.3799	0.2959	33.999	10.059
19	3.6165	0.2765	37.379	10.336
20	3.8697	0.2584	40.995	10.594
21	4.1406	0.2415	44.865	10.836
22	4.4304	0.2257	49.006	11.061
23	4.7405	0.2109	53.436	11.272
24	5.0724	0.1971	58.177	11.469
25	5.4274	0.1842	63.249	11.654
26	5.8074	0.1722	68.676	11.826
27	6.2139	0.1609	74.484	11.987
28	6.6488	0.1504	80.698	12.137
29	7.1143	0.1406	87.346	12.278
30	7.6123	0.1314	94.461	12.409
31	8.1451	0.1228	102.073	12.532
32	8.7153	0.1147	110.218	12.647
33	9.3253	0.1072	118.933	12.754
34	9.9781	0.1002	128.259	12.854
35	10.6766	0.0937	138.237	12.948
36	11.4239	0.0875	148.913	13.035
37	12.2236	0.0818	160.337	13.117
38	13.0793	0.0765	172.561	13.193
39	13.9948	0.0715	185.640	13.265
40	14.9744	0.0668	199.635	13.332

8 per cent

n	$(1+i)^n$	v^n	$S_{\overline{n}\rvert}$	$a_{\overline{n}\rvert}$
1	1.0800	0.9259	1.000	0.926
2	1.1664	0.8573	2.080	1.783
3	1.2597	0.7938	3.246	2.577
4	1.3605	0.7350	4.506	3.312
5	1.4693	0.6806	5.867	3.993
6	1.5869	0.6302	7.336	4.623
7	1.7138	0.5835	8.923	5.206
8	1.8509	0.5403	10.637	5.747
9	1.9990	0.5002	12.488	6.247
10	2.1589	0.4632	14.487	6.710
11	2.3316	0.4289	16.645	7.139
12	2.5182	0.3971	18.977	7.536
13	2.7196	0.3677	21.495	7.904
14	2.9372	0.3405	24.215	8.244
15	3.1722	0.3152	27.152	8.559
16	3.4259	0.2919	30.324	8.851
17	3.7000	0.2703	33.750	9.122
18	3.9960	0.2502	37.450	9.372
19	4.3157	0.2317	41.446	9.604
20	4.6610	0.2145	45.762	9.818
21	5.0338	0.1987	50.423	10.017
22	5.4365	0.1839	55.457	10.201
23	5.8715	0.1703	60.893	10.371
24	6.3412	0.1577	66.765	10.529
25	6.8485	0.1460	73.106	10.675
26	7.3964	0.1352	79.954	10.810
27	7.9881	0.1252	87.351	10.935
28	8.6271	0.1159	95.339	11.051
29	9.3173	0.1073	103.966	11.158
30	10.0627	0.0994	113.283	11.258
31	10.8677	0.0920	123.346	11.350
32	11.7371	0.0852	134.213	11.435
33	12.6760	0.0789	145.951	11.514
34	13.6901	0.0730	158.627	11.587
35	14.7853	0.0676	172.317	11.655
36	15.9682	0.0626	187.102	11.717
37	17.2456	0.0580	203.070	11.775
38	18.6253	0.0537	220.316	11.829
39	20.1153	0.0497	238.941	11.879
40	21.7245	0.0460	259.056	11.925

9 per cent

n	$(1 + i)^n$	v^n	$S_{\overline{n}\vert}$	$a_{\overline{n}\vert}$
1	1.0900	0.9174	1.000	0.917
2	1.1881	0.8417	2.090	1.759
3	1.2950	0.7722	3.278	2.531
4	1.4116	0.7084	4.573	3.240
5	1.5386	0.6499	5.985	3.890
6	1.6771	0.5963	7.523	4.486
7	1.8280	0.5470	9.200	5.033
8	1.9926	0.5019	11.028	5.535
9	2.1719	0.4604	13.021	5.995
10	2.3674	0.4224	15.193	6.419
11	2.5804	0.3875	17.560	6.805
12	2.8127	0.3555	20.141	7.161
13	3.0658	0.3262	22.953	7.487
14	3.3417	0.2992	26.019	7.786
15	3.6425	0.2745	29.361	8.061
16	3.9703	0.2519	33.003	8.313
17	4.3276	0.2311	36.974	8.544
18	4.7171	0.2120	41.301	8.756
19	5.1417	0.1945	46.018	8.950
20	5.6044	0.1784	51.160	9.129
21	6.1088	0.1637	56.765	9.292
22	6.6586	0.1502	62.873	9.442
23	7.2579	0.1378	69.532	9.580
24	7.9111	0.1264	76.790	9.707
25	8.6231	0.1160	84.701	9.823
26	9.3992	0.1064	93.324	9.929
27	10.2451	0.0976	102.723	10.027
28	11.1671	0.0895	112.968	10.116
29	12.1722	0.0822	124.135	10.198
30	13.2677	0.0754	136.307	10.274
31	14.4618	0.0691	149.575	10.343
32	15.7633	0.0634	164.037	10.406
33	17.1820	0.0582	179.800	10.464
34	18.7284	0.0534	196.982	10.518
35	20.4140	0.0490	215.711	10.567
36	22.2512	0.0449	236.125	10.612
37	24.2538	0.0412	258.376	10.653
38	26.4367	0.0378	282.630	10.691
39	28.8160	0.0347	309.066	10.726
40	31.4094	0.0318	337.882	10.757

10 per cent

n	$(1 + i)^n$	v^n	$S_{\overline{n}\rceil}$	$a_{\overline{n}\rceil}$
1	1.1000	0.9091	1.000	0.909
2	1.2100	0.8264	2.100	1.736
3	1.3310	0.7513	3.310	2.487
4	1.4641	0.6830	4.641	3.170
5	1.6105	0.6209	6.105	3.791
6	1.7716	0.5645	7.716	4.355
7	1.9487	0.5132	9.487	4.868
8	2.1436	0.4665	11.436	5.335
9	2.3579	0.4241	13.579	5.759
10	2.5937	0.3855	15.937	6.145
11	2.8531	0.3505	18.531	6.495
12	3.1384	0.3186	21.384	6.814
13	3.4523	0.2897	24.523	7.103
14	3.7975	0.2633	27.975	7.367
15	4.1772	0.2394	31.772	7.606
16	4.5950	0.2176	35.950	7.824
17	5.0545	0.1978	40.545	8.022
18	5.5599	0.1799	45.599	8.201
19	6.1159	0.1635	51.159	8.365
20	6.7275	0.1486	57.275	8.514
21	7.4002	0.1351	64.002	8.649
22	8.1403	0.1228	71.403	8.772
23	8.9543	0.1117	79.543	8.883
24	9.8497	0.1015	88.497	8.985
25	10.8347	0.0923	98.347	9.077
26	11.9182	0.0839	109.182	9.161
27	13.1100	0.0763	121.100	9.237
28	14.4210	0.0693	134.210	9.307
29	15.8631	0.0630	148.631	9.370
30	17.4494	0.0573	164.494	9.427
31	19.1943	0.0521	181.943	9.479
32	21.1138	0.0474	201.138	9.526
33	23.2251	0.0431	222.251	9.569
34	25.5477	0.0391	245.477	9.609
35	28.1024	0.0356	271.024	9.644
36	30.9127	0.0323	299.127	9.677
37	34.0039	0.0294	330.039	9.706
38	37.4043	0.0267	364.043	9.733
39	41.1448	0.0243	401.448	9.757
40	45.2592	0.0221	442.592	9.779

Index